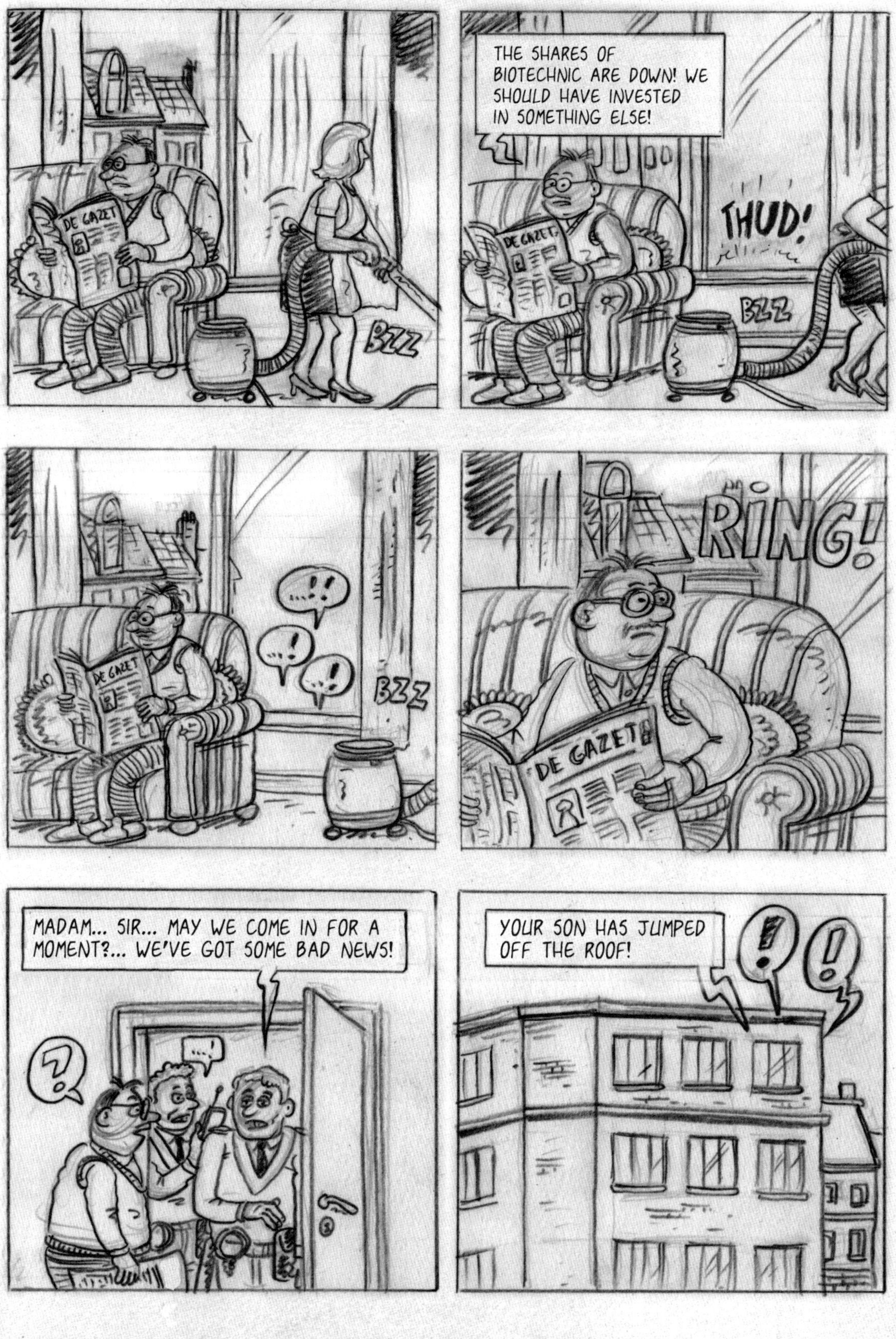
DE GAZET
BZZ
THE SHARES OF BIOTECHNIC ARE DOWN! WE SHOULD HAVE INVESTED IN SOMETHING ELSE!
THUD!
BZZ
...!!
...!
...!
BZZ
RING!
MADAM... SIR... MAY WE COME IN FOR A MOMENT?... WE'VE GOT SOME BAD NEWS!
?
...!
YOUR SON HAS JUMPED OFF THE ROOF!
!
!

Years of the Elephant Introduction

The years may pass, but elephants never forget. And how could any parent forget the loss of their child from suicide? There's no escape from the constant reminders and unanswered questions. But if you're a cartoonist, being able to tell stories in words and pictures can provide a way to escape reality; or reshape and control it. With ink and imagination, perhaps its possible to face the turmoil of emotions about your child taking his own life, and express these feelings through comics. This is what Willy Linthout attempts to do here in his poignant, unflinchingly candid graphic memoir.

Autobiography has found its perfect medium of expression in comics, an outlet often for one person, both writer and artist, to work things out on paper. Many of the finest graphic novels of this type, from Art Spiegelman's Maus to Alison Bechdel's Fun Home, deal with the complexities of relationships between father and child. But while Spiegelman and Bechdel told their stories from a son or daughter's perspective, Linthout speaks out from the point of view of a grown man who is a parent, a father, a husband, a brother and a breadwinner of his family. He adopts a similar approach to Eddie Campbell in Alec: The Years Have Pants or Yoshihiro Tatsumi in A Drifting Life, and uses a thinly disguised alter ego, Charles Germonprez. But there is no disguising the autobiographical heartfelt genuineness of this bereaved father's emotions.

The language of comics is richly flexible and playful, ideally suited to the strange and surreal. As a best-selling cartoonist of some 130 zany Urbanus albums, Willy uses his skills brilliantly to convey a rollercoaster-ride of bewilderment, grief, anger, despair, paranoia and ultimately enduring love for his son. He makes some astute choices and constraints to strengthen its impact. For instance, he omits all captions, giving the reader no grounding in place or time, reality or fantasy, from one panel to the next, and instilling a similar sort of disorientation and confusion as his floundering protagonist is going through. Similarly, to make us share in his feelings of extreme isolation, even from his own wife, he decides almost never to portray her in these panels. Reflecting his troubled mental state, anything is possible and the stuff of nightmares or madness can suddenly invade the everyday.

And then in a master stroke, he solves the question of how to represent and personify his own dead son by using the chalk outline of his fallen body. And in turn, this leads to his decision not to complete his sketched, uninked drawings but to leave them in their unrefined, pencilled state, urgent, vulnerable, as if to emphasise the human hand and heart behind them. This looser, unfussy, unpolished approach, also found in Joe Kubert's Yossel and Jeffrey Brown's Clumsy, seems to reinforce the honesty and intimacy of autobiographical comics. As Willy puts it, "Sam's life didn't get the chance to go all the way, it stayed unfinished, so the same goes for my pencils."

But now, by finishing this cathartic graphic novel, instigated as self-therapy, Willy has given himself a way to remember. He is also giving others, especially those who experience a similar seismic family trauma, a way to come to terms with such depths of loss. Like an elephant, this cartoonist will never forget his son's death, nor his son's life. And neither will we.

Paul Gravett, author of *Graphic Novels: Stories to Change Your Life*
and director of the Comica Festival, London
www.paulgravett.com

The author wishes to thank the following people:

- his brother Theo for being there for him.

- Steven de Rie and Serge Baeken for helping out and being real friends.

- Steve Coburn for providing a rough translation allowing me to offer this book to foreign publishers.

YEARS OF THE ELEPHANT

Willy Linthout

With assistance from Theo Linthout

Translation - Michiel Horn
poetry by Theo Linthout translated by Serge Baeken

FANFARE · PONENT MON

CHAPTER 1 - CONTINUOUS THREAD

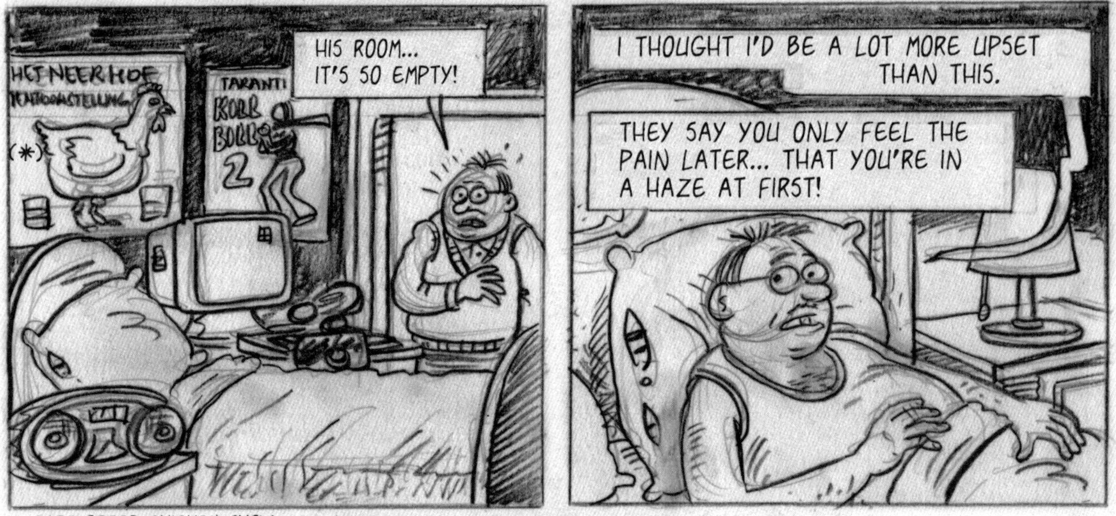
HET NEERHOF
TENTOONSTELLING
(*)
HIS ROOM... IT'S SO EMPTY!
I THOUGHT I'D BE A LOT MORE UPSET THAN THIS.
THEY SAY YOU ONLY FEEL THE PAIN LATER... THAT YOU'RE IN A HAZE AT FIRST!

* RARE BREED CHICKEN SHOW

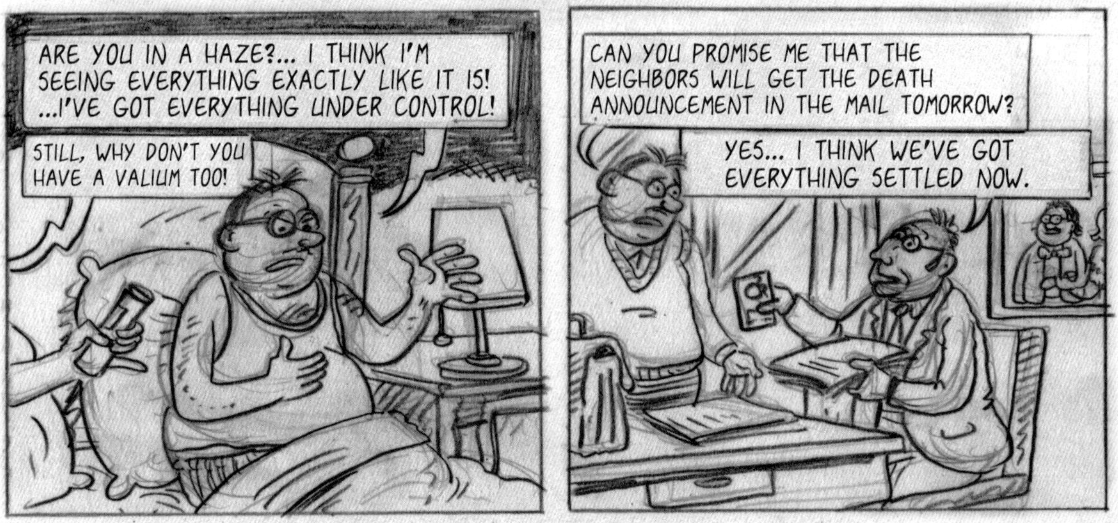
ARE YOU IN A HAZE?... I THINK I'M SEEING EVERYTHING EXACTLY LIKE IT IS! ...I'VE GOT EVERYTHING UNDER CONTROL!
STILL, WHY DON'T YOU HAVE A VALIUM TOO!
CAN YOU PROMISE ME THAT THE NEIGHBORS WILL GET THE DEATH ANNOUNCEMENT IN THE MAIL TOMORROW?
YES... I THINK WE'VE GOT EVERYTHING SETTLED NOW.

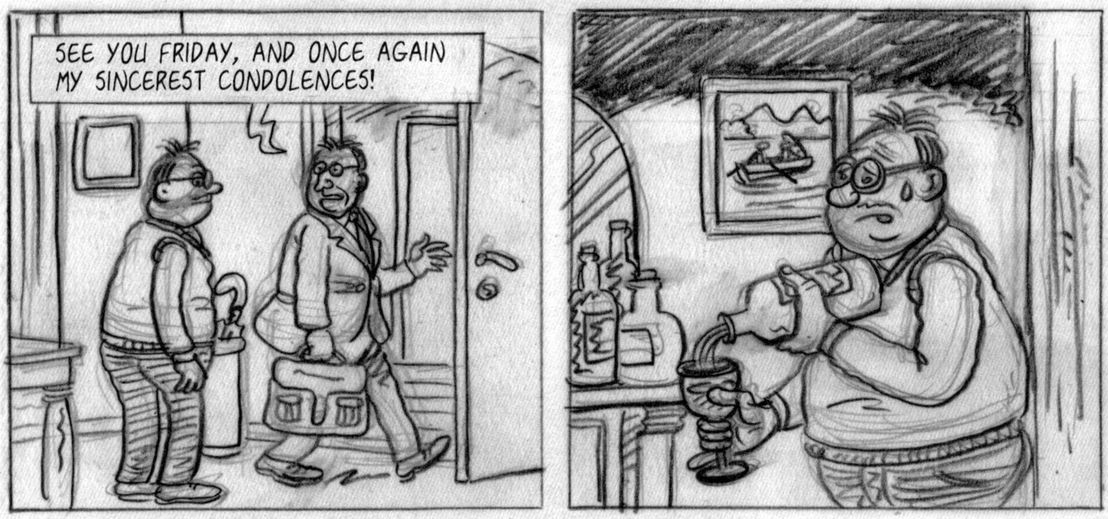
SEE YOU FRIDAY, AND ONCE AGAIN MY SINCEREST CONDOLENCES!

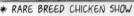

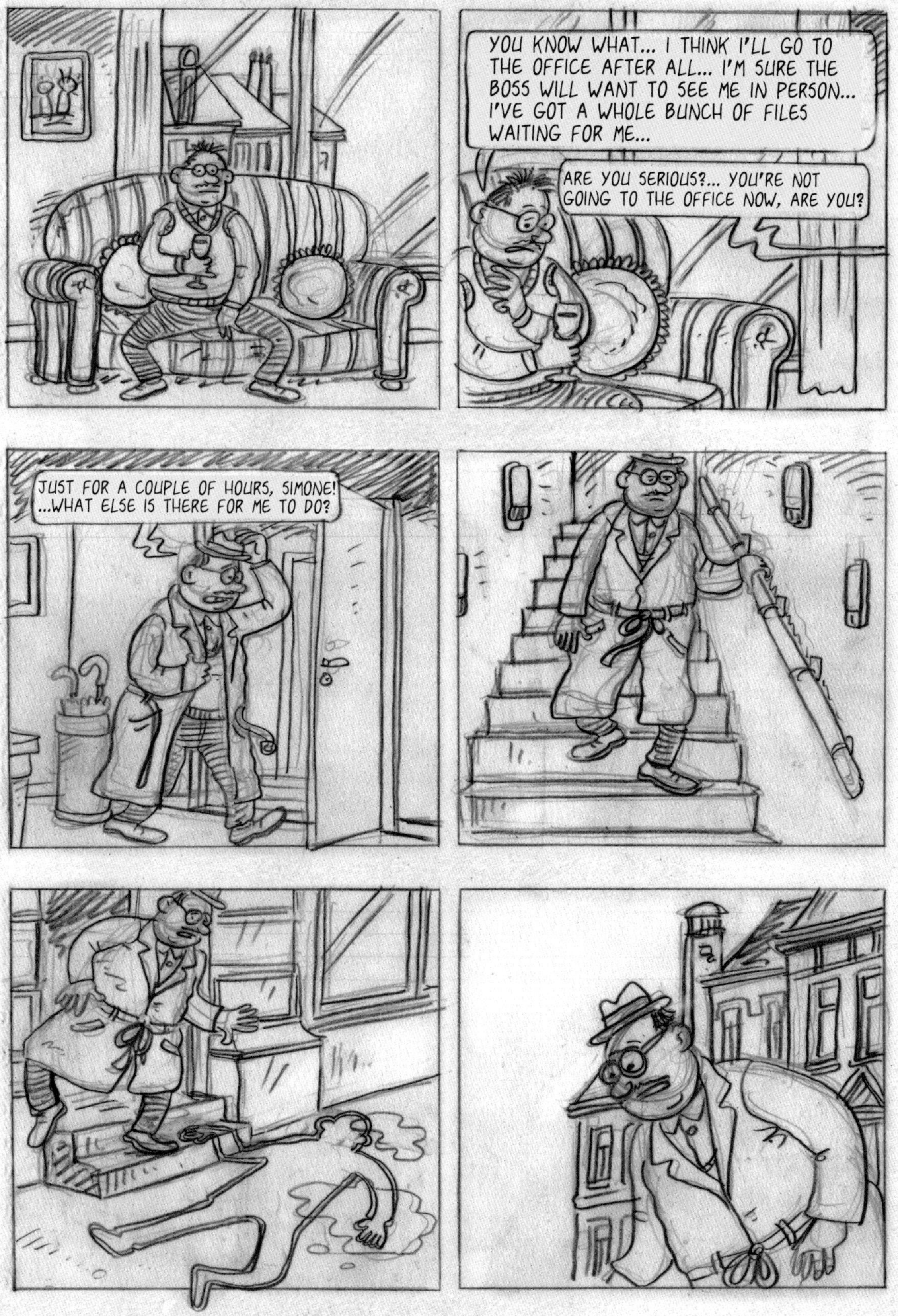
YOU KNOW WHAT... I THINK I'LL GO TO THE OFFICE AFTER ALL... I'M SURE THE BOSS WILL WANT TO SEE ME IN PERSON... I'VE GOT A WHOLE BUNCH OF FILES WAITING FOR ME...
ARE YOU SERIOUS?... YOU'RE NOT GOING TO THE OFFICE NOW, ARE YOU?
JUST FOR A COUPLE OF HOURS, SIMONE! ...WHAT ELSE IS THERE FOR ME TO DO?

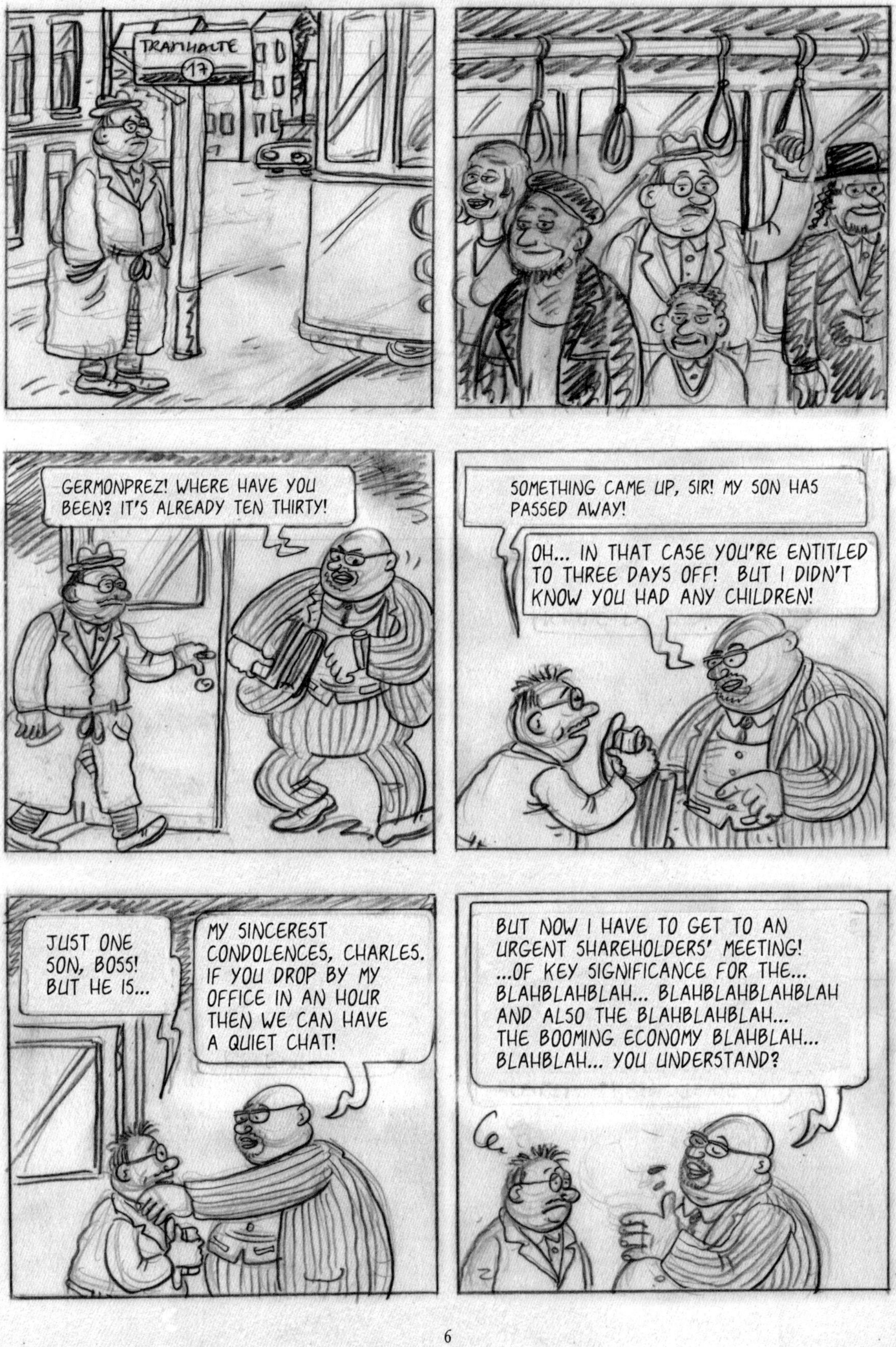
TRAMHALTE
17
GERMONPREZ! WHERE HAVE YOU BEEN? IT'S ALREADY TEN THIRTY!
SOMETHING CAME UP, SIR! MY SON HAS PASSED AWAY!
OH... IN THAT CASE YOU'RE ENTITLED TO THREE DAYS OFF! BUT I DIDN'T KNOW YOU HAD ANY CHILDREN!
JUST ONE SON, BOSS! BUT HE IS...
MY SINCEREST CONDOLENCES, CHARLES. IF YOU DROP BY MY OFFICE IN AN HOUR THEN WE CAN HAVE A QUIET CHAT!
BUT NOW I HAVE TO GET TO AN URGENT SHAREHOLDERS' MEETING! ...OF KEY SIGNIFICANCE FOR THE... BLAHBLAHBLAH... BLAHBLAHBLAHBLAH AND ALSO THE BLAHBLAHBLAH... THE BOOMING ECONOMY BLAHBLAH... BLAHBLAH... YOU UNDERSTAND?

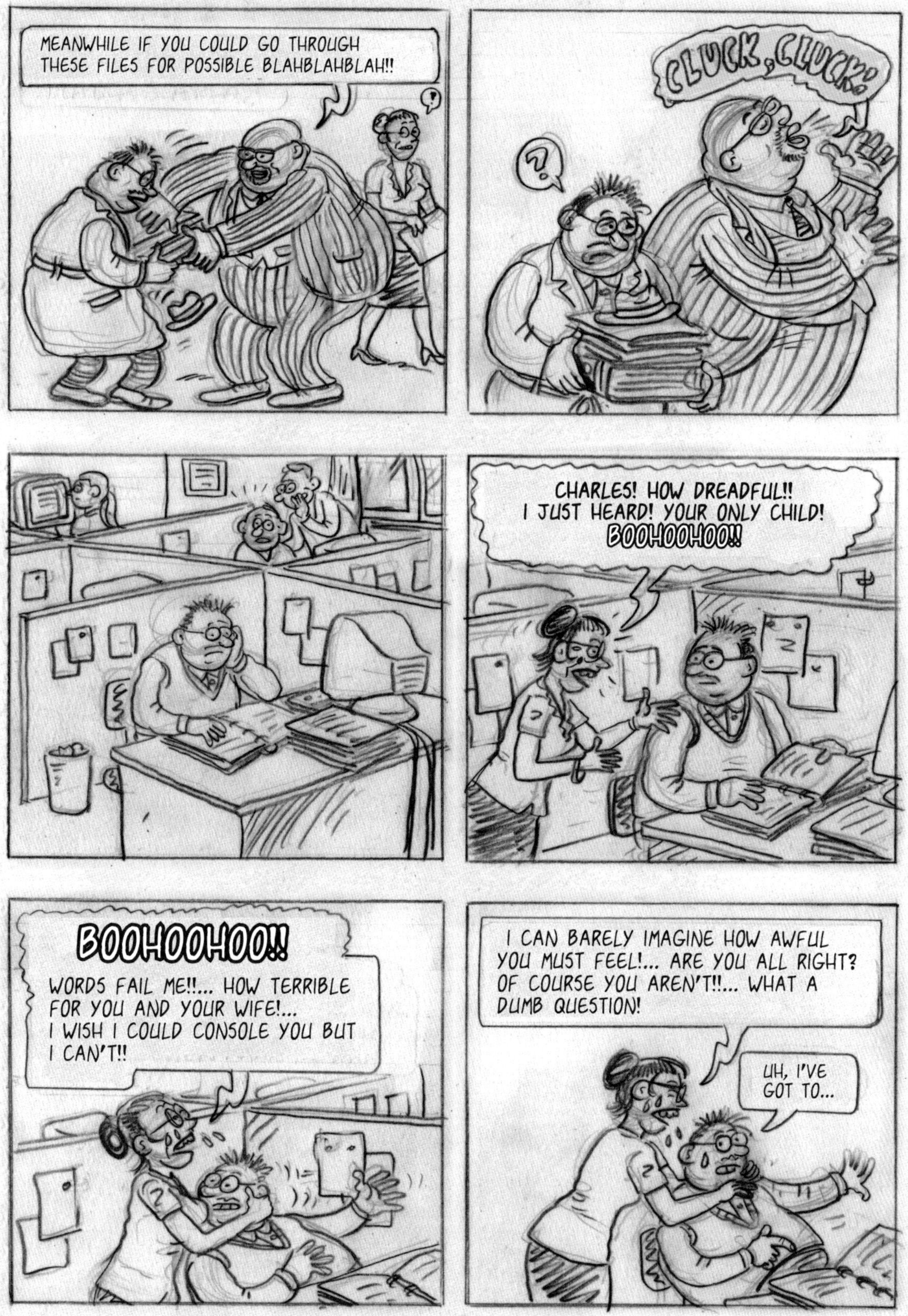
MEANWHILE IF YOU COULD GO THROUGH THESE FILES FOR POSSIBLE BLAHBLAHBLAH!!
CLUCK, CLUCK!
CHARLES! HOW DREADFUL!! I JUST HEARD! YOUR ONLY CHILD! BOOHOOHOO!!
BOOHOOHOO!!
WORDS FAIL ME!!... HOW TERRIBLE FOR YOU AND YOUR WIFE!... I WISH I COULD CONSOLE YOU BUT I CAN'T!!
I CAN BARELY IMAGINE HOW AWFUL YOU MUST FEEL!... ARE YOU ALL RIGHT? OF COURSE YOU AREN'T!!... WHAT A DUMB QUESTION!
UH, I'VE GOT TO...

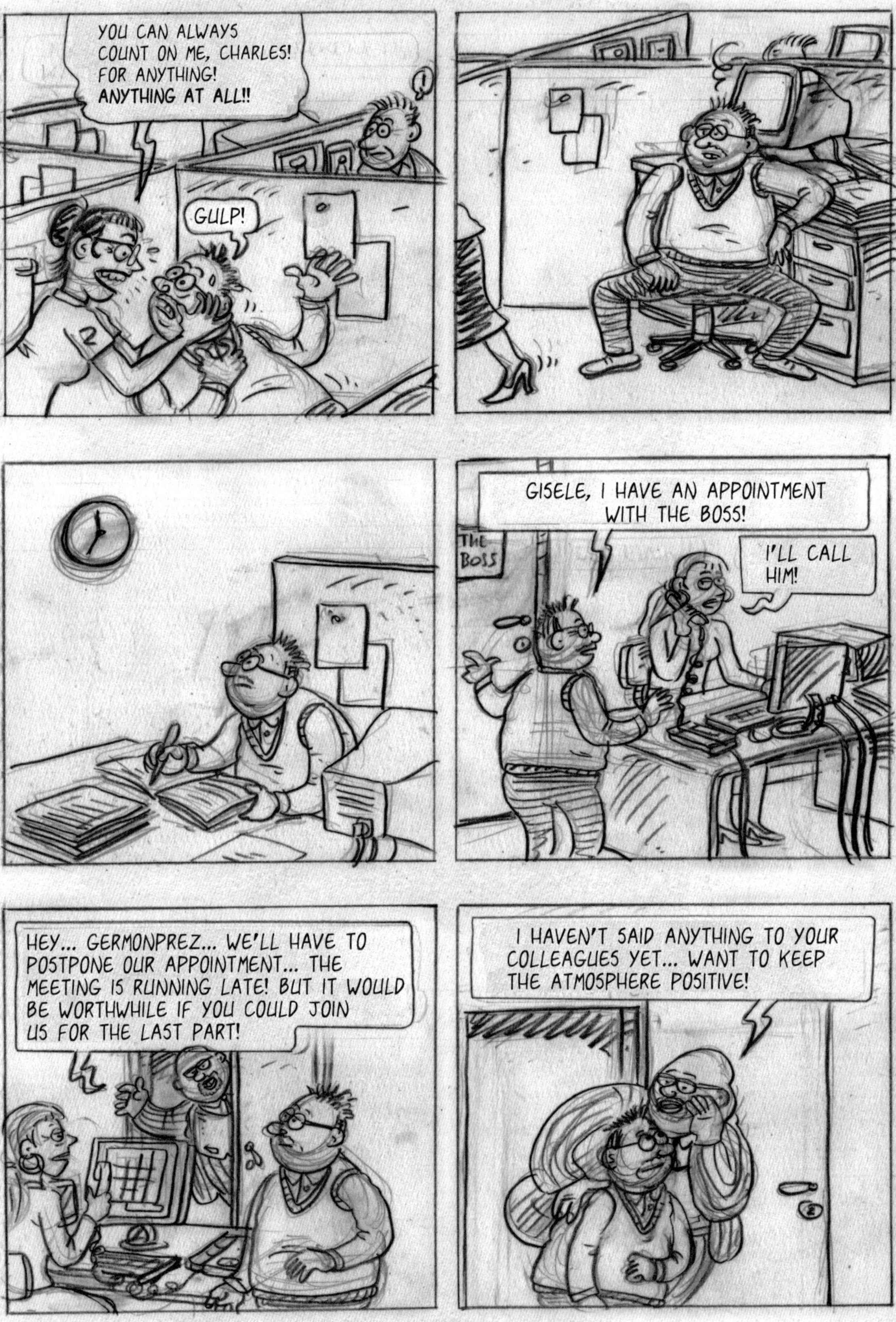
YOU CAN ALWAYS COUNT ON ME, CHARLES! FOR ANYTHING! ANYTHING AT ALL!!
!
GULP!
GISELE, I HAVE AN APPOINTMENT WITH THE BOSS!
THE BOSS
I'LL CALL HIM!
HEY... GERMONPREZ... WE'LL HAVE TO POSTPONE OUR APPOINTMENT... THE MEETING IS RUNNING LATE! BUT IT WOULD BE WORTHWHILE IF YOU COULD JOIN US FOR THE LAST PART!
I HAVEN'T SAID ANYTHING TO YOUR COLLEAGUES YET... WANT TO KEEP THE ATMOSPHERE POSITIVE!

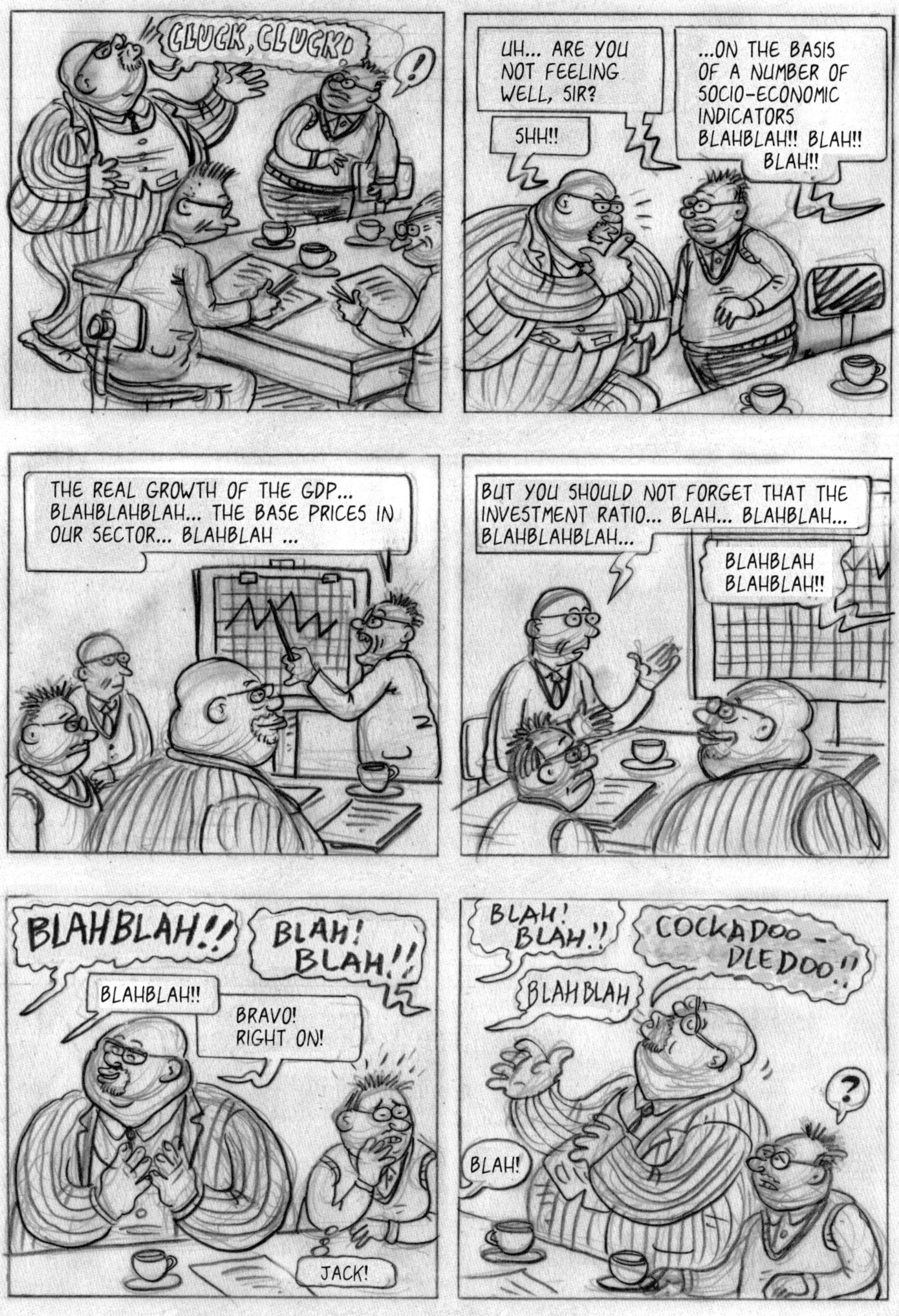
CLUCK, CLUCK!
!
UH... ARE YOU NOT FEELING WELL, SIR?
SHH!!
...ON THE BASIS OF A NUMBER OF SOCIO-ECONOMIC INDICATORS BLAHBLAH!! BLAH!! BLAH!!
THE REAL GROWTH OF THE GDP... BLAHBLAHBLAH... THE BASE PRICES IN OUR SECTOR... BLAHBLAH ...
BUT YOU SHOULD NOT FORGET THAT THE INVESTMENT RATIO... BLAH... BLAHBLAH... BLAHBLAHBLAH...
BLAHBLAH BLAHBLAH!!
BLAHBLAH!!
BLAH! BLAH!!
BLAHBLAH!!
BRAVO! RIGHT ON!
JACK!
BLAH! BLAH!!
COCKADOO-DLEDOO!!
BLAHBLAH
BLAH!
?

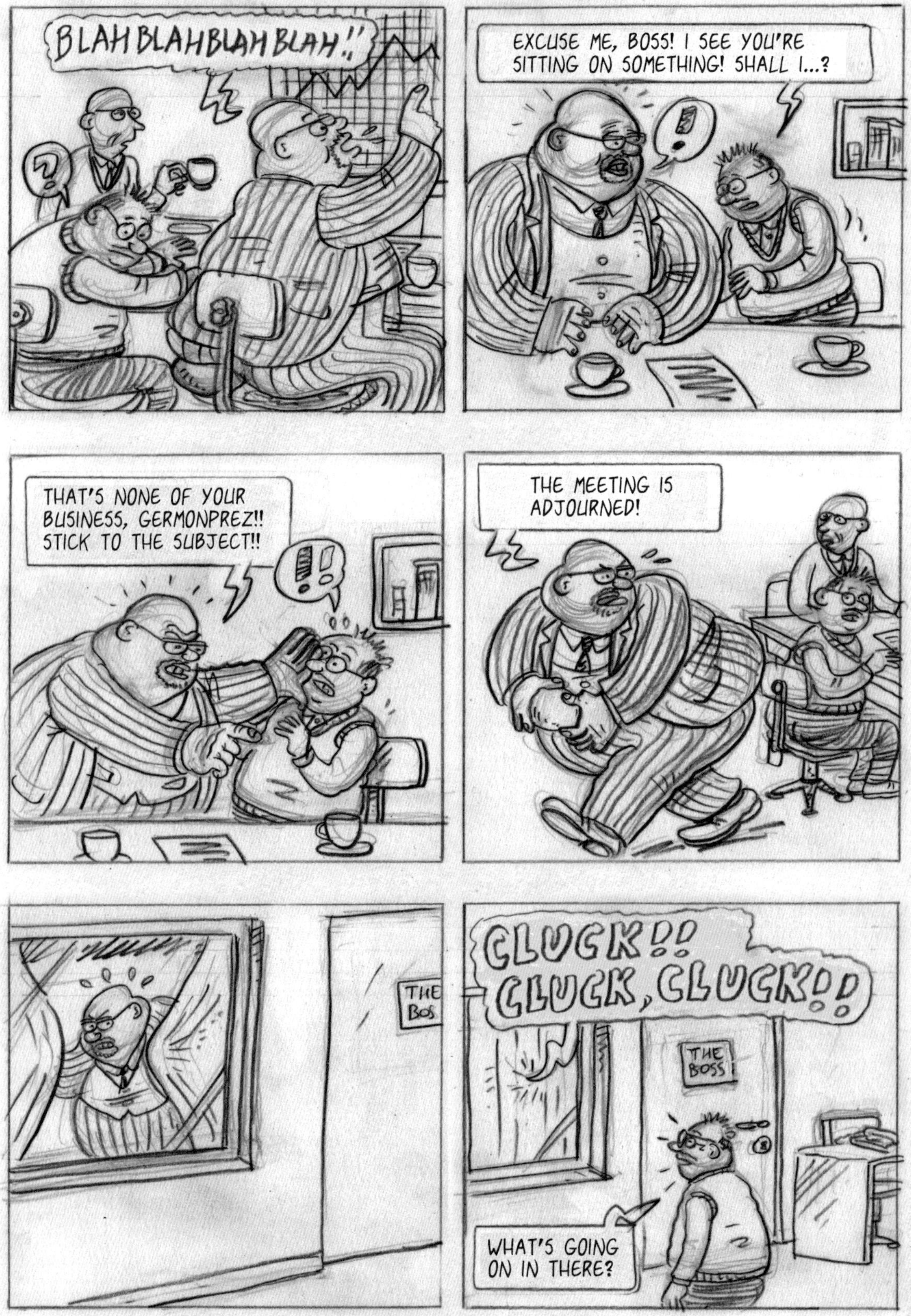
BLAH BLAH BLAH BLAH!!
EXCUSE ME, BOSS! I SEE YOU'RE SITTING ON SOMETHING! SHALL I...?
THAT'S NONE OF YOUR BUSINESS, GERMONPREZ!! STICK TO THE SUBJECT!!
THE MEETING IS ADJOURNED!
THE BOS
CLUCK!! CLUCK, CLUCK!!
THE BOSS
WHAT'S GOING ON IN THERE?

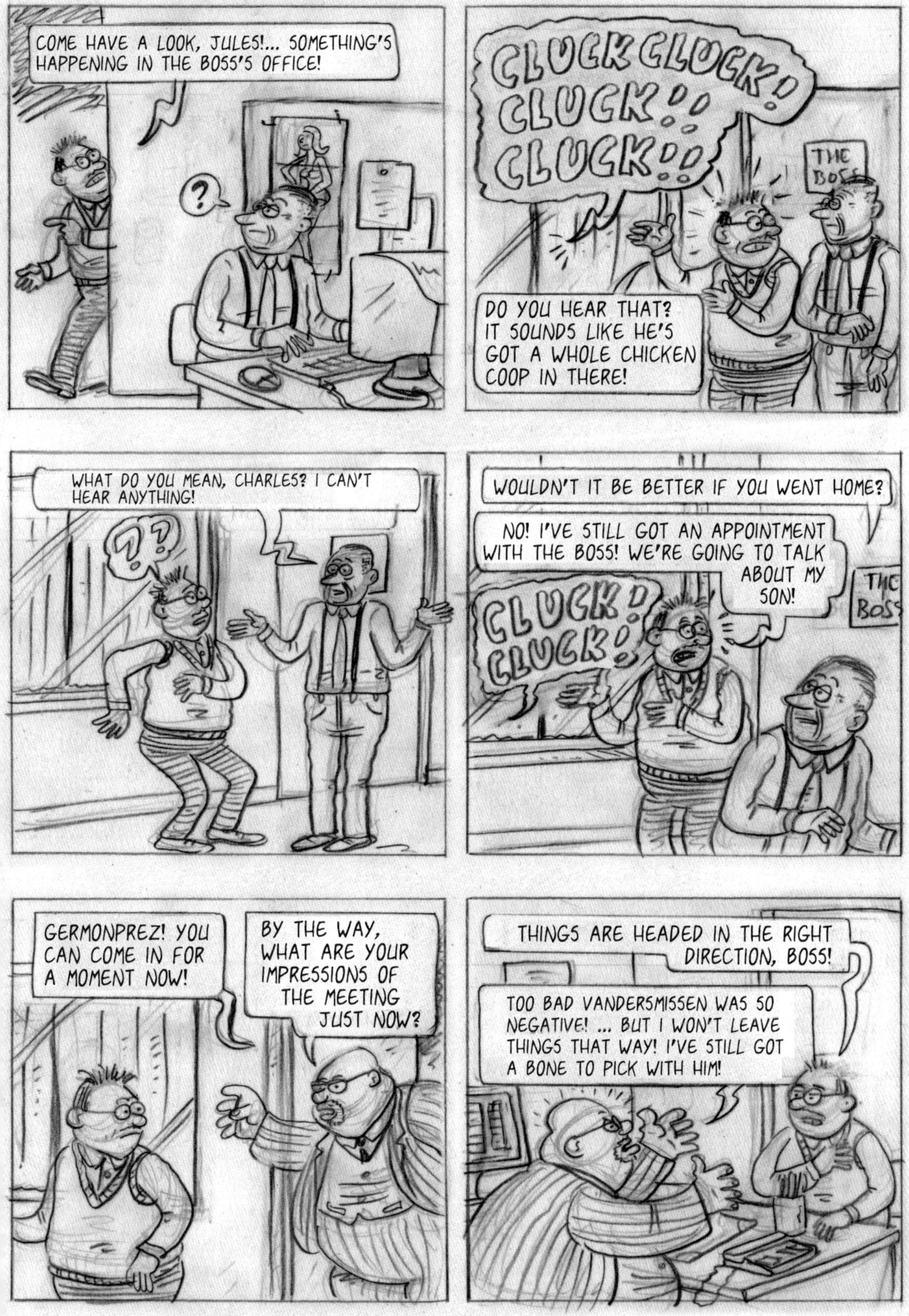

COME HAVE A LOOK, JULES!... SOMETHING'S HAPPENING IN THE BOSS'S OFFICE!
?
CLUCK CLUCK! CLUCK!! CLUCK!!
THE BOSS
DO YOU HEAR THAT? IT SOUNDS LIKE HE'S GOT A WHOLE CHICKEN COOP IN THERE!
WHAT DO YOU MEAN, CHARLES? I CAN'T HEAR ANYTHING!
??
WOULDN'T IT BE BETTER IF YOU WENT HOME?
NO! I'VE STILL GOT AN APPOINTMENT WITH THE BOSS! WE'RE GOING TO TALK ABOUT MY SON!
CLUCK! CLUCK!
THE BOSS
GERMONPREZ! YOU CAN COME IN FOR A MOMENT NOW!
BY THE WAY, WHAT ARE YOUR IMPRESSIONS OF THE MEETING JUST NOW?
THINGS ARE HEADED IN THE RIGHT DIRECTION, BOSS!
TOO BAD VANDERSMISSEN WAS SO NEGATIVE! ... BUT I WON'T LEAVE THINGS THAT WAY! I'VE STILL GOT A BONE TO PICK WITH HIM!

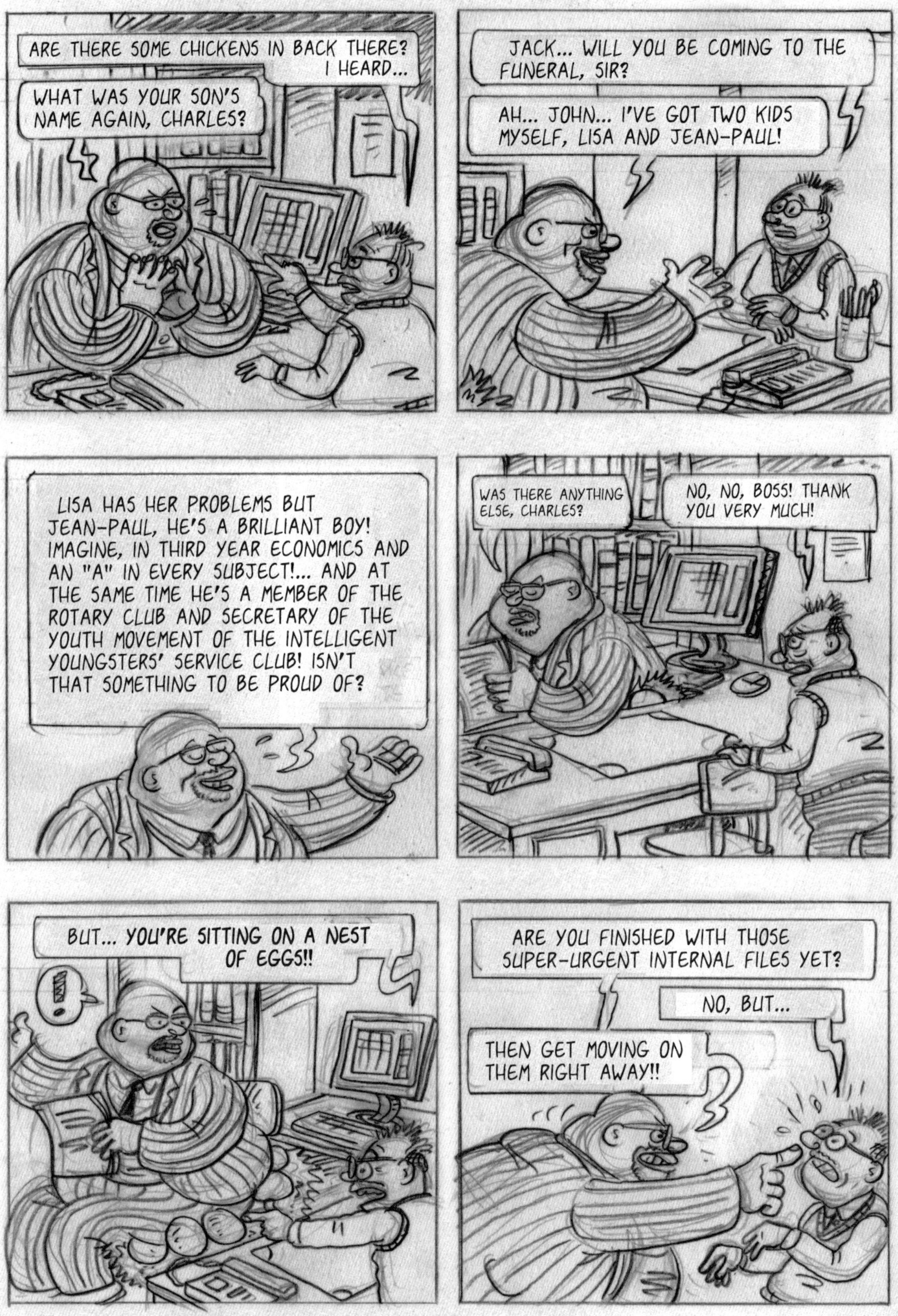
ARE THERE SOME CHICKENS IN BACK THERE? I HEARD...
WHAT WAS YOUR SON'S NAME AGAIN, CHARLES?
JACK... WILL YOU BE COMING TO THE FUNERAL, SIR?
AH... JOHN... I'VE GOT TWO KIDS MYSELF, LISA AND JEAN-PAUL!
LISA HAS HER PROBLEMS BUT JEAN-PAUL, HE'S A BRILLIANT BOY! IMAGINE, IN THIRD YEAR ECONOMICS AND AN "A" IN EVERY SUBJECT!... AND AT THE SAME TIME HE'S A MEMBER OF THE ROTARY CLUB AND SECRETARY OF THE YOUTH MOVEMENT OF THE INTELLIGENT YOUNGSTERS' SERVICE CLUB! ISN'T THAT SOMETHING TO BE PROUD OF?
WAS THERE ANYTHING ELSE, CHARLES?
NO, NO, BOSS! THANK YOU VERY MUCH!
BUT... YOU'RE SITTING ON A NEST OF EGGS!!
!
ARE YOU FINISHED WITH THOSE SUPER-URGENT INTERNAL FILES YET?
NO, BUT...
THEN GET MOVING ON THEM RIGHT AWAY!!

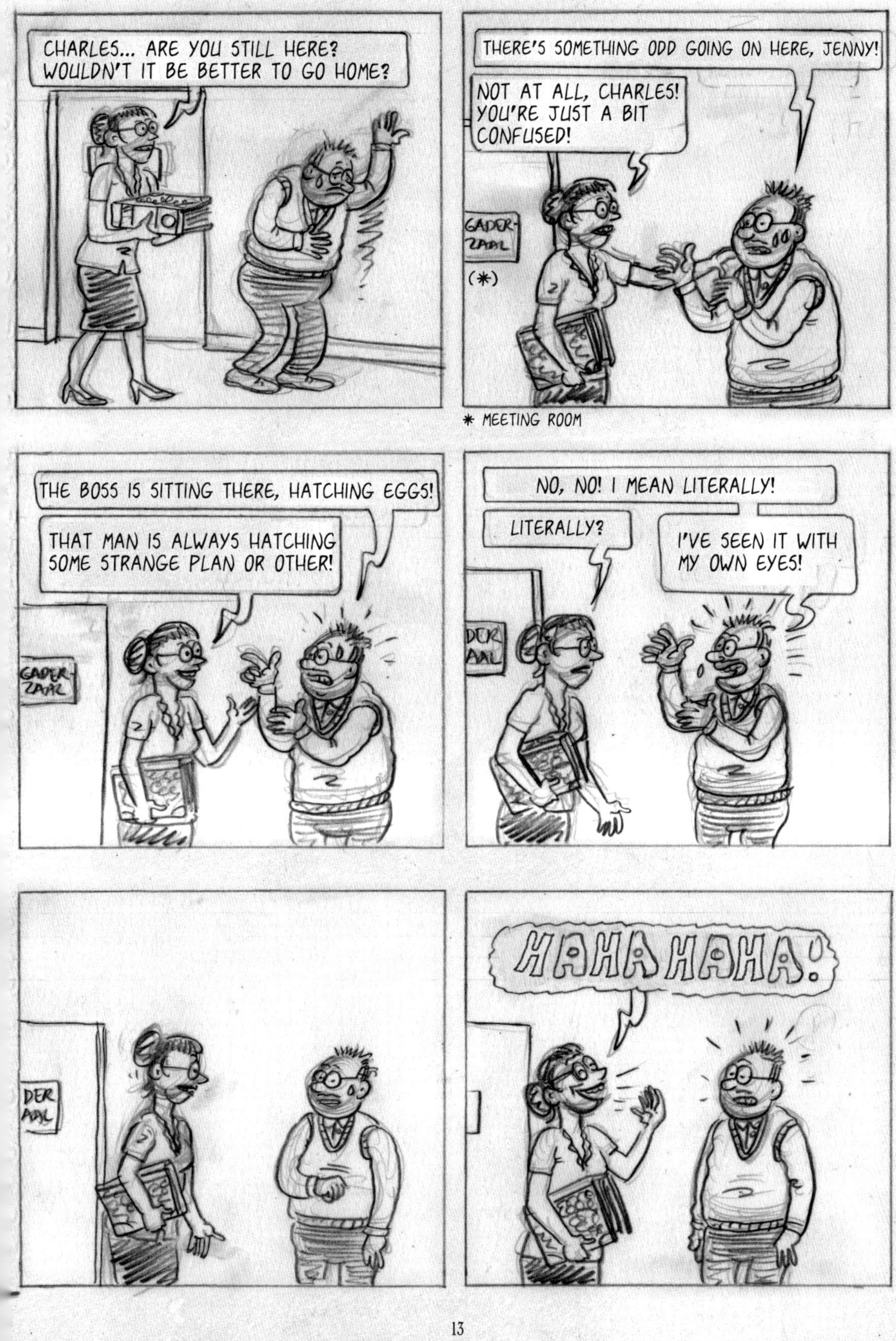
CHARLES... ARE YOU STILL HERE? WOULDN'T IT BE BETTER TO GO HOME?
THERE'S SOMETHING ODD GOING ON HERE, JENNY!
NOT AT ALL, CHARLES! YOU'RE JUST A BIT CONFUSED!
GADER-ZAAL
(*)
* MEETING ROOM
THE BOSS IS SITTING THERE, HATCHING EGGS!
THAT MAN IS ALWAYS HATCHING SOME STRANGE PLAN OR OTHER!
GADER-ZAAL
NO, NO! I MEAN LITERALLY!
LITERALLY?
I'VE SEEN IT WITH MY OWN EYES!
HAHAHAHAHA!

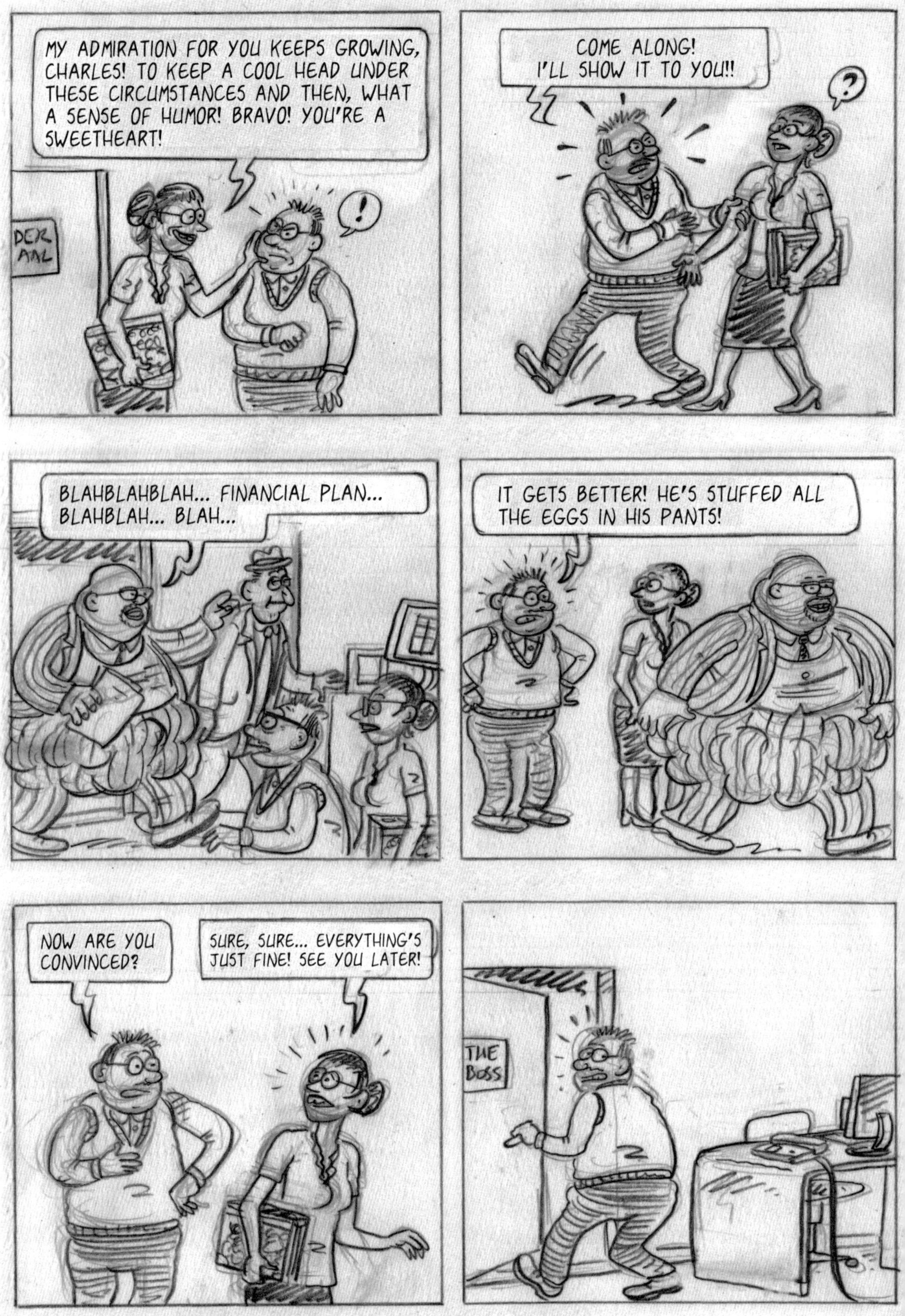
MY ADMIRATION FOR YOU KEEPS GROWING, CHARLES! TO KEEP A COOL HEAD UNDER THESE CIRCUMSTANCES AND THEN, WHAT A SENSE OF HUMOR! BRAVO! YOU'RE A SWEETHEART!
DER AAL
!
COME ALONG! I'LL SHOW IT TO YOU!!
?
BLAHBLAHBLAH... FINANCIAL PLAN... BLAHBLAH... BLAH...
IT GETS BETTER! HE'S STUFFED ALL THE EGGS IN HIS PANTS!
NOW ARE YOU CONVINCED?
SURE, SURE... EVERYTHING'S JUST FINE! SEE YOU LATER!
THE BOSS

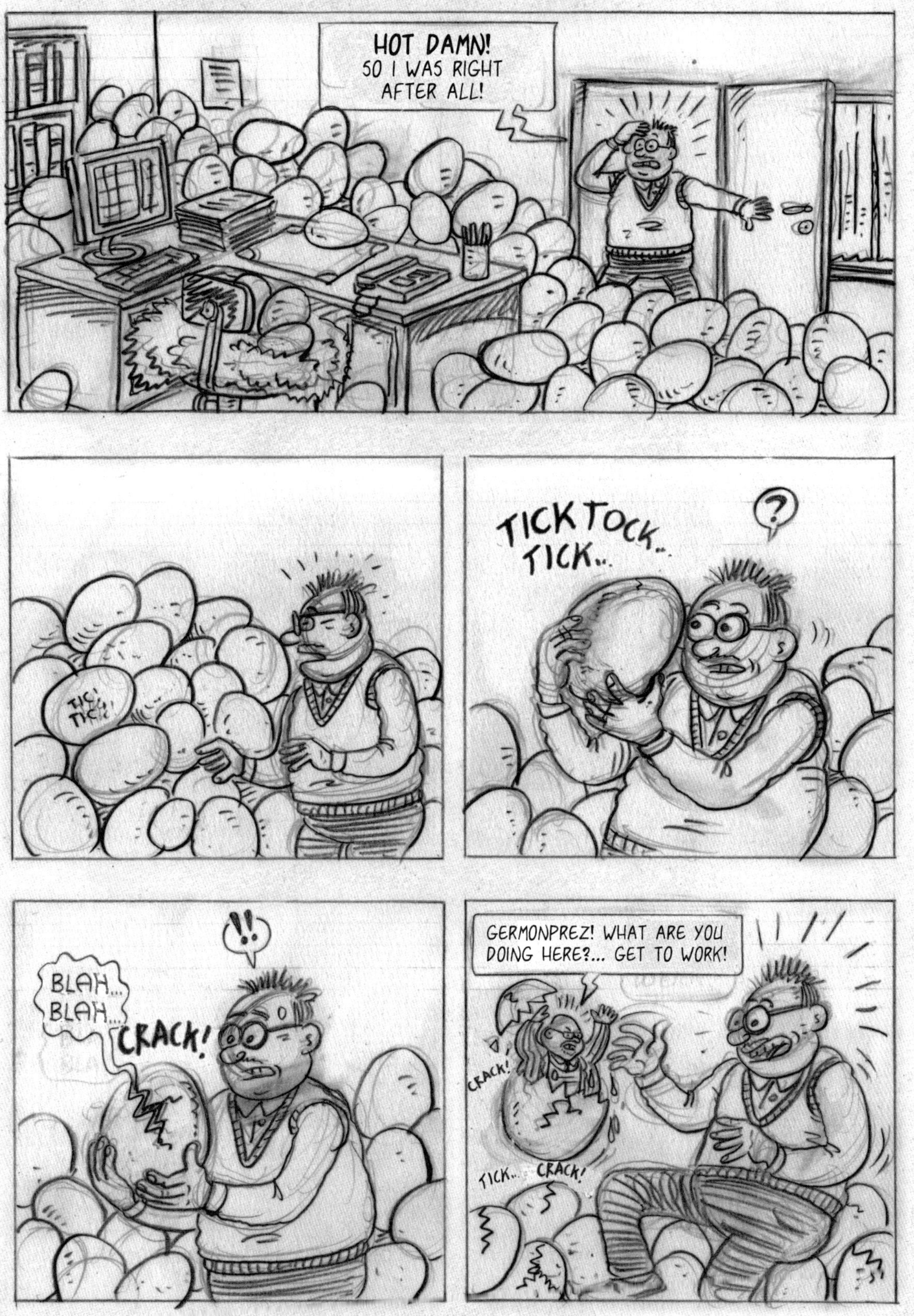
HOT DAMN!
SO I WAS RIGHT AFTER ALL!
TIC! TICK
TICK TOCK..
TICK..
?
!!
BLAH...
BLAH...
CRACK!
GERMONPREZ! WHAT ARE YOU DOING HERE?... GET TO WORK!
CRACK!
TICK...
CRACK!

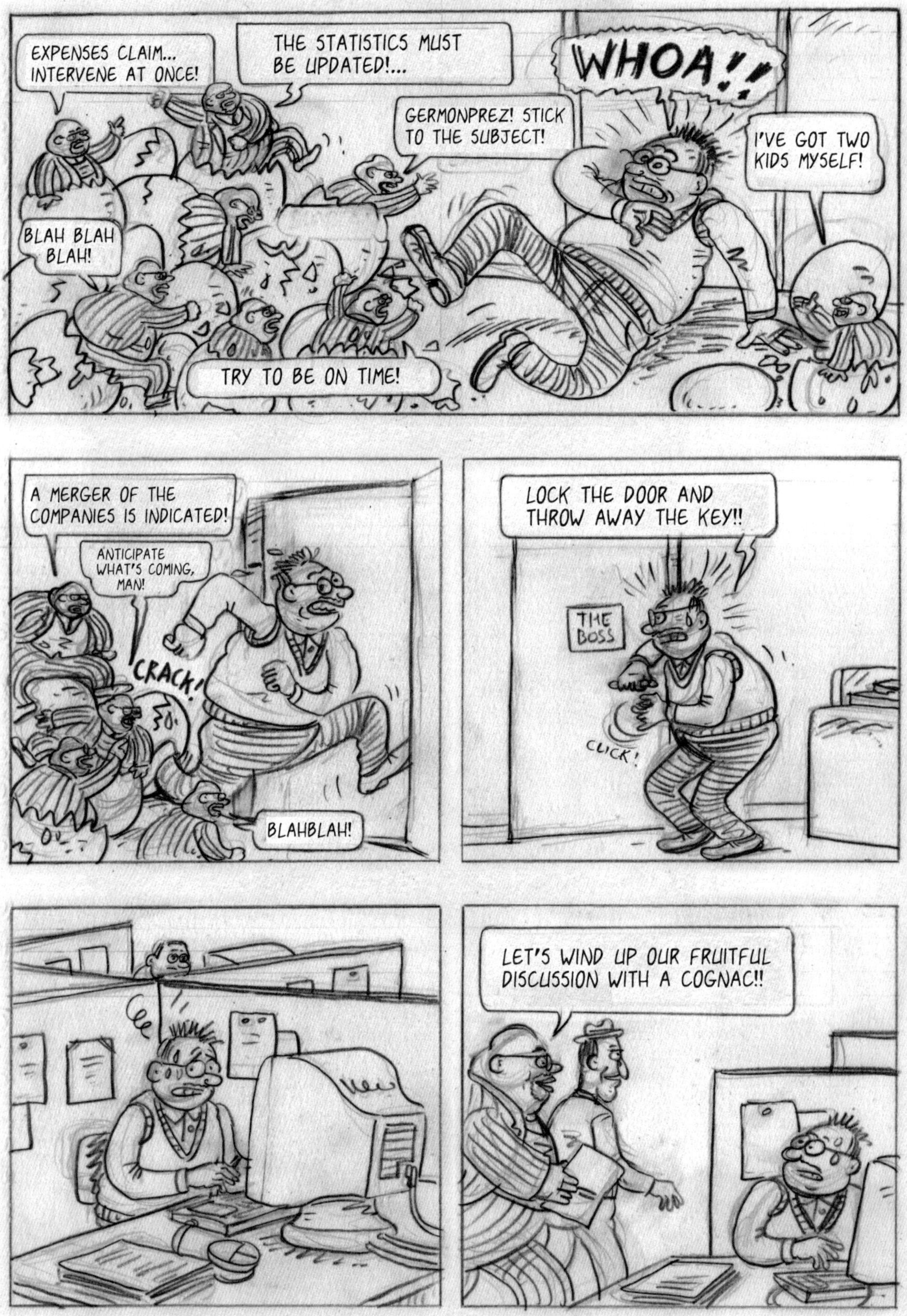
EXPENSES CLAIM... INTERVENE AT ONCE!
THE STATISTICS MUST BE UPDATED!...
WHOA!!
GERMONPREZ! STICK TO THE SUBJECT!
I'VE GOT TWO KIDS MYSELF!
BLAH BLAH BLAH!
TRY TO BE ON TIME!
A MERGER OF THE COMPANIES IS INDICATED!
ANTICIPATE WHAT'S COMING, MAN!
CRACK!
BLAHBLAH!
LOCK THE DOOR AND THROW AWAY THE KEY!!
THE BOSS
CLICK!
LET'S WIND UP OUR FRUITFUL DISCUSSION WITH A COGNAC!!

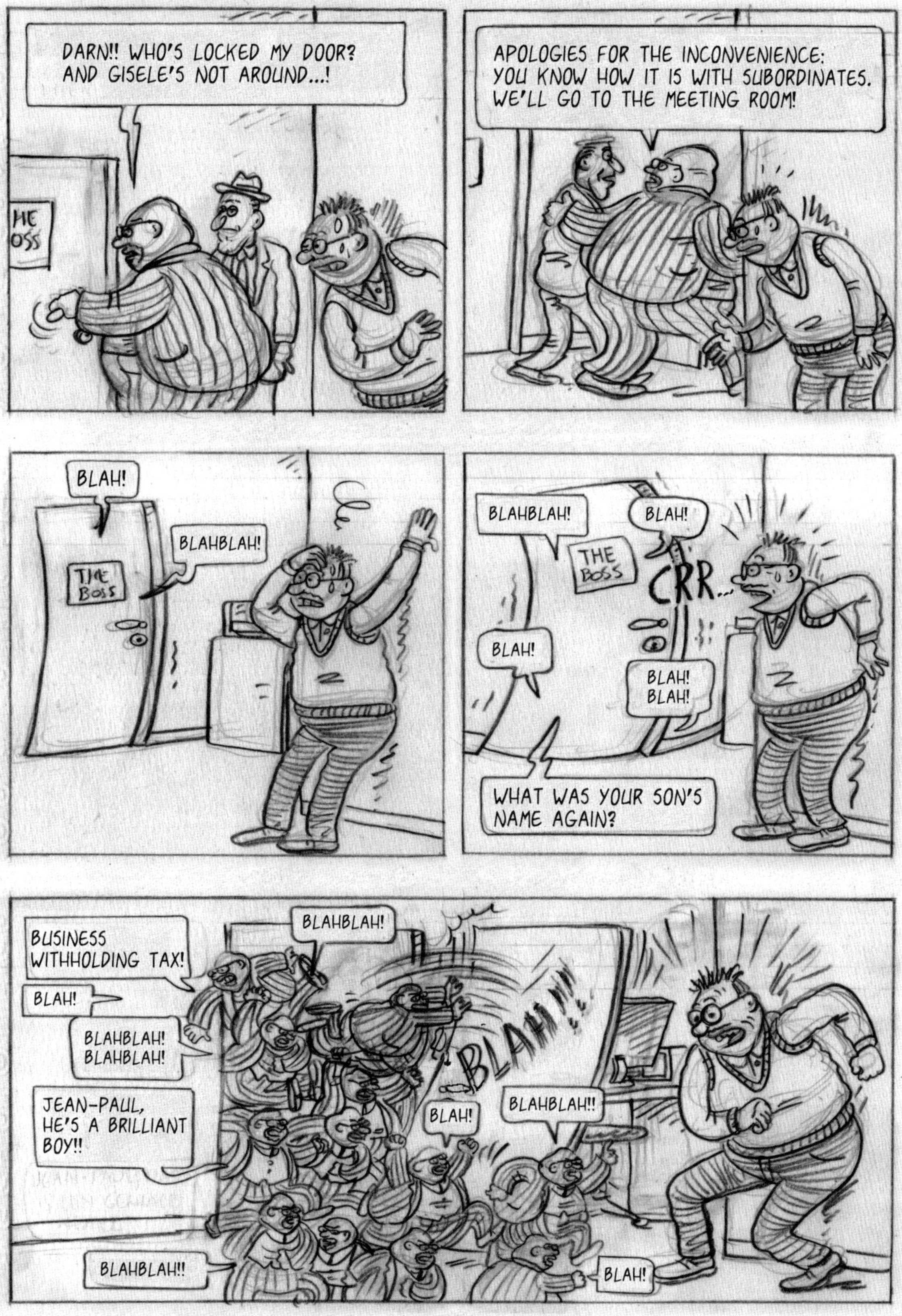
DARN!! WHO'S LOCKED MY DOOR? AND GISELE'S NOT AROUND...!
APOLOGIES FOR THE INCONVENIENCE: YOU KNOW HOW IT IS WITH SUBORDINATES. WE'LL GO TO THE MEETING ROOM!
BLAH!
THE BOSS
BLAHBLAH!
BLAHBLAH!
BLAH!
THE BOSS
CRR...
BLAH!
BLAH! BLAH!
WHAT WAS YOUR SON'S NAME AGAIN?
BUSINESS WITHHOLDING TAX!
BLAHBLAH!
BLAH!
BLAHBLAH! BLAHBLAH!
BLAH!!!
JEAN-PAUL, HE'S A BRILLIANT BOY!!
BLAH!
BLAHBLAH!!
BLAHBLAH!!
BLAH!

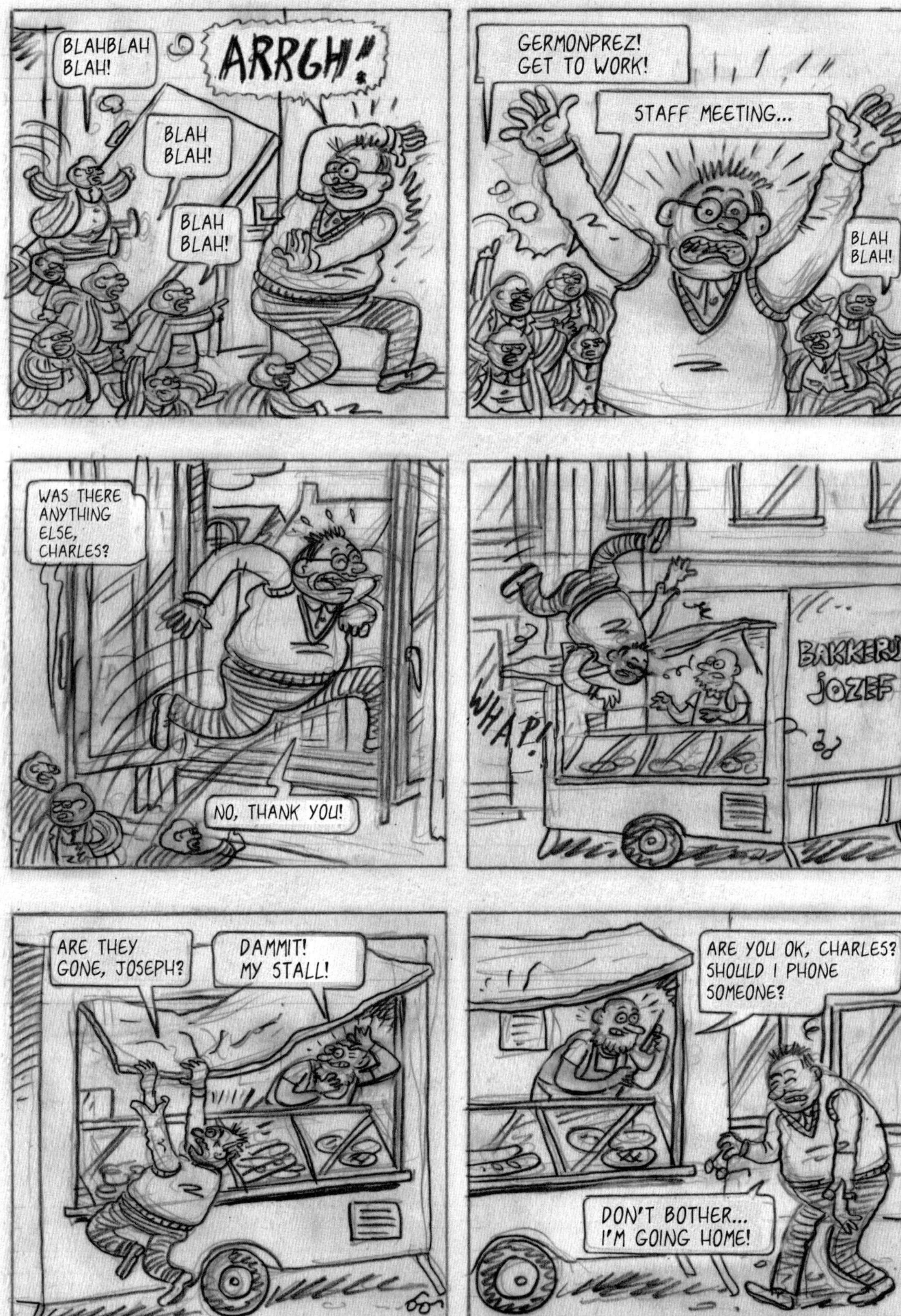

BLAHBLAH BLAH!
ARRGH!
BLAH BLAH!
BLAH BLAH!
GERMONPREZ! GET TO WORK!
STAFF MEETING...
BLAH BLAH!
WAS THERE ANYTHING ELSE, CHARLES?
NO, THANK YOU!
WHAP!
BAKKERIJ JOZEF
ARE THEY GONE, JOSEPH?
DAMMIT! MY STALL!
ARE YOU OK, CHARLES? SHOULD I PHONE SOMEONE?
DON'T BOTHER... I'M GOING HOME!

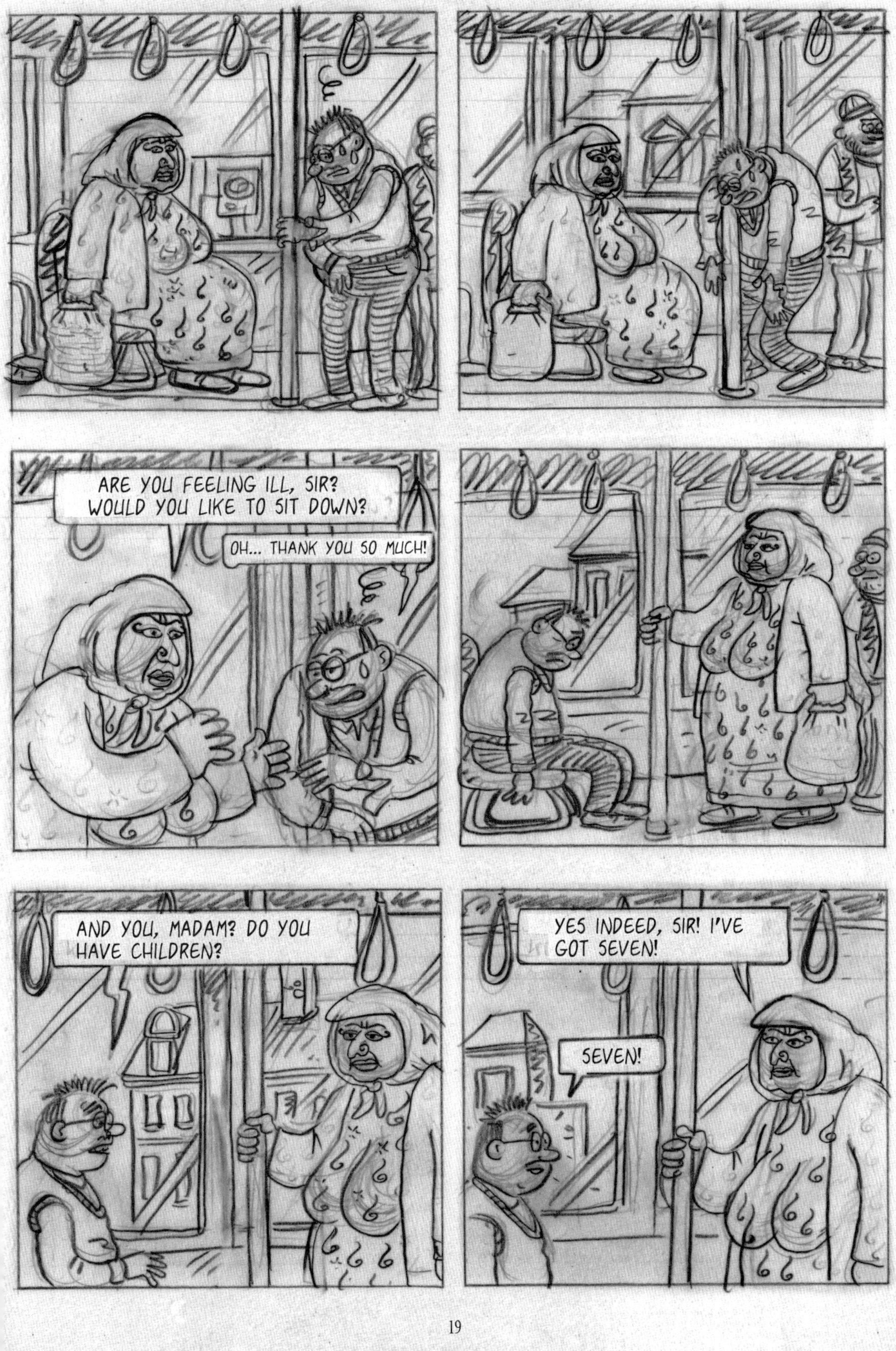
ARE YOU FEELING ILL, SIR? WOULD YOU LIKE TO SIT DOWN?
OH... THANK YOU SO MUCH!
AND YOU, MADAM? DO YOU HAVE CHILDREN?
YES INDEED, SIR! I'VE GOT SEVEN!
SEVEN!

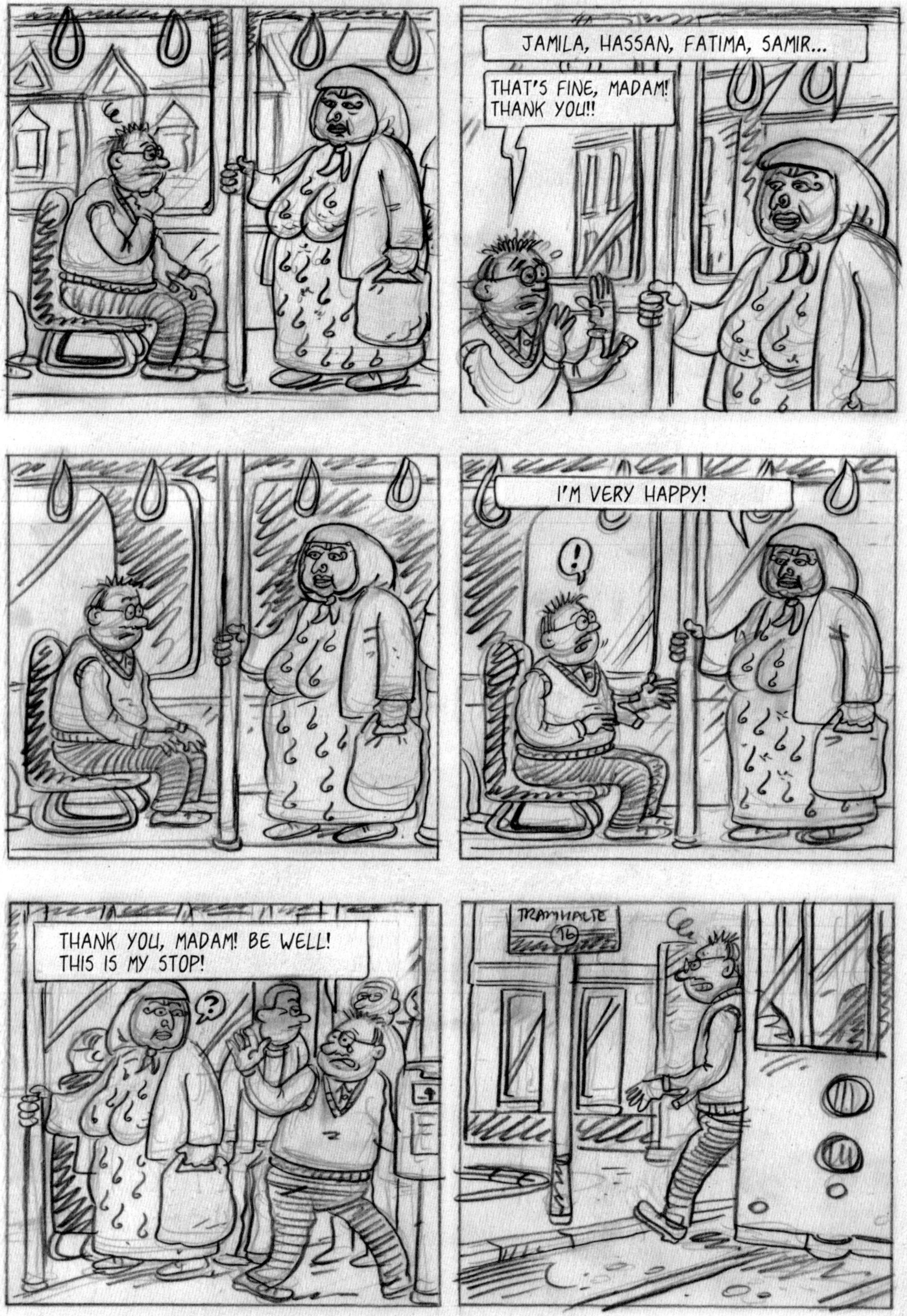
JAMILA, HASSAN, FATIMA, SAMIR...
THAT'S FINE, MADAM! THANK YOU!!
I'M VERY HAPPY!
!
THANK YOU, MADAM! BE WELL! THIS IS MY STOP!
?
TRAMHALTE
16

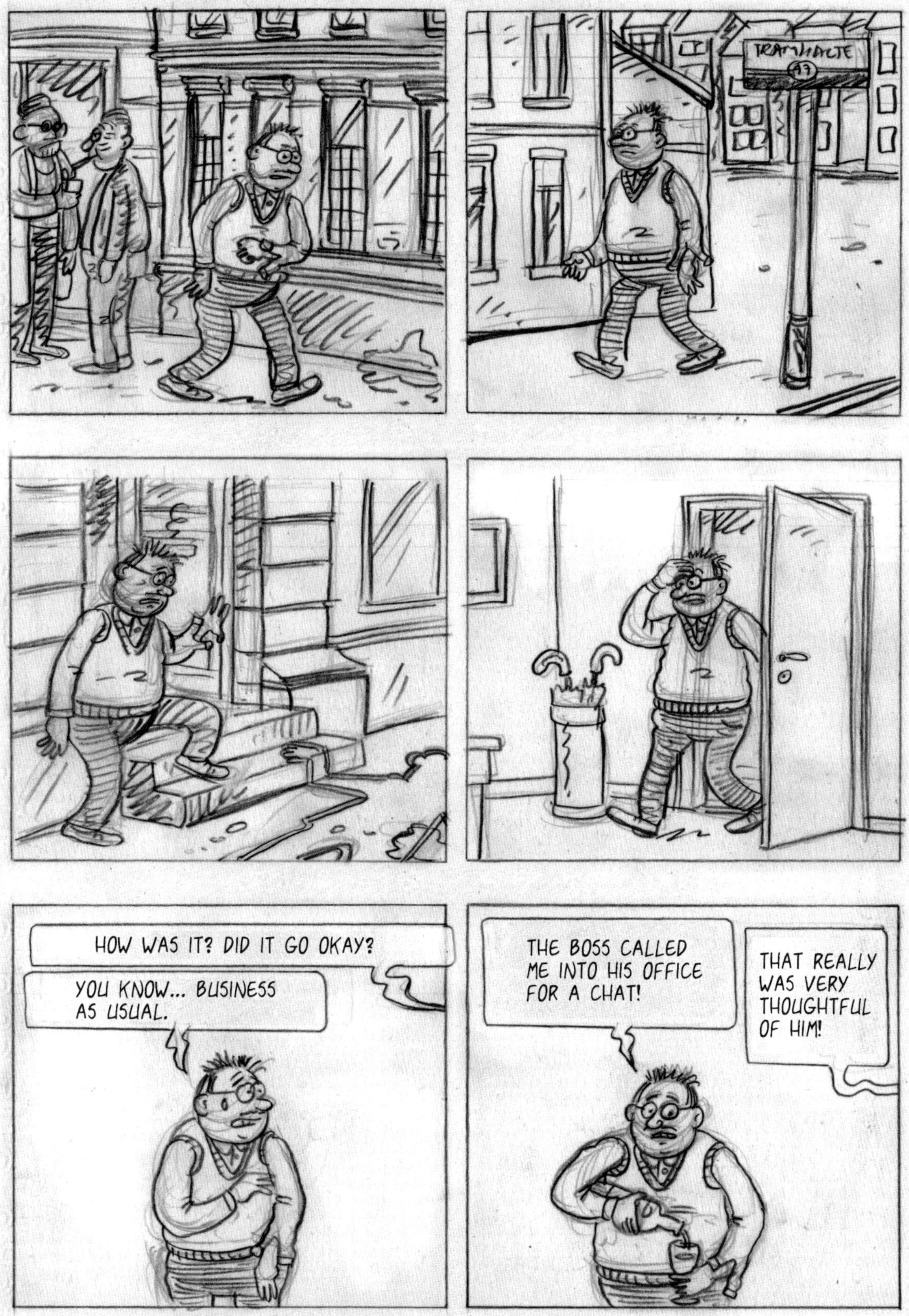
HOW WAS IT? DID IT GO OKAY?
YOU KNOW... BUSINESS AS USUAL.
THE BOSS CALLED ME INTO HIS OFFICE FOR A CHAT!
THAT REALLY WAS VERY THOUGHTFUL OF HIM!

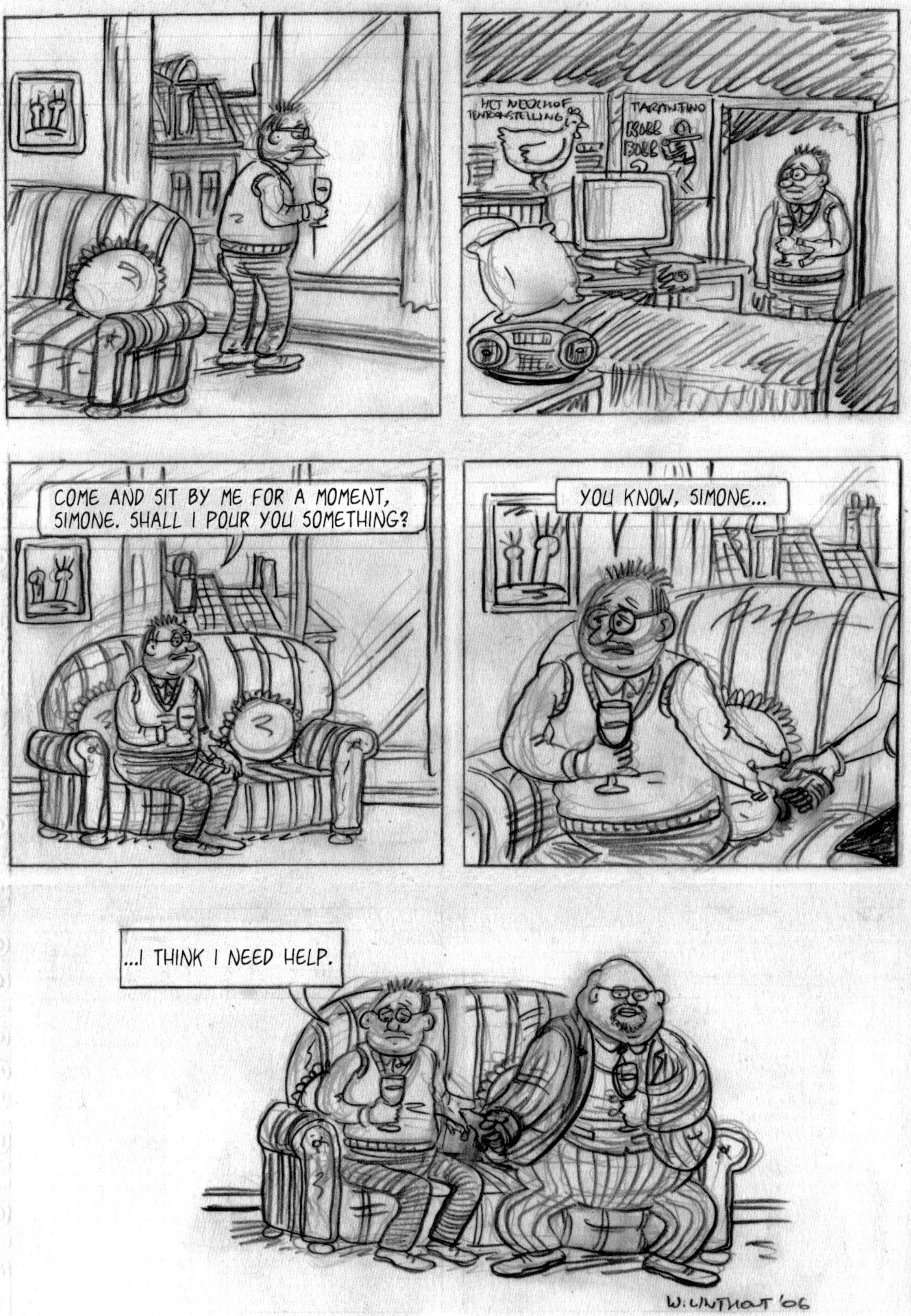
COME AND SIT BY ME FOR A MOMENT, SIMONE. SHALL I POUR YOU SOMETHING?
YOU KNOW, SIMONE...
...I THINK I NEED HELP.

CHAPTER 2 - THERE IS ONLY ONE COLOR

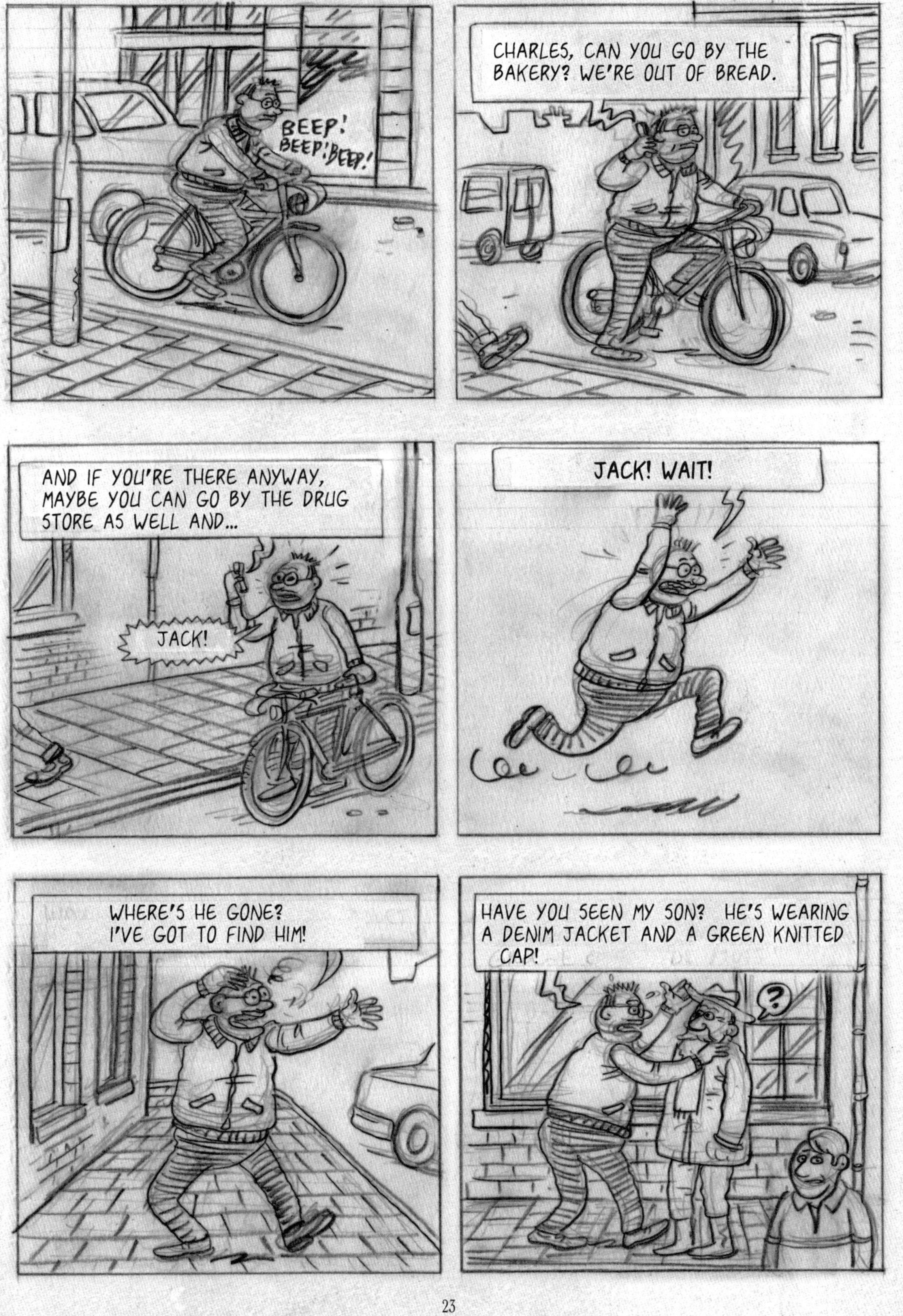
BEEP! BEEP! BEEP!
CHARLES, CAN YOU GO BY THE BAKERY? WE'RE OUT OF BREAD.
AND IF YOU'RE THERE ANYWAY, MAYBE YOU CAN GO BY THE DRUG STORE AS WELL AND...
JACK!
JACK! WAIT!
WHERE'S HE GONE? I'VE GOT TO FIND HIM!
HAVE YOU SEEN MY SON? HE'S WEARING A DENIM JACKET AND A GREEN KNITTED CAP!
?

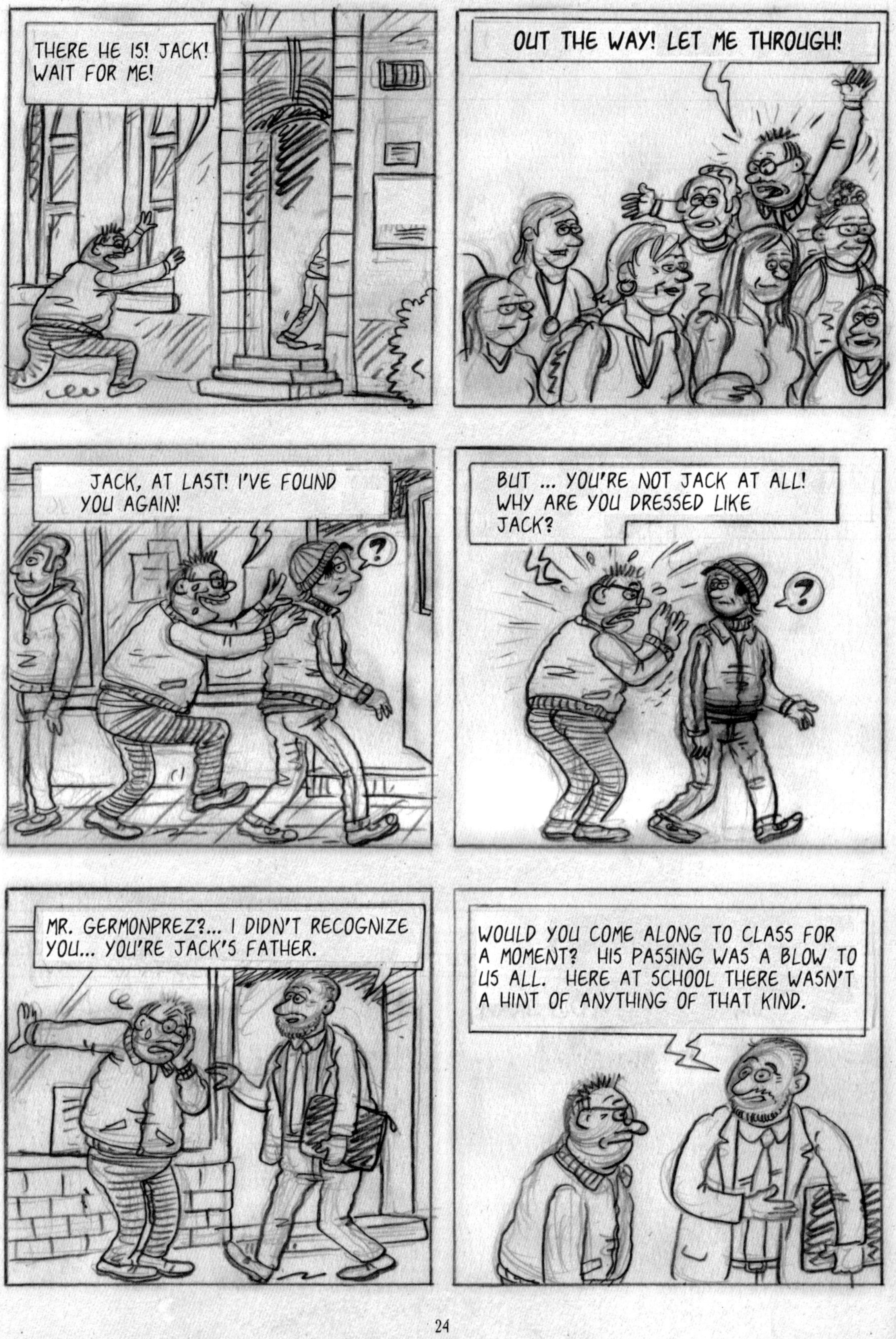
THERE HE IS! JACK! WAIT FOR ME!
OUT THE WAY! LET ME THROUGH!
JACK, AT LAST! I'VE FOUND YOU AGAIN!
?
BUT ... YOU'RE NOT JACK AT ALL! WHY ARE YOU DRESSED LIKE JACK?
?
MR. GERMONPREZ?... I DIDN'T RECOGNIZE YOU... YOU'RE JACK'S FATHER.
WOULD YOU COME ALONG TO CLASS FOR A MOMENT? HIS PASSING WAS A BLOW TO US ALL. HERE AT SCHOOL THERE WASN'T A HINT OF ANYTHING OF THAT KIND.

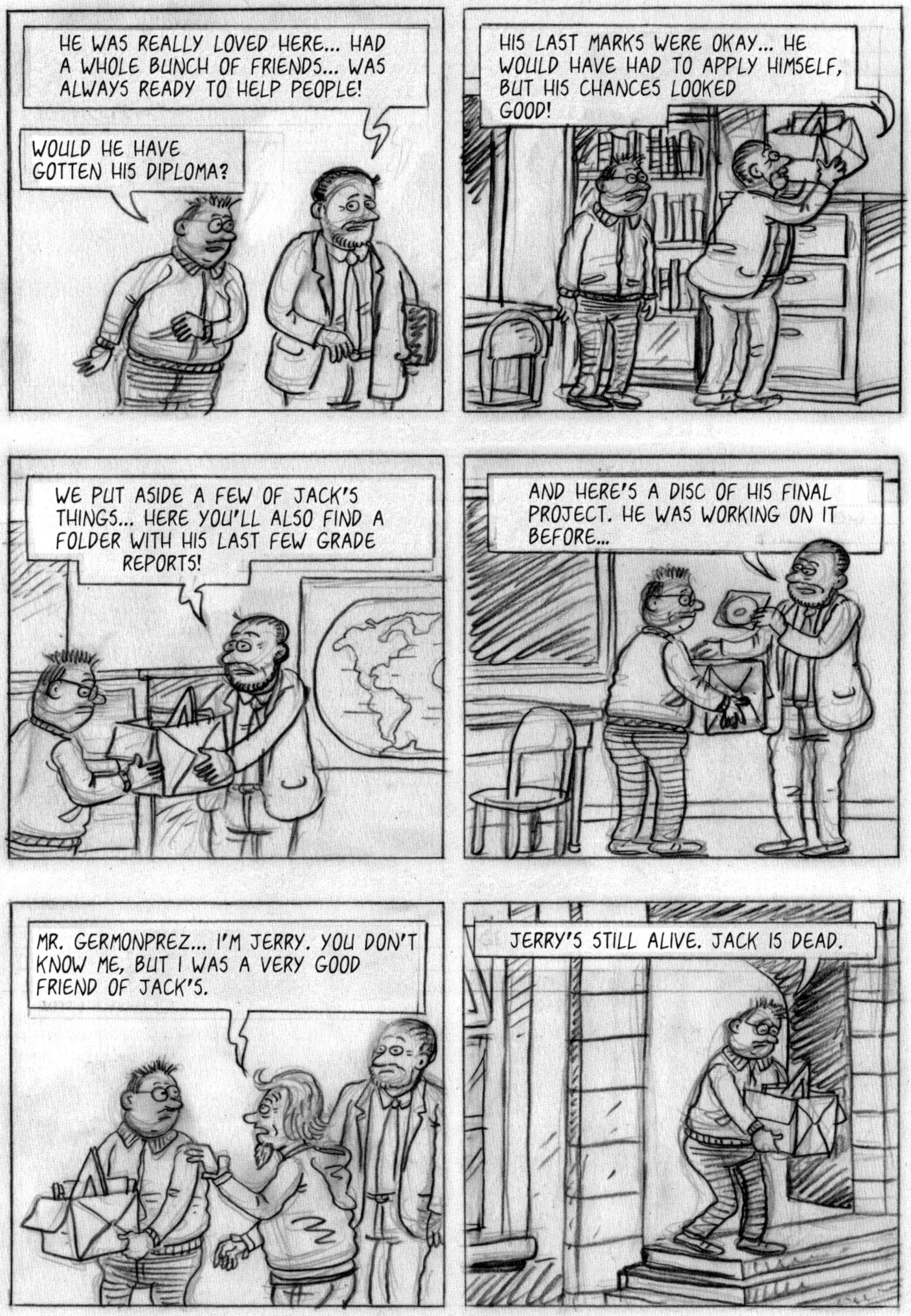
HE WAS REALLY LOVED HERE... HAD A WHOLE BUNCH OF FRIENDS... WAS ALWAYS READY TO HELP PEOPLE!
WOULD HE HAVE GOTTEN HIS DIPLOMA?
HIS LAST MARKS WERE OKAY... HE WOULD HAVE HAD TO APPLY HIMSELF, BUT HIS CHANCES LOOKED GOOD!
WE PUT ASIDE A FEW OF JACK'S THINGS... HERE YOU'LL ALSO FIND A FOLDER WITH HIS LAST FEW GRADE REPORTS!
AND HERE'S A DISC OF HIS FINAL PROJECT. HE WAS WORKING ON IT BEFORE...
MR. GERMONPREZ... I'M JERRY. YOU DON'T KNOW ME, BUT I WAS A VERY GOOD FRIEND OF JACK'S.
JERRY'S STILL ALIVE. JACK IS DEAD.

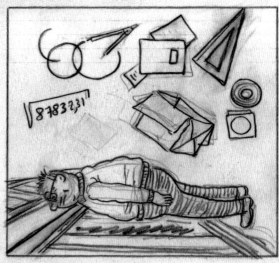

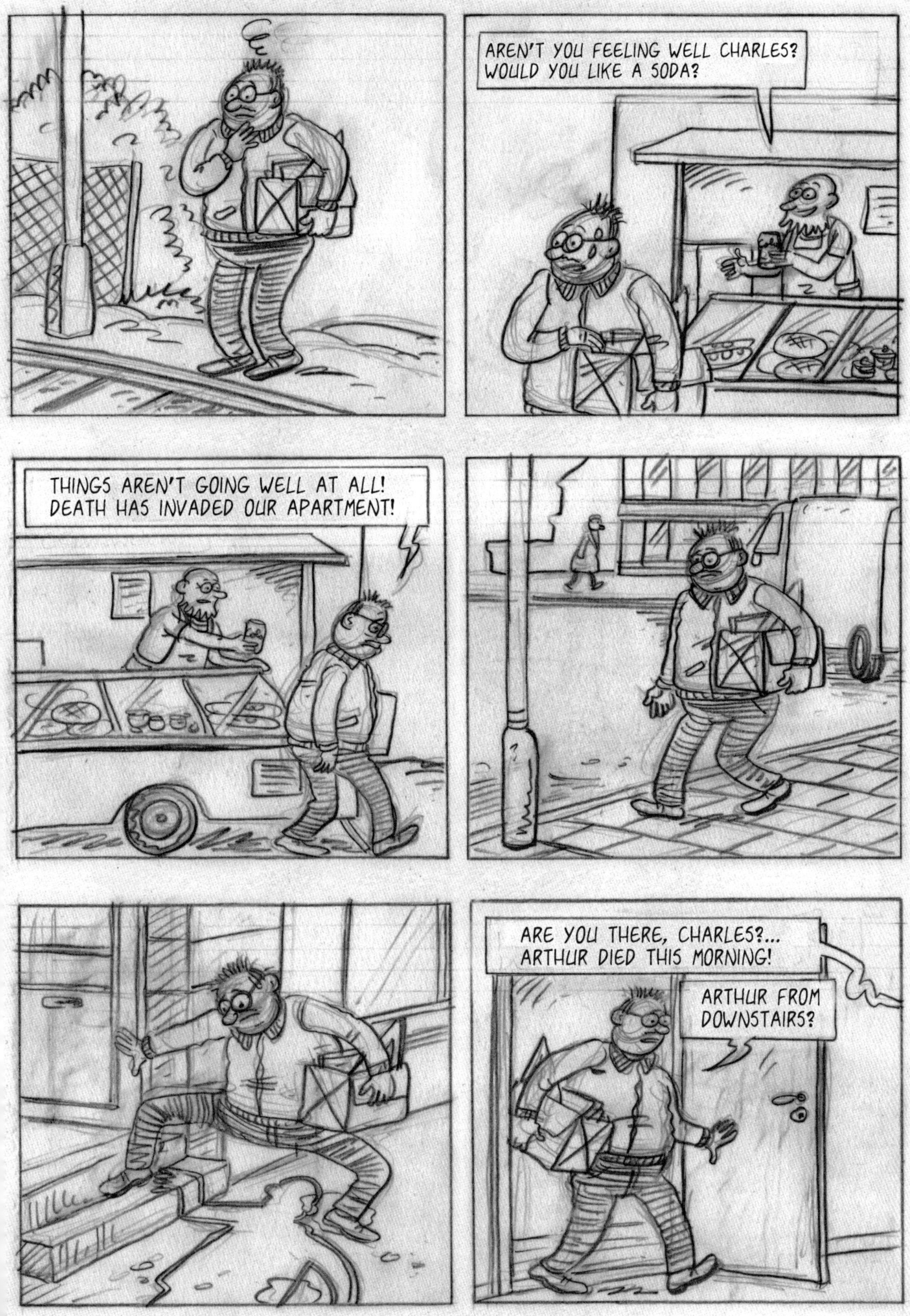
AREN'T YOU FEELING WELL CHARLES? WOULD YOU LIKE A SODA?
THINGS AREN'T GOING WELL AT ALL! DEATH HAS INVADED OUR APARTMENT!
ARE YOU THERE, CHARLES?... ARTHUR DIED THIS MORNING!
ARTHUR FROM DOWNSTAIRS?

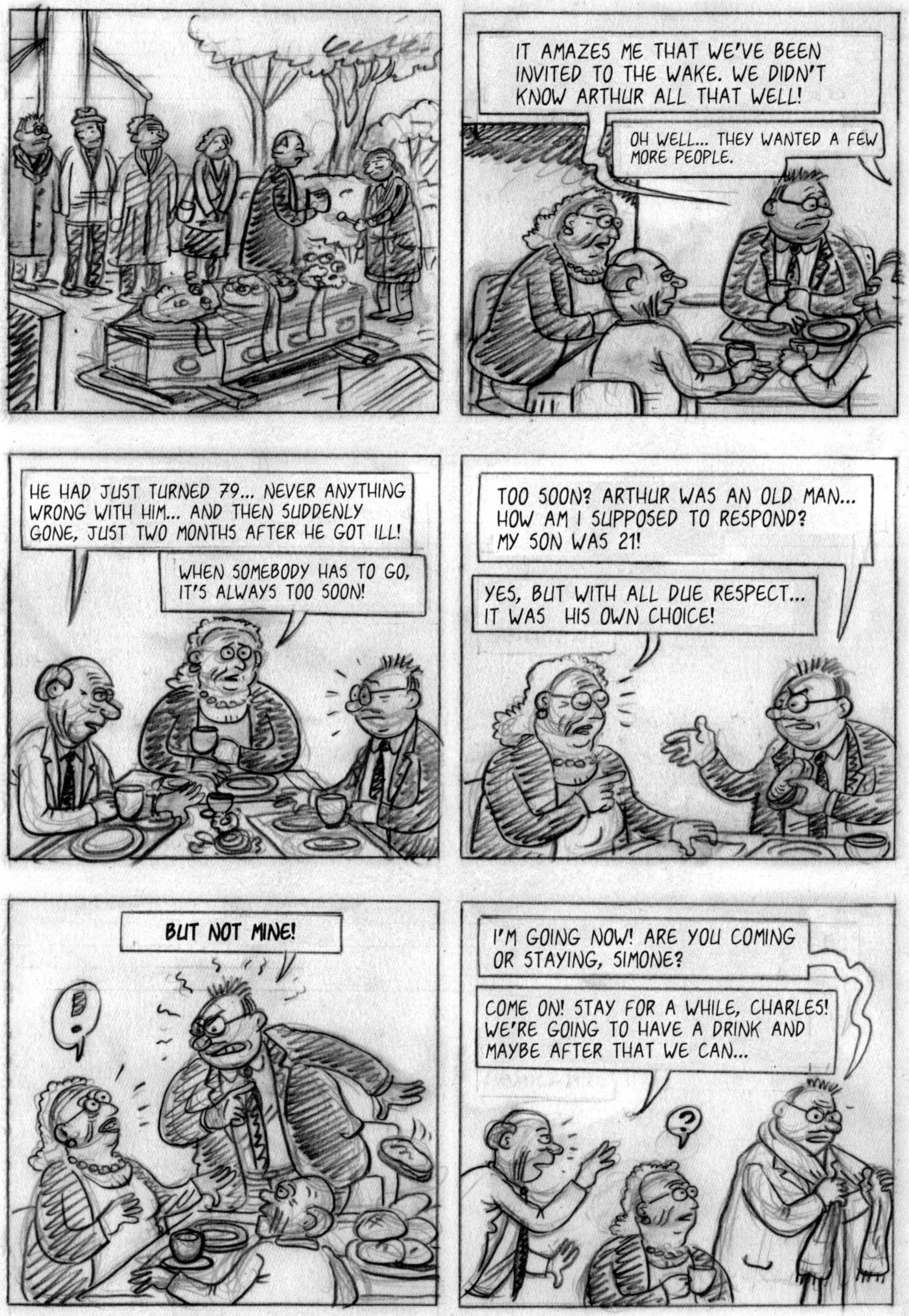
IT AMAZES ME THAT WE'VE BEEN INVITED TO THE WAKE. WE DIDN'T KNOW ARTHUR ALL THAT WELL!
OH WELL... THEY WANTED A FEW MORE PEOPLE.
HE HAD JUST TURNED 79... NEVER ANYTHING WRONG WITH HIM... AND THEN SUDDENLY GONE, JUST TWO MONTHS AFTER HE GOT ILL!
WHEN SOMEBODY HAS TO GO, IT'S ALWAYS TOO SOON!
TOO SOON? ARTHUR WAS AN OLD MAN... HOW AM I SUPPOSED TO RESPOND? MY SON WAS 21!
YES, BUT WITH ALL DUE RESPECT... IT WAS HIS OWN CHOICE!
BUT NOT MINE!
!
I'M GOING NOW! ARE YOU COMING OR STAYING, SIMONE?
COME ON! STAY FOR A WHILE, CHARLES! WE'RE GOING TO HAVE A DRINK AND MAYBE AFTER THAT WE CAN...
?

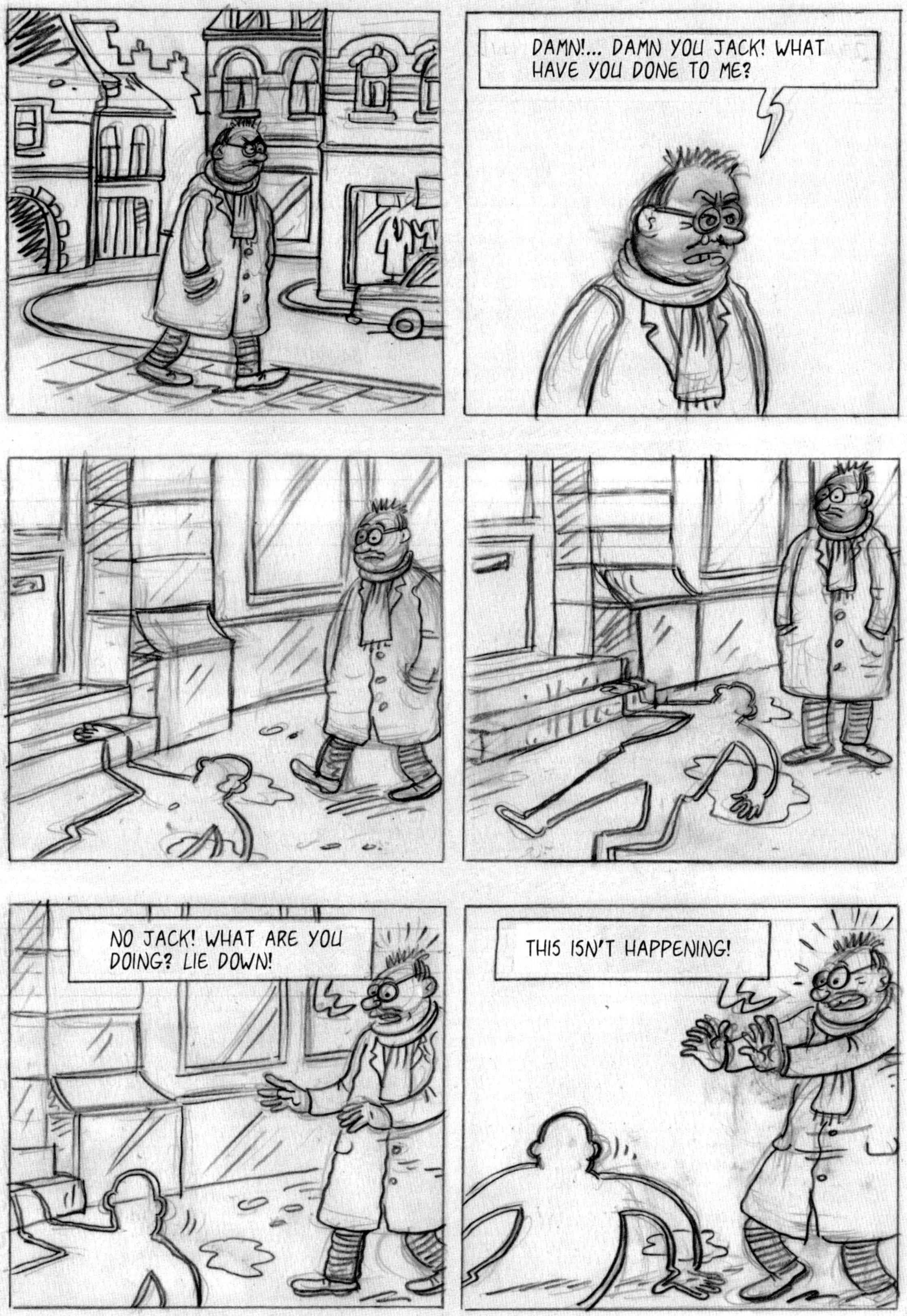
DAMN!... DAMN YOU JACK! WHAT HAVE YOU DONE TO ME?
NO JACK! WHAT ARE YOU DOING? LIE DOWN!
THIS ISN'T HAPPENING!

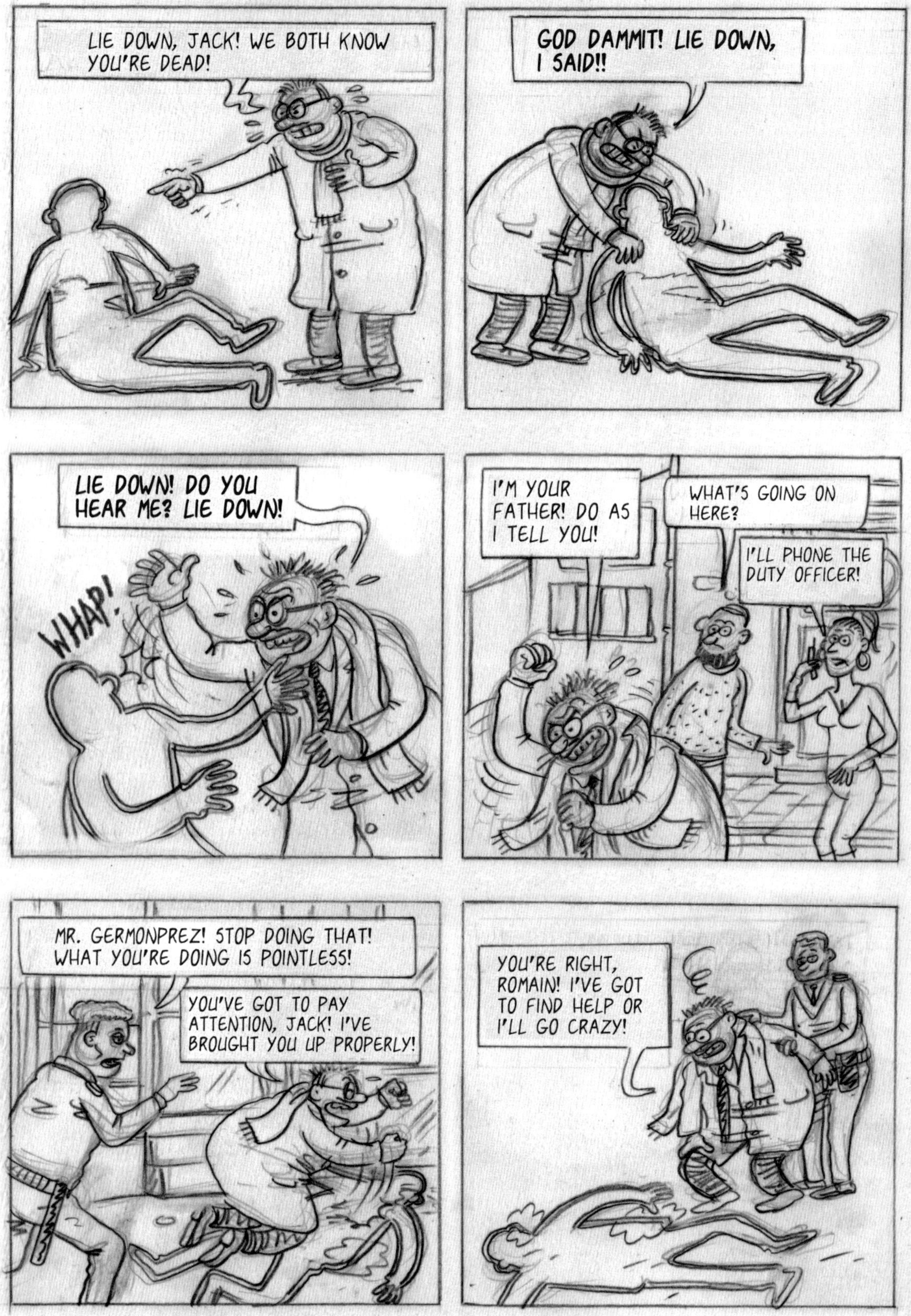
LIE DOWN, JACK! WE BOTH KNOW YOU'RE DEAD!
GOD DAMMIT! LIE DOWN, I SAID!!
LIE DOWN! DO YOU HEAR ME? LIE DOWN!
WHAP!
I'M YOUR FATHER! DO AS I TELL YOU!
WHAT'S GOING ON HERE?
I'LL PHONE THE DUTY OFFICER!
MR. GERMONPREZ! STOP DOING THAT! WHAT YOU'RE DOING IS POINTLESS!
YOU'VE GOT TO PAY ATTENTION, JACK! I'VE BROUGHT YOU UP PROPERLY!
YOU'RE RIGHT, ROMAIN! I'VE GOT TO FIND HELP OR I'LL GO CRAZY!

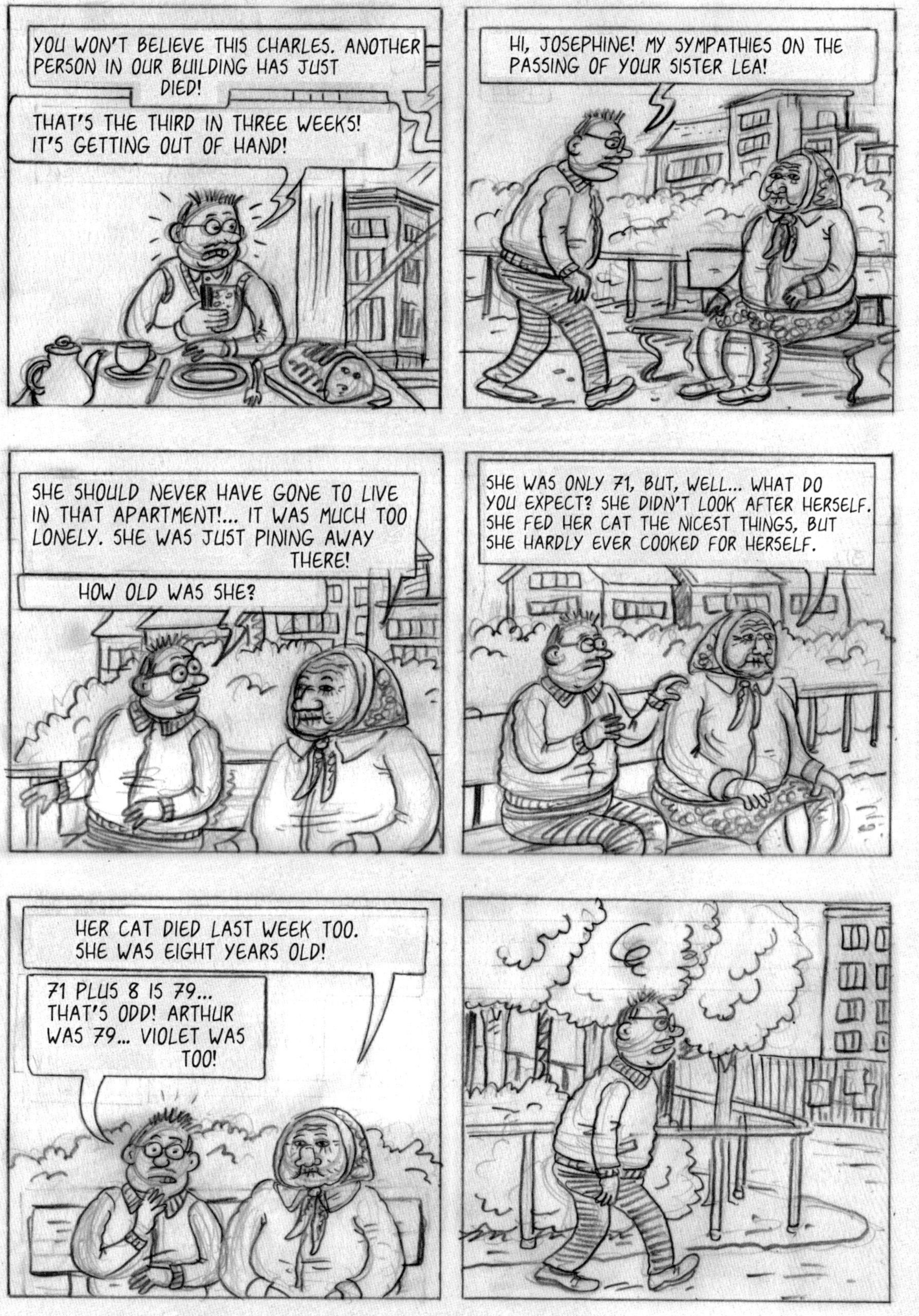
YOU WON'T BELIEVE THIS CHARLES. ANOTHER PERSON IN OUR BUILDING HAS JUST DIED!
THAT'S THE THIRD IN THREE WEEKS! IT'S GETTING OUT OF HAND!
HI, JOSEPHINE! MY SYMPATHIES ON THE PASSING OF YOUR SISTER LEA!
SHE SHOULD NEVER HAVE GONE TO LIVE IN THAT APARTMENT!... IT WAS MUCH TOO LONELY. SHE WAS JUST PINING AWAY THERE!
HOW OLD WAS SHE?
SHE WAS ONLY 71, BUT, WELL... WHAT DO YOU EXPECT? SHE DIDN'T LOOK AFTER HERSELF. SHE FED HER CAT THE NICEST THINGS, BUT SHE HARDLY EVER COOKED FOR HERSELF.
HER CAT DIED LAST WEEK TOO. SHE WAS EIGHT YEARS OLD!
71 PLUS 8 IS 79... THAT'S ODD! ARTHUR WAS 79... VIOLET WAS TOO!

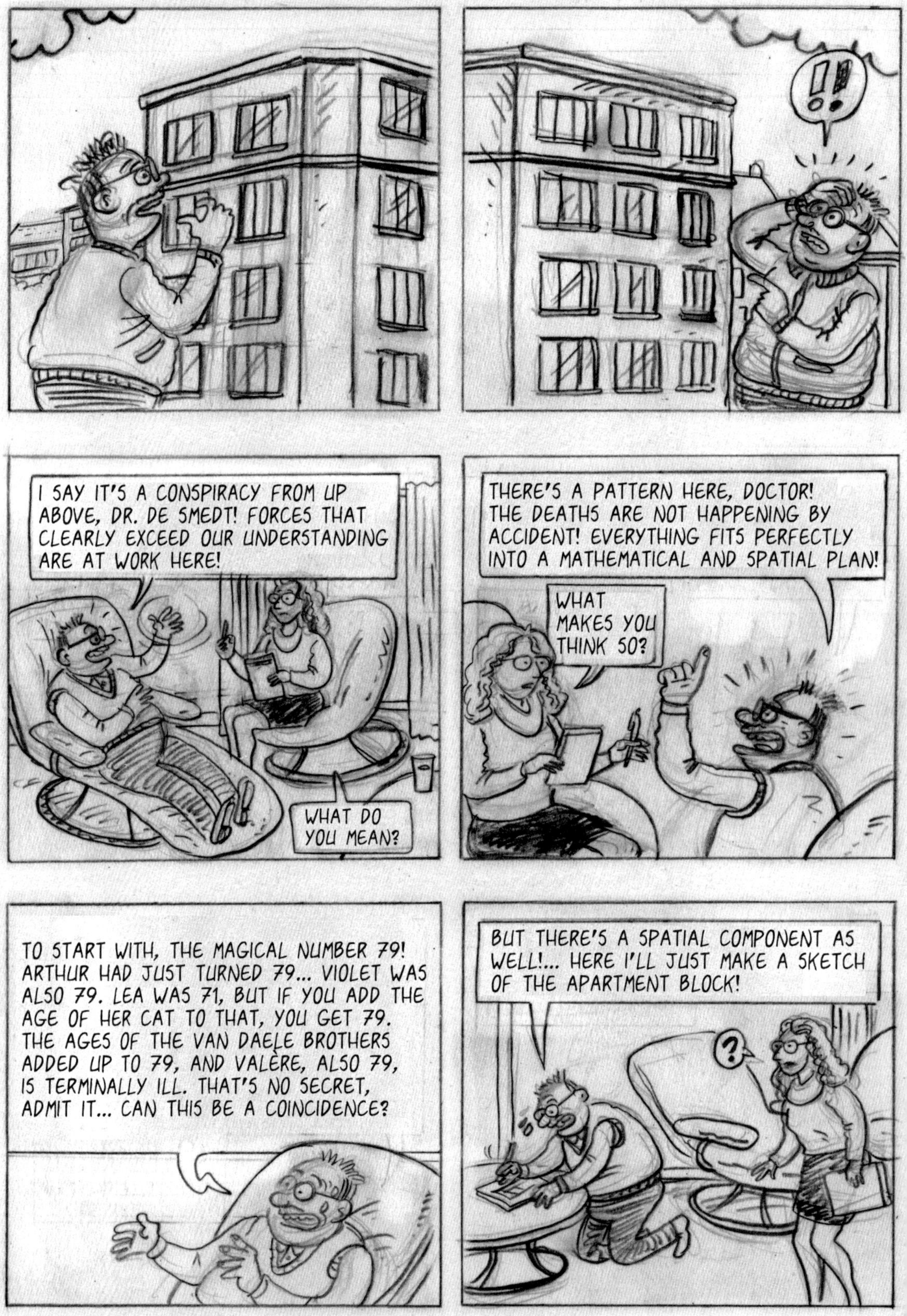
!!
I SAY IT'S A CONSPIRACY FROM UP ABOVE, DR. DE SMEDT! FORCES THAT CLEARLY EXCEED OUR UNDERSTANDING ARE AT WORK HERE!
WHAT DO YOU MEAN?
THERE'S A PATTERN HERE, DOCTOR! THE DEATHS ARE NOT HAPPENING BY ACCIDENT! EVERYTHING FITS PERFECTLY INTO A MATHEMATICAL AND SPATIAL PLAN!
WHAT MAKES YOU THINK SO?
TO START WITH, THE MAGICAL NUMBER 79! ARTHUR HAD JUST TURNED 79... VIOLET WAS ALSO 79. LEA WAS 71, BUT IF YOU ADD THE AGE OF HER CAT TO THAT, YOU GET 79. THE AGES OF THE VAN DAELE BROTHERS ADDED UP TO 79, AND VALÈRE, ALSO 79, IS TERMINALLY ILL. THAT'S NO SECRET, ADMIT IT... CAN THIS BE A COINCIDENCE?
BUT THERE'S A SPATIAL COMPONENT AS WELL!... HERE I'LL JUST MAKE A SKETCH OF THE APARTMENT BLOCK!
?

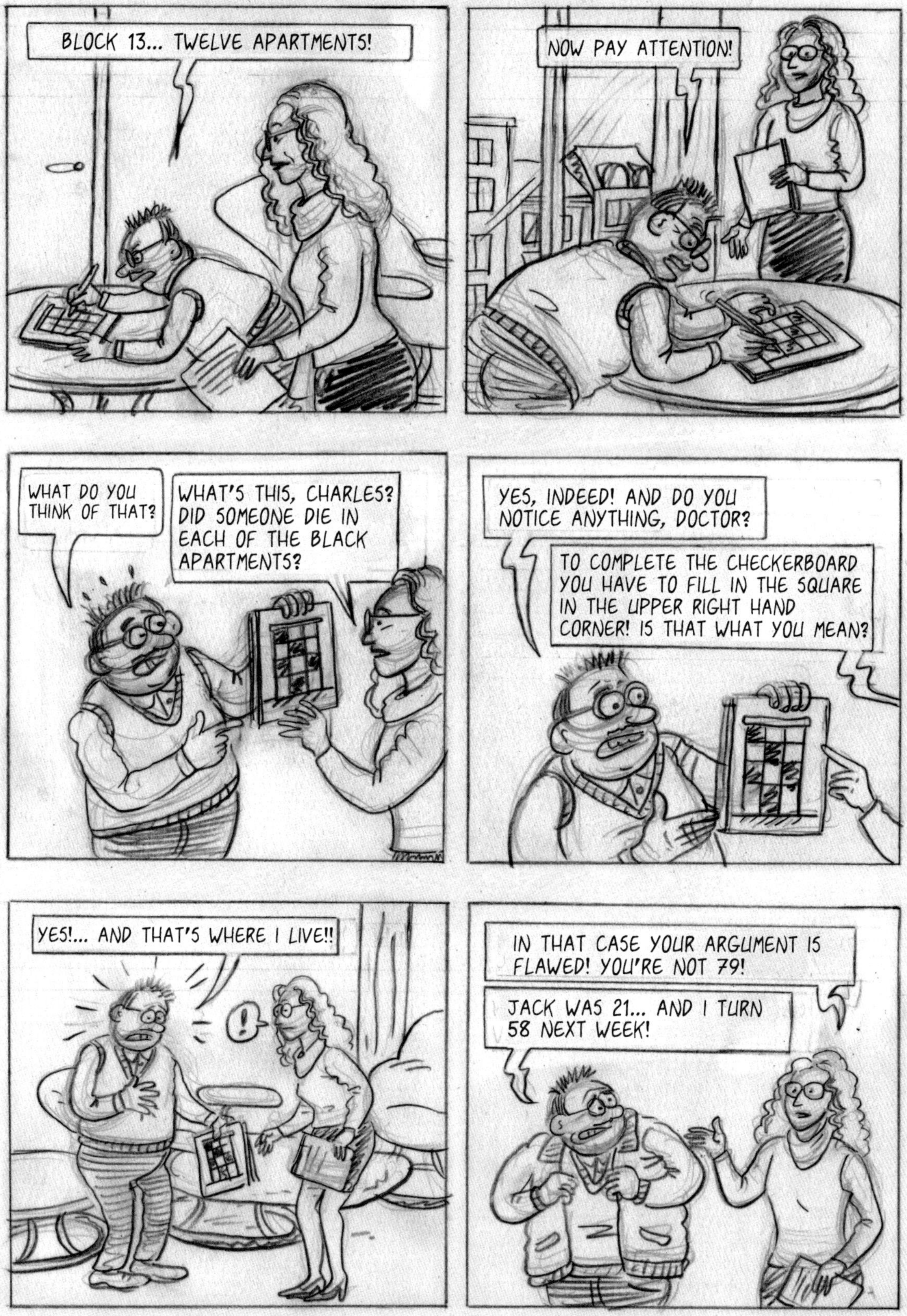
BLOCK 13... TWELVE APARTMENTS!
NOW PAY ATTENTION!
WHAT DO YOU THINK OF THAT?
WHAT'S THIS, CHARLES? DID SOMEONE DIE IN EACH OF THE BLACK APARTMENTS?
YES, INDEED! AND DO YOU NOTICE ANYTHING, DOCTOR?
TO COMPLETE THE CHECKERBOARD YOU HAVE TO FILL IN THE SQUARE IN THE UPPER RIGHT HAND CORNER! IS THAT WHAT YOU MEAN?
YES!... AND THAT'S WHERE I LIVE!!
!
IN THAT CASE YOUR ARGUMENT IS FLAWED! YOU'RE NOT 79!
JACK WAS 21... AND I TURN 58 NEXT WEEK!

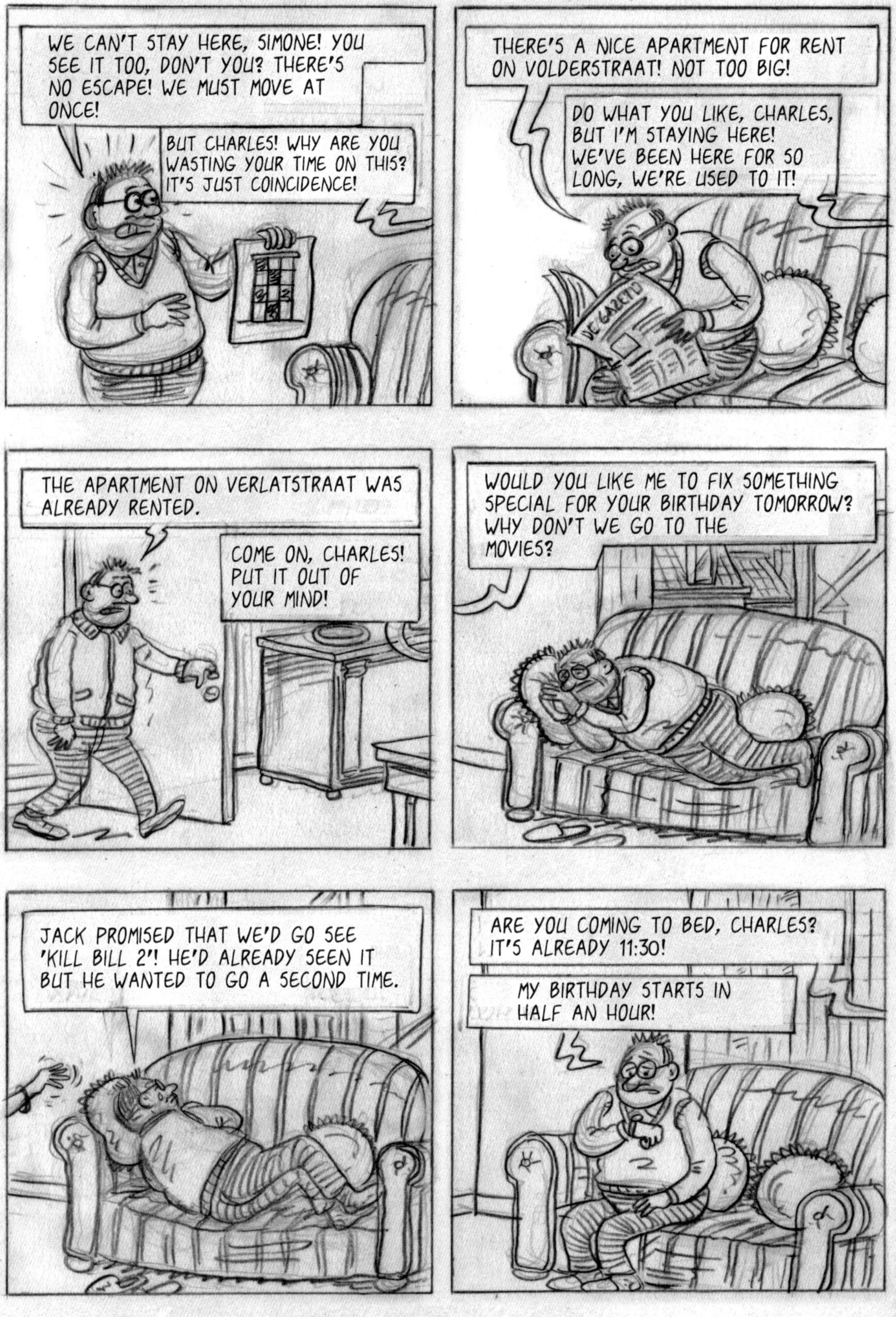
WE CAN'T STAY HERE, SIMONE! YOU SEE IT TOO, DON'T YOU? THERE'S NO ESCAPE! WE MUST MOVE AT ONCE!
BUT CHARLES! WHY ARE YOU WASTING YOUR TIME ON THIS? IT'S JUST COINCIDENCE!
THERE'S A NICE APARTMENT FOR RENT ON VOLDERSTRAAT! NOT TOO BIG!
DO WHAT YOU LIKE, CHARLES, BUT I'M STAYING HERE! WE'VE BEEN HERE FOR SO LONG, WE'RE USED TO IT!
DE GAZETTE
THE APARTMENT ON VERLATSTRAAT WAS ALREADY RENTED.
COME ON, CHARLES! PUT IT OUT OF YOUR MIND!
WOULD YOU LIKE ME TO FIX SOMETHING SPECIAL FOR YOUR BIRTHDAY TOMORROW? WHY DON'T WE GO TO THE MOVIES?
JACK PROMISED THAT WE'D GO SEE 'KILL BILL 2'! HE'D ALREADY SEEN IT BUT HE WANTED TO GO A SECOND TIME.
ARE YOU COMING TO BED, CHARLES? IT'S ALREADY 11:30!
MY BIRTHDAY STARTS IN HALF AN HOUR!

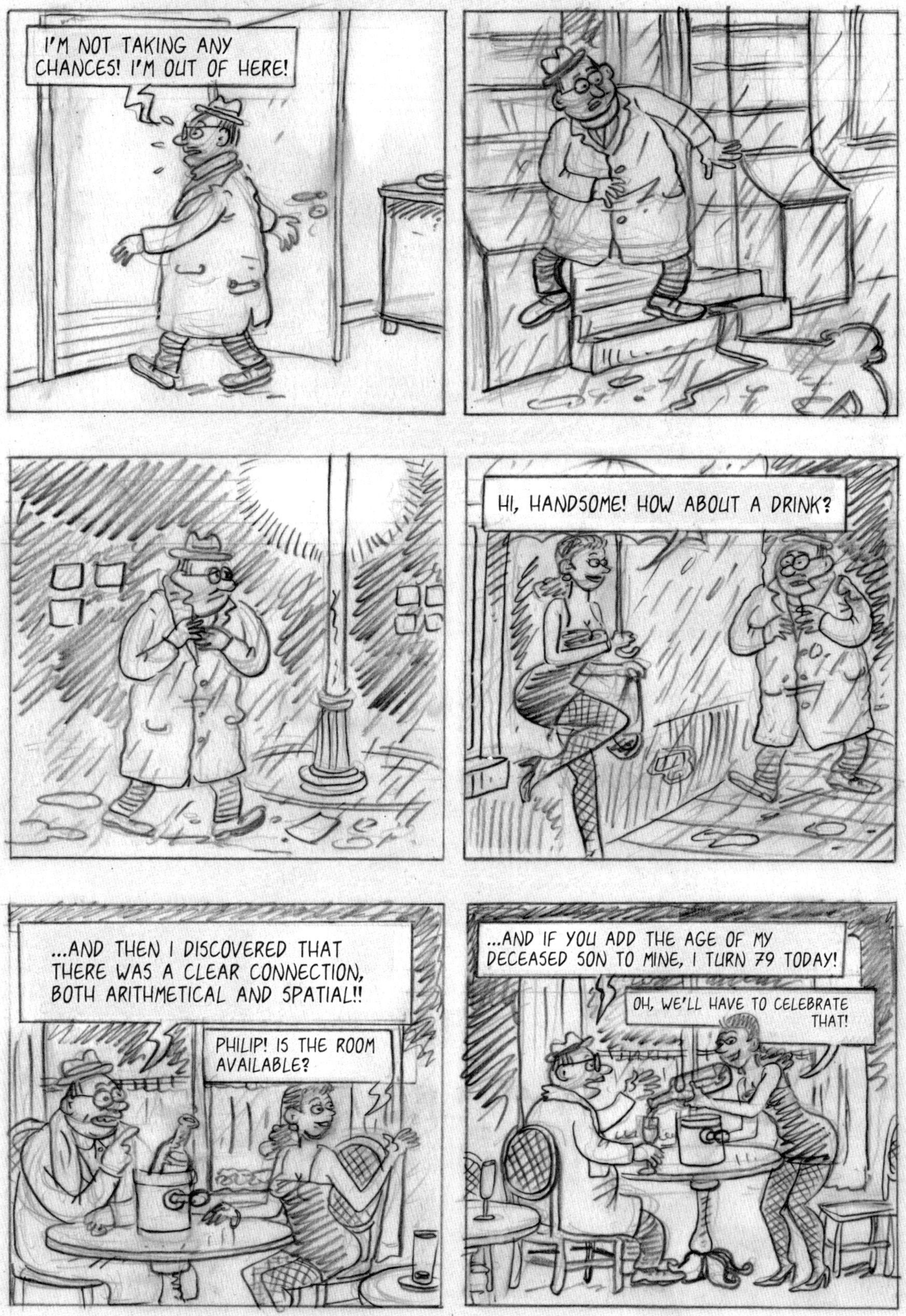
I'M NOT TAKING ANY CHANCES! I'M OUT OF HERE!
HI, HANDSOME! HOW ABOUT A DRINK?
...AND THEN I DISCOVERED THAT THERE WAS A CLEAR CONNECTION, BOTH ARITHMETICAL AND SPATIAL!!
PHILIP! IS THE ROOM AVAILABLE?
...AND IF YOU ADD THE AGE OF MY DECEASED SON TO MINE, I TURN 79 TODAY!
OH, WE'LL HAVE TO CELEBRATE THAT!

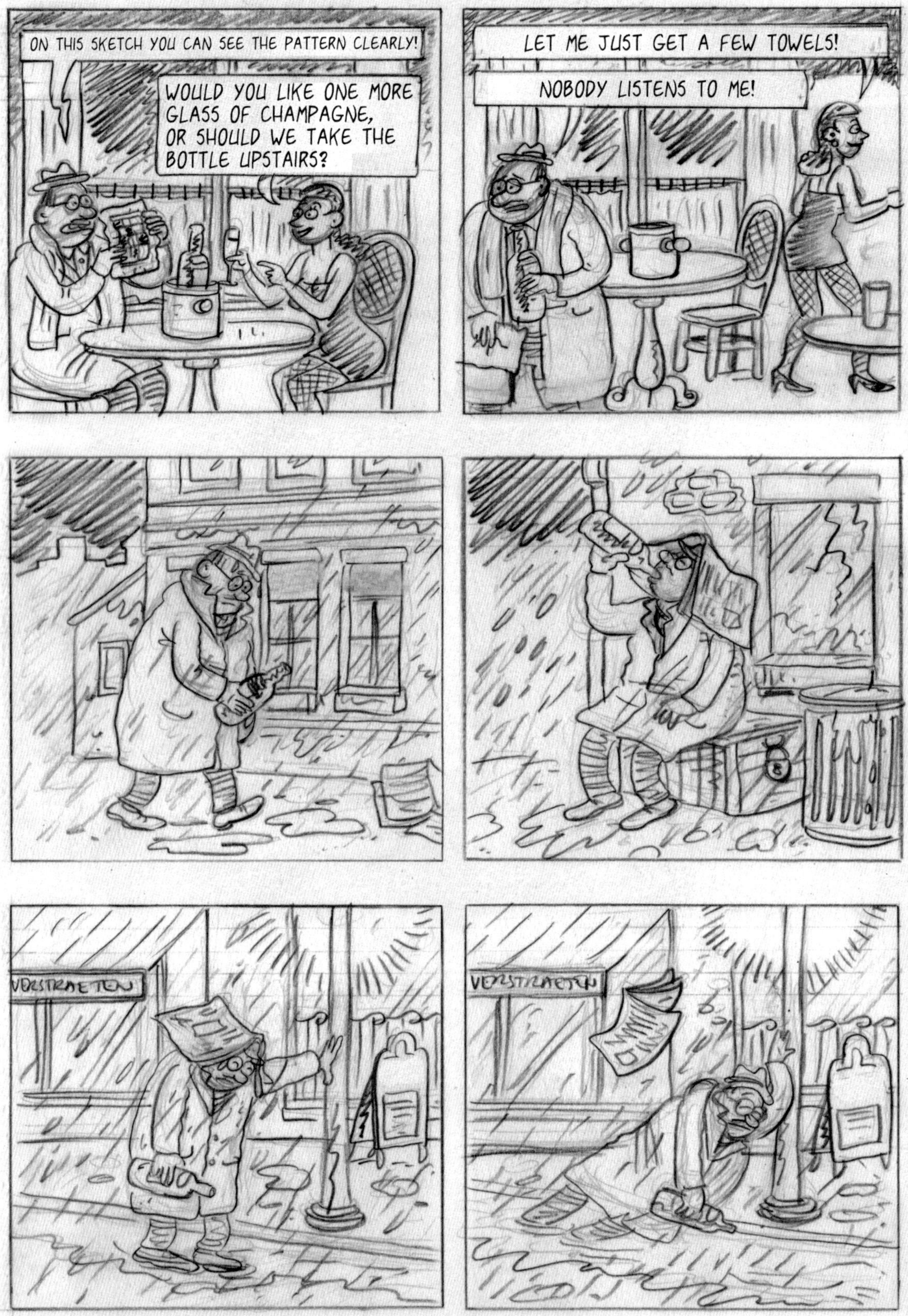
ON THIS SKETCH YOU CAN SEE THE PATTERN CLEARLY!
WOULD YOU LIKE ONE MORE GLASS OF CHAMPAGNE, OR SHOULD WE TAKE THE BOTTLE UPSTAIRS?
LET ME JUST GET A FEW TOWELS!
NOBODY LISTENS TO ME!
VERSTRAETEN
VERSTRAETEN

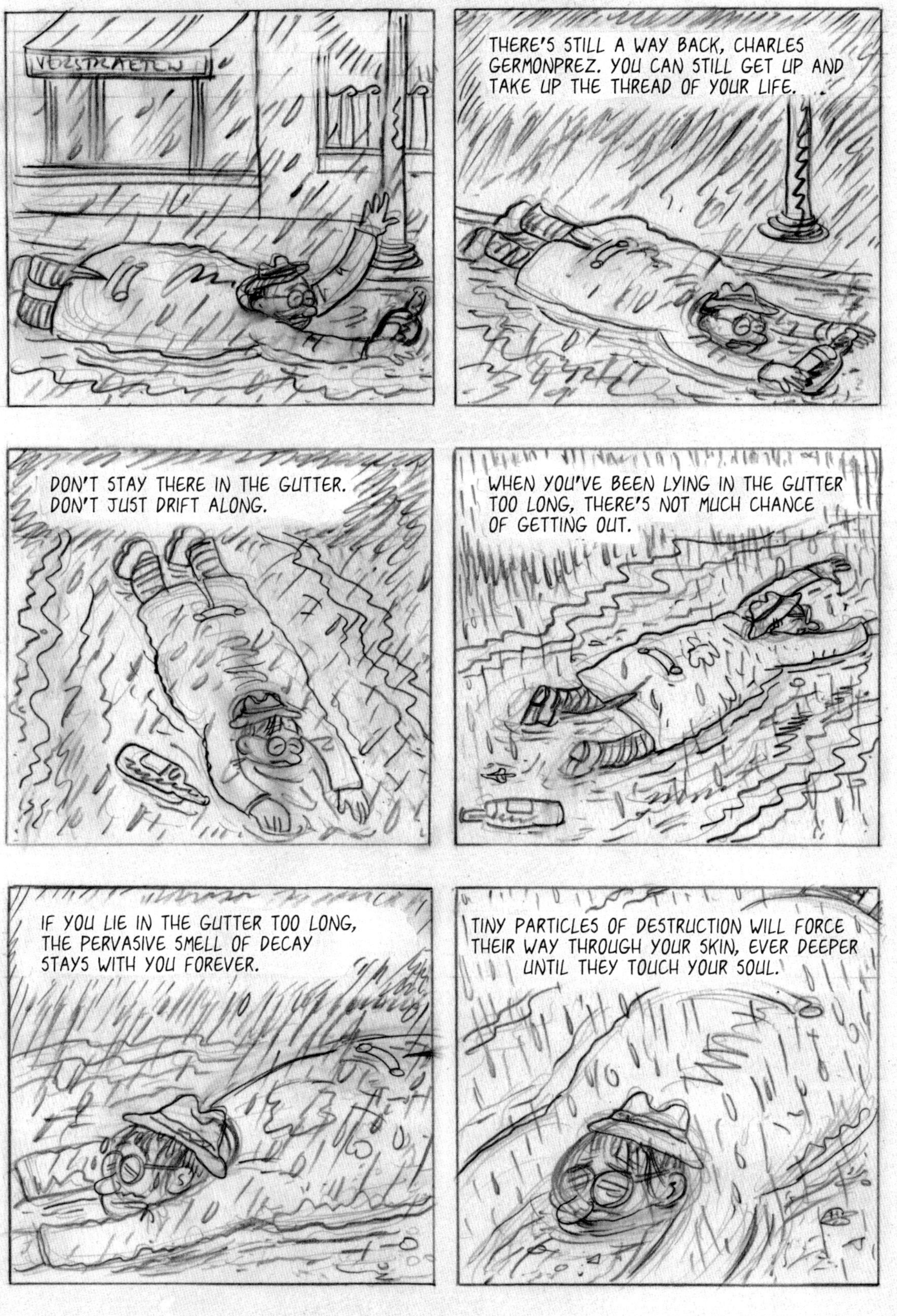
THERE'S STILL A WAY BACK, CHARLES GERMONPREZ. YOU CAN STILL GET UP AND TAKE UP THE THREAD OF YOUR LIFE.
DON'T STAY THERE IN THE GUTTER. DON'T JUST DRIFT ALONG.
WHEN YOU'VE BEEN LYING IN THE GUTTER TOO LONG, THERE'S NOT MUCH CHANCE OF GETTING OUT.
IF YOU LIE IN THE GUTTER TOO LONG, THE PERVASIVE SMELL OF DECAY STAYS WITH YOU FOREVER.
TINY PARTICLES OF DESTRUCTION WILL FORCE THEIR WAY THROUGH YOUR SKIN, EVER DEEPER UNTIL THEY TOUCH YOUR SOUL.

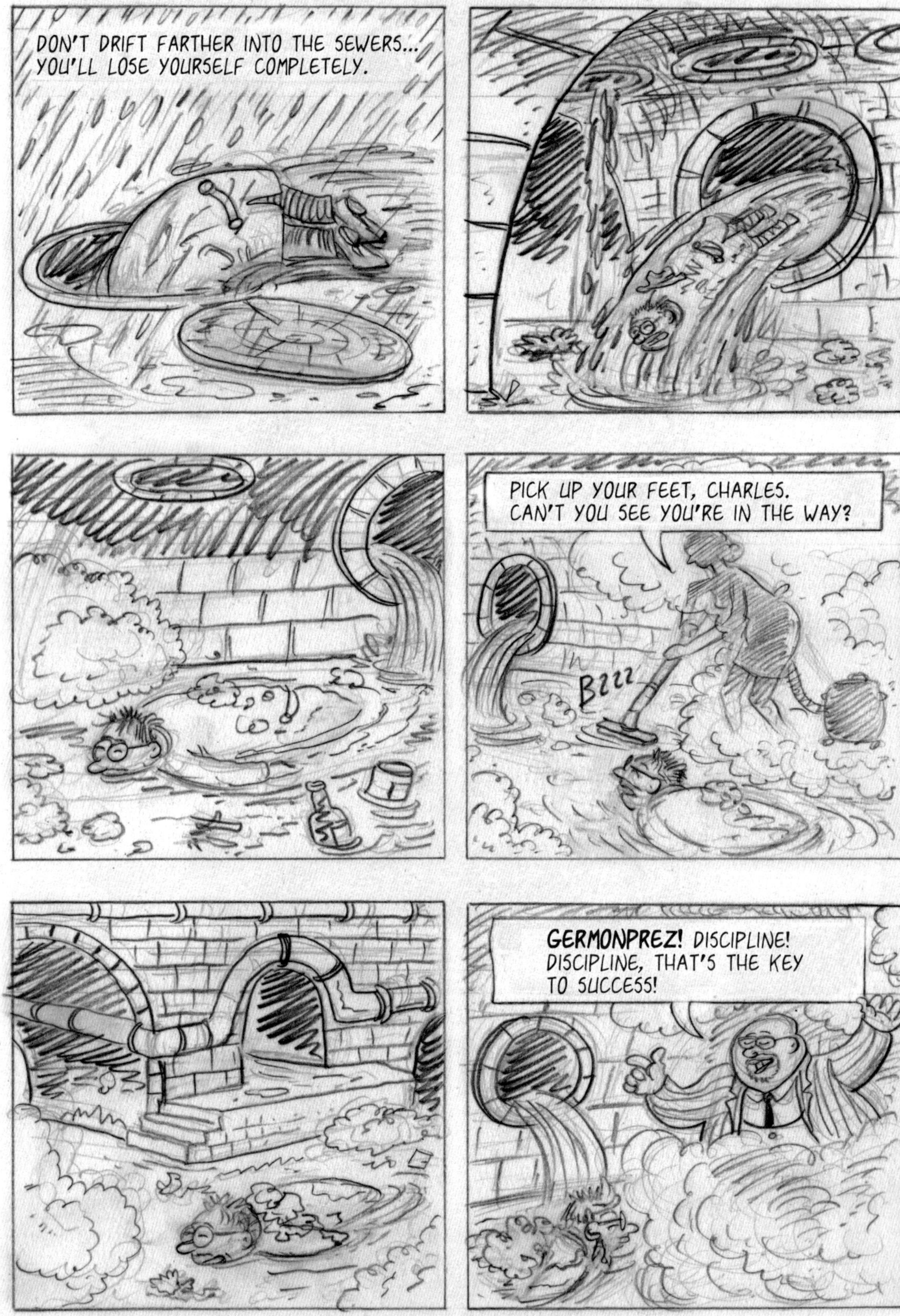
DON'T DRIFT FARTHER INTO THE SEWERS... YOU'LL LOSE YOURSELF COMPLETELY.
PICK UP YOUR FEET, CHARLES. CAN'T YOU SEE YOU'RE IN THE WAY?
Bzzz
GERMONPREZ! DISCIPLINE! DISCIPLINE, THAT'S THE KEY TO SUCCESS!

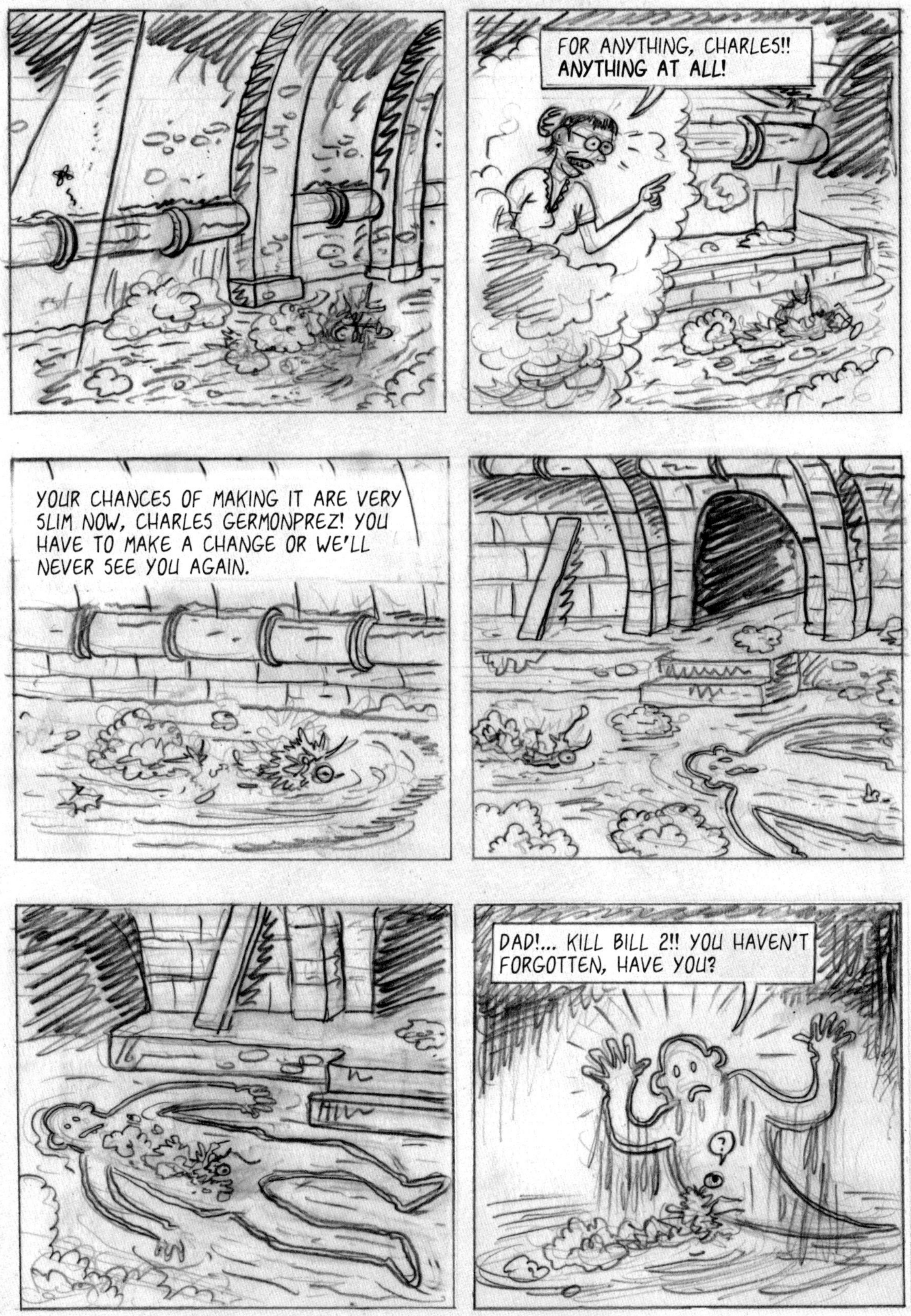
FOR ANYTHING, CHARLES!!
ANYTHING AT ALL!
YOUR CHANCES OF MAKING IT ARE VERY SLIM NOW, CHARLES GERMONPREZ! YOU HAVE TO MAKE A CHANGE OR WE'LL NEVER SEE YOU AGAIN.
DAD!... KILL BILL 2!! YOU HAVEN'T FORGOTTEN, HAVE YOU?
?

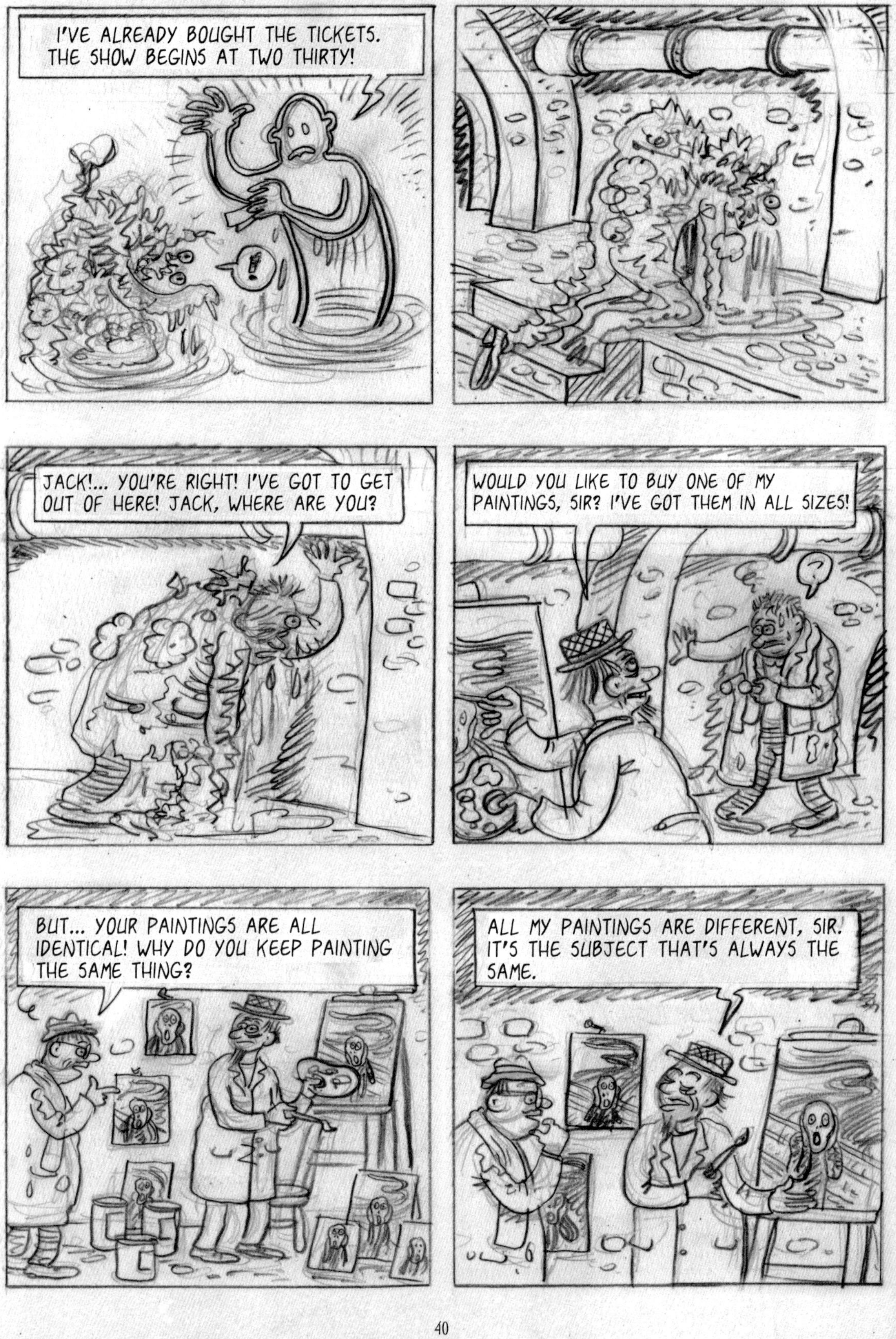
I'VE ALREADY BOUGHT THE TICKETS. THE SHOW BEGINS AT TWO THIRTY!
!
JACK!... YOU'RE RIGHT! I'VE GOT TO GET OUT OF HERE! JACK, WHERE ARE YOU?
WOULD YOU LIKE TO BUY ONE OF MY PAINTINGS, SIR? I'VE GOT THEM IN ALL SIZES!
?
BUT... YOUR PAINTINGS ARE ALL IDENTICAL! WHY DO YOU KEEP PAINTING THE SAME THING?
ALL MY PAINTINGS ARE DIFFERENT, SIR. IT'S THE SUBJECT THAT'S ALWAYS THE SAME.

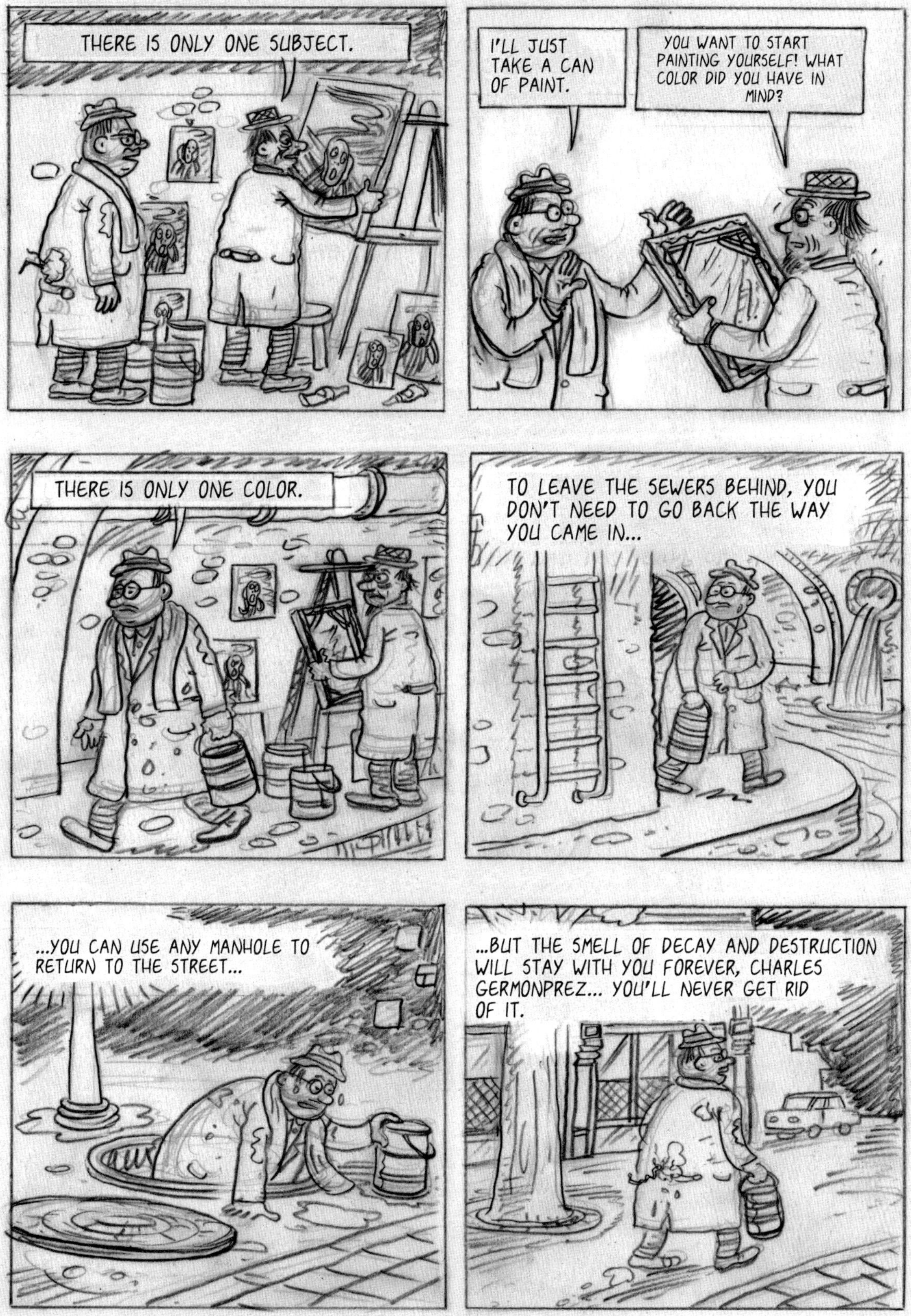
THERE IS ONLY ONE SUBJECT.
I'LL JUST TAKE A CAN OF PAINT.
YOU WANT TO START PAINTING YOURSELF! WHAT COLOR DID YOU HAVE IN MIND?
THERE IS ONLY ONE COLOR.
TO LEAVE THE SEWERS BEHIND, YOU DON'T NEED TO GO BACK THE WAY YOU CAME IN...
...YOU CAN USE ANY MANHOLE TO RETURN TO THE STREET...
...BUT THE SMELL OF DECAY AND DESTRUCTION WILL STAY WITH YOU FOREVER, CHARLES GERMONPREZ... YOU'LL NEVER GET RID OF IT.

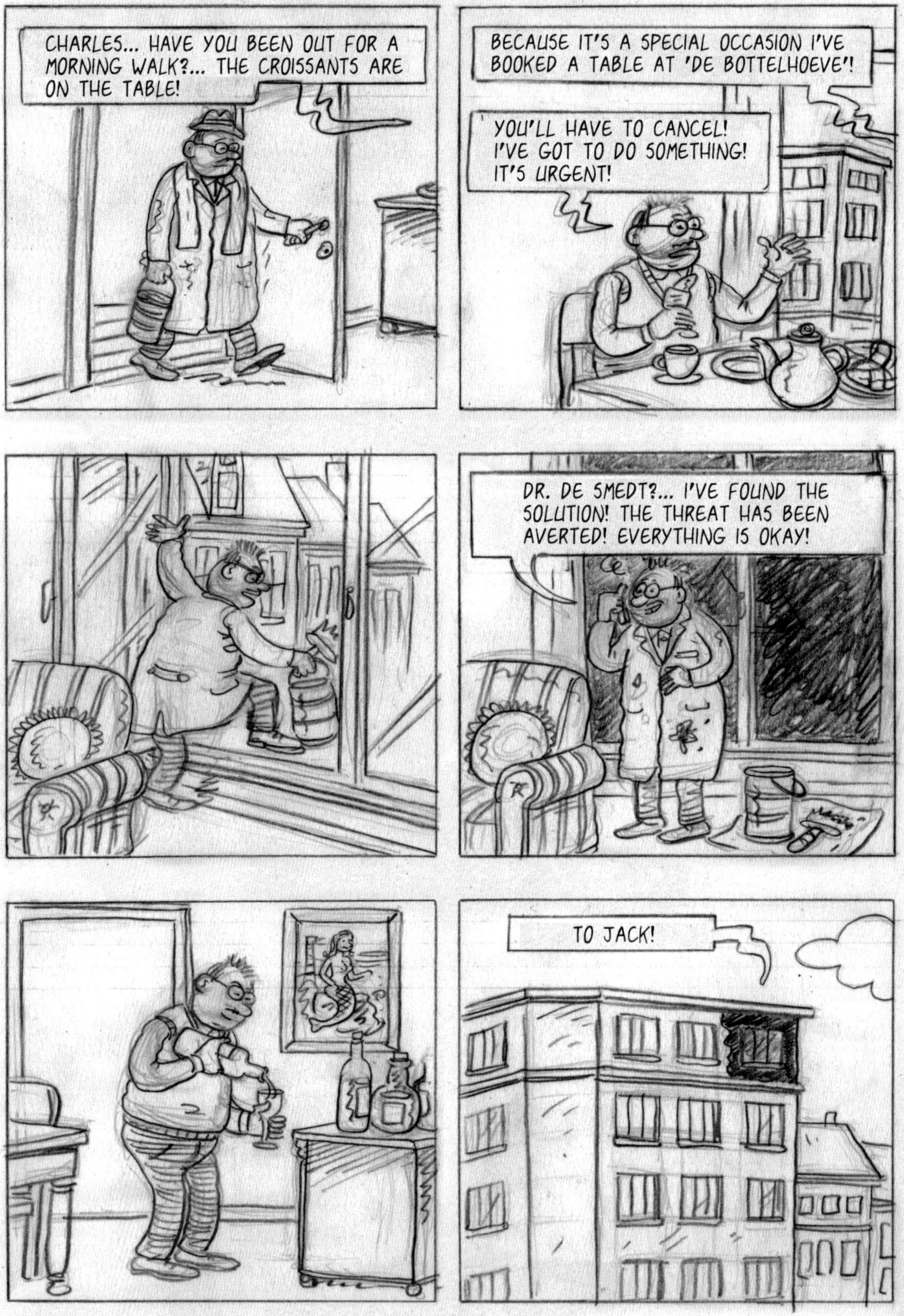
CHARLES... HAVE YOU BEEN OUT FOR A MORNING WALK?... THE CROISSANTS ARE ON THE TABLE!
BECAUSE IT'S A SPECIAL OCCASION I'VE BOOKED A TABLE AT 'DE BOTTELHOEVE'!
YOU'LL HAVE TO CANCEL! I'VE GOT TO DO SOMETHING! IT'S URGENT!
DR. DE SMEDT?... I'VE FOUND THE SOLUTION! THE THREAT HAS BEEN AVERTED! EVERYTHING IS OKAY!
TO JACK!

CHAPTER 3 - TROUBLE BREATHING

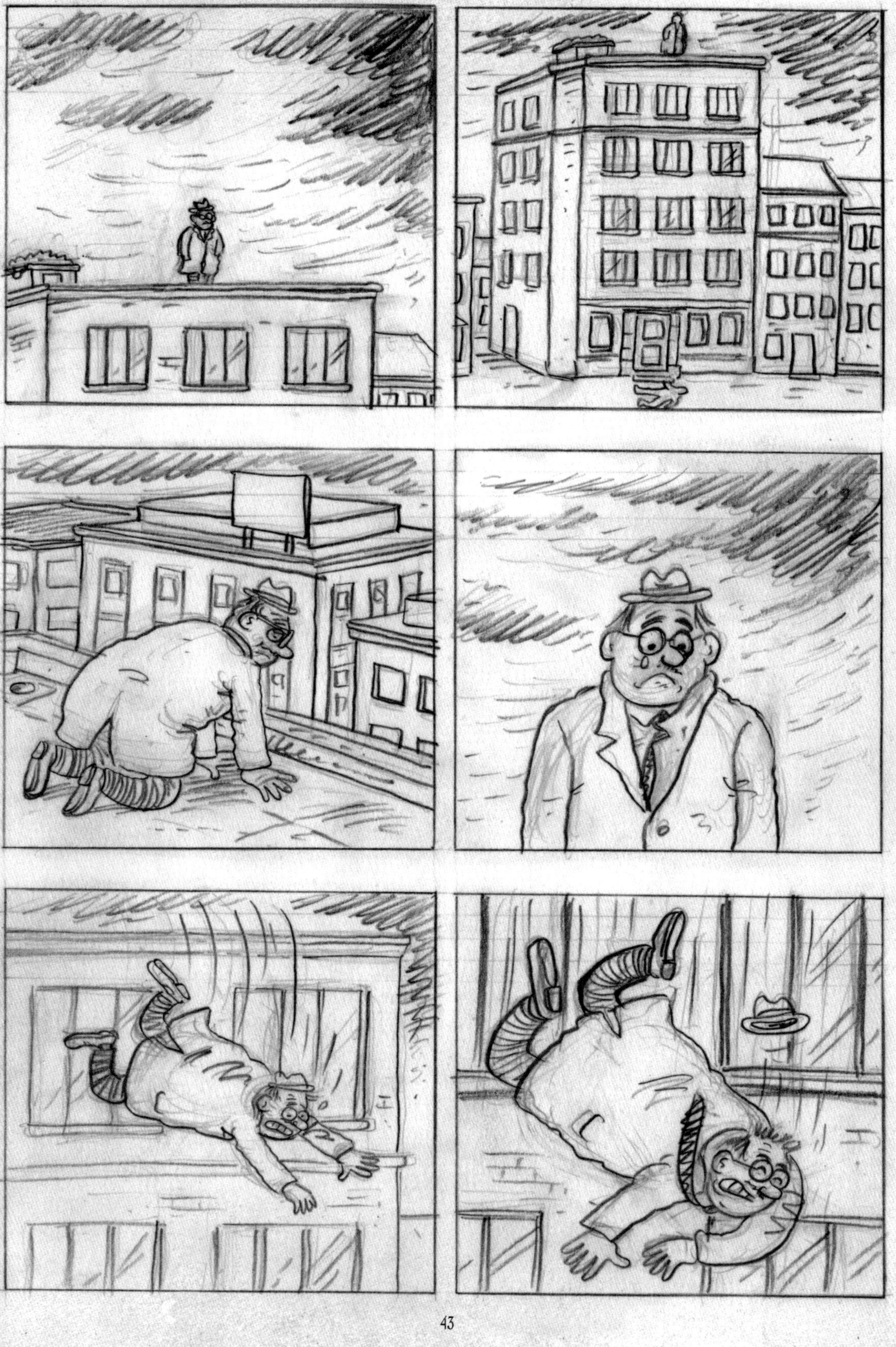

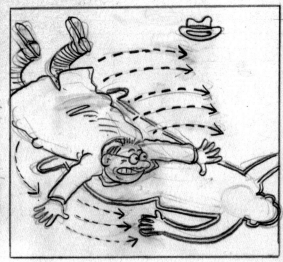

TRY AGAIN... CORRECT THE COURSE!

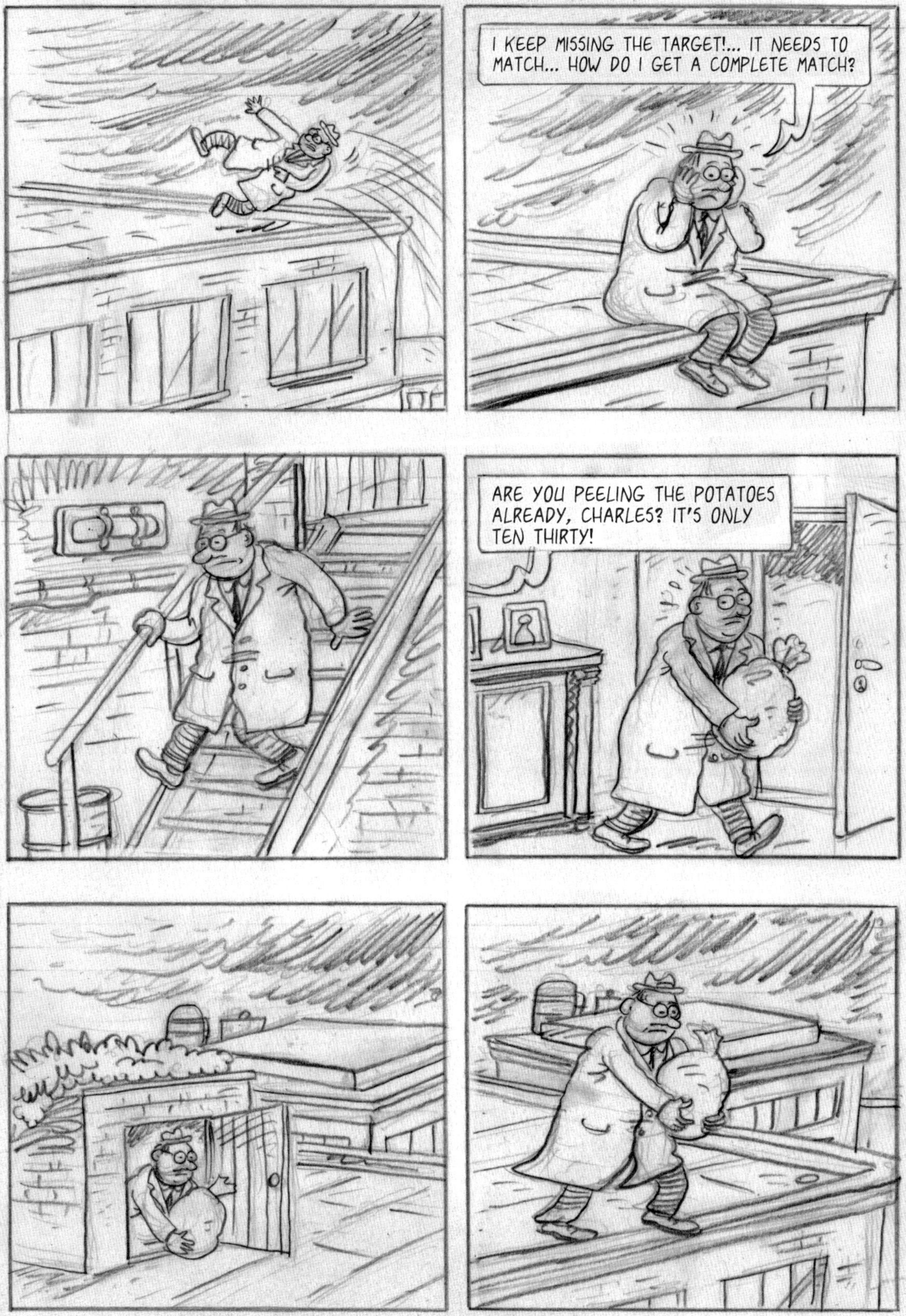
I KEEP MISSING THE TARGET!... IT NEEDS TO MATCH... HOW DO I GET A COMPLETE MATCH?
ARE YOU PEELING THE POTATOES ALREADY, CHARLES? IT'S ONLY TEN THIRTY!

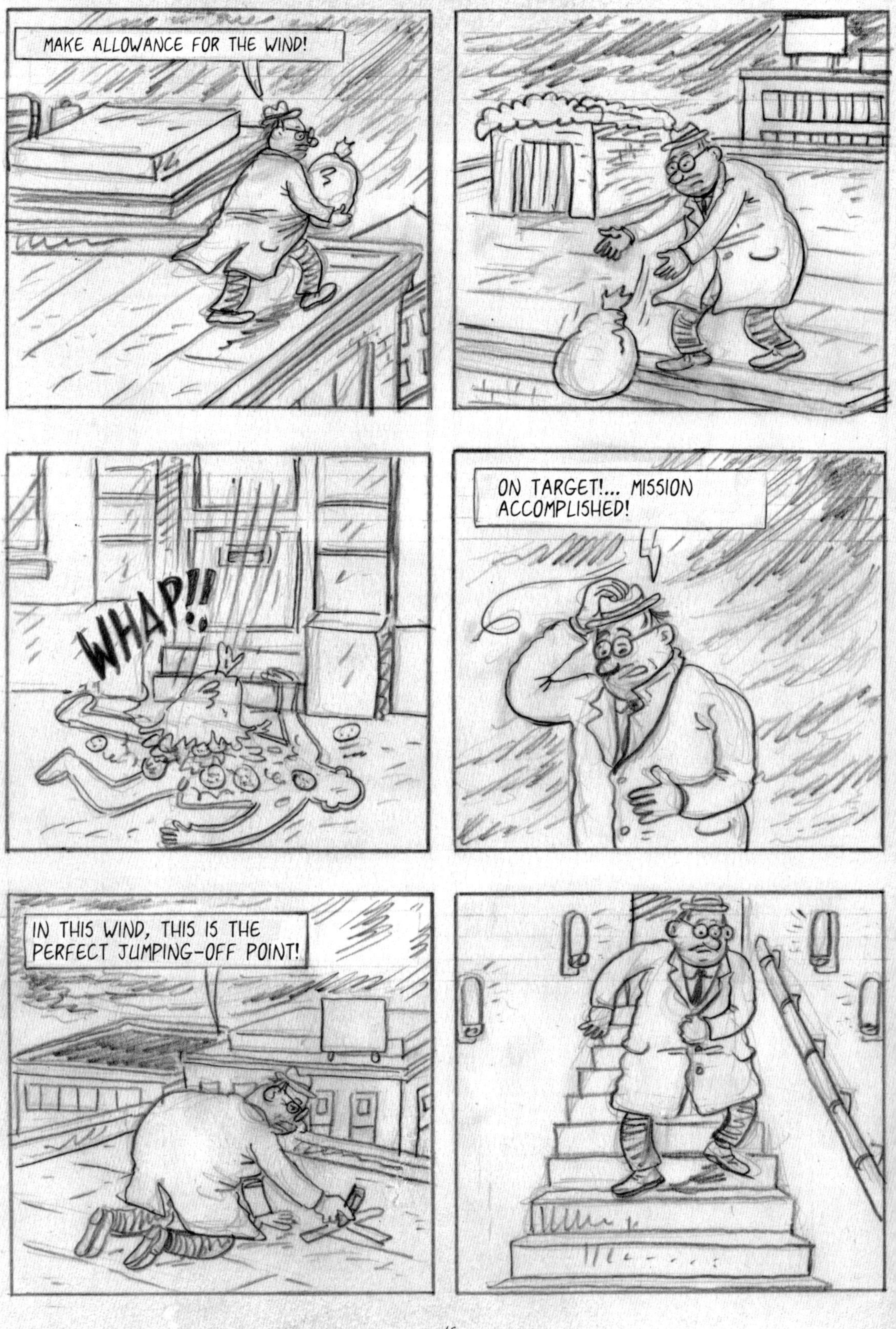
MAKE ALLOWANCE FOR THE WIND!
WHAP!!
ON TARGET!... MISSION ACCOMPLISHED!
IN THIS WIND, THIS IS THE PERFECT JUMPING-OFF POINT!

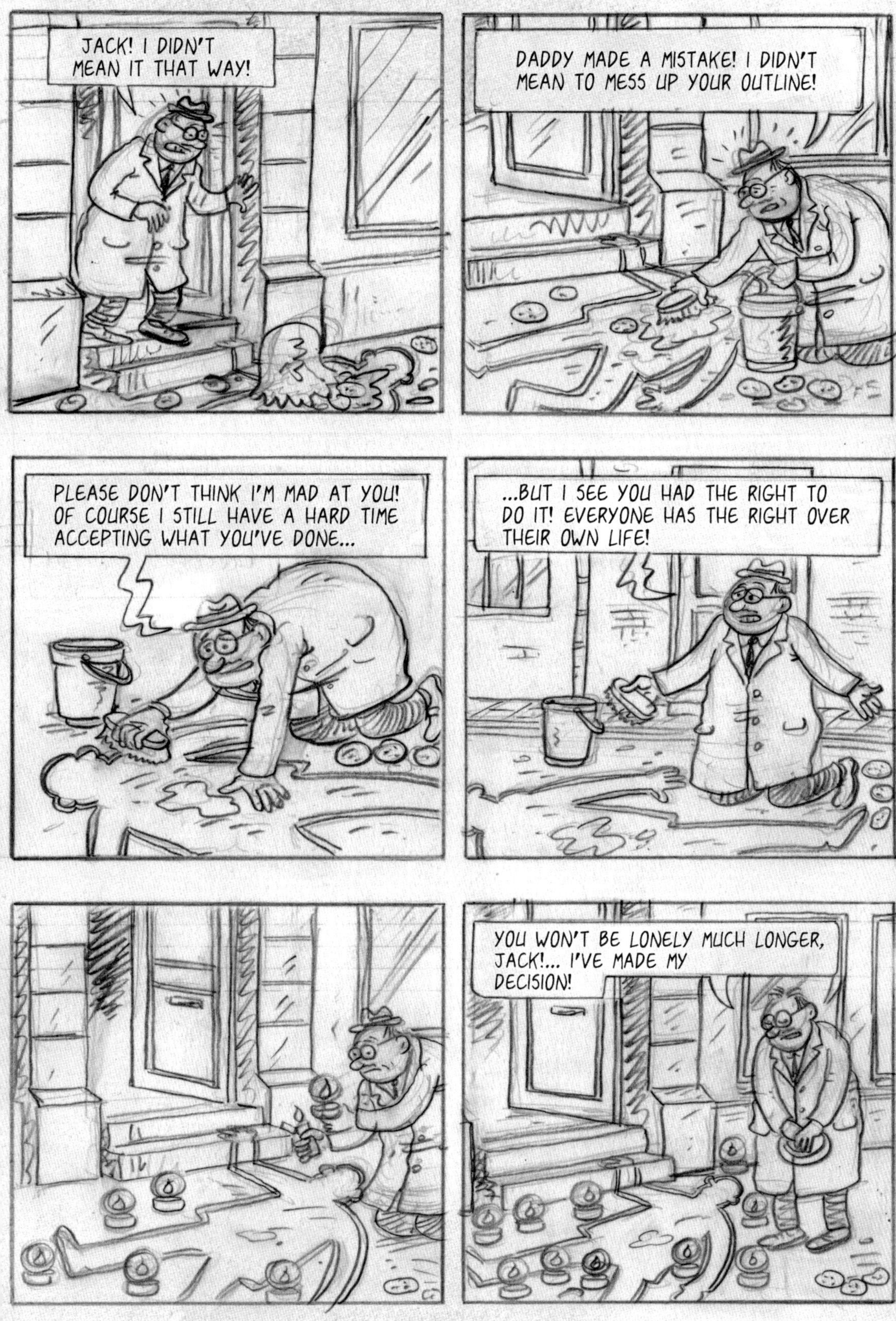
JACK! I DIDN'T MEAN IT THAT WAY!
DADDY MADE A MISTAKE! I DIDN'T MEAN TO MESS UP YOUR OUTLINE!
PLEASE DON'T THINK I'M MAD AT YOU! OF COURSE I STILL HAVE A HARD TIME ACCEPTING WHAT YOU'VE DONE...
...BUT I SEE YOU HAD THE RIGHT TO DO IT! EVERYONE HAS THE RIGHT OVER THEIR OWN LIFE!
YOU WON'T BE LONELY MUCH LONGER, JACK!... I'VE MADE MY DECISION!

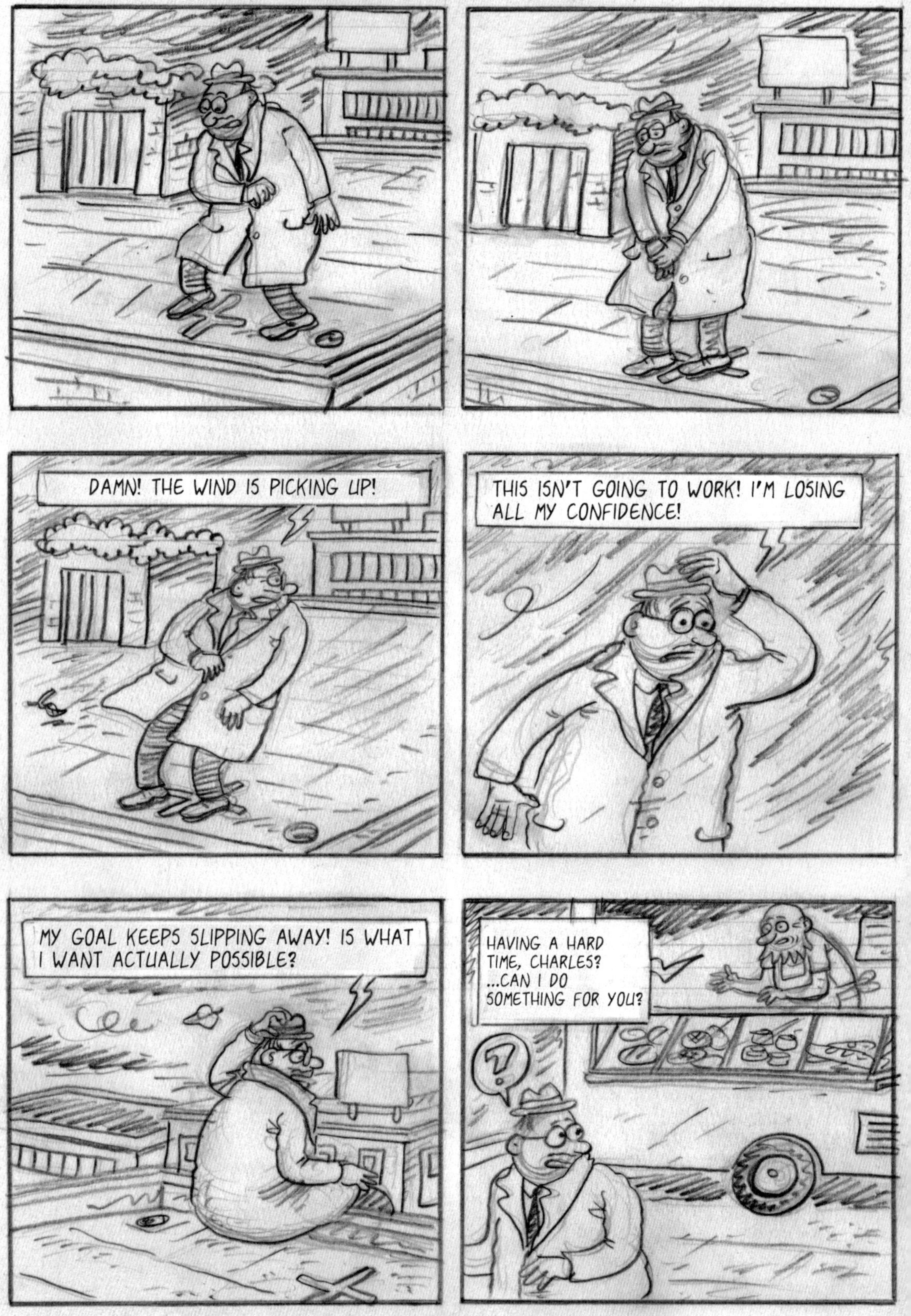
DAMN! THE WIND IS PICKING UP!
THIS ISN'T GOING TO WORK! I'M LOSING ALL MY CONFIDENCE!
MY GOAL KEEPS SLIPPING AWAY! IS WHAT I WANT ACTUALLY POSSIBLE?
HAVING A HARD TIME, CHARLES? ...CAN I DO SOMETHING FOR YOU?
?

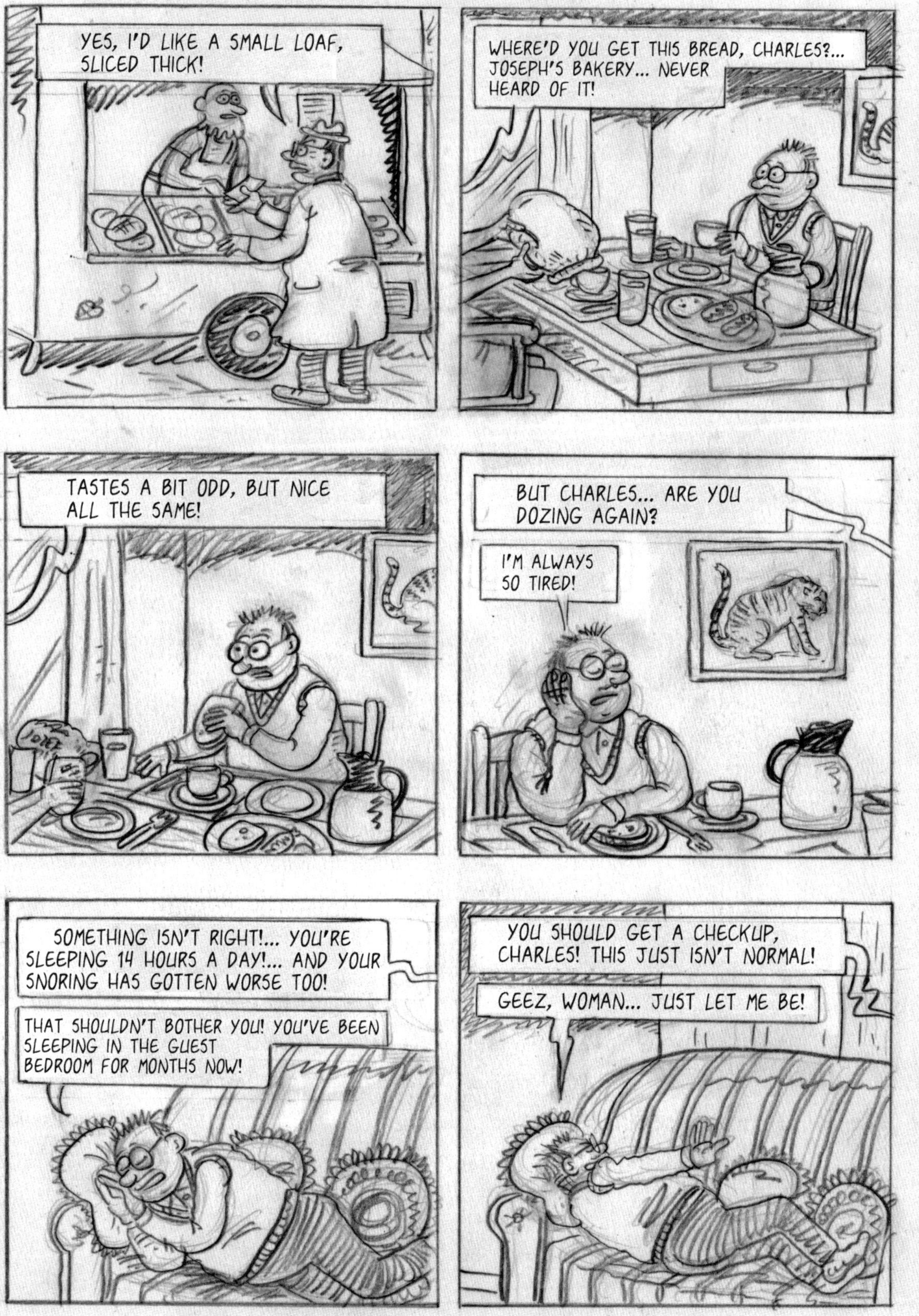
YES, I'D LIKE A SMALL LOAF, SLICED THICK!
WHERE'D YOU GET THIS BREAD, CHARLES?... JOSEPH'S BAKERY... NEVER HEARD OF IT!
TASTES A BIT ODD, BUT NICE ALL THE SAME!
BUT CHARLES... ARE YOU DOZING AGAIN?
I'M ALWAYS SO TIRED!
SOMETHING ISN'T RIGHT!... YOU'RE SLEEPING 14 HOURS A DAY!... AND YOUR SNORING HAS GOTTEN WORSE TOO!
THAT SHOULDN'T BOTHER YOU! YOU'VE BEEN SLEEPING IN THE GUEST BEDROOM FOR MONTHS NOW!
YOU SHOULD GET A CHECKUP, CHARLES! THIS JUST ISN'T NORMAL!
GEEZ, WOMAN... JUST LET ME BE!

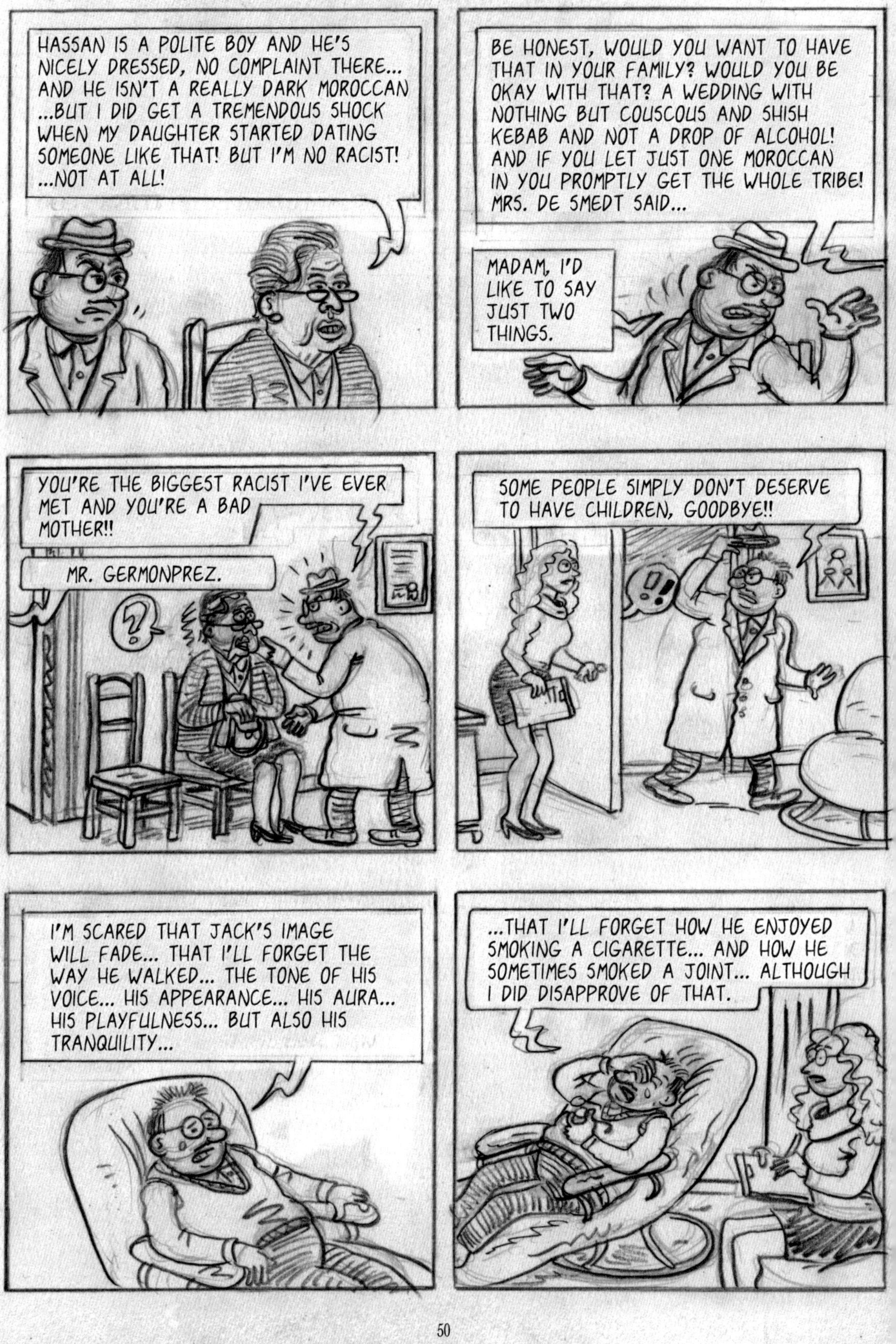
HASSAN IS A POLITE BOY AND HE'S NICELY DRESSED, NO COMPLAINT THERE... AND HE ISN'T A REALLY DARK MOROCCAN ...BUT I DID GET A TREMENDOUS SHOCK WHEN MY DAUGHTER STARTED DATING SOMEONE LIKE THAT! BUT I'M NO RACIST! ...NOT AT ALL!
BE HONEST, WOULD YOU WANT TO HAVE THAT IN YOUR FAMILY? WOULD YOU BE OKAY WITH THAT? A WEDDING WITH NOTHING BUT COUSCOUS AND SHISH KEBAB AND NOT A DROP OF ALCOHOL! AND IF YOU LET JUST ONE MOROCCAN IN YOU PROMPTLY GET THE WHOLE TRIBE! MRS. DE SMEDT SAID...
MADAM, I'D LIKE TO SAY JUST TWO THINGS.
YOU'RE THE BIGGEST RACIST I'VE EVER MET AND YOU'RE A BAD MOTHER!!
MR. GERMONPREZ.
?
SOME PEOPLE SIMPLY DON'T DESERVE TO HAVE CHILDREN, GOODBYE!!
?!
I'M SCARED THAT JACK'S IMAGE WILL FADE... THAT I'LL FORGET THE WAY HE WALKED... THE TONE OF HIS VOICE... HIS APPEARANCE... HIS AURA... HIS PLAYFULNESS... BUT ALSO HIS TRANQUILITY...
...THAT I'LL FORGET HOW HE ENJOYED SMOKING A CIGARETTE... AND HOW HE SOMETIMES SMOKED A JOINT... ALTHOUGH I DID DISAPPROVE OF THAT.

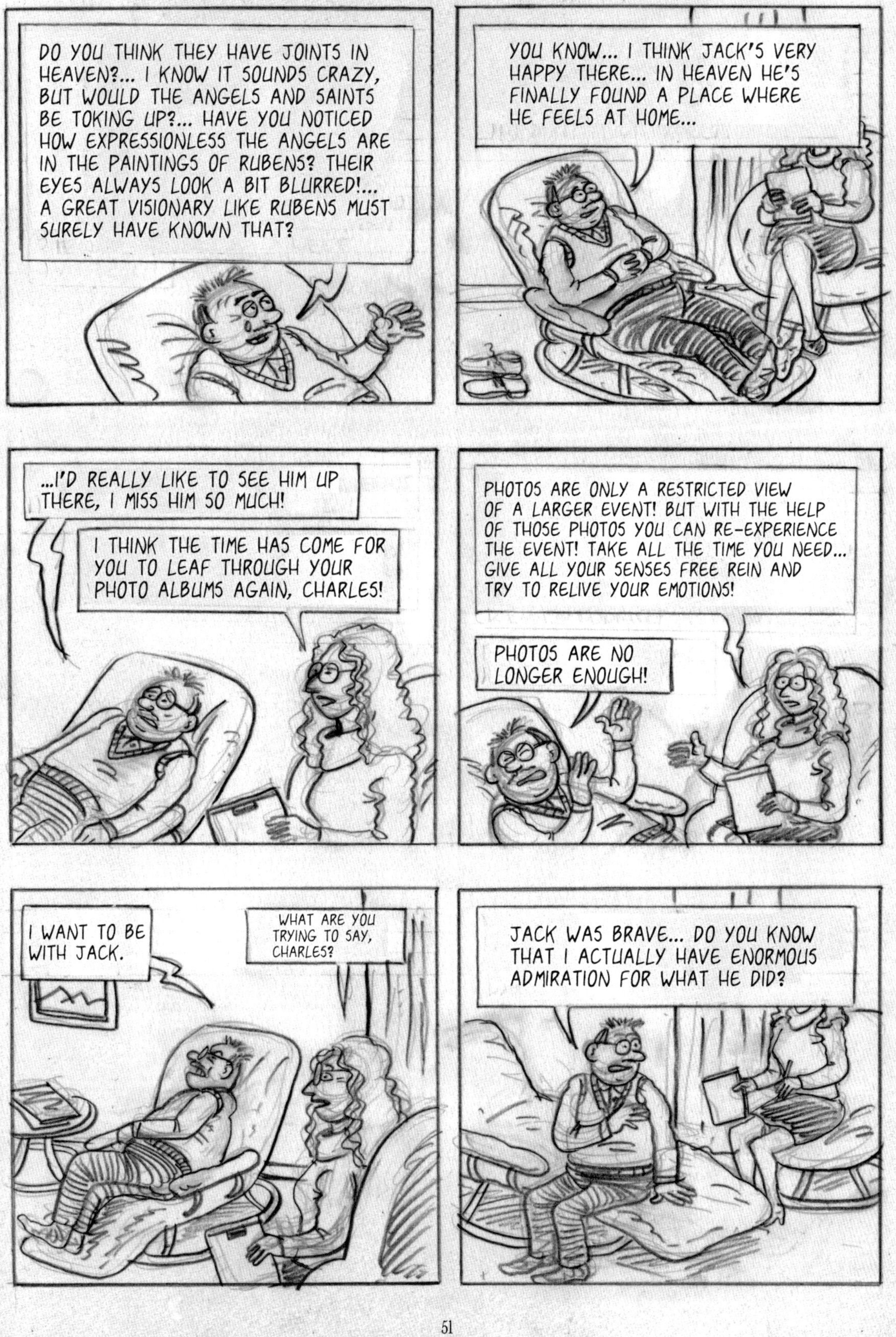
DO YOU THINK THEY HAVE JOINTS IN HEAVEN?... I KNOW IT SOUNDS CRAZY, BUT WOULD THE ANGELS AND SAINTS BE TOKING UP?... HAVE YOU NOTICED HOW EXPRESSIONLESS THE ANGELS ARE IN THE PAINTINGS OF RUBENS? THEIR EYES ALWAYS LOOK A BIT BLURRED!... A GREAT VISIONARY LIKE RUBENS MUST SURELY HAVE KNOWN THAT?
YOU KNOW... I THINK JACK'S VERY HAPPY THERE... IN HEAVEN HE'S FINALLY FOUND A PLACE WHERE HE FEELS AT HOME...
...I'D REALLY LIKE TO SEE HIM UP THERE, I MISS HIM SO MUCH!
I THINK THE TIME HAS COME FOR YOU TO LEAF THROUGH YOUR PHOTO ALBUMS AGAIN, CHARLES!
PHOTOS ARE ONLY A RESTRICTED VIEW OF A LARGER EVENT! BUT WITH THE HELP OF THOSE PHOTOS YOU CAN RE-EXPERIENCE THE EVENT! TAKE ALL THE TIME YOU NEED... GIVE ALL YOUR SENSES FREE REIN AND TRY TO RELIVE YOUR EMOTIONS!
PHOTOS ARE NO LONGER ENOUGH!
I WANT TO BE WITH JACK.
WHAT ARE YOU TRYING TO SAY, CHARLES?
JACK WAS BRAVE... DO YOU KNOW THAT I ACTUALLY HAVE ENORMOUS ADMIRATION FOR WHAT HE DID?

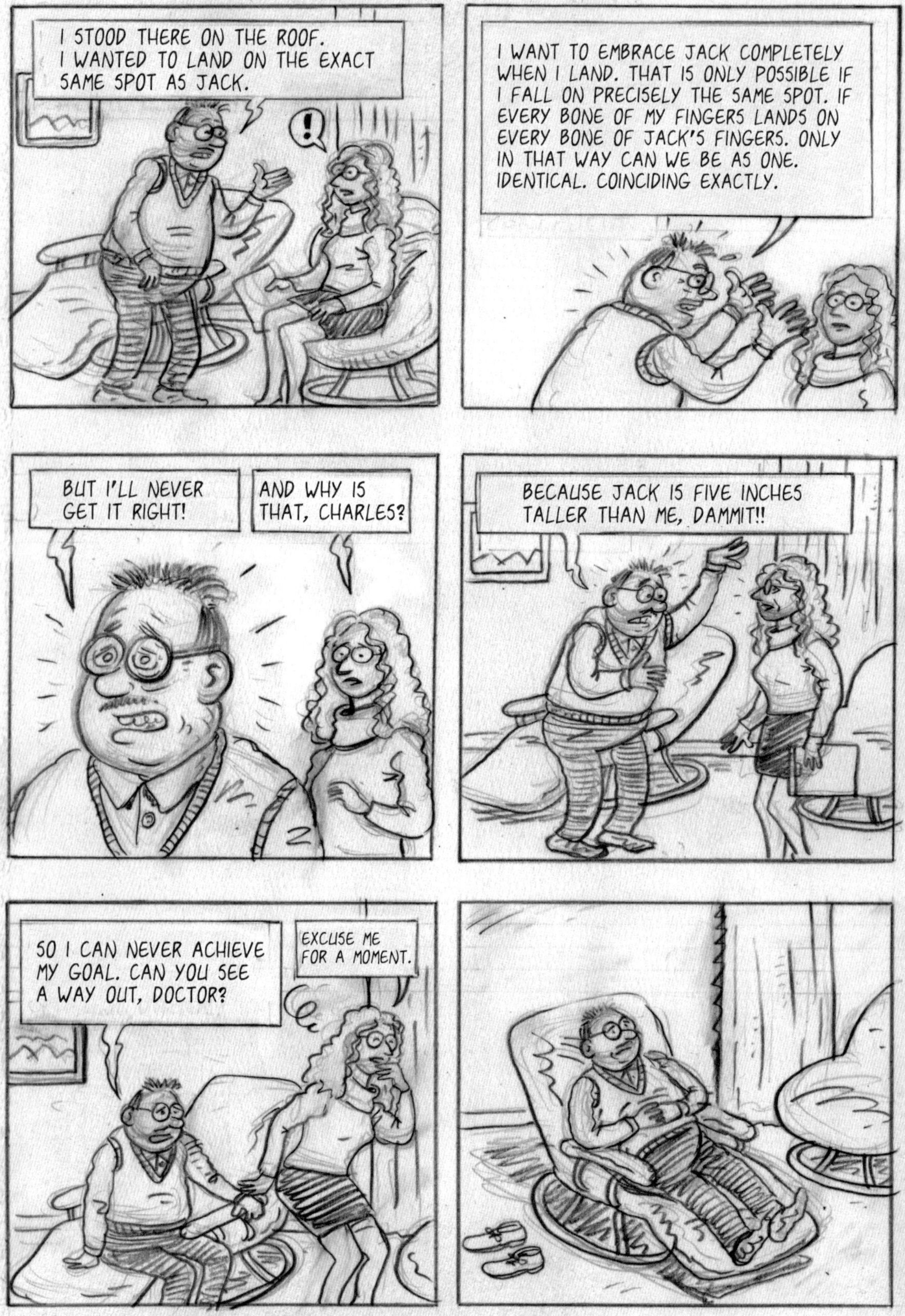
I STOOD THERE ON THE ROOF. I WANTED TO LAND ON THE EXACT SAME SPOT AS JACK.
!
I WANT TO EMBRACE JACK COMPLETELY WHEN I LAND. THAT IS ONLY POSSIBLE IF I FALL ON PRECISELY THE SAME SPOT. IF EVERY BONE OF MY FINGERS LANDS ON EVERY BONE OF JACK'S FINGERS. ONLY IN THAT WAY CAN WE BE AS ONE. IDENTICAL. COINCIDING EXACTLY.
BUT I'LL NEVER GET IT RIGHT!
AND WHY IS THAT, CHARLES?
BECAUSE JACK IS FIVE INCHES TALLER THAN ME, DAMMIT!!
SO I CAN NEVER ACHIEVE MY GOAL. CAN YOU SEE A WAY OUT, DOCTOR?
EXCUSE ME FOR A MOMENT.

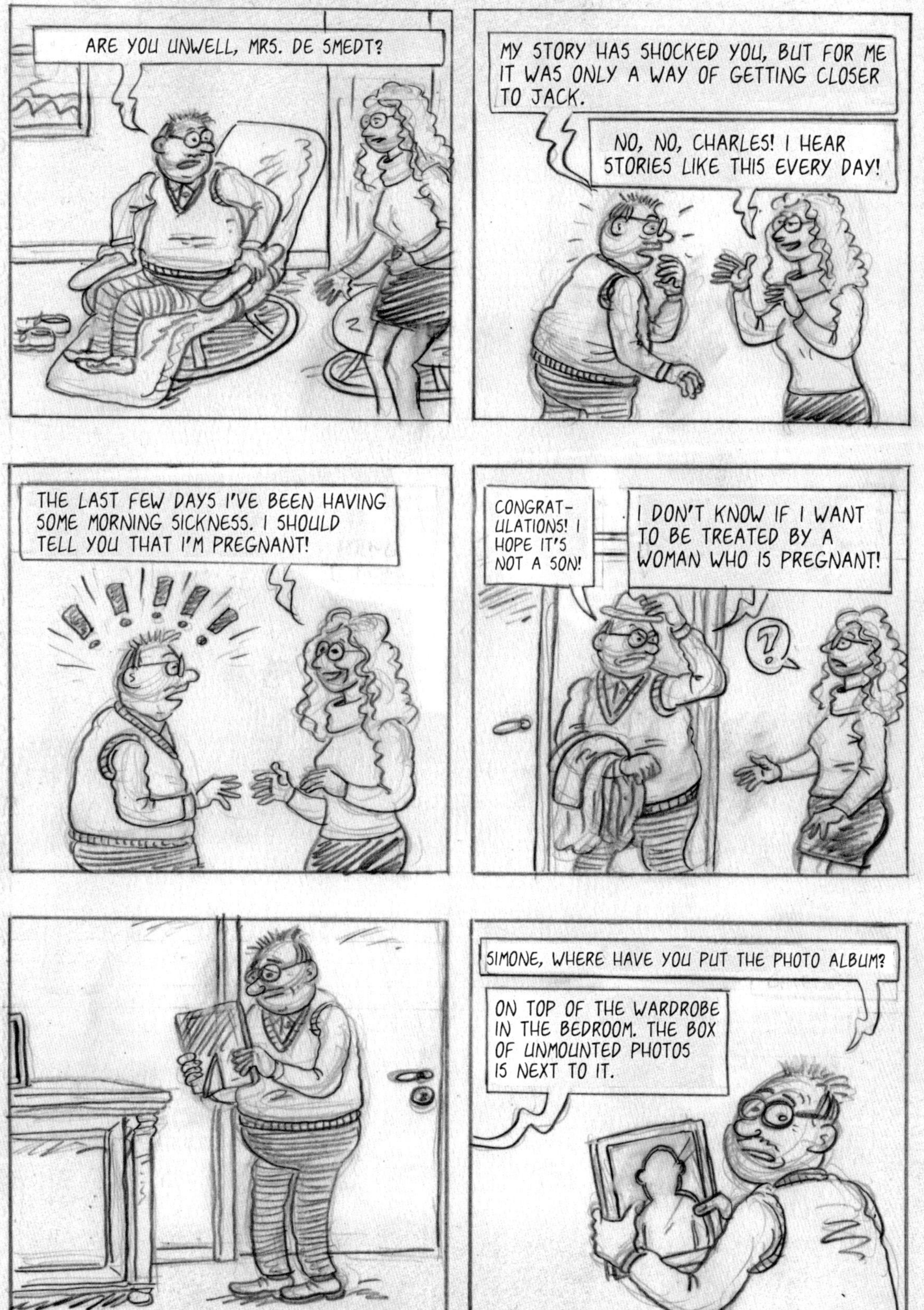
ARE YOU UNWELL, MRS. DE SMEDT?
MY STORY HAS SHOCKED YOU, BUT FOR ME IT WAS ONLY A WAY OF GETTING CLOSER TO JACK.
NO, NO, CHARLES! I HEAR STORIES LIKE THIS EVERY DAY!
THE LAST FEW DAYS I'VE BEEN HAVING SOME MORNING SICKNESS. I SHOULD TELL YOU THAT I'M PREGNANT!
CONGRAT-ULATIONS! I HOPE IT'S NOT A SON!
I DON'T KNOW IF I WANT TO BE TREATED BY A WOMAN WHO IS PREGNANT!
?
SIMONE, WHERE HAVE YOU PUT THE PHOTO ALBUM?
ON TOP OF THE WARDROBE IN THE BEDROOM. THE BOX OF UNMOUNTED PHOTOS IS NEXT TO IT.

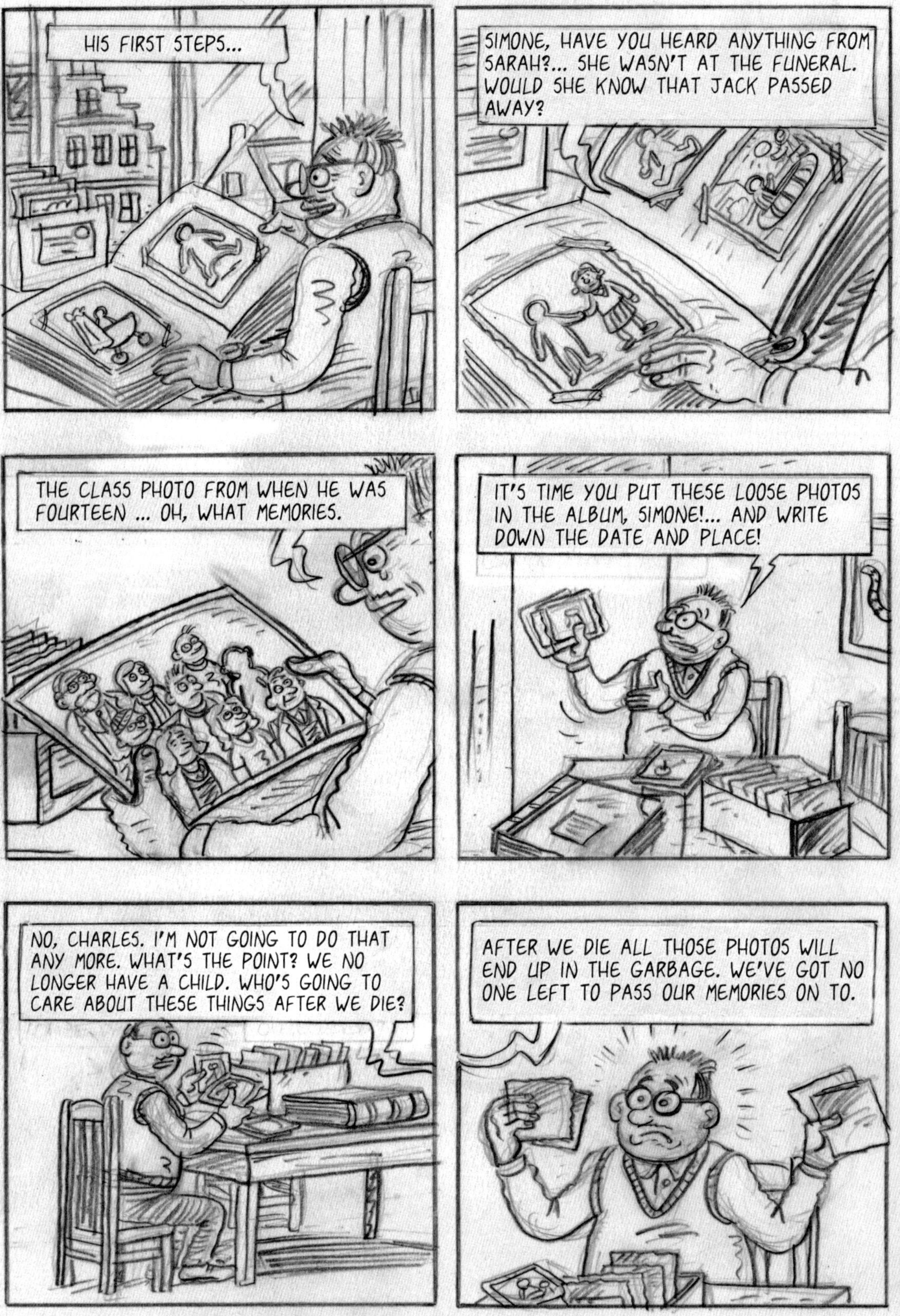
HIS FIRST STEPS...
SIMONE, HAVE YOU HEARD ANYTHING FROM SARAH?... SHE WASN'T AT THE FUNERAL. WOULD SHE KNOW THAT JACK PASSED AWAY?
THE CLASS PHOTO FROM WHEN HE WAS FOURTEEN ... OH, WHAT MEMORIES.
IT'S TIME YOU PUT THESE LOOSE PHOTOS IN THE ALBUM, SIMONE!... AND WRITE DOWN THE DATE AND PLACE!
NO, CHARLES. I'M NOT GOING TO DO THAT ANY MORE. WHAT'S THE POINT? WE NO LONGER HAVE A CHILD. WHO'S GOING TO CARE ABOUT THESE THINGS AFTER WE DIE?
AFTER WE DIE ALL THOSE PHOTOS WILL END UP IN THE GARBAGE. WE'VE GOT NO ONE LEFT TO PASS OUR MEMORIES ON TO.

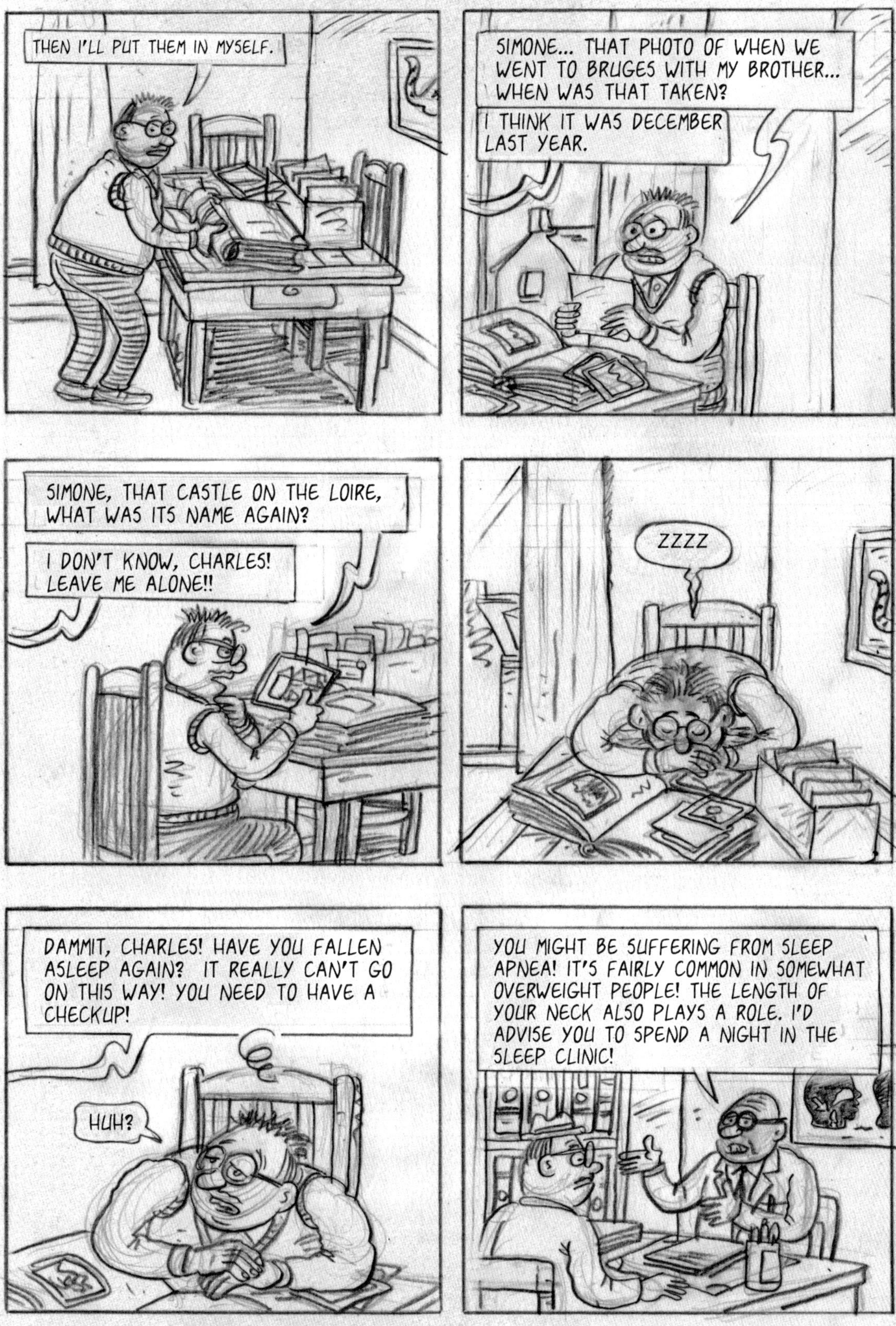
THEN I'LL PUT THEM IN MYSELF.
SIMONE... THAT PHOTO OF WHEN WE WENT TO BRUGES WITH MY BROTHER... WHEN WAS THAT TAKEN?
I THINK IT WAS DECEMBER LAST YEAR.
SIMONE, THAT CASTLE ON THE LOIRE, WHAT WAS ITS NAME AGAIN?
I DON'T KNOW, CHARLES! LEAVE ME ALONE!!
ZZZZ
DAMMIT, CHARLES! HAVE YOU FALLEN ASLEEP AGAIN? IT REALLY CAN'T GO ON THIS WAY! YOU NEED TO HAVE A CHECKUP!
HUH?
YOU MIGHT BE SUFFERING FROM SLEEP APNEA! IT'S FAIRLY COMMON IN SOMEWHAT OVERWEIGHT PEOPLE! THE LENGTH OF YOUR NECK ALSO PLAYS A ROLE. I'D ADVISE YOU TO SPEND A NIGHT IN THE SLEEP CLINIC!

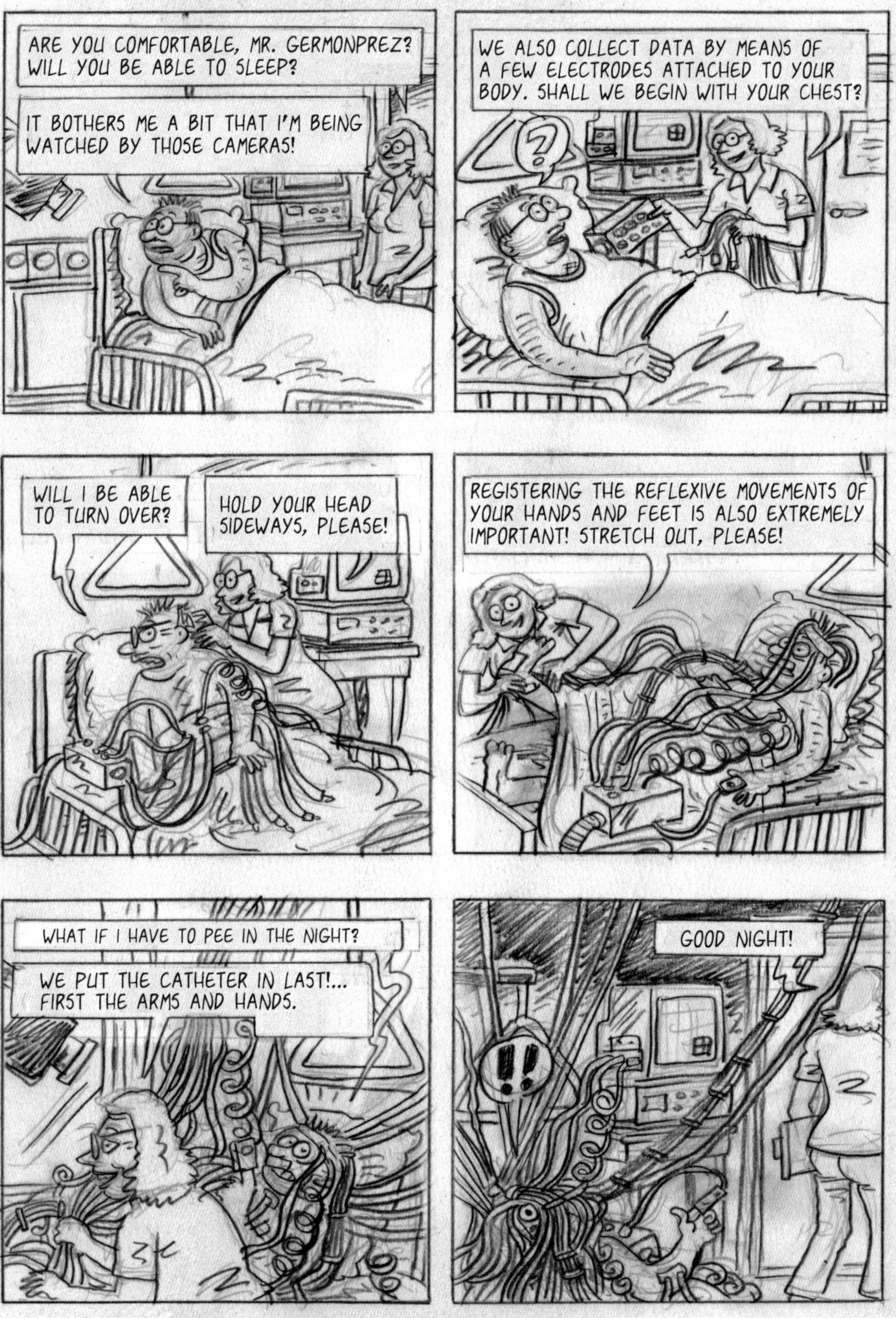
ARE YOU COMFORTABLE, MR. GERMONPREZ? WILL YOU BE ABLE TO SLEEP?
IT BOTHERS ME A BIT THAT I'M BEING WATCHED BY THOSE CAMERAS!
WE ALSO COLLECT DATA BY MEANS OF A FEW ELECTRODES ATTACHED TO YOUR BODY. SHALL WE BEGIN WITH YOUR CHEST?
?
WILL I BE ABLE TO TURN OVER?
HOLD YOUR HEAD SIDEWAYS, PLEASE!
REGISTERING THE REFLEXIVE MOVEMENTS OF YOUR HANDS AND FEET IS ALSO EXTREMELY IMPORTANT! STRETCH OUT, PLEASE!
WHAT IF I HAVE TO PEE IN THE NIGHT?
WE PUT THE CATHETER IN LAST!... FIRST THE ARMS AND HANDS.
GOOD NIGHT!
!!

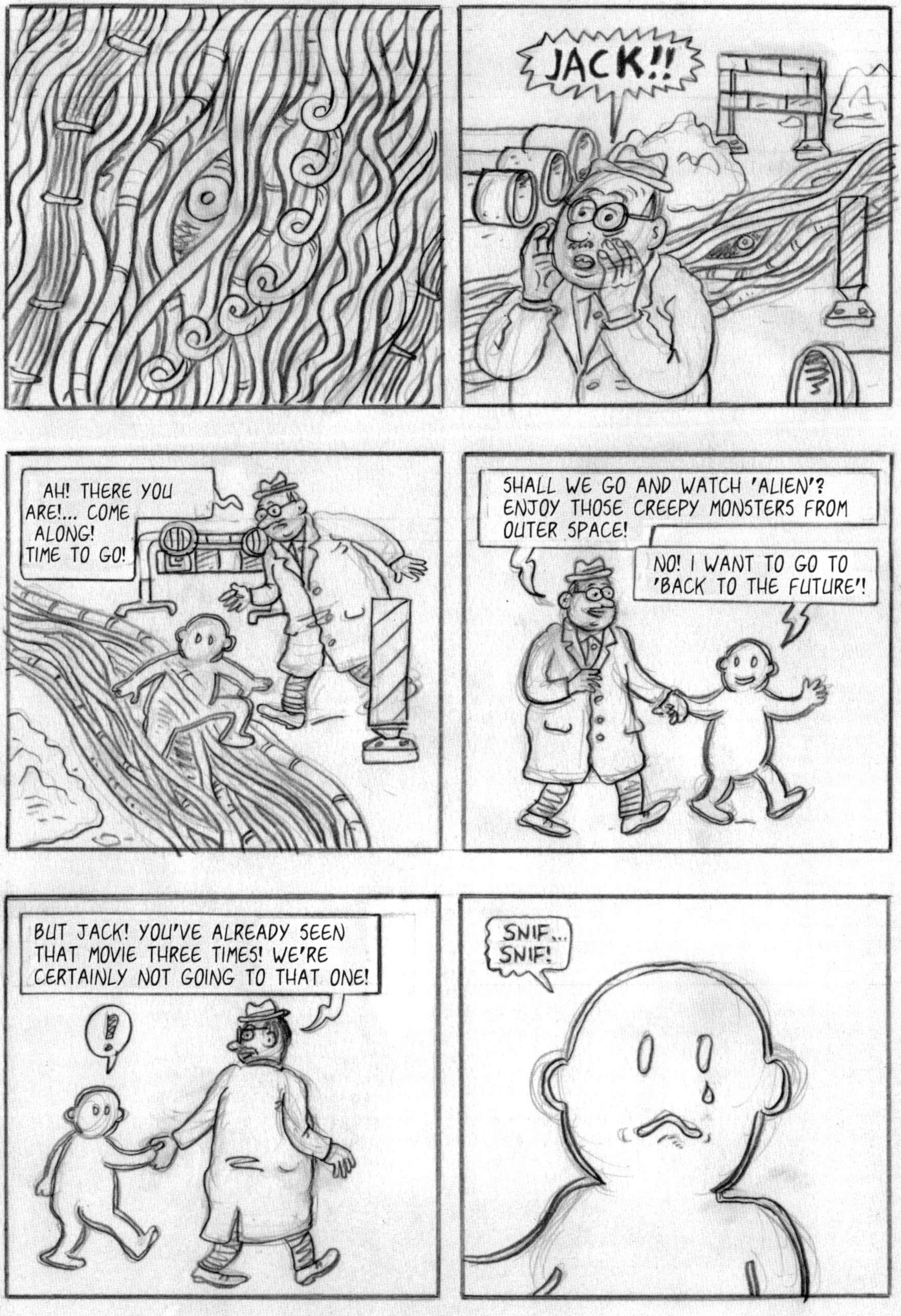
JACK!!
AH! THERE YOU ARE!... COME ALONG! TIME TO GO!
SHALL WE GO AND WATCH 'ALIEN'? ENJOY THOSE CREEPY MONSTERS FROM OUTER SPACE!
NO! I WANT TO GO TO 'BACK TO THE FUTURE'!
BUT JACK! YOU'VE ALREADY SEEN THAT MOVIE THREE TIMES! WE'RE CERTAINLY NOT GOING TO THAT ONE!
!
SNIF... SNIF!

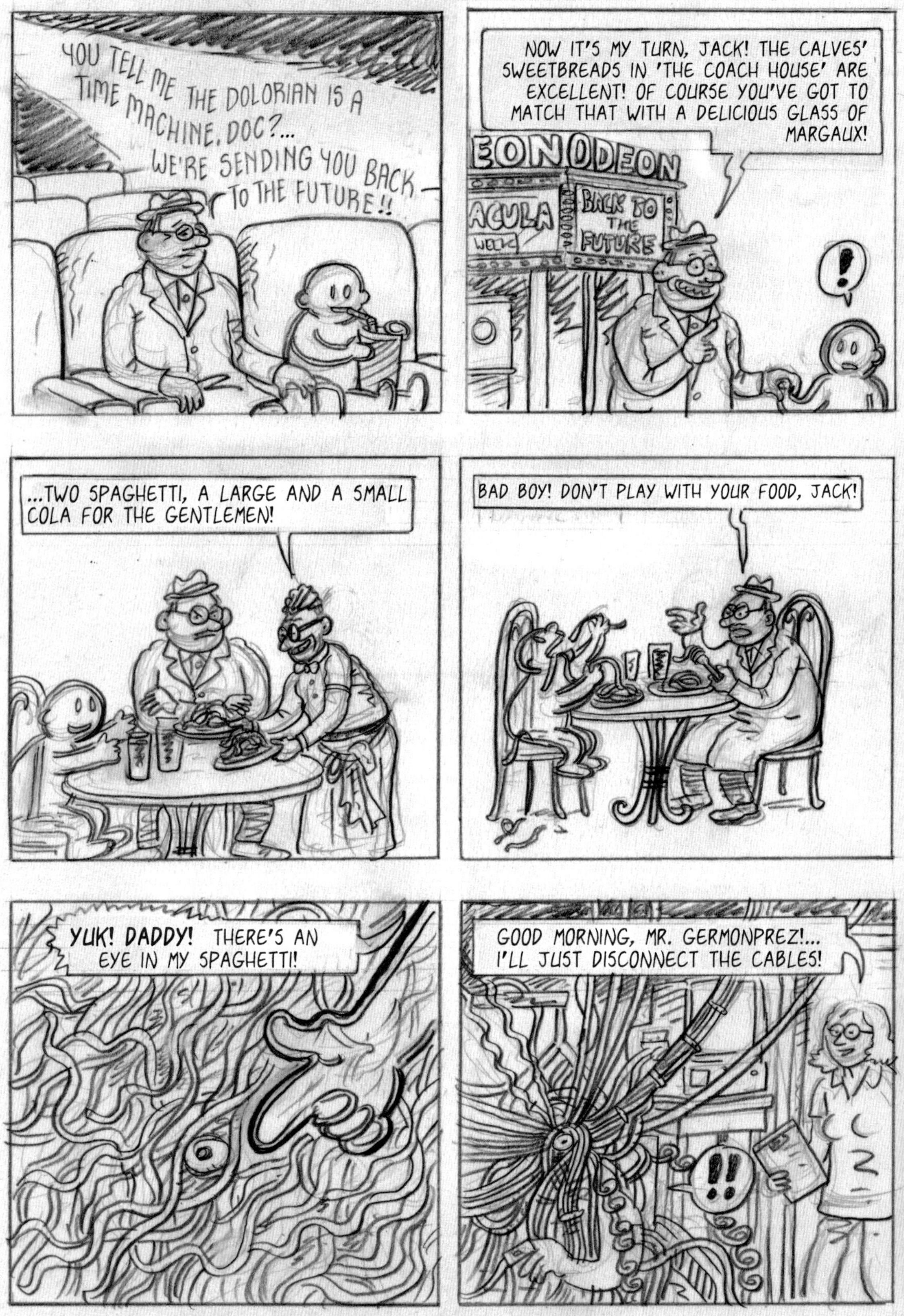
YOU TELL ME THE DOLORIAN IS A TIME MACHINE, DOC?...
WE'RE SENDING YOU BACK TO THE FUTURE!!
NOW IT'S MY TURN, JACK! THE CALVES' SWEETBREADS IN 'THE COACH HOUSE' ARE EXCELLENT! OF COURSE YOU'VE GOT TO MATCH THAT WITH A DELICIOUS GLASS OF MARGAUX!
EONODEON
ACULA
WEEK
BACK TO THE FUTURE
!
...TWO SPAGHETTI, A LARGE AND A SMALL COLA FOR THE GENTLEMEN!
BAD BOY! DON'T PLAY WITH YOUR FOOD, JACK!
YUK! DADDY! THERE'S AN EYE IN MY SPAGHETTI!
GOOD MORNING, MR. GERMONPREZ!... I'LL JUST DISCONNECT THE CABLES!
!!

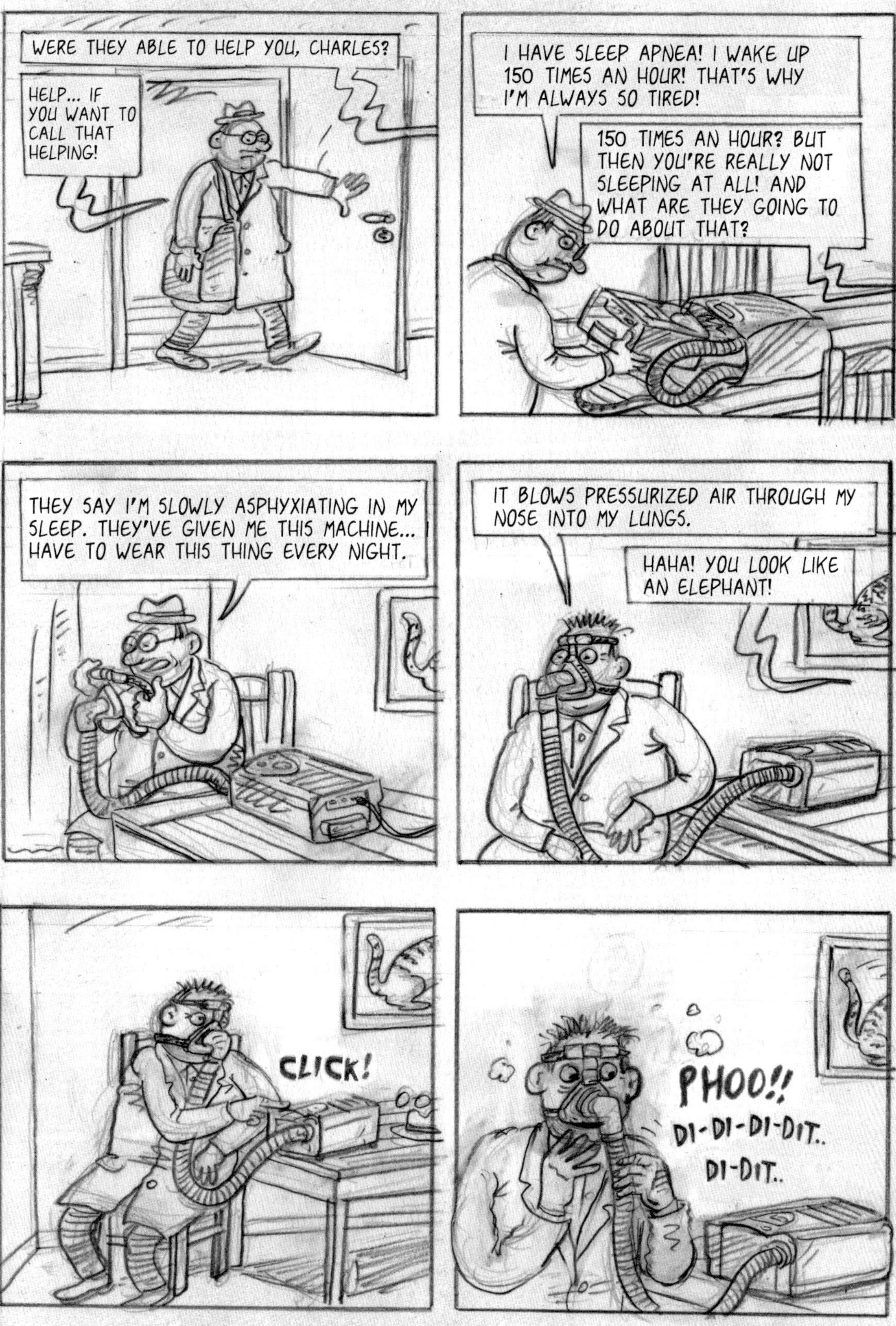
WERE THEY ABLE TO HELP YOU, CHARLES?
HELP... IF YOU WANT TO CALL THAT HELPING!
I HAVE SLEEP APNEA! I WAKE UP 150 TIMES AN HOUR! THAT'S WHY I'M ALWAYS SO TIRED!
150 TIMES AN HOUR? BUT THEN YOU'RE REALLY NOT SLEEPING AT ALL! AND WHAT ARE THEY GOING TO DO ABOUT THAT?
THEY SAY I'M SLOWLY ASPHYXIATING IN MY SLEEP. THEY'VE GIVEN ME THIS MACHINE... HAVE TO WEAR THIS THING EVERY NIGHT.
IT BLOWS PRESSURIZED AIR THROUGH MY NOSE INTO MY LUNGS.
HAHA! YOU LOOK LIKE AN ELEPHANT!
CLICK!
PHOO!!
DI-DI-DI-DIT..
DI-DIT..

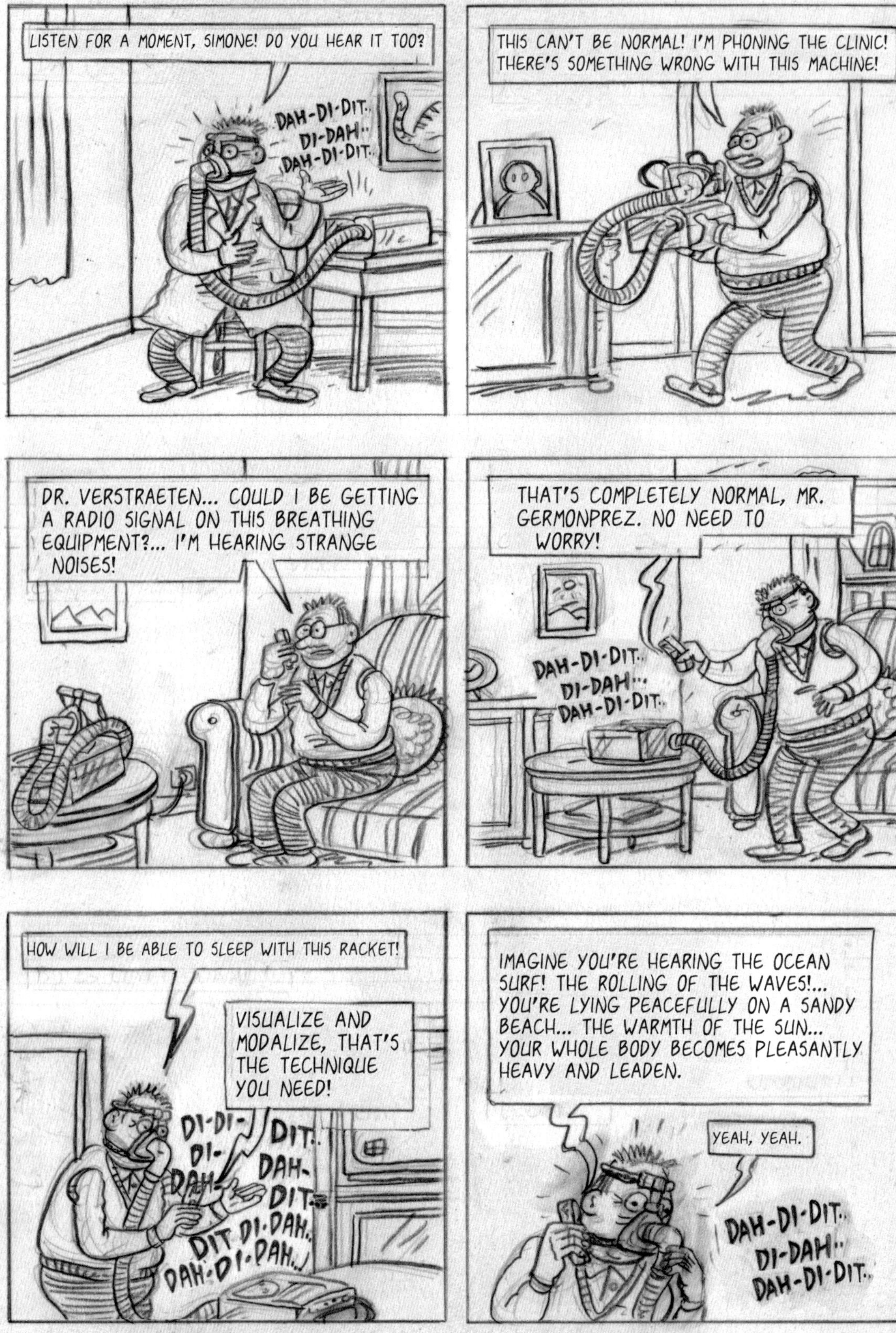
LISTEN FOR A MOMENT, SIMONE! DO YOU HEAR IT TOO?
DAH-DI-DIT.. DI-DAH.. DAH-DI-DIT..
THIS CAN'T BE NORMAL! I'M PHONING THE CLINIC! THERE'S SOMETHING WRONG WITH THIS MACHINE!
DR. VERSTRAETEN... COULD I BE GETTING A RADIO SIGNAL ON THIS BREATHING EQUIPMENT?... I'M HEARING STRANGE NOISES!
THAT'S COMPLETELY NORMAL, MR. GERMONPREZ. NO NEED TO WORRY!
DAH-DI-DIT.. DI-DAH.. DAH-DI-DIT..
HOW WILL I BE ABLE TO SLEEP WITH THIS RACKET!
VISUALIZE AND MODALIZE, THAT'S THE TECHNIQUE YOU NEED!
DI-DI-DI-DAH DIT.. DAH-DIT DIT DI-DAH.. DAH-DI-DAH..
IMAGINE YOU'RE HEARING THE OCEAN SURF! THE ROLLING OF THE WAVES!... YOU'RE LYING PEACEFULLY ON A SANDY BEACH... THE WARMTH OF THE SUN... YOUR WHOLE BODY BECOMES PLEASANTLY HEAVY AND LEADEN.
YEAH, YEAH.
DAH-DI-DIT.. DI-DAH.. DAH-DI-DIT..

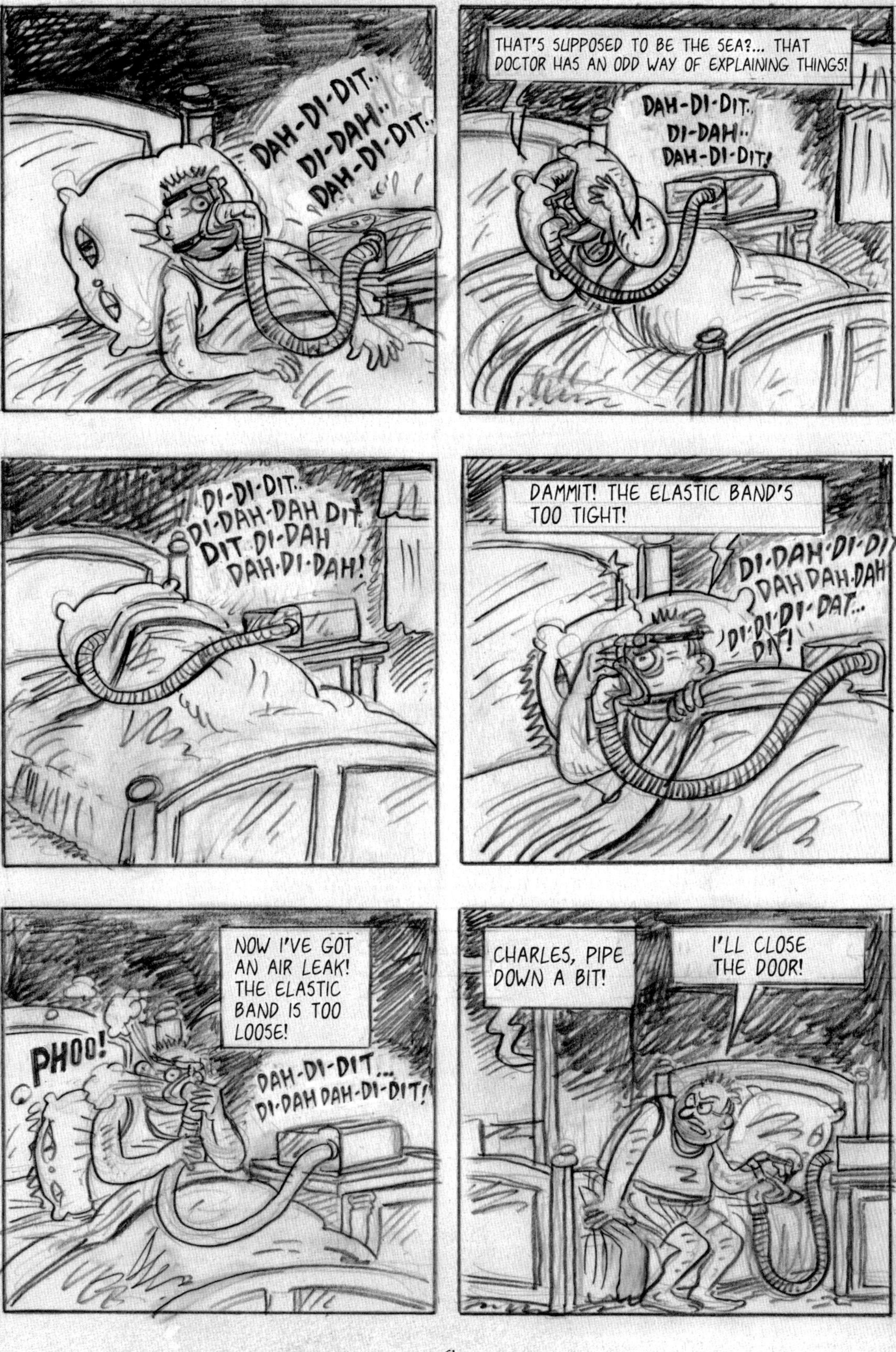
DAH-DI-DIT..
DI-DAH..
DAH-DI-DIT..
THAT'S SUPPOSED TO BE THE SEA?... THAT DOCTOR HAS AN ODD WAY OF EXPLAINING THINGS!
DAH-DI-DIT..
DI-DAH..
DAH-DI-DIT!
DI-DI-DIT..
DI-DAH-DAH DIT
DIT DI-DAH
DAH-DI-DAH!
DAMMIT! THE ELASTIC BAND'S TOO TIGHT!
DI-DAH-DI-DIT
DAH DAH-DAH
DI-DI-DI-DAT...
DIT!
NOW I'VE GOT AN AIR LEAK! THE ELASTIC BAND IS TOO LOOSE!
PHOO!
DAH-DI-DIT...
DI-DAH DAH-DI-DIT!
CHARLES, PIPE DOWN A BIT!
I'LL CLOSE THE DOOR!

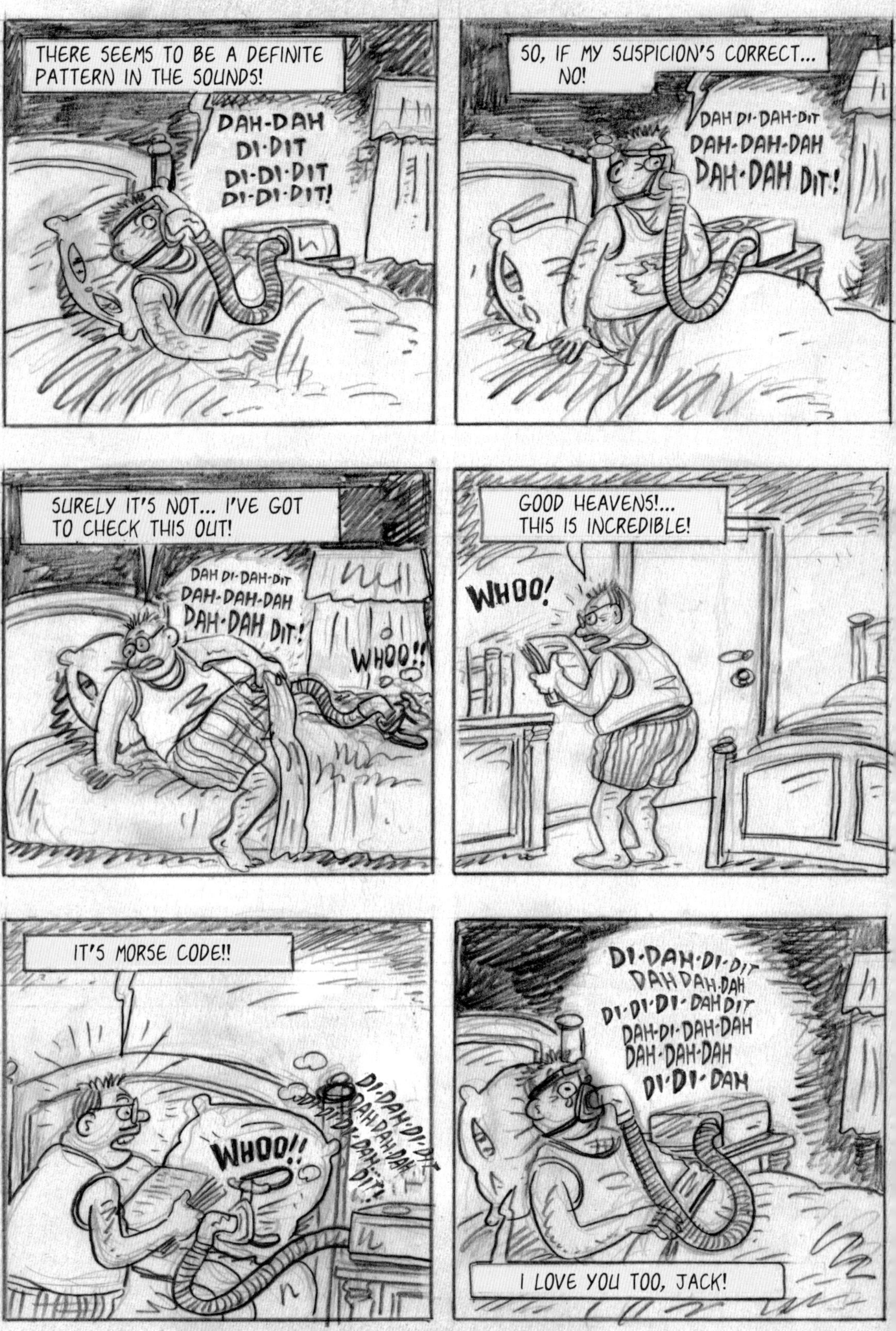

THERE SEEMS TO BE A DEFINITE PATTERN IN THE SOUNDS!
DAH-DAH DI-DIT DI-DI-DIT DI-DI-DIT!
SO, IF MY SUSPICION'S CORRECT... NO!
DAH DI-DAH-DIT DAH-DAH-DAH DAH-DAH DIT!
SURELY IT'S NOT... I'VE GOT TO CHECK THIS OUT!
DAH DI-DAH-DIT DAH-DAH-DAH DAH-DAH DIT!
WHOO!!
GOOD HEAVENS!... THIS IS INCREDIBLE!
WHOO!
IT'S MORSE CODE!!
WHOO!!
DI-DAH-DI-DIT DAH DAH-DAH DI-DI-DI-DAH DIT DAH-DI-DAH-DAH DAH-DAH-DAH DI-DI-DAH
I LOVE YOU TOO, JACK!

CHAPTER 4 – BAD CONNECTION

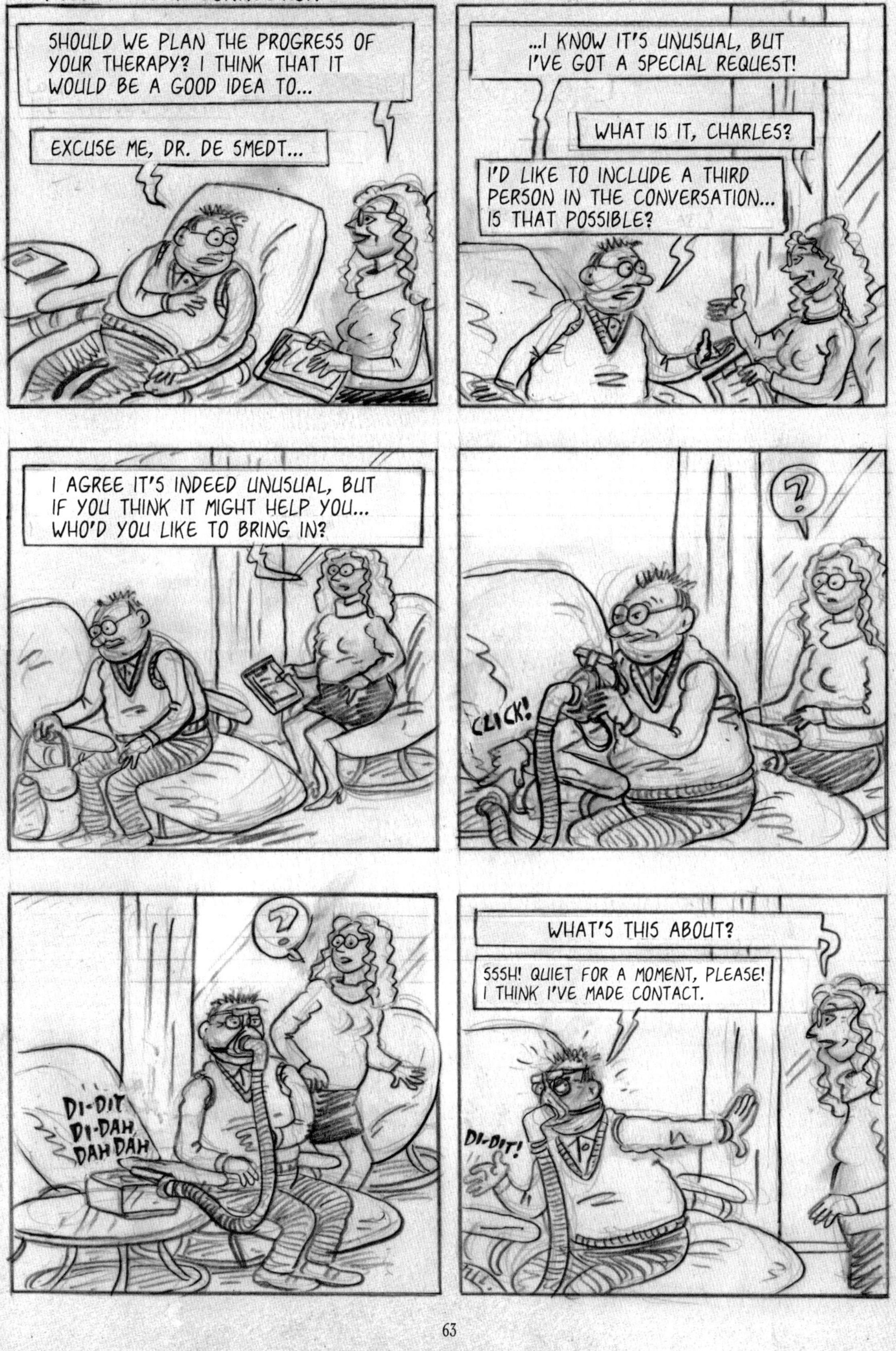
SHOULD WE PLAN THE PROGRESS OF YOUR THERAPY? I THINK THAT IT WOULD BE A GOOD IDEA TO...
EXCUSE ME, DR. DE SMEDT...
...I KNOW IT'S UNUSUAL, BUT I'VE GOT A SPECIAL REQUEST!
WHAT IS IT, CHARLES?
I'D LIKE TO INCLUDE A THIRD PERSON IN THE CONVERSATION... IS THAT POSSIBLE?
I AGREE IT'S INDEED UNUSUAL, BUT IF YOU THINK IT MIGHT HELP YOU... WHO'D YOU LIKE TO BRING IN?
?
CLICK!
?
DI-DIT DI-DAH DAH DAH
WHAT'S THIS ABOUT?
SSSH! QUIET FOR A MOMENT, PLEASE! I THINK I'VE MADE CONTACT.
DI-DIT!

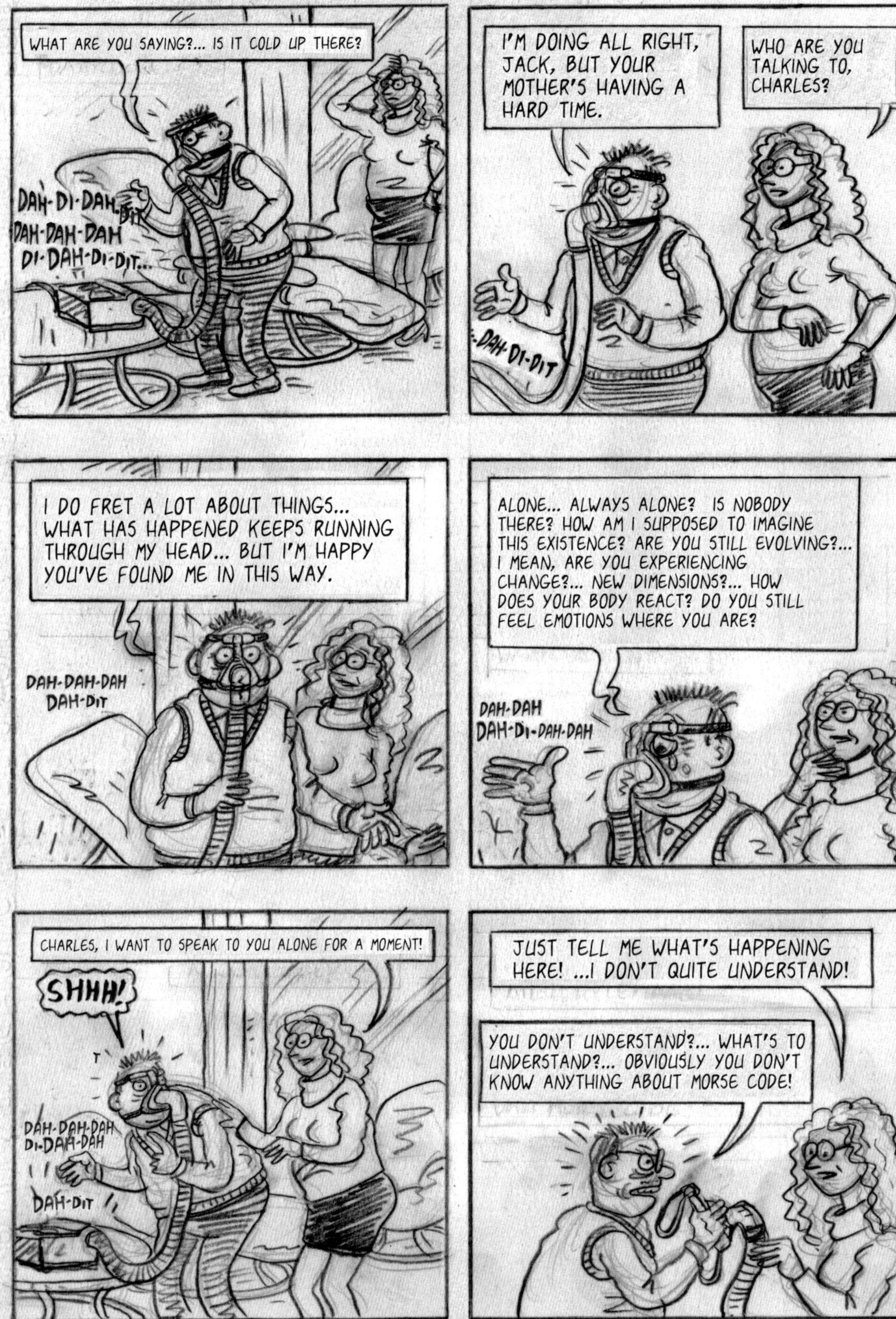
WHAT ARE YOU SAYING?... IS IT COLD UP THERE?
DAH-DI-DAH-DIT
DAH-DAH-DAH
DI-DAH-DI-DIT...
I'M DOING ALL RIGHT, JACK, BUT YOUR MOTHER'S HAVING A HARD TIME.
WHO ARE YOU TALKING TO, CHARLES?
...DAH-DI-DIT
I DO FRET A LOT ABOUT THINGS... WHAT HAS HAPPENED KEEPS RUNNING THROUGH MY HEAD... BUT I'M HAPPY YOU'VE FOUND ME IN THIS WAY.
DAH-DAH-DAH
DAH-DIT
ALONE... ALWAYS ALONE? IS NOBODY THERE? HOW AM I SUPPOSED TO IMAGINE THIS EXISTENCE? ARE YOU STILL EVOLVING?... I MEAN, ARE YOU EXPERIENCING CHANGE?... NEW DIMENSIONS?... HOW DOES YOUR BODY REACT? DO YOU STILL FEEL EMOTIONS WHERE YOU ARE?
DAH-DAH
DAH-DI-DAH-DAH
CHARLES, I WANT TO SPEAK TO YOU ALONE FOR A MOMENT!
SHHH!
DAH-DAH-DAH
DI-DAH-DAH
DAH-DIT
JUST TELL ME WHAT'S HAPPENING HERE! ...I DON'T QUITE UNDERSTAND!
YOU DON'T UNDERSTAND?... WHAT'S TO UNDERSTAND?... OBVIOUSLY YOU DON'T KNOW ANYTHING ABOUT MORSE CODE!

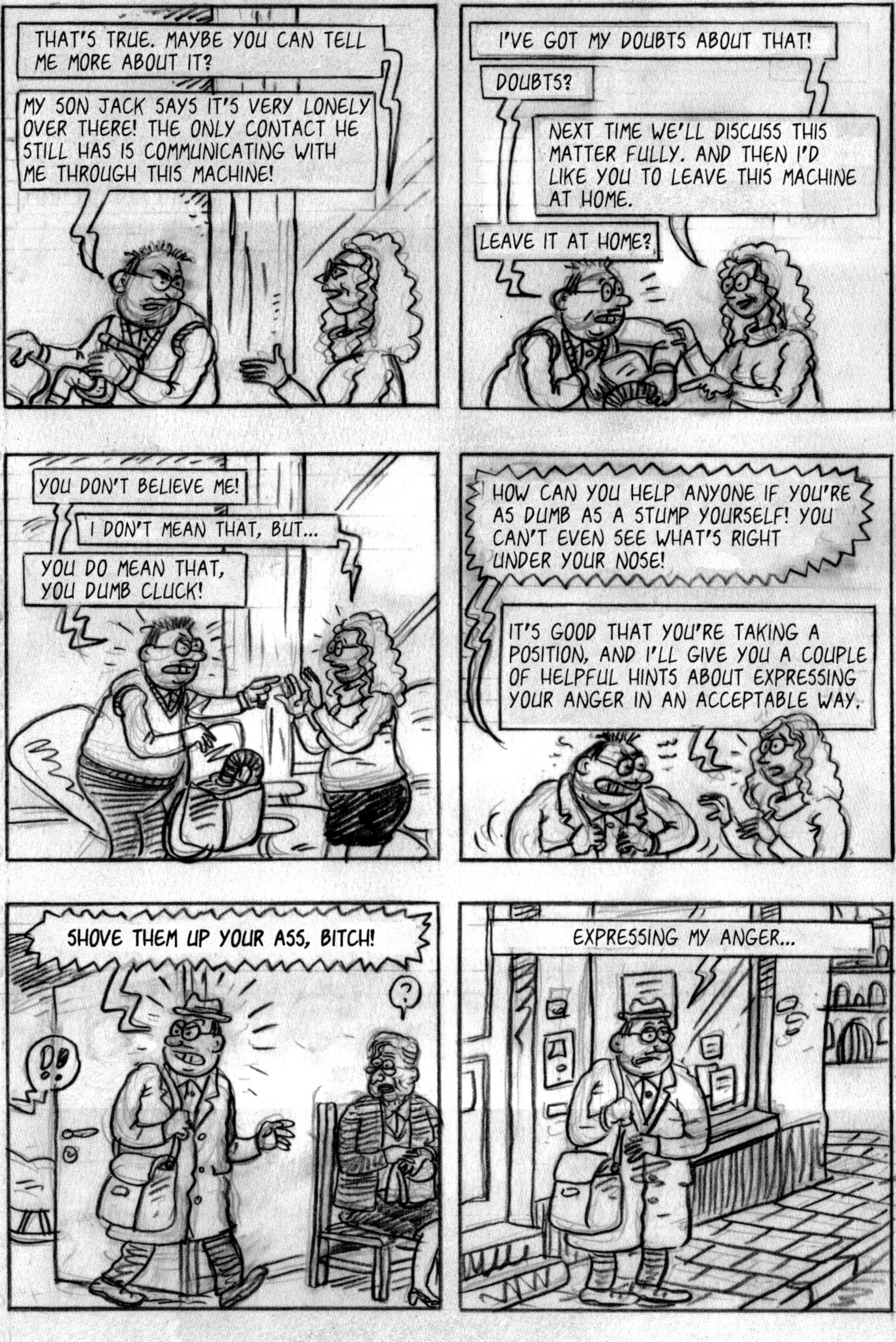
THAT'S TRUE. MAYBE YOU CAN TELL ME MORE ABOUT IT?
MY SON JACK SAYS IT'S VERY LONELY OVER THERE! THE ONLY CONTACT HE STILL HAS IS COMMUNICATING WITH ME THROUGH THIS MACHINE!
I'VE GOT MY DOUBTS ABOUT THAT!
DOUBTS?
NEXT TIME WE'LL DISCUSS THIS MATTER FULLY. AND THEN I'D LIKE YOU TO LEAVE THIS MACHINE AT HOME.
LEAVE IT AT HOME?
YOU DON'T BELIEVE ME!
I DON'T MEAN THAT, BUT...
YOU DO MEAN THAT, YOU DUMB CLUCK!
HOW CAN YOU HELP ANYONE IF YOU'RE AS DUMB AS A STUMP YOURSELF! YOU CAN'T EVEN SEE WHAT'S RIGHT UNDER YOUR NOSE!
IT'S GOOD THAT YOU'RE TAKING A POSITION, AND I'LL GIVE YOU A COUPLE OF HELPFUL HINTS ABOUT EXPRESSING YOUR ANGER IN AN ACCEPTABLE WAY.
SHOVE THEM UP YOUR ASS, BITCH!
?
!?
EXPRESSING MY ANGER...

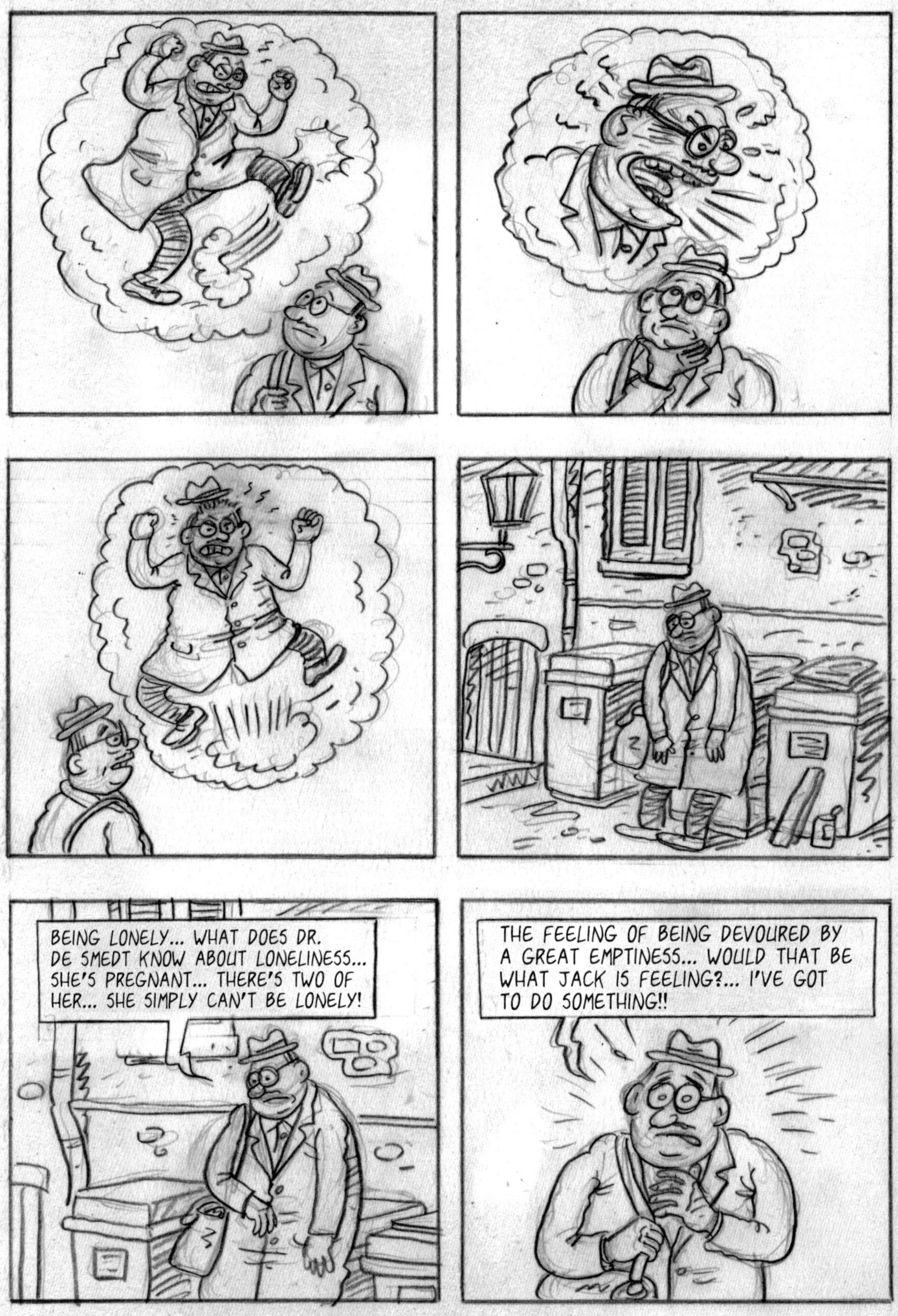
BEING LONELY... WHAT DOES DR. DE SMEDT KNOW ABOUT LONELINESS... SHE'S PREGNANT... THERE'S TWO OF HER... SHE SIMPLY CAN'T BE LONELY!
THE FEELING OF BEING DEVOURED BY A GREAT EMPTINESS... WOULD THAT BE WHAT JACK IS FEELING?... I'VE GOT TO DO SOMETHING!!

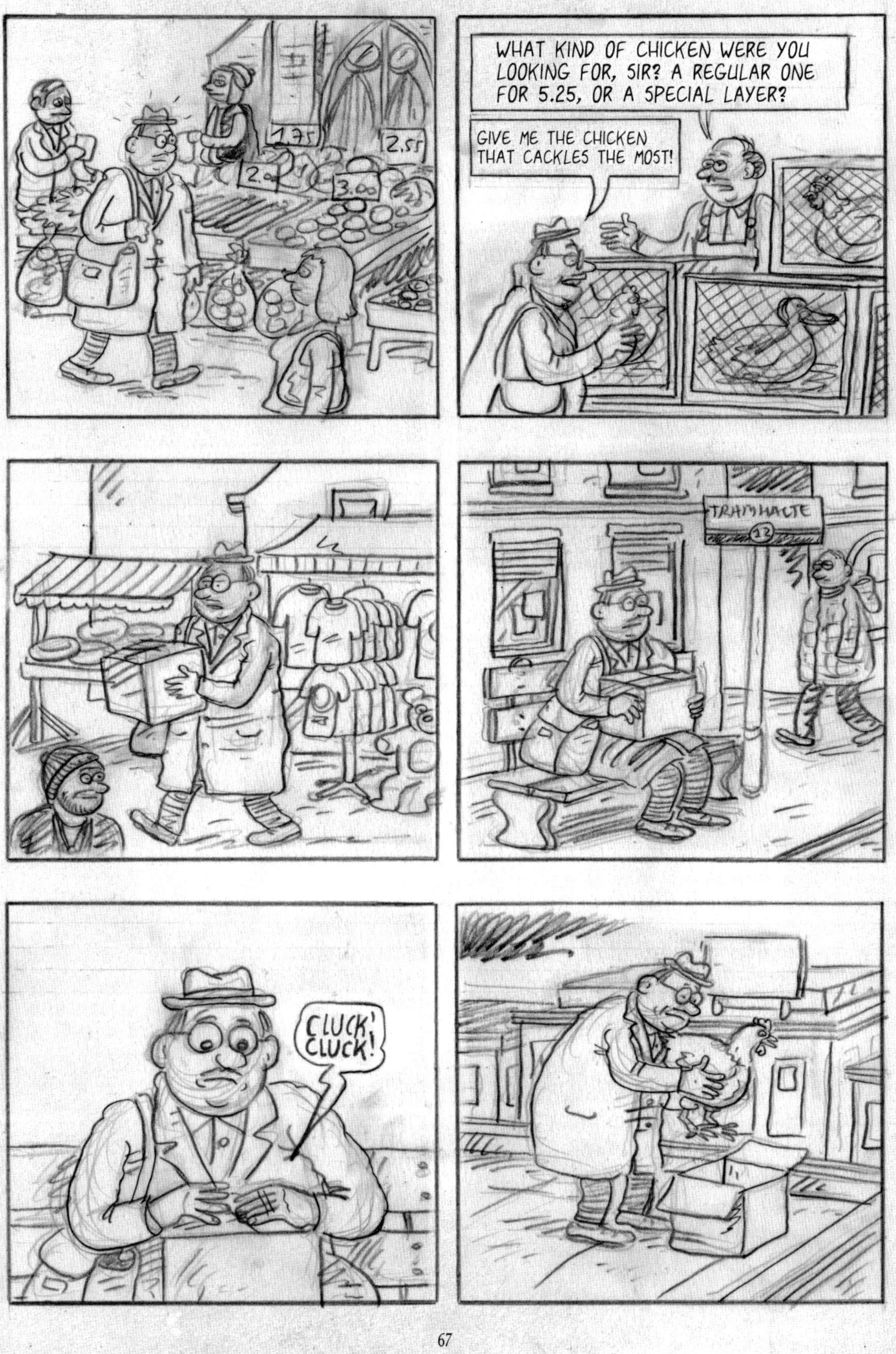
1.75
2.55
2.00
3.00
WHAT KIND OF CHICKEN WERE YOU LOOKING FOR, SIR? A REGULAR ONE FOR 5.25, OR A SPECIAL LAYER?
GIVE ME THE CHICKEN THAT CACKLES THE MOST!
TRAMHALTE
12
CLUCK! CLUCK!

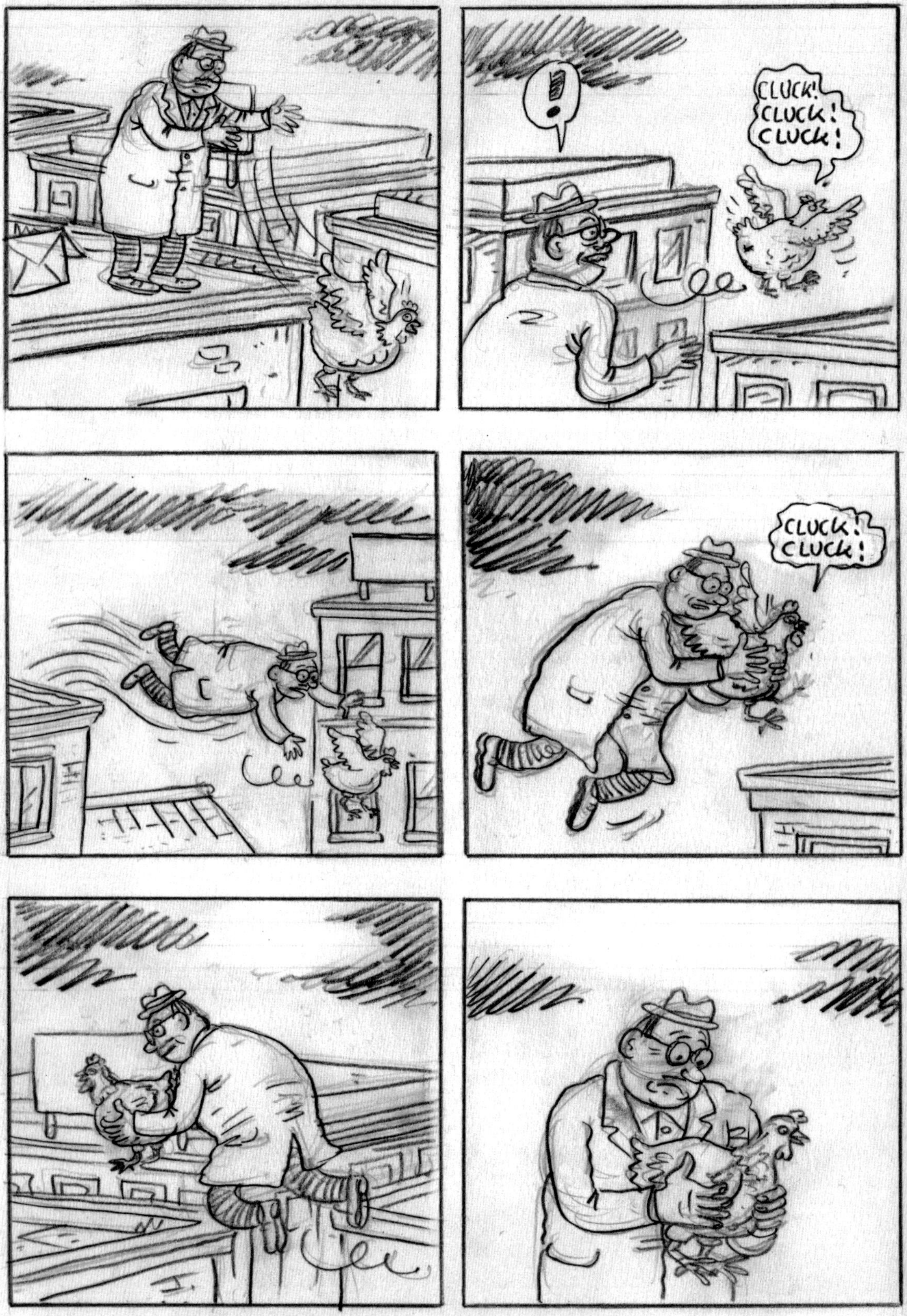
!
CLUCK! CLUCK! CLUCK!
CLUCK! CLUCK!

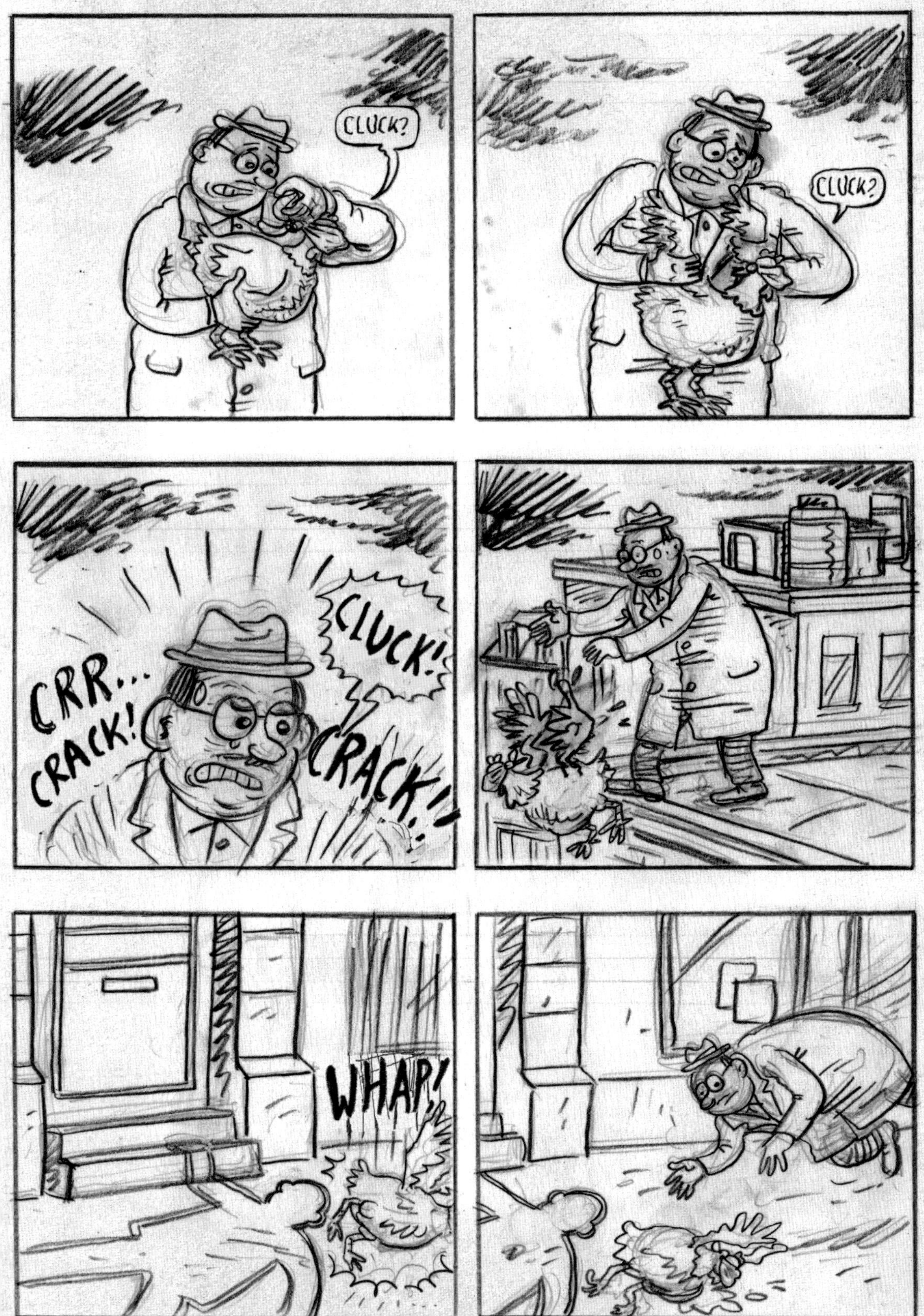
CLUCK?
CLUCK?
CRR... CRACK!
CLUCK!
CRACK!!
WHAP!

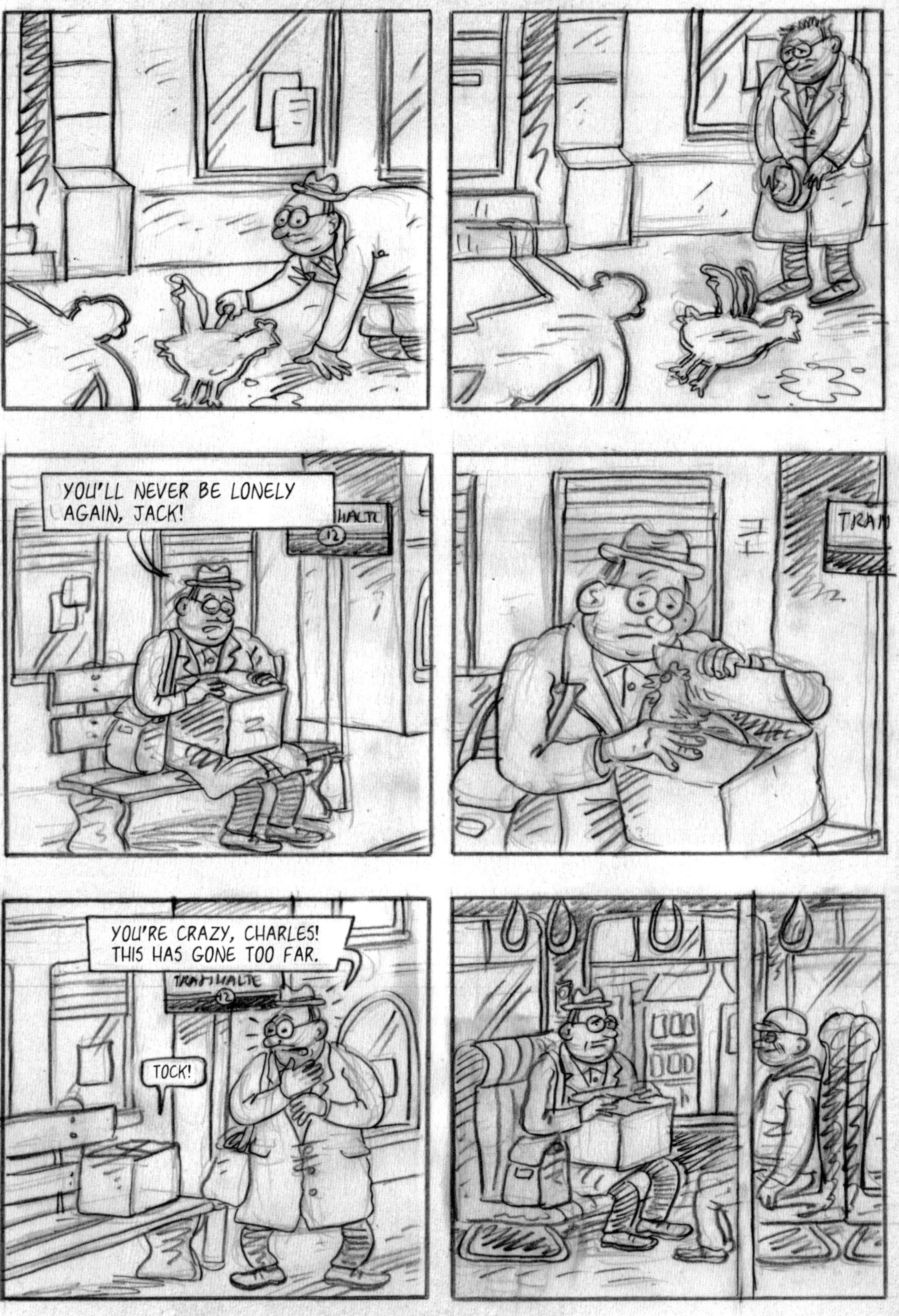
YOU'LL NEVER BE LONELY AGAIN, JACK!
TRAM
YOU'RE CRAZY, CHARLES! THIS HAS GONE TOO FAR.
TOCK!

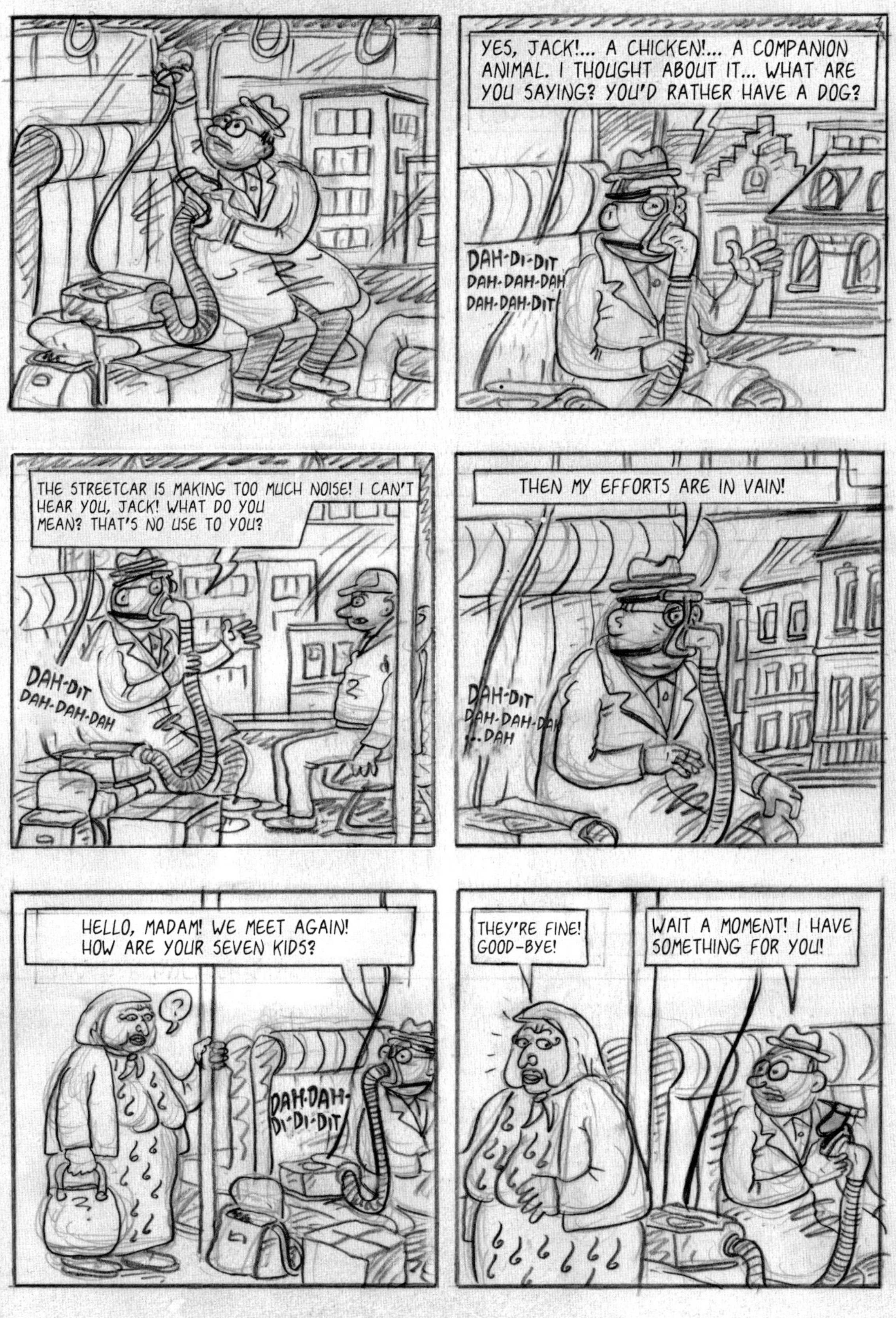
YES, JACK!... A CHICKEN!... A COMPANION ANIMAL. I THOUGHT ABOUT IT... WHAT ARE YOU SAYING? YOU'D RATHER HAVE A DOG?
DAH-DI-DIT
DAH-DAH-DAH
DAH-DAH-DIT
THE STREETCAR IS MAKING TOO MUCH NOISE! I CAN'T HEAR YOU, JACK! WHAT DO YOU MEAN? THAT'S NO USE TO YOU?
DAH-DIT
DAH-DAH-DAH
THEN MY EFFORTS ARE IN VAIN!
DAH-DIT
DAH-DAH-DAH
...DAH
HELLO, MADAM! WE MEET AGAIN! HOW ARE YOUR SEVEN KIDS?
?
DAH-DAH-
DI-DI-DIT
THEY'RE FINE! GOOD-BYE!
WAIT A MOMENT! I HAVE SOMETHING FOR YOU!

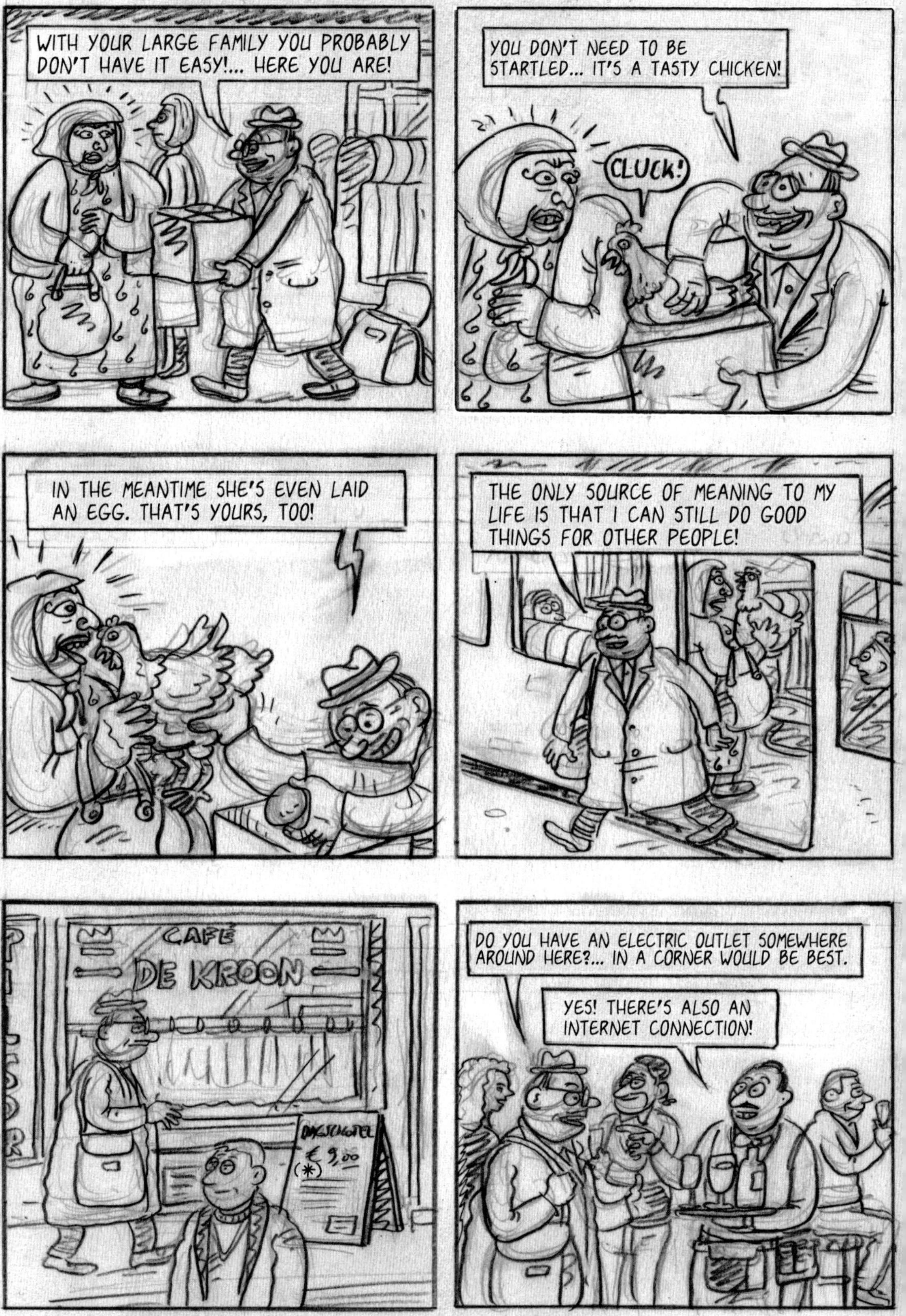

WITH YOUR LARGE FAMILY YOU PROBABLY DON'T HAVE IT EASY!... HERE YOU ARE!
YOU DON'T NEED TO BE STARTLED... IT'S A TASTY CHICKEN!
CLUCK!
IN THE MEANTIME SHE'S EVEN LAID AN EGG. THAT'S YOURS, TOO!
THE ONLY SOURCE OF MEANING TO MY LIFE IS THAT I CAN STILL DO GOOD THINGS FOR OTHER PEOPLE!
CAFÉ
DE KROON
€ 9,00
(*)
DO YOU HAVE AN ELECTRIC OUTLET SOMEWHERE AROUND HERE?... IN A CORNER WOULD BE BEST.
YES! THERE'S ALSO AN INTERNET CONNECTION!

* TODAY'S SPECIAL

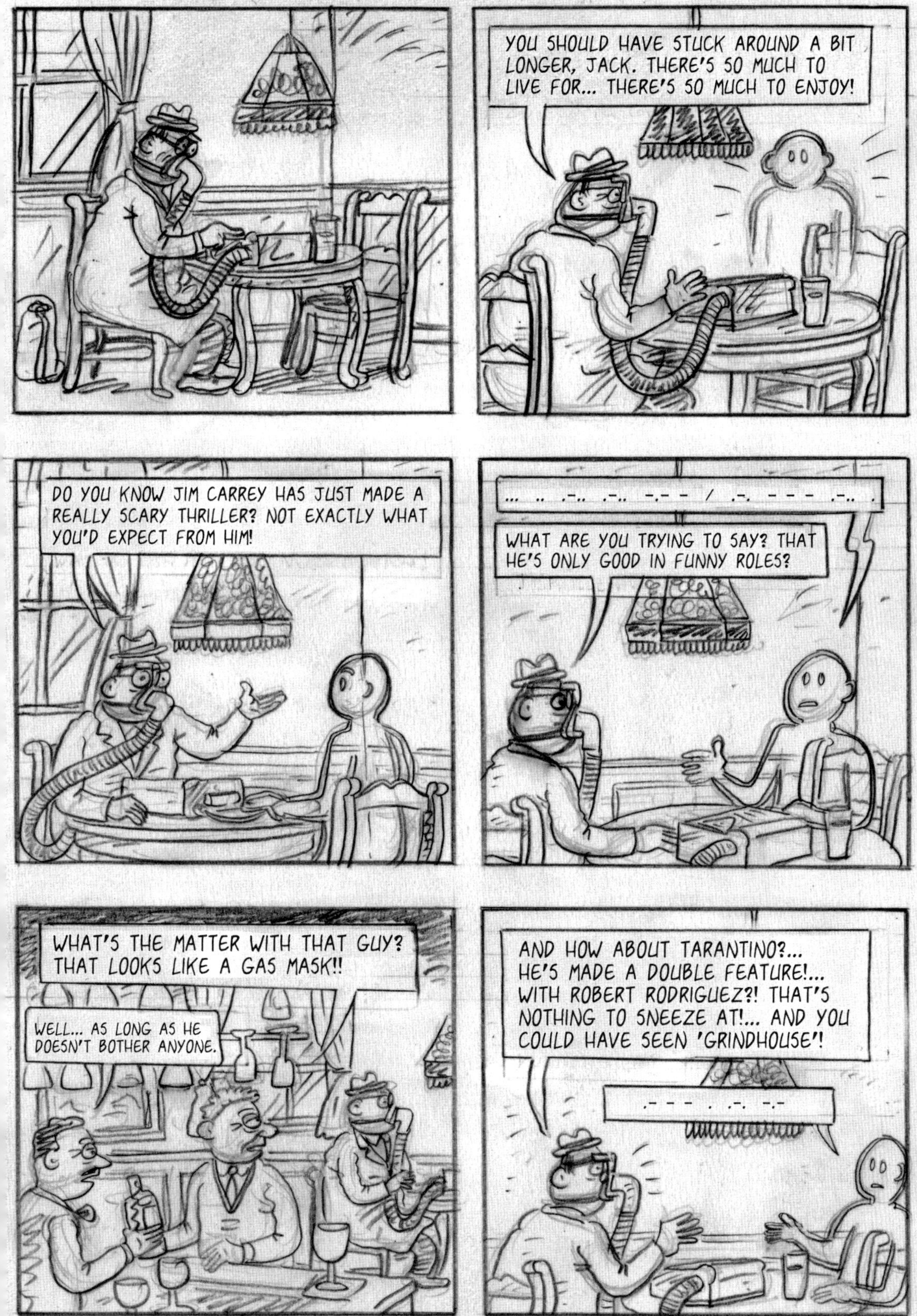
YOU SHOULD HAVE STUCK AROUND A BIT LONGER, JACK. THERE'S SO MUCH TO LIVE FOR... THERE'S SO MUCH TO ENJOY!
DO YOU KNOW JIM CARREY HAS JUST MADE A REALLY SCARY THRILLER? NOT EXACTLY WHAT YOU'D EXPECT FROM HIM!
... .. .-.. .-.. -.-- / .-. --- .-.. .
WHAT ARE YOU TRYING TO SAY? THAT HE'S ONLY GOOD IN FUNNY ROLES?
WHAT'S THE MATTER WITH THAT GUY? THAT LOOKS LIKE A GAS MASK!!
WELL... AS LONG AS HE DOESN'T BOTHER ANYONE.
AND HOW ABOUT TARANTINO?... HE'S MADE A DOUBLE FEATURE!... WITH ROBERT RODRIGUEZ?! THAT'S NOTHING TO SNEEZE AT!... AND YOU COULD HAVE SEEN 'GRINDHOUSE'!
.--- . .-. -.-

SARAH DROPPED BY LAST WEEK. SHE WASN'T AT THE FUNERAL SERVICE, BUT SHE CAME TO TELL US IN PERSON THAT SHE WAS VERY FOND OF YOU AND THAT SHE THOUGHT YOU WERE NICE!

YOU COULD HAVE STARTED SOMETHING BEAUTIFUL WITH HER!

-.---!!

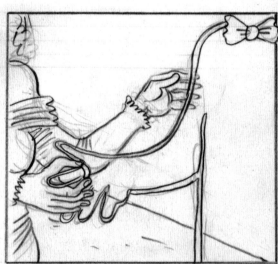

WHAT ARE YOU SAYING?... YOU'RE LAUGHING AT ME!! YOU THINK IT'S ALL BULLSHIT! MY BOY, I'M TRYING TO TEACH YOU SOME VALUES!

.... .- / .... .- !!
..- ..- !!

SARAH ISN'T FAT AT ALL!... SHE HAPPENS TO BE A VERY SWEET, ATTRACTIVE GIRL, BUT YOU DIDN'T WANT TO SEE THAT! ...IF YOU CAN'T CONDUCT A SERIOUS CONVERSATION I'D RATHER YOU LEFT RIGHT NOW!!

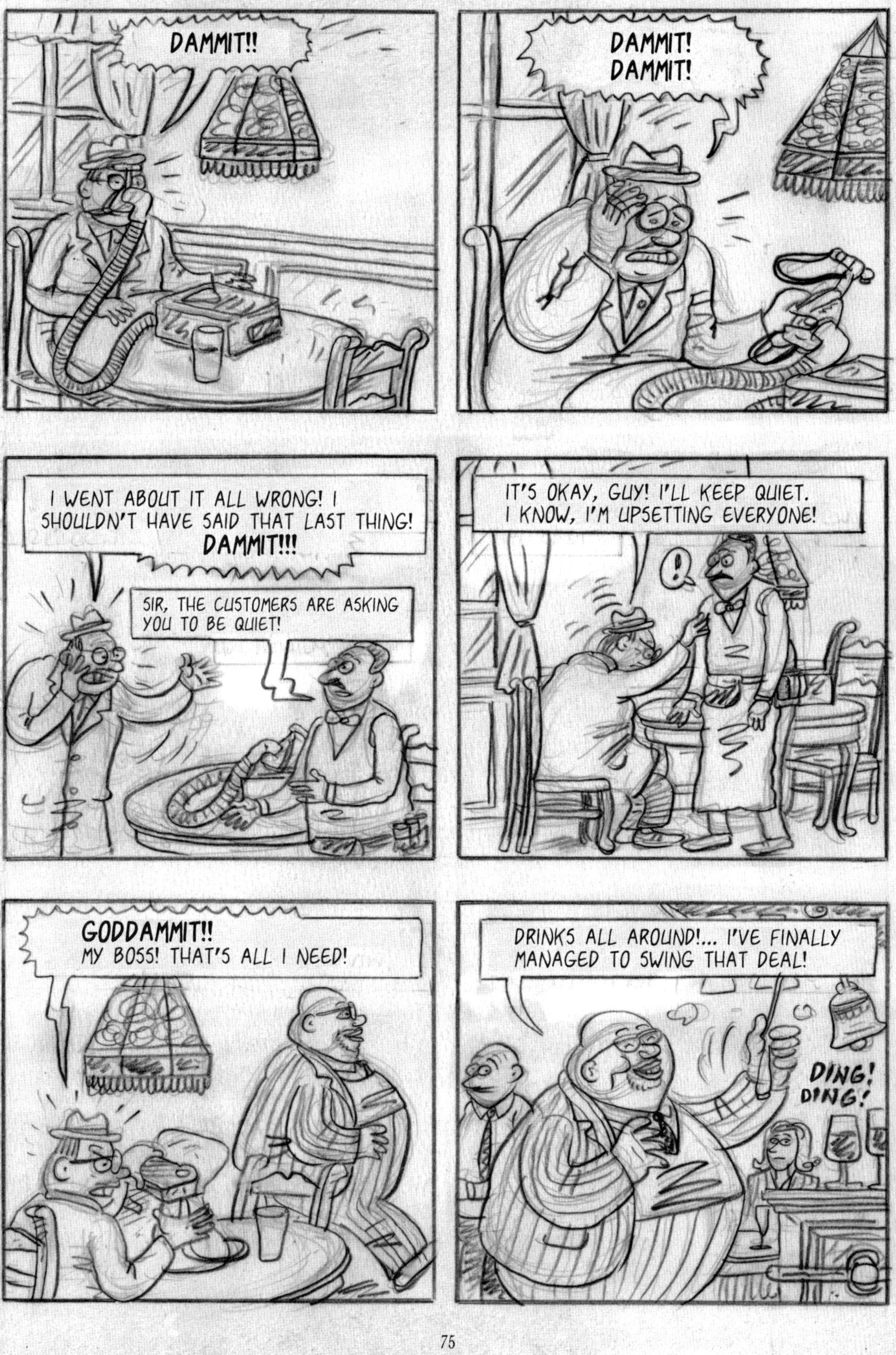
DAMMIT!!
DAMMIT! DAMMIT!
I WENT ABOUT IT ALL WRONG! I SHOULDN'T HAVE SAID THAT LAST THING! DAMMIT!!!
SIR, THE CUSTOMERS ARE ASKING YOU TO BE QUIET!
IT'S OKAY, GUY! I'LL KEEP QUIET. I KNOW, I'M UPSETTING EVERYONE!
!
GODDAMMIT!! MY BOSS! THAT'S ALL I NEED!
DRINKS ALL AROUND!... I'VE FINALLY MANAGED TO SWING THAT DEAL!
DING! DING!

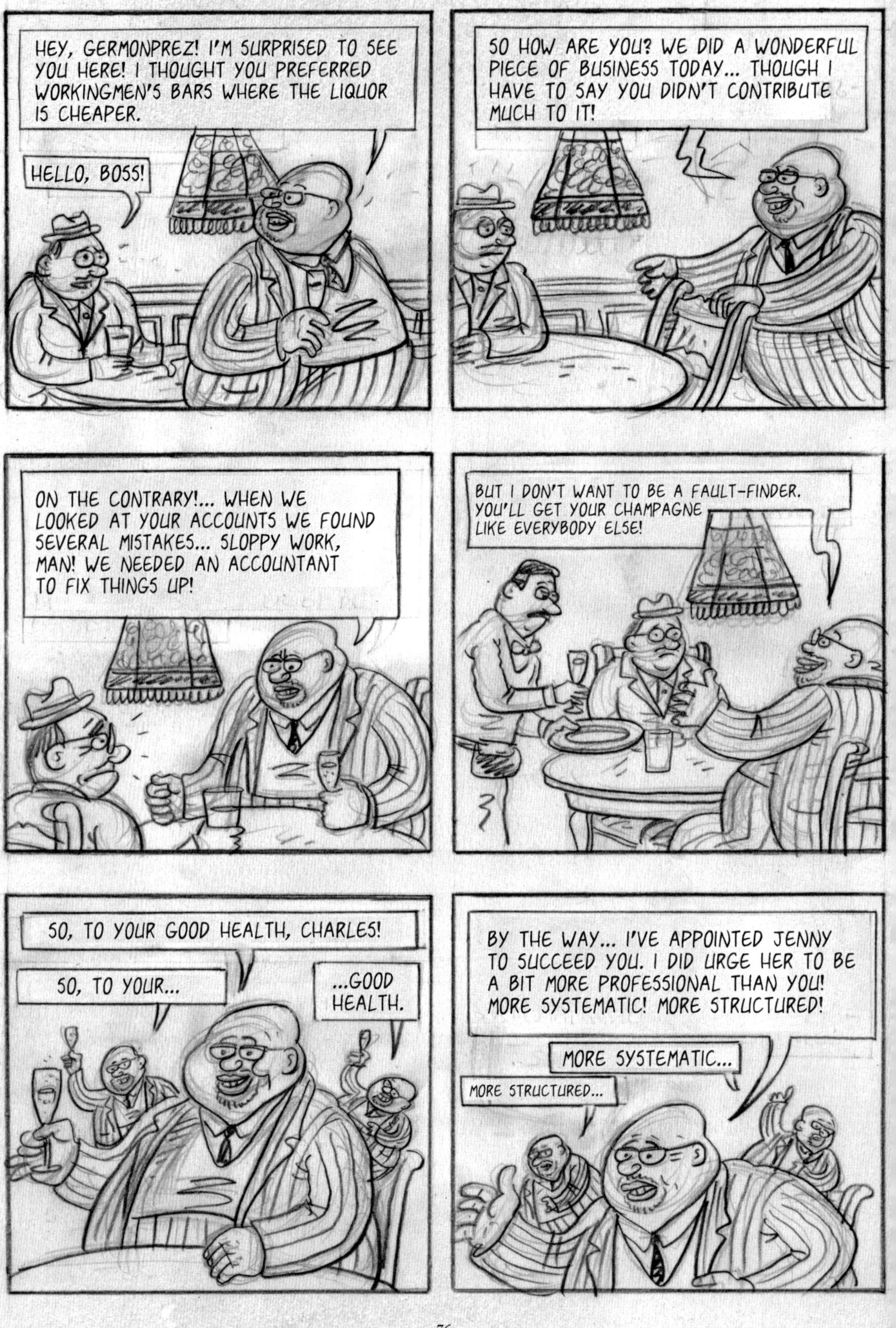
HEY, GERMONPREZ! I'M SURPRISED TO SEE YOU HERE! I THOUGHT YOU PREFERRED WORKINGMEN'S BARS WHERE THE LIQUOR IS CHEAPER.
HELLO, BOSS!
SO HOW ARE YOU? WE DID A WONDERFUL PIECE OF BUSINESS TODAY... THOUGH I HAVE TO SAY YOU DIDN'T CONTRIBUTE MUCH TO IT!
ON THE CONTRARY!... WHEN WE LOOKED AT YOUR ACCOUNTS WE FOUND SEVERAL MISTAKES... SLOPPY WORK, MAN! WE NEEDED AN ACCOUNTANT TO FIX THINGS UP!
BUT I DON'T WANT TO BE A FAULT-FINDER. YOU'LL GET YOUR CHAMPAGNE LIKE EVERYBODY ELSE!
SO, TO YOUR GOOD HEALTH, CHARLES!
SO, TO YOUR...
...GOOD HEALTH.
BY THE WAY... I'VE APPOINTED JENNY TO SUCCEED YOU. I DID URGE HER TO BE A BIT MORE PROFESSIONAL THAN YOU! MORE SYSTEMATIC! MORE STRUCTURED!
MORE SYSTEMATIC...
MORE STRUCTURED...

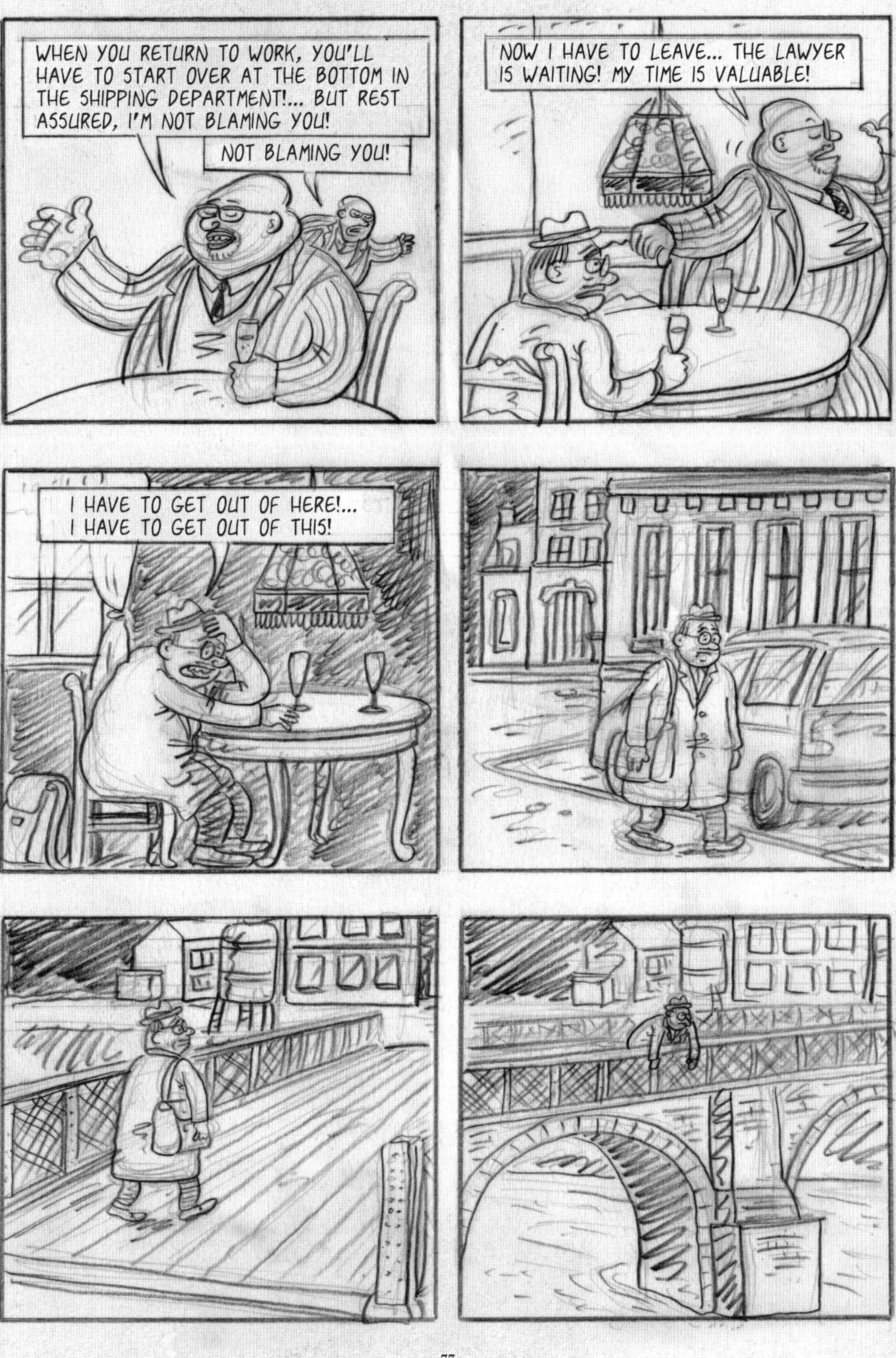
WHEN YOU RETURN TO WORK, YOU'LL HAVE TO START OVER AT THE BOTTOM IN THE SHIPPING DEPARTMENT!... BUT REST ASSURED, I'M NOT BLAMING YOU!
NOT BLAMING YOU!
NOW I HAVE TO LEAVE... THE LAWYER IS WAITING! MY TIME IS VALUABLE!
I HAVE TO GET OUT OF HERE!... I HAVE TO GET OUT OF THIS!

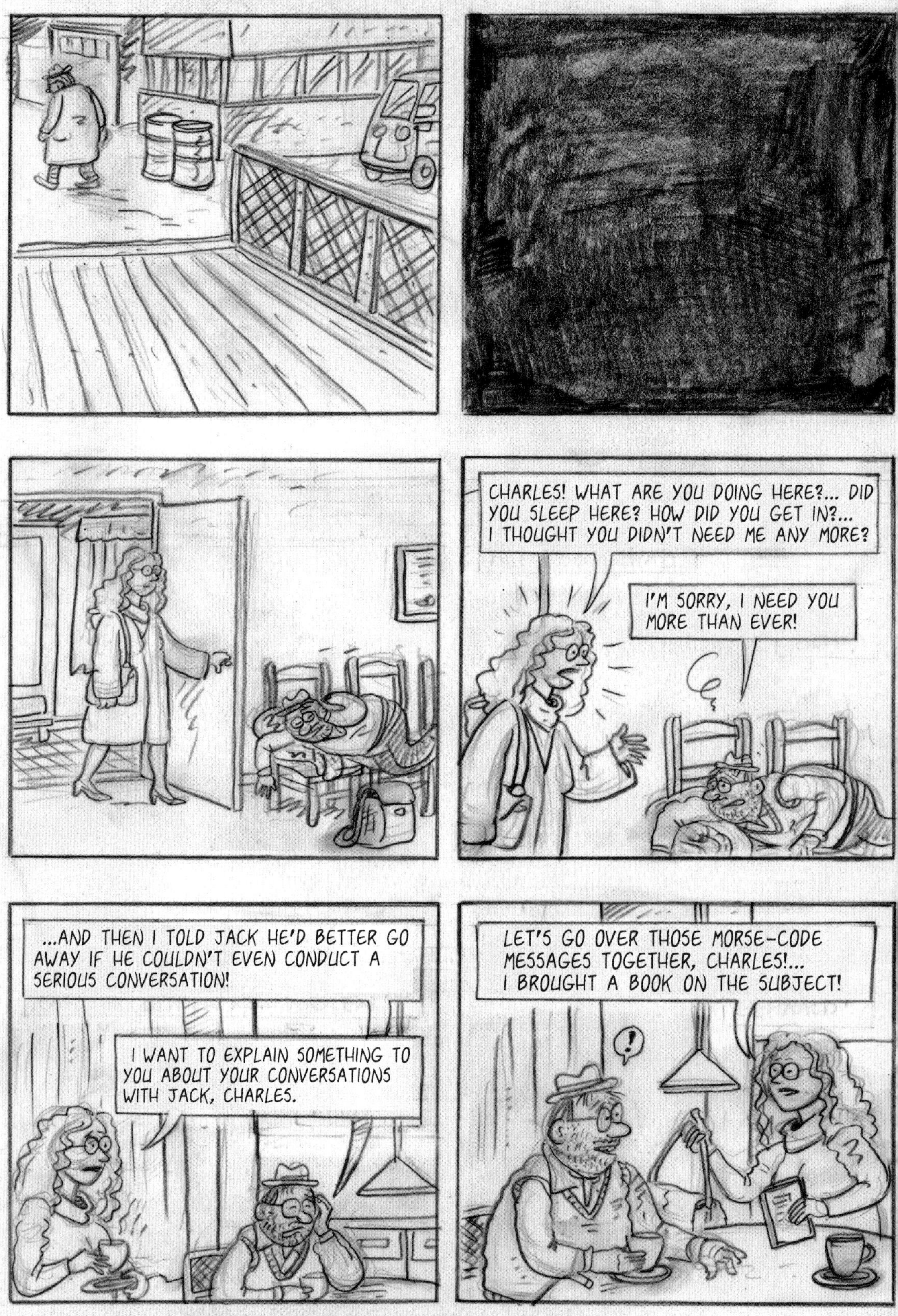
CHARLES! WHAT ARE YOU DOING HERE?... DID YOU SLEEP HERE? HOW DID YOU GET IN?... I THOUGHT YOU DIDN'T NEED ME ANY MORE?
I'M SORRY, I NEED YOU MORE THAN EVER!
...AND THEN I TOLD JACK HE'D BETTER GO AWAY IF HE COULDN'T EVEN CONDUCT A SERIOUS CONVERSATION!
I WANT TO EXPLAIN SOMETHING TO YOU ABOUT YOUR CONVERSATIONS WITH JACK, CHARLES.
LET'S GO OVER THOSE MORSE-CODE MESSAGES TOGETHER, CHARLES!... I BROUGHT A BOOK ON THE SUBJECT!
!

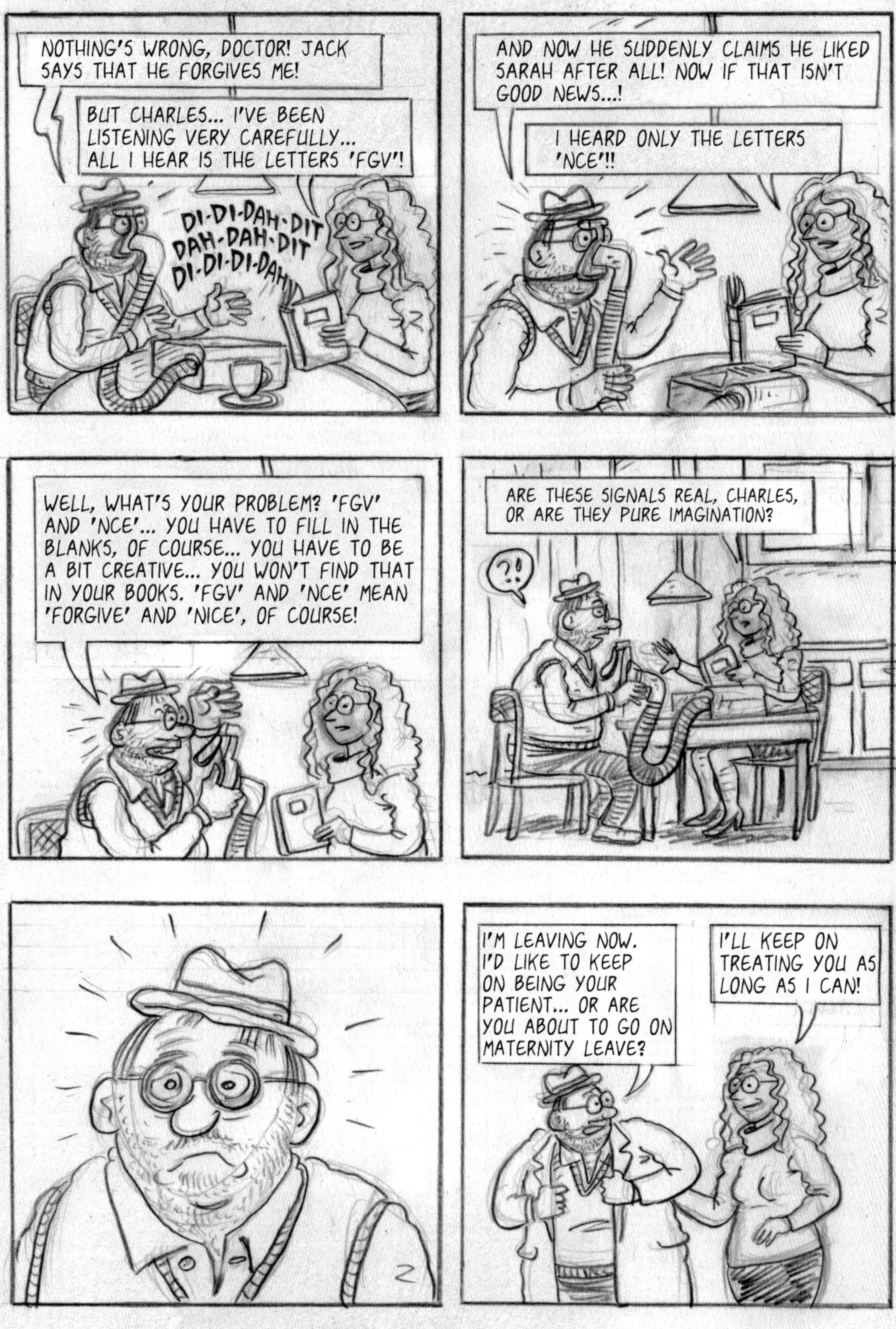
NOTHING'S WRONG, DOCTOR! JACK SAYS THAT HE FORGIVES ME!
BUT CHARLES... I'VE BEEN LISTENING VERY CAREFULLY... ALL I HEAR IS THE LETTERS 'FGV'!
DI-DI-DAH-DIT DAH-DAH-DIT DI-DI-DI-DAH
AND NOW HE SUDDENLY CLAIMS HE LIKED SARAH AFTER ALL! NOW IF THAT ISN'T GOOD NEWS...!
I HEARD ONLY THE LETTERS 'NCE'!!
WELL, WHAT'S YOUR PROBLEM? 'FGV' AND 'NCE'... YOU HAVE TO FILL IN THE BLANKS, OF COURSE... YOU HAVE TO BE A BIT CREATIVE... YOU WON'T FIND THAT IN YOUR BOOKS. 'FGV' AND 'NCE' MEAN 'FORGIVE' AND 'NICE', OF COURSE!
ARE THESE SIGNALS REAL, CHARLES, OR ARE THEY PURE IMAGINATION?
?!
I'M LEAVING NOW. I'D LIKE TO KEEP ON BEING YOUR PATIENT... OR ARE YOU ABOUT TO GO ON MATERNITY LEAVE?
I'LL KEEP ON TREATING YOU AS LONG AS I CAN!

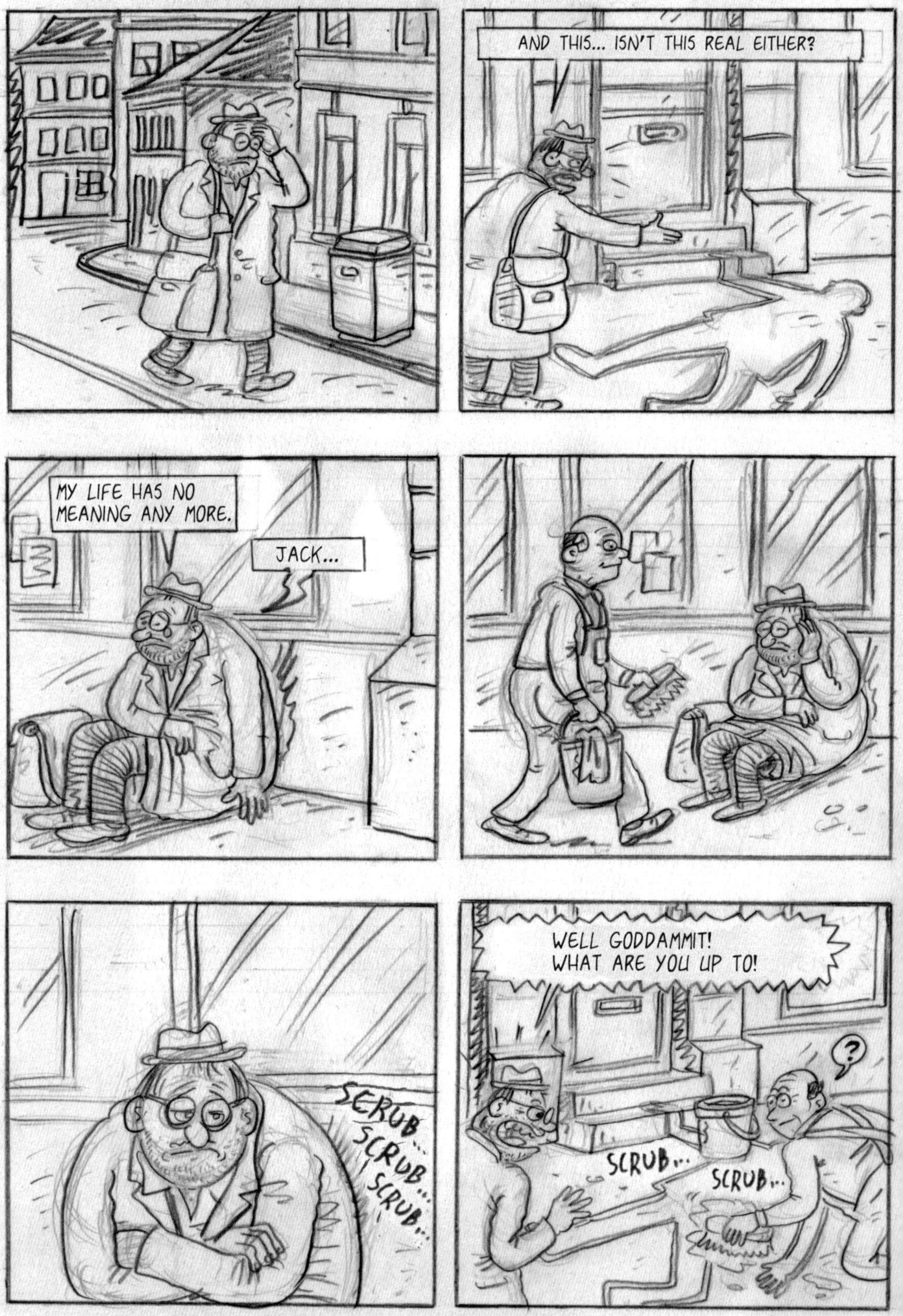
AND THIS... ISN'T THIS REAL EITHER?
MY LIFE HAS NO MEANING ANY MORE.
JACK...
SCRUB... SCRUB... SCRUB...
WELL GODDAMMIT! WHAT ARE YOU UP TO!
?
SCRUB...
SCRUB...

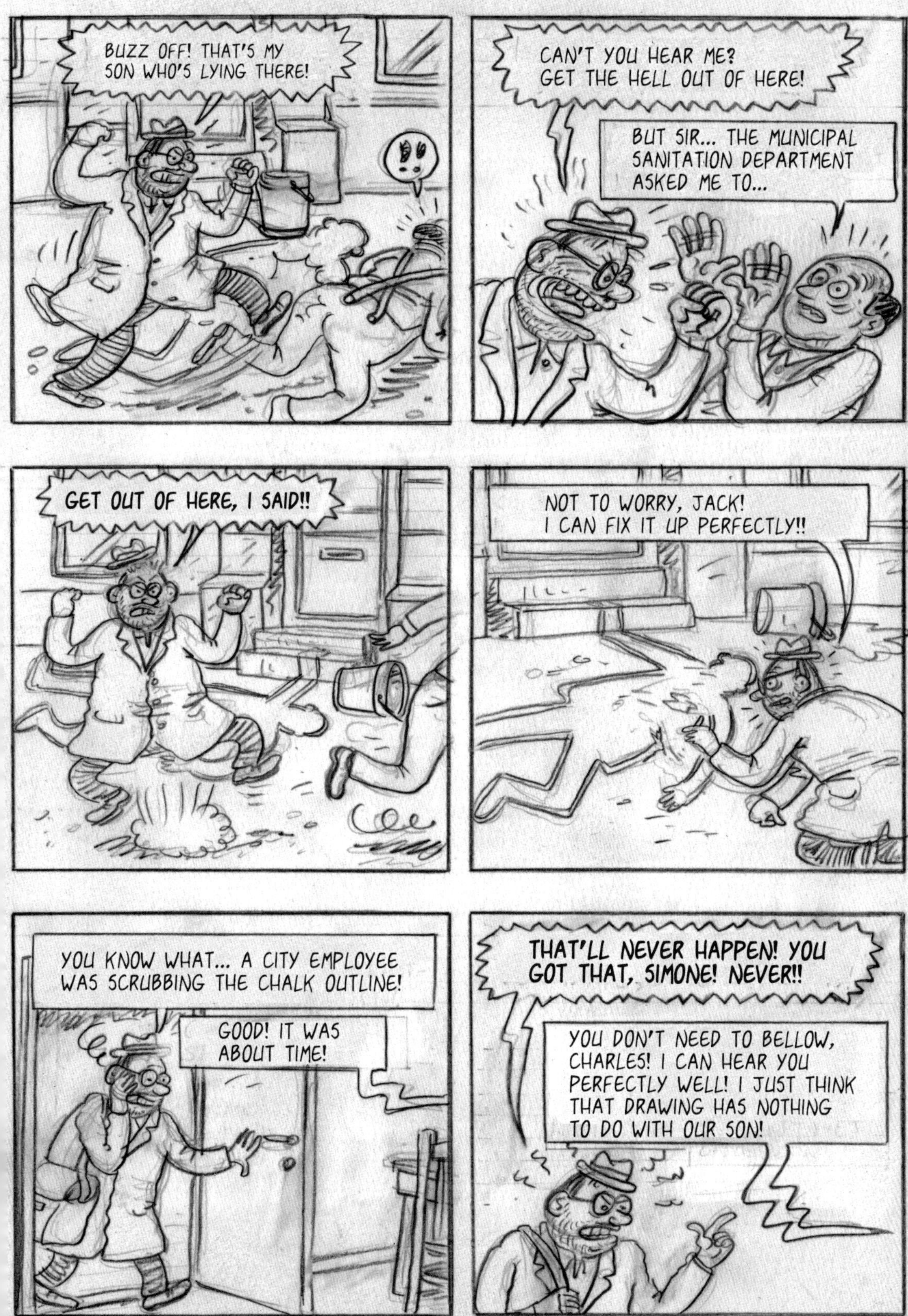
BUZZ OFF! THAT'S MY SON WHO'S LYING THERE!
CAN'T YOU HEAR ME? GET THE HELL OUT OF HERE!
BUT SIR... THE MUNICIPAL SANITATION DEPARTMENT ASKED ME TO...
GET OUT OF HERE, I SAID!!
NOT TO WORRY, JACK! I CAN FIX IT UP PERFECTLY!!
YOU KNOW WHAT... A CITY EMPLOYEE WAS SCRUBBING THE CHALK OUTLINE!
GOOD! IT WAS ABOUT TIME!
THAT'LL NEVER HAPPEN! YOU GOT THAT, SIMONE! NEVER!!
YOU DON'T NEED TO BELLOW, CHARLES! I CAN HEAR YOU PERFECTLY WELL! I JUST THINK THAT DRAWING HAS NOTHING TO DO WITH OUR SON!

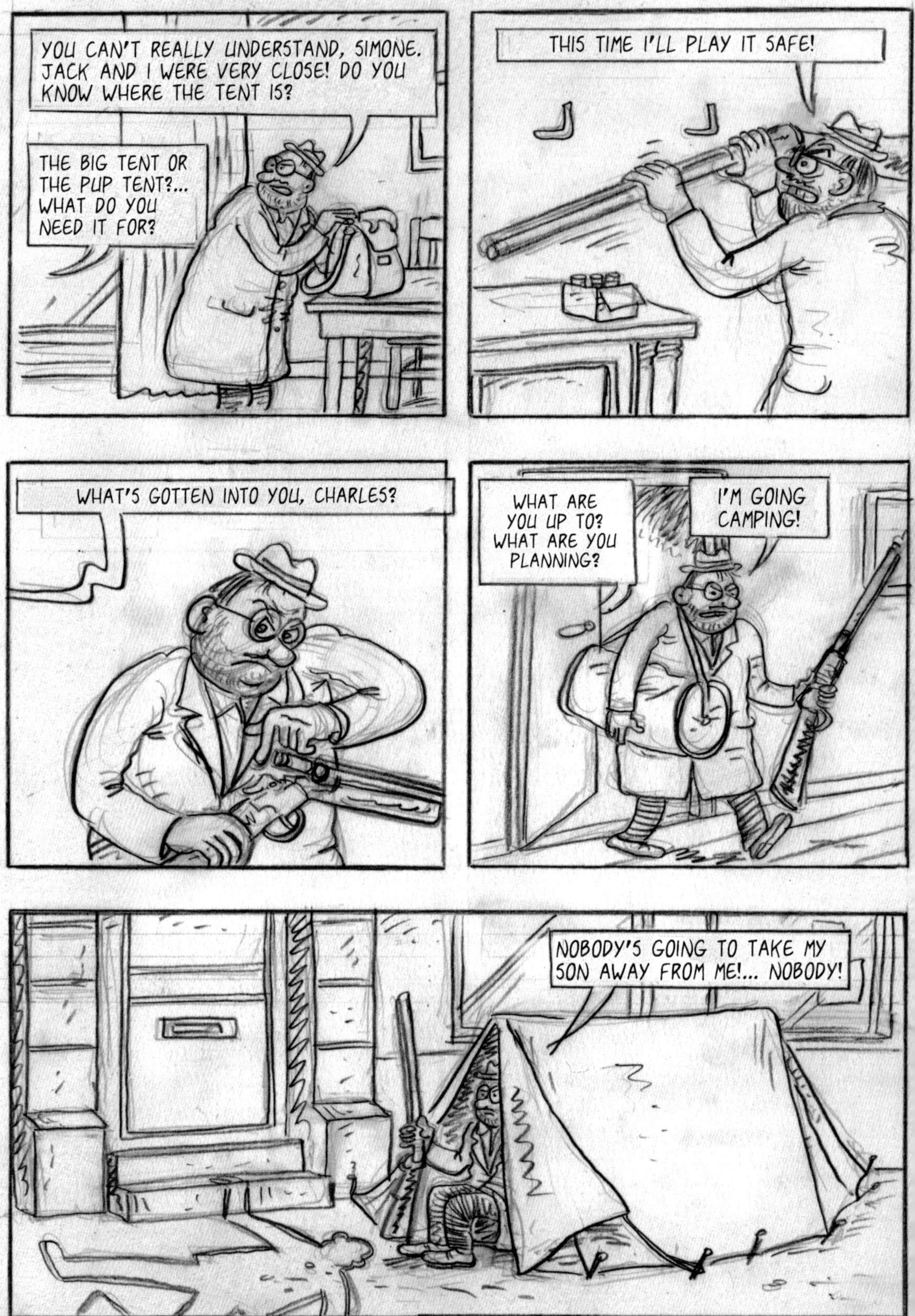
YOU CAN'T REALLY UNDERSTAND, SIMONE. JACK AND I WERE VERY CLOSE! DO YOU KNOW WHERE THE TENT IS?
THE BIG TENT OR THE PUP TENT?... WHAT DO YOU NEED IT FOR?
THIS TIME I'LL PLAY IT SAFE!
WHAT'S GOTTEN INTO YOU, CHARLES?
WHAT ARE YOU UP TO? WHAT ARE YOU PLANNING?
I'M GOING CAMPING!
NOBODY'S GOING TO TAKE MY SON AWAY FROM ME!... NOBODY!

CHAPTER 5 - THE IMPORTANCE OF DETAILS

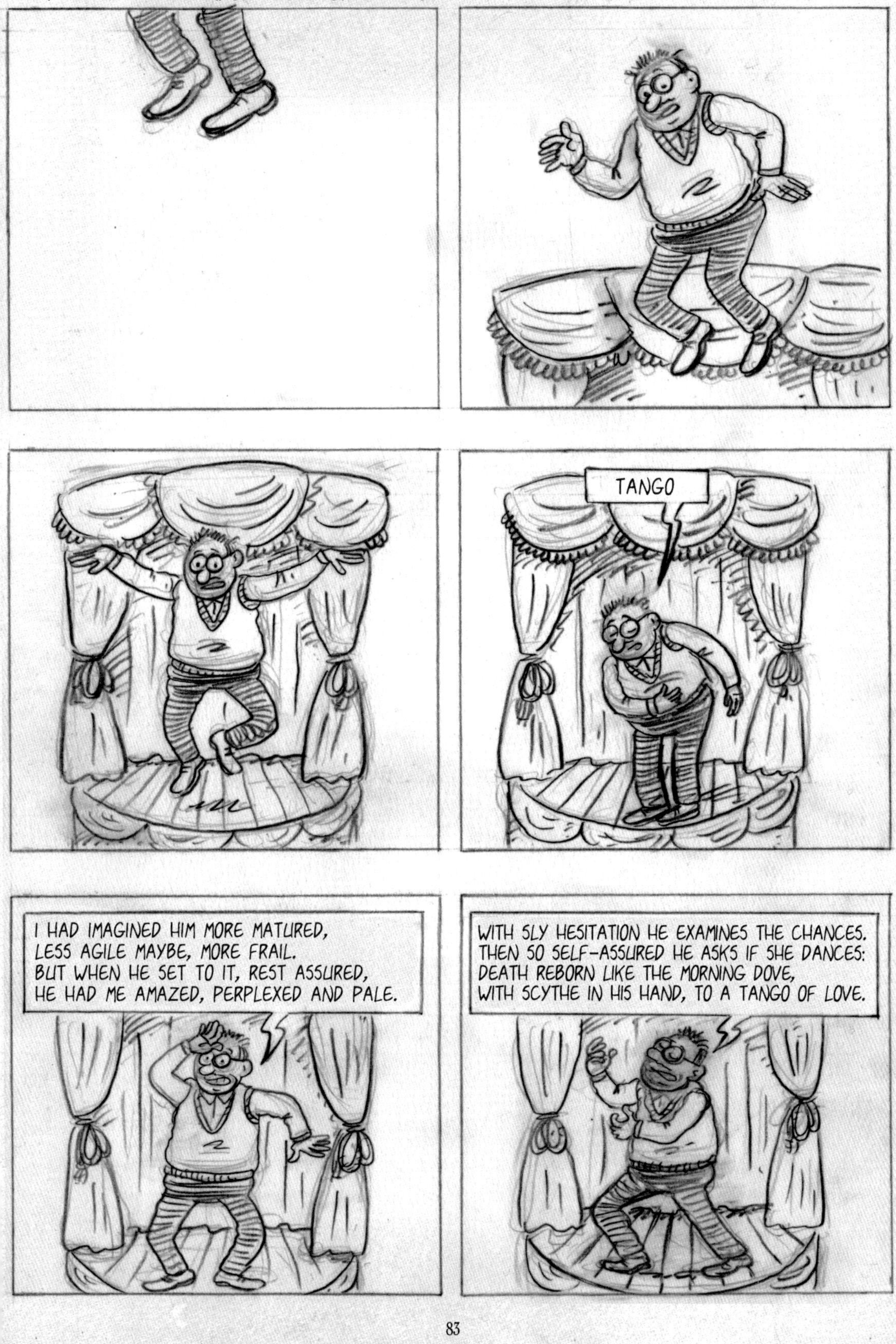
TANGO
I HAD IMAGINED HIM MORE MATURED,
LESS AGILE MAYBE, MORE FRAIL.
BUT WHEN HE SET TO IT, REST ASSURED,
HE HAD ME AMAZED, PERPLEXED AND PALE.
WITH SLY HESITATION HE EXAMINES THE CHANCES.
THEN SO SELF-ASSURED HE ASKS IF SHE DANCES:
DEATH REBORN LIKE THE MORNING DOVE,
WITH SCYTHE IN HIS HAND, TO A TANGO OF LOVE.

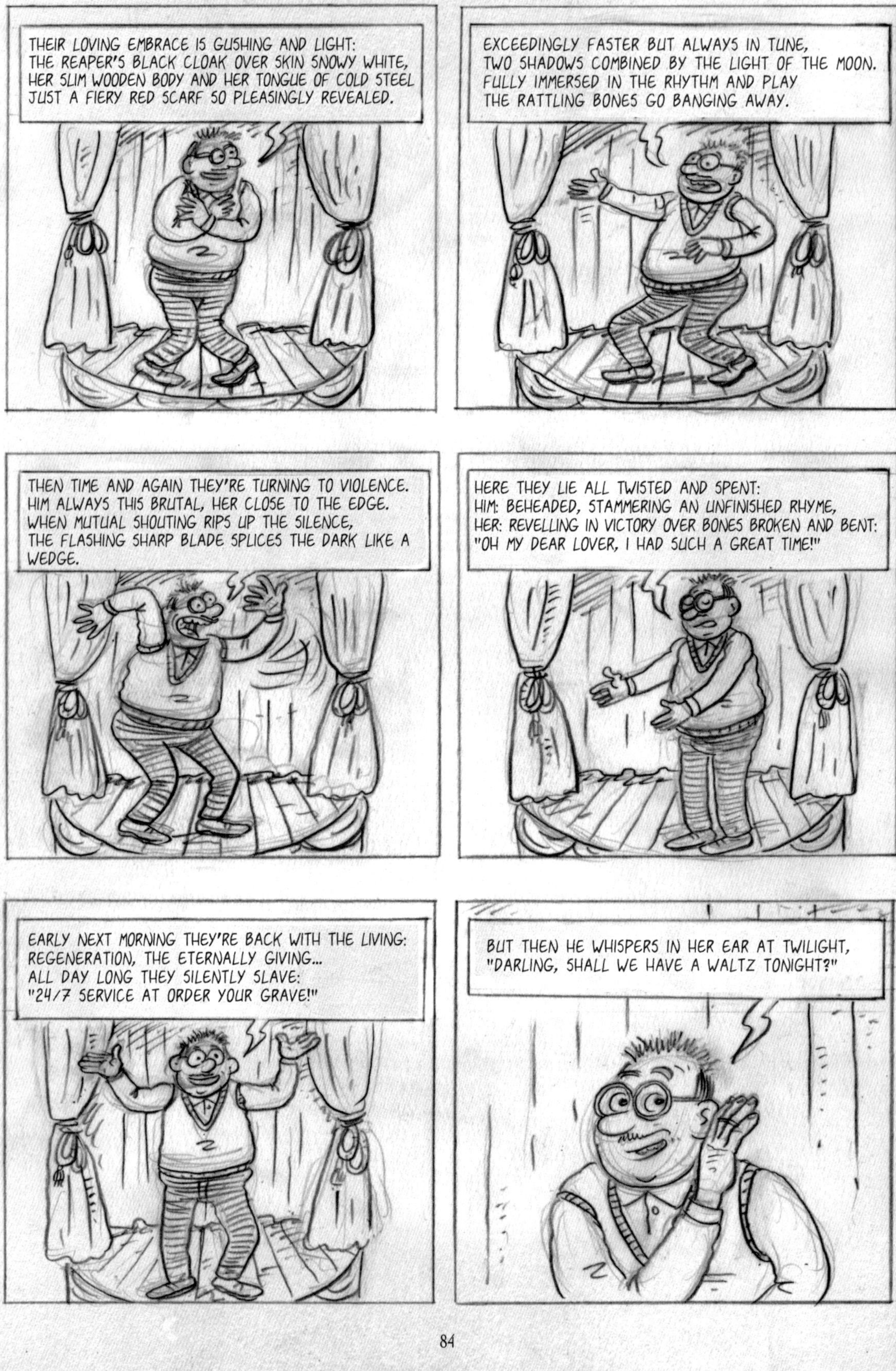
THEIR LOVING EMBRACE IS GUSHING AND LIGHT: THE REAPER'S BLACK CLOAK OVER SKIN SNOWY WHITE, HER SLIM WOODEN BODY AND HER TONGUE OF COLD STEEL JUST A FIERY RED SCARF SO PLEASINGLY REVEALED.
EXCEEDINGLY FASTER BUT ALWAYS IN TUNE, TWO SHADOWS COMBINED BY THE LIGHT OF THE MOON. FULLY IMMERSED IN THE RHYTHM AND PLAY THE RATTLING BONES GO BANGING AWAY.
THEN TIME AND AGAIN THEY'RE TURNING TO VIOLENCE. HIM ALWAYS THIS BRUTAL, HER CLOSE TO THE EDGE. WHEN MUTUAL SHOUTING RIPS UP THE SILENCE, THE FLASHING SHARP BLADE SPLICES THE DARK LIKE A WEDGE.
HERE THEY LIE ALL TWISTED AND SPENT: HIM: BEHEADED, STAMMERING AN UNFINISHED RHYME, HER: REVELLING IN VICTORY OVER BONES BROKEN AND BENT: "OH MY DEAR LOVER, I HAD SUCH A GREAT TIME!"
EARLY NEXT MORNING THEY'RE BACK WITH THE LIVING: REGENERATION, THE ETERNALLY GIVING... ALL DAY LONG THEY SILENTLY SLAVE: "24/7 SERVICE AT ORDER YOUR GRAVE!"
BUT THEN HE WHISPERS IN HER EAR AT TWILIGHT, "DARLING, SHALL WE HAVE A WALTZ TONIGHT?"

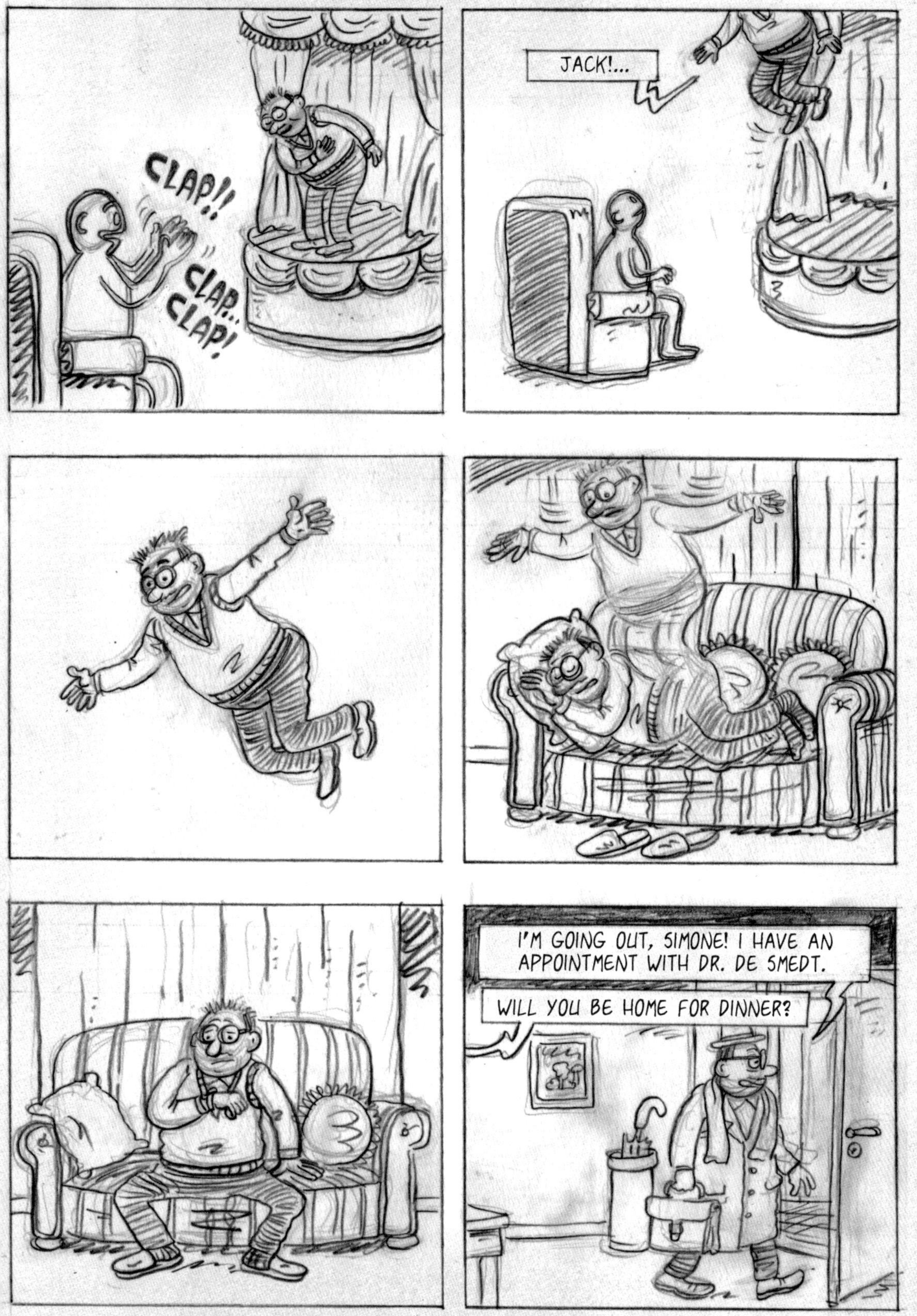
CLAP!!
CLAP...
CLAP!
JACK!...
I'M GOING OUT, SIMONE! I HAVE AN APPOINTMENT WITH DR. DE SMEDT.
WILL YOU BE HOME FOR DINNER?

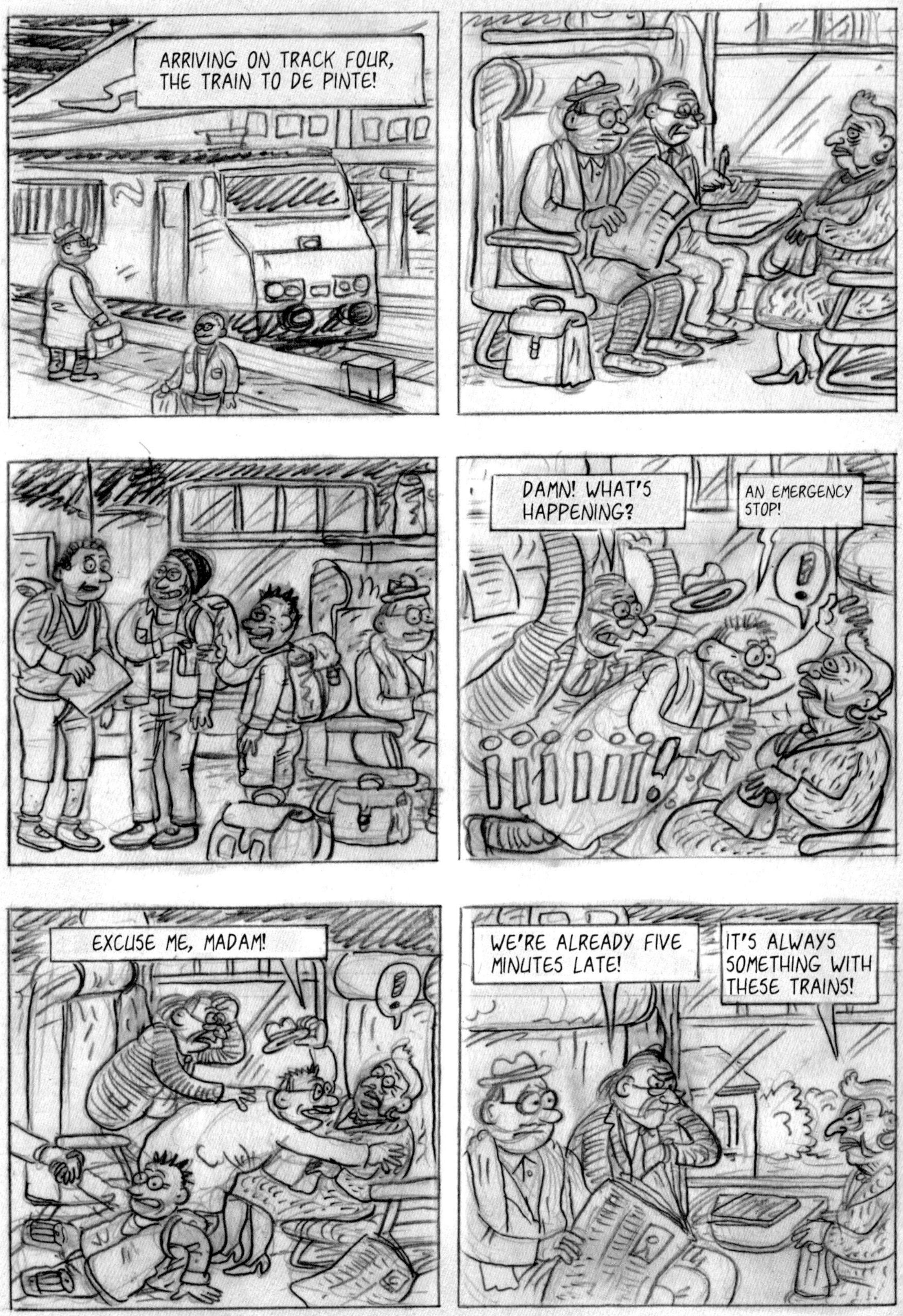
ARRIVING ON TRACK FOUR, THE TRAIN TO DE PINTE!
DAMN! WHAT'S HAPPENING?
AN EMERGENCY STOP!
!
EXCUSE ME, MADAM!
!
WE'RE ALREADY FIVE MINUTES LATE!
IT'S ALWAYS SOMETHING WITH THESE TRAINS!

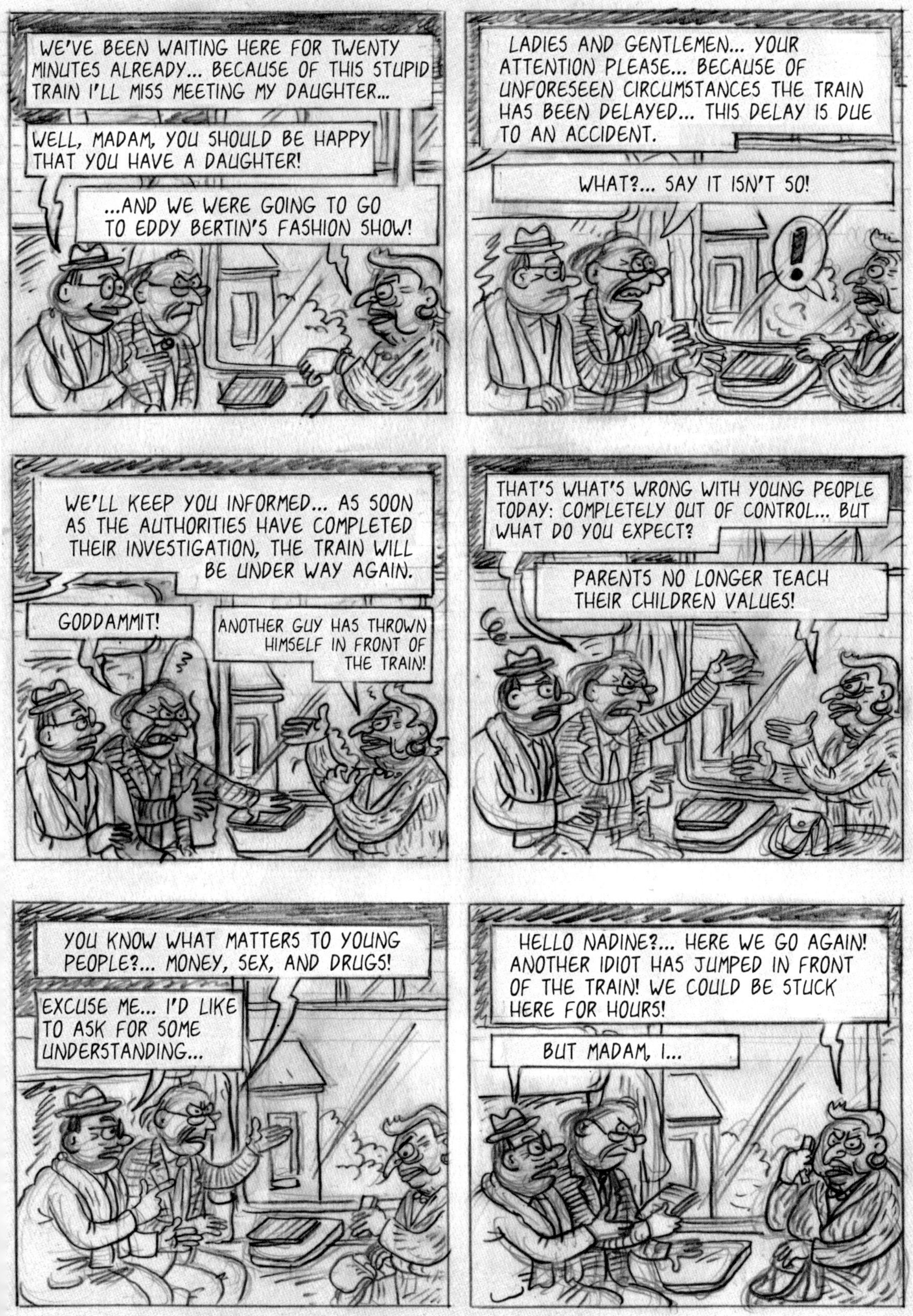
WE'VE BEEN WAITING HERE FOR TWENTY MINUTES ALREADY... BECAUSE OF THIS STUPID TRAIN I'LL MISS MEETING MY DAUGHTER...
WELL, MADAM, YOU SHOULD BE HAPPY THAT YOU HAVE A DAUGHTER!
...AND WE WERE GOING TO GO TO EDDY BERTIN'S FASHION SHOW!
LADIES AND GENTLEMEN... YOUR ATTENTION PLEASE... BECAUSE OF UNFORESEEN CIRCUMSTANCES THE TRAIN HAS BEEN DELAYED... THIS DELAY IS DUE TO AN ACCIDENT.
WHAT?... SAY IT ISN'T SO!
!
WE'LL KEEP YOU INFORMED... AS SOON AS THE AUTHORITIES HAVE COMPLETED THEIR INVESTIGATION, THE TRAIN WILL BE UNDER WAY AGAIN.
GODDAMMIT!
ANOTHER GUY HAS THROWN HIMSELF IN FRONT OF THE TRAIN!
THAT'S WHAT'S WRONG WITH YOUNG PEOPLE TODAY: COMPLETELY OUT OF CONTROL... BUT WHAT DO YOU EXPECT?
PARENTS NO LONGER TEACH THEIR CHILDREN VALUES!
YOU KNOW WHAT MATTERS TO YOUNG PEOPLE?... MONEY, SEX, AND DRUGS!
EXCUSE ME... I'D LIKE TO ASK FOR SOME UNDERSTANDING...
HELLO NADINE?... HERE WE GO AGAIN! ANOTHER IDIOT HAS JUMPED IN FRONT OF THE TRAIN! WE COULD BE STUCK HERE FOR HOURS!
BUT MADAM, I...

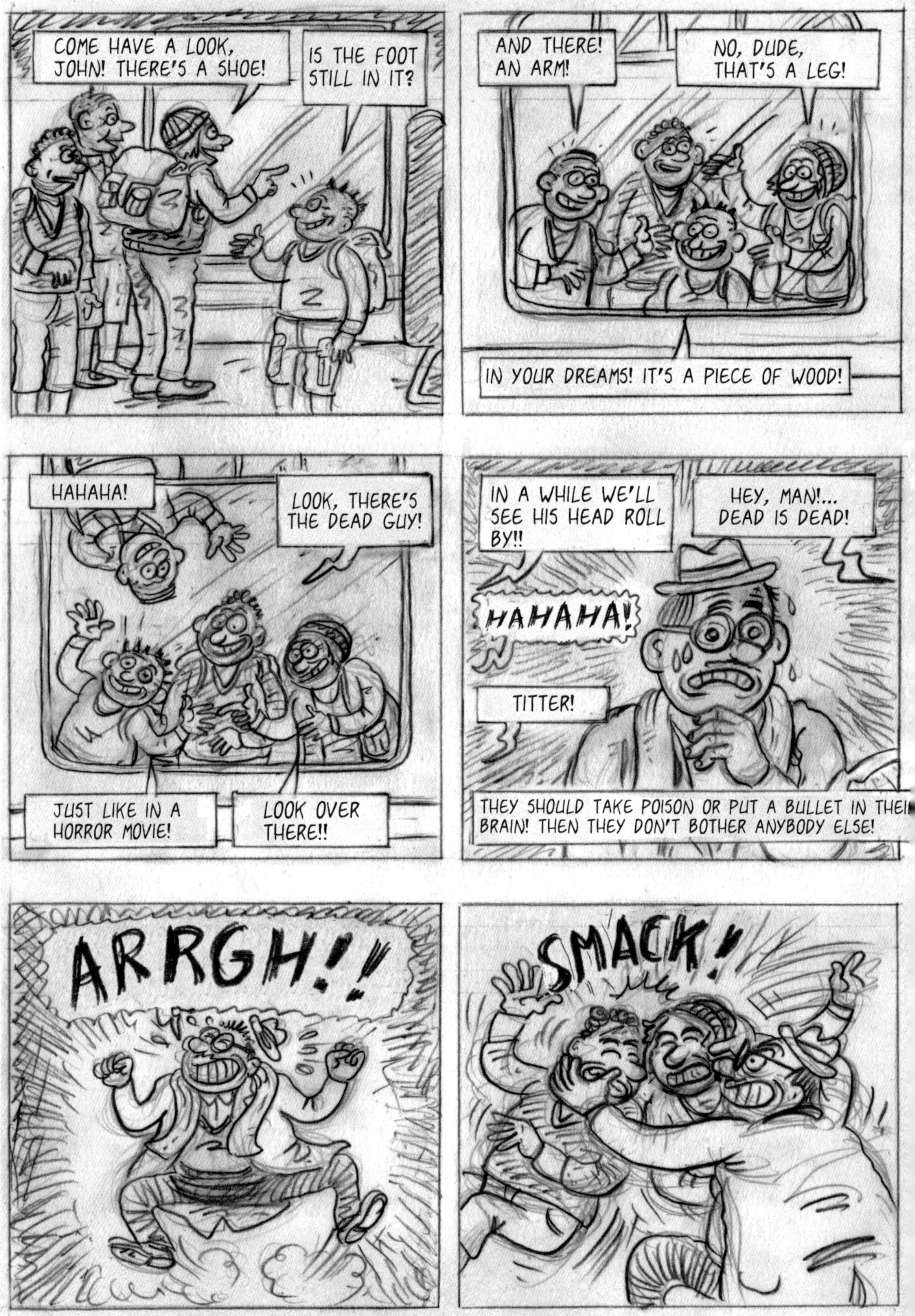
COME HAVE A LOOK, JOHN! THERE'S A SHOE!
IS THE FOOT STILL IN IT?
AND THERE! AN ARM!
NO, DUDE, THAT'S A LEG!
IN YOUR DREAMS! IT'S A PIECE OF WOOD!
HAHAHA!
LOOK, THERE'S THE DEAD GUY!
JUST LIKE IN A HORROR MOVIE!
LOOK OVER THERE!!
IN A WHILE WE'LL SEE HIS HEAD ROLL BY!!
HEY, MAN!... DEAD IS DEAD!
HAHAHA!
TITTER!
THEY SHOULD TAKE POISON OR PUT A BULLET IN THEI
BRAIN! THEN THEY DON'T BOTHER ANYBODY ELSE!
ARRGH!!
SMACK!

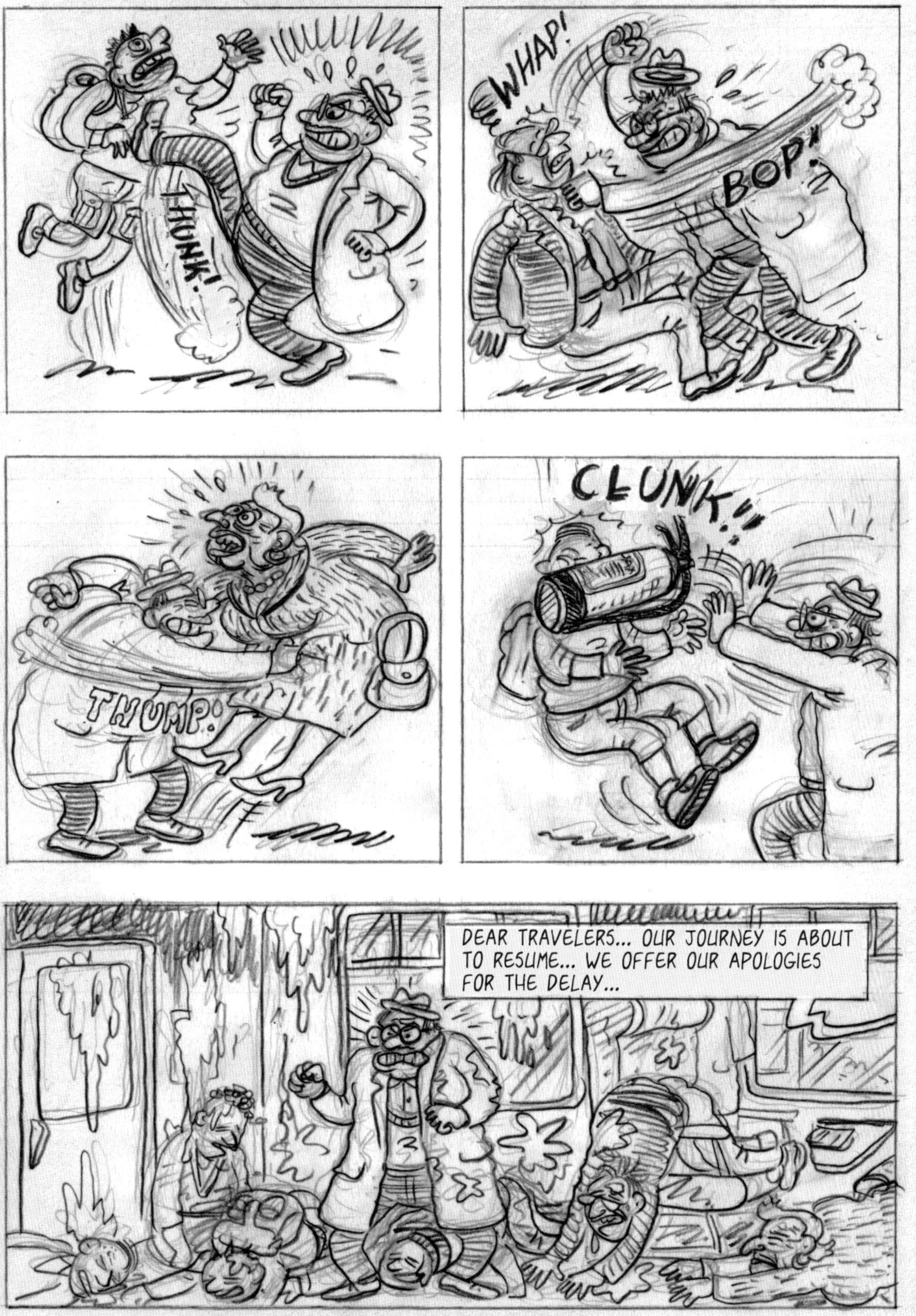
THUNK!
WHAP!
BOP!
THUMP!
CLUNK!!
DEAR TRAVELERS... OUR JOURNEY IS ABOUT TO RESUME... WE OFFER OUR APOLOGIES FOR THE DELAY...

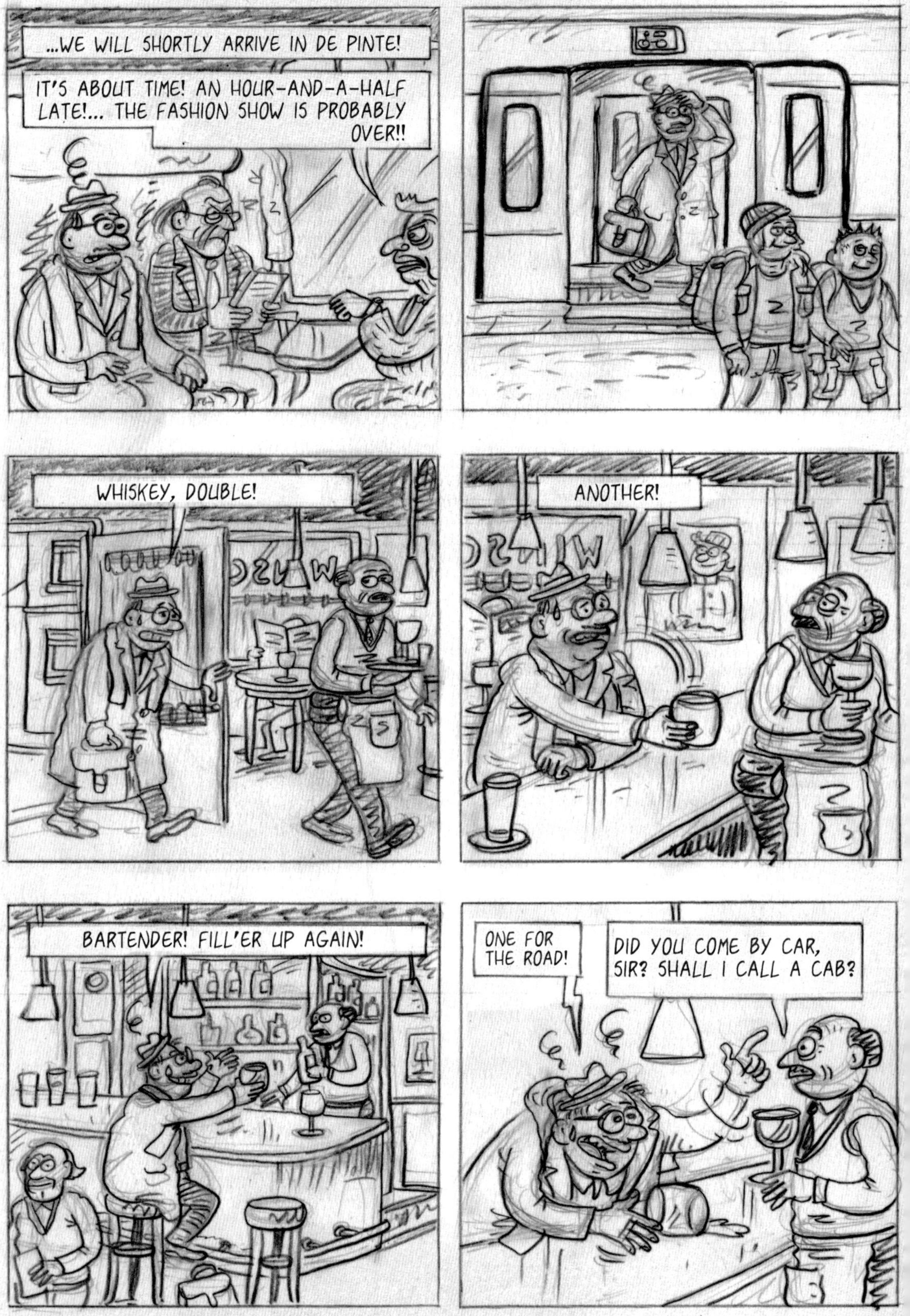
...WE WILL SHORTLY ARRIVE IN DE PINTE!
IT'S ABOUT TIME! AN HOUR-AND-A-HALF LATE!... THE FASHION SHOW IS PROBABLY OVER!!
WHISKEY, DOUBLE!
ANOTHER!
BARTENDER! FILL'ER UP AGAIN!
ONE FOR THE ROAD!
DID YOU COME BY CAR, SIR? SHALL I CALL A CAB?

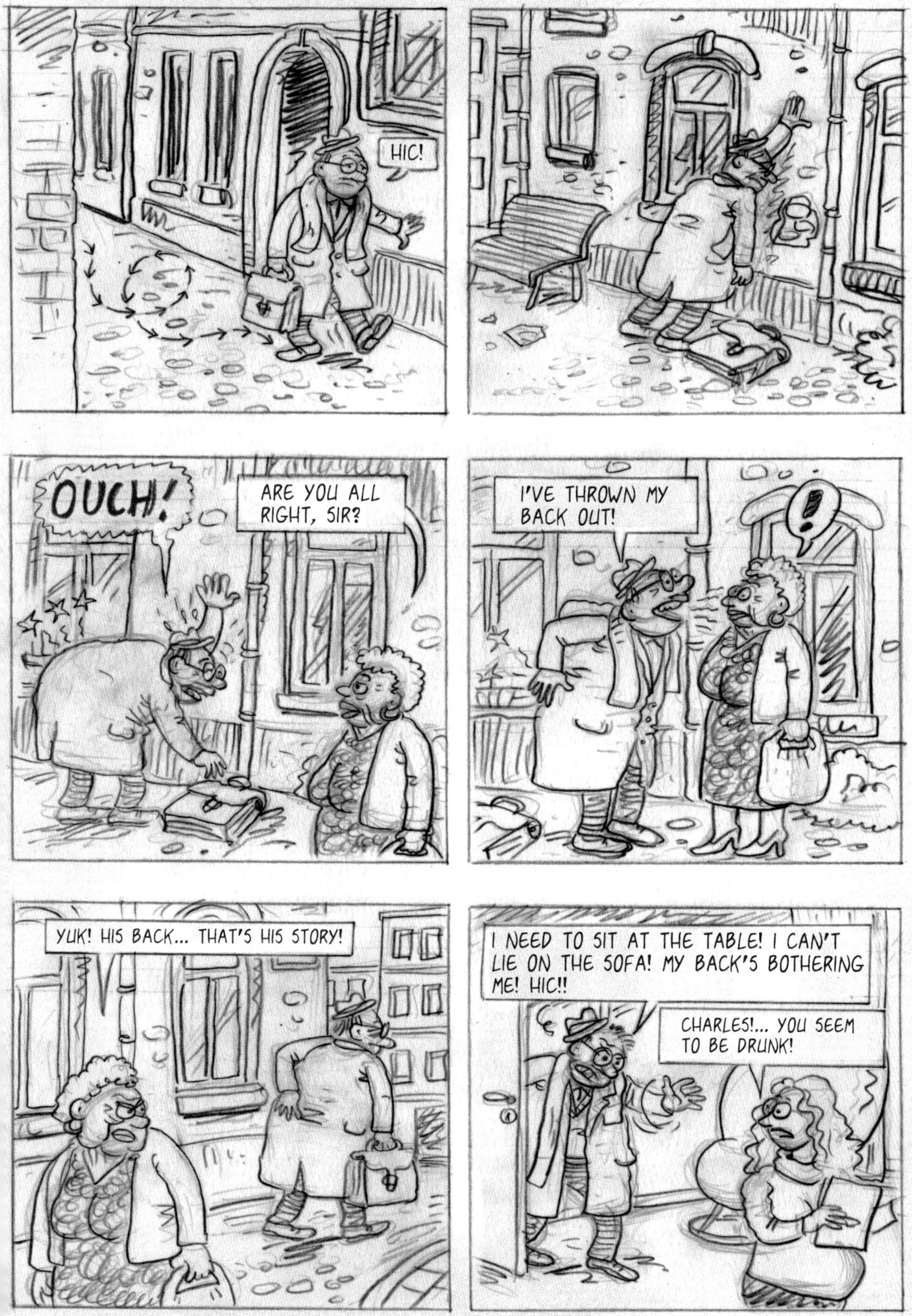

HIC!
OUCH!
ARE YOU ALL RIGHT, SIR?
I'VE THROWN MY BACK OUT!
!
YUK! HIS BACK... THAT'S HIS STORY!
I NEED TO SIT AT THE TABLE! I CAN'T LIE ON THE SOFA! MY BACK'S BOTHERING ME! HIC!!
CHARLES!... YOU SEEM TO BE DRUNK!

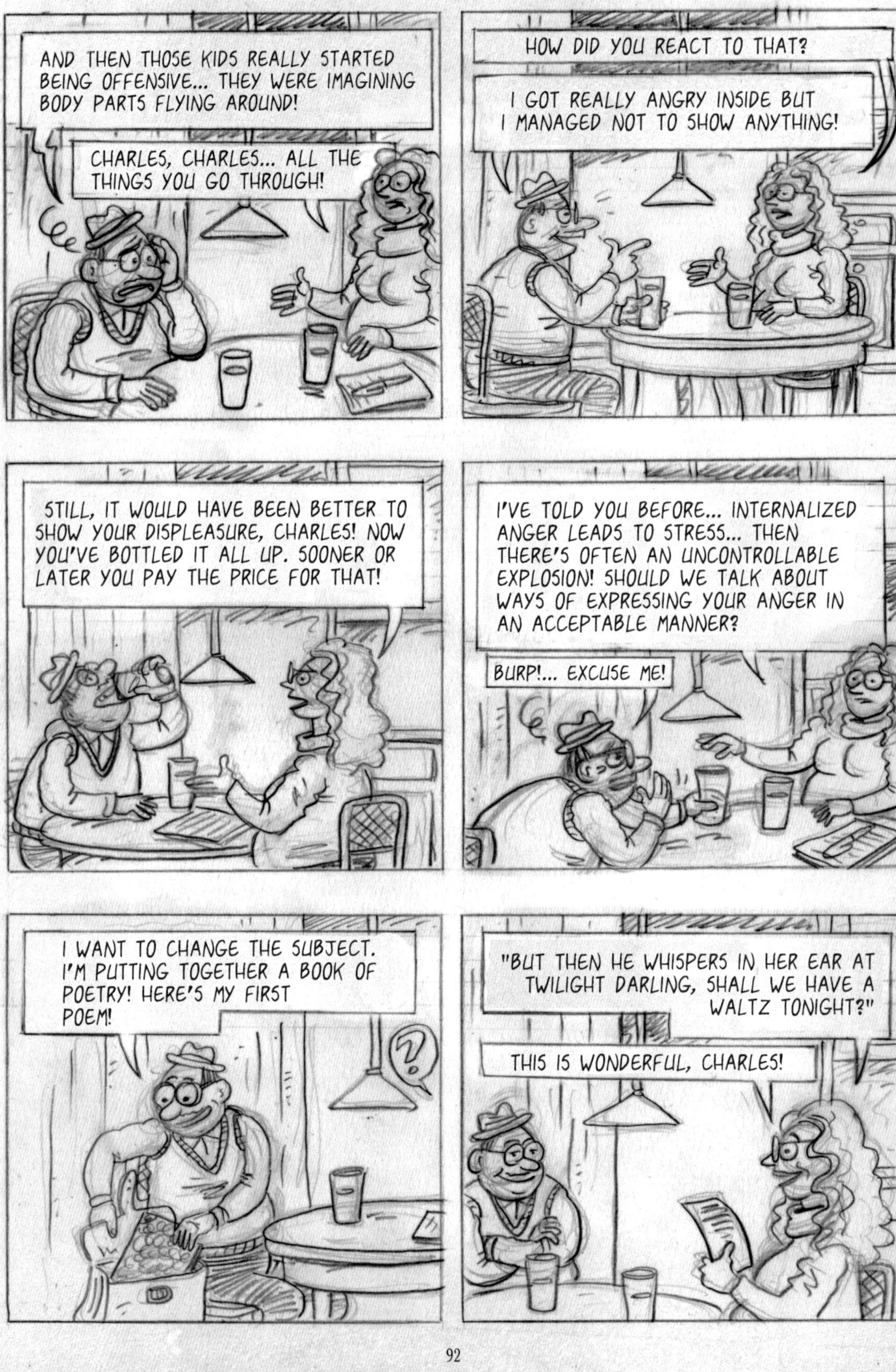
AND THEN THOSE KIDS REALLY STARTED BEING OFFENSIVE... THEY WERE IMAGINING BODY PARTS FLYING AROUND!
CHARLES, CHARLES... ALL THE THINGS YOU GO THROUGH!
HOW DID YOU REACT TO THAT?
I GOT REALLY ANGRY INSIDE BUT I MANAGED NOT TO SHOW ANYTHING!
STILL, IT WOULD HAVE BEEN BETTER TO SHOW YOUR DISPLEASURE, CHARLES! NOW YOU'VE BOTTLED IT ALL UP. SOONER OR LATER YOU PAY THE PRICE FOR THAT!
I'VE TOLD YOU BEFORE... INTERNALIZED ANGER LEADS TO STRESS... THEN THERE'S OFTEN AN UNCONTROLLABLE EXPLOSION! SHOULD WE TALK ABOUT WAYS OF EXPRESSING YOUR ANGER IN AN ACCEPTABLE MANNER?
BURP!... EXCUSE ME!
I WANT TO CHANGE THE SUBJECT. I'M PUTTING TOGETHER A BOOK OF POETRY! HERE'S MY FIRST POEM!
?
"BUT THEN HE WHISPERS IN HER EAR AT TWILIGHT DARLING, SHALL WE HAVE A WALTZ TONIGHT?"
THIS IS WONDERFUL, CHARLES!

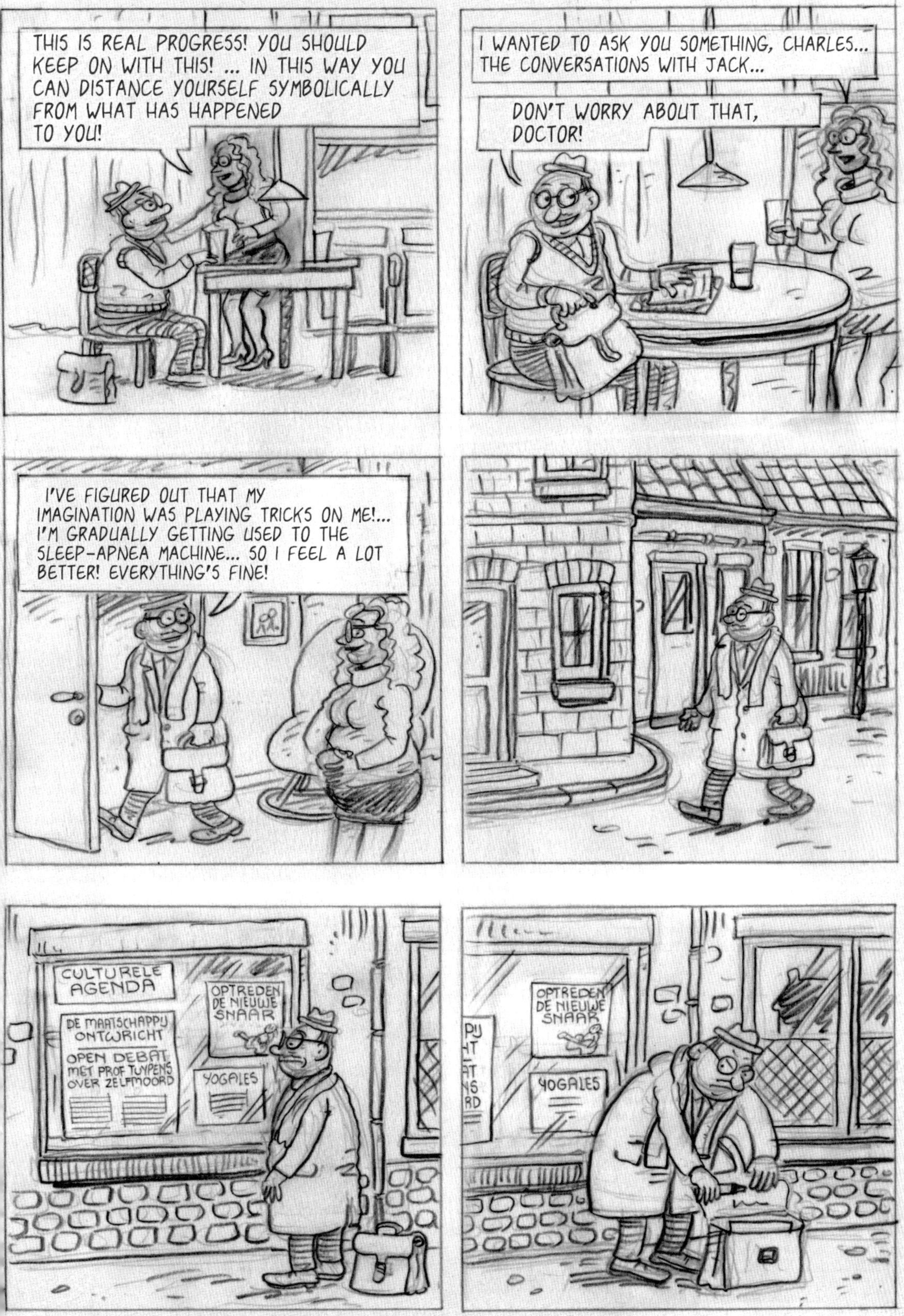

THIS IS REAL PROGRESS! YOU SHOULD KEEP ON WITH THIS! ... IN THIS WAY YOU CAN DISTANCE YOURSELF SYMBOLICALLY FROM WHAT HAS HAPPENED TO YOU!
I WANTED TO ASK YOU SOMETHING, CHARLES... THE CONVERSATIONS WITH JACK...
DON'T WORRY ABOUT THAT, DOCTOR!
I'VE FIGURED OUT THAT MY IMAGINATION WAS PLAYING TRICKS ON ME!... I'M GRADUALLY GETTING USED TO THE SLEEP-APNEA MACHINE... SO I FEEL A LOT BETTER! EVERYTHING'S FINE!
CULTURELE AGENDA
DE MAATSCHAPPIJ ONTWRICHT
OPEN DEBAT MET PROF TUYPENS OVER ZELFMOORD
OPTREDEN DE NIEUWE SNAAR
YOGALES
OPTREDEN DE NIEUWE SNAAR
YOGALES

CULTURAL AGENDA / SOCIAL BREAKDOWN / PUBLIC DEBATE WITH PROF. TUYPENS ABOUT SUICIDE / PERFORMANCE THE NEW CHORD / YOGA LESSONS

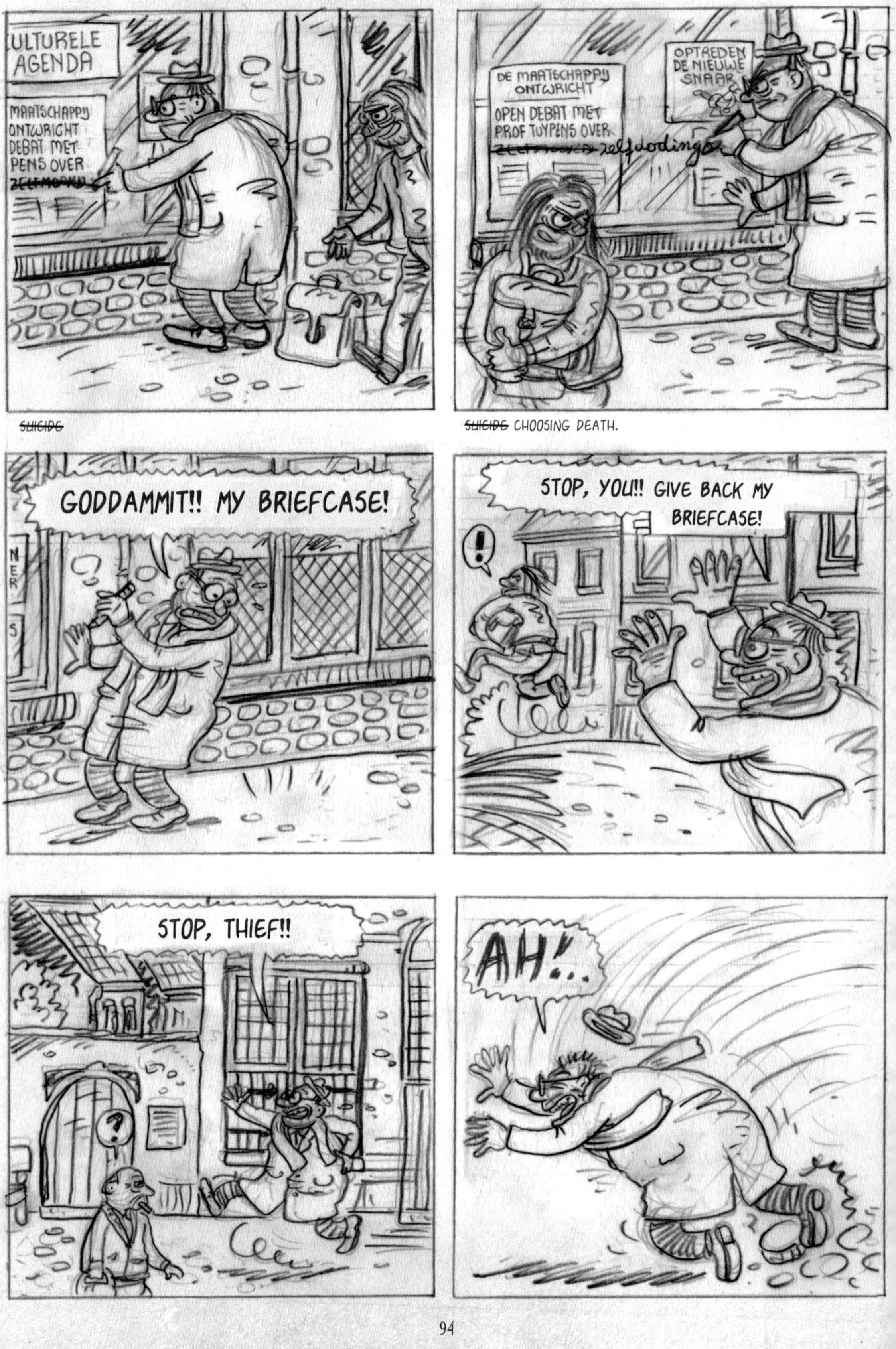
ULTURELE
AGENDA
MAATSCHAPPIJ ONTWRICHT
DEBAT MET
PENS OVER
SUICIDE
DE MAATSCHAPPIJ ONTWRICHT
OPEN DEBAT MET
PROF TUYPENS OVER
zelfdoding
OPTREDEN
DE NIEUWE
SNAAR
SUICIDE CHOOSING DEATH.
GODDAMMIT!! MY BRIEFCASE!
STOP, YOU!! GIVE BACK MY BRIEFCASE!
!
STOP, THIEF!!
?
AH!..

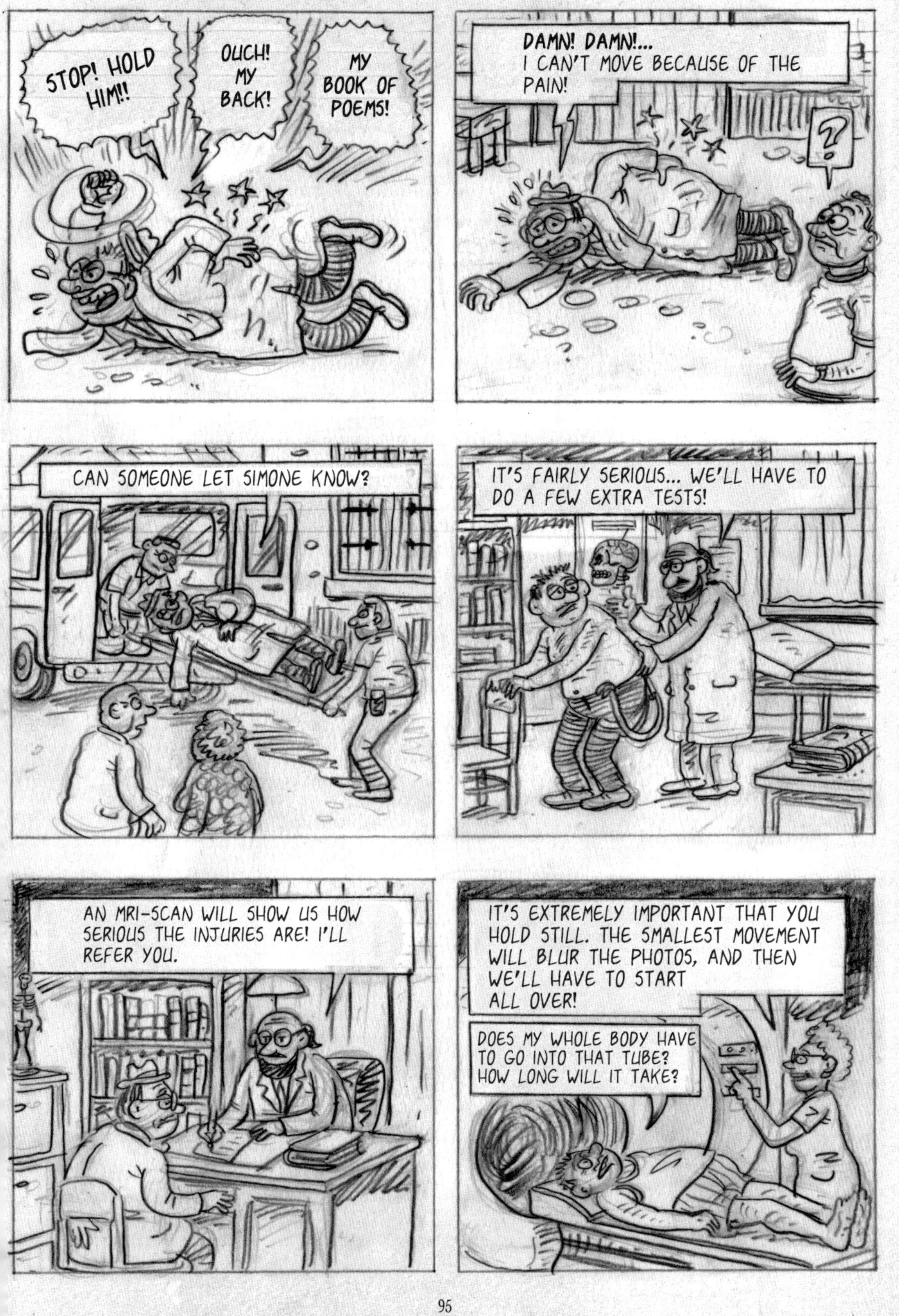
STOP! HOLD HIM!!
OUCH! MY BACK!
MY BOOK OF POEMS!
DAMN! DAMN!... I CAN'T MOVE BECAUSE OF THE PAIN!
?
CAN SOMEONE LET SIMONE KNOW?
IT'S FAIRLY SERIOUS... WE'LL HAVE TO DO A FEW EXTRA TESTS!
AN MRI-SCAN WILL SHOW US HOW SERIOUS THE INJURIES ARE! I'LL REFER YOU.
IT'S EXTREMELY IMPORTANT THAT YOU HOLD STILL. THE SMALLEST MOVEMENT WILL BLUR THE PHOTOS, AND THEN WE'LL HAVE TO START ALL OVER!
DOES MY WHOLE BODY HAVE TO GO INTO THAT TUBE? HOW LONG WILL IT TAKE?

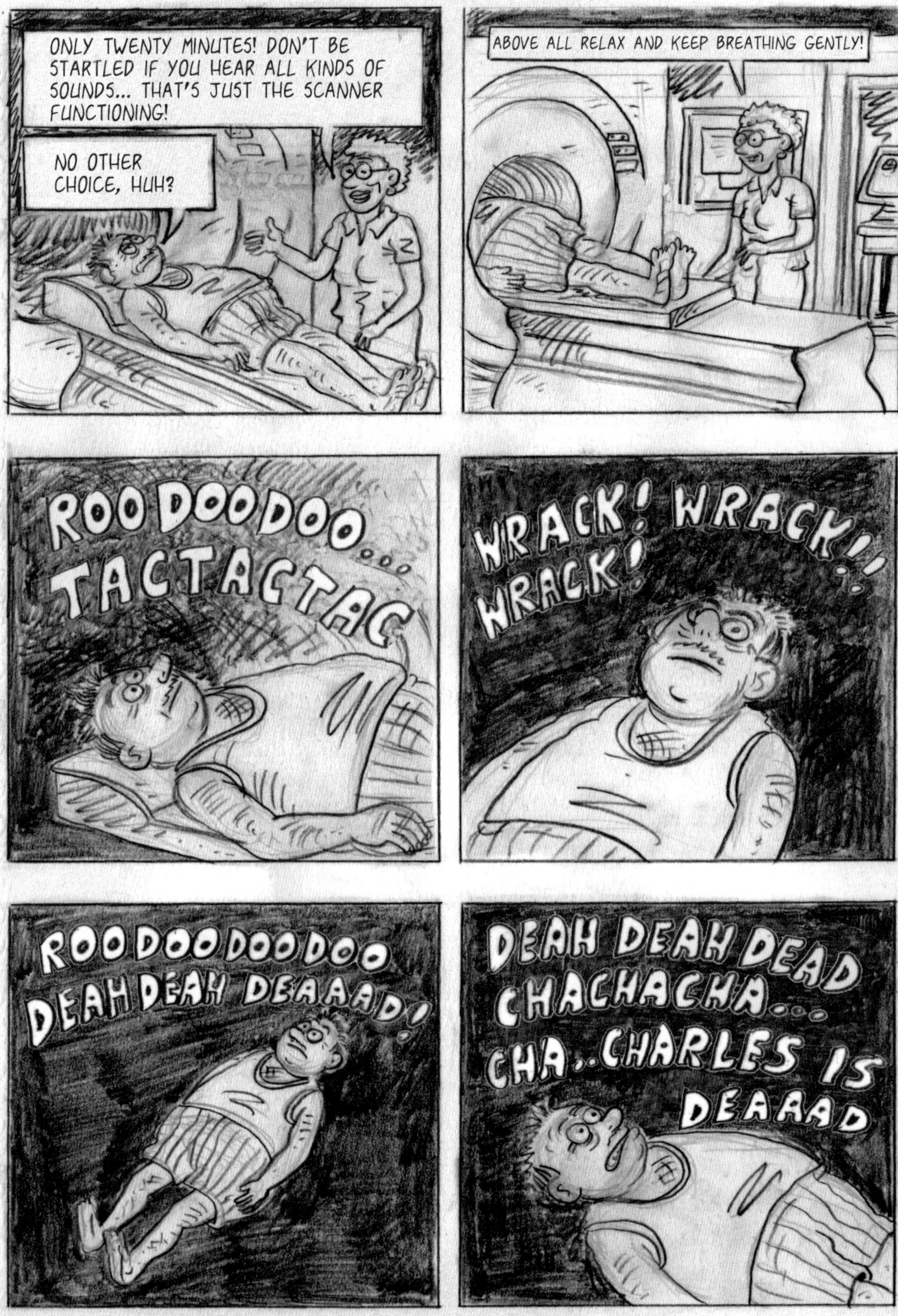
ONLY TWENTY MINUTES! DON'T BE STARTLED IF YOU HEAR ALL KINDS OF SOUNDS... THAT'S JUST THE SCANNER FUNCTIONING!
NO OTHER CHOICE, HUH?
ABOVE ALL RELAX AND KEEP BREATHING GENTLY!
ROO DOO DOO... TACTACTAC
WRACK! WRACK!! WRACK!
ROO DOO DOO DOO DEAH DEAH DEAAAD!
DEAH DEAH DEAD CHACHACHA... CHA..CHARLES IS DEAAAD

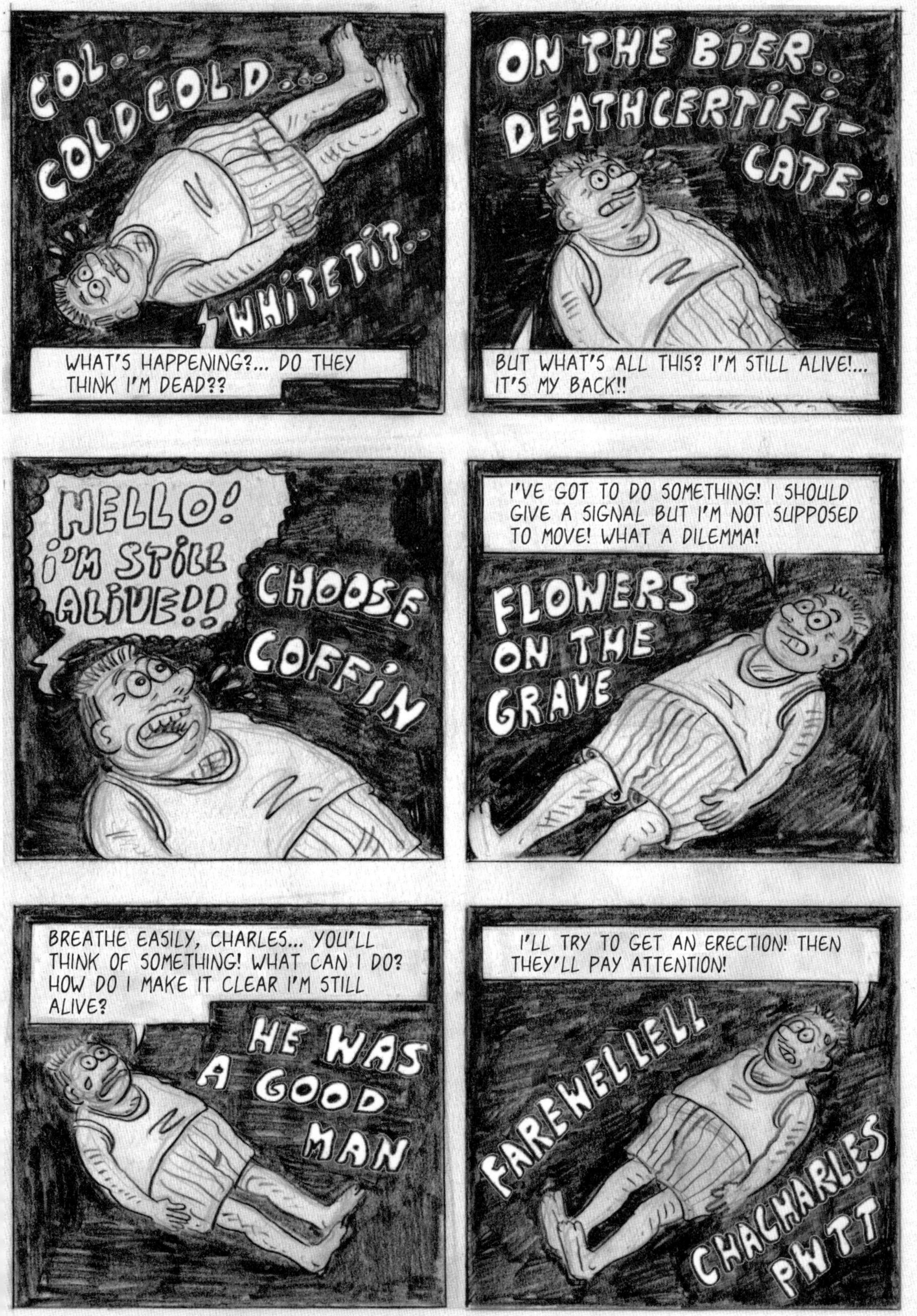
COL... COLDCOLD...
WHITETIT...
WHAT'S HAPPENING?... DO THEY THINK I'M DEAD??
ON THE BIER... DEATHCERTIFI-CATE.
BUT WHAT'S ALL THIS? I'M STILL ALIVE!... IT'S MY BACK!!
HELLO! I'M STILL ALIVE!!
CHOOSE COFFIN
I'VE GOT TO DO SOMETHING! I SHOULD GIVE A SIGNAL BUT I'M NOT SUPPOSED TO MOVE! WHAT A DILEMMA!
FLOWERS ON THE GRAVE
BREATHE EASILY, CHARLES... YOU'LL THINK OF SOMETHING! WHAT CAN I DO? HOW DO I MAKE IT CLEAR I'M STILL ALIVE?
HE WAS A GOOD MAN
I'LL TRY TO GET AN ERECTION! THEN THEY'LL PAY ATTENTION!
FAREWELLELL
CHACHARLES
PHTT

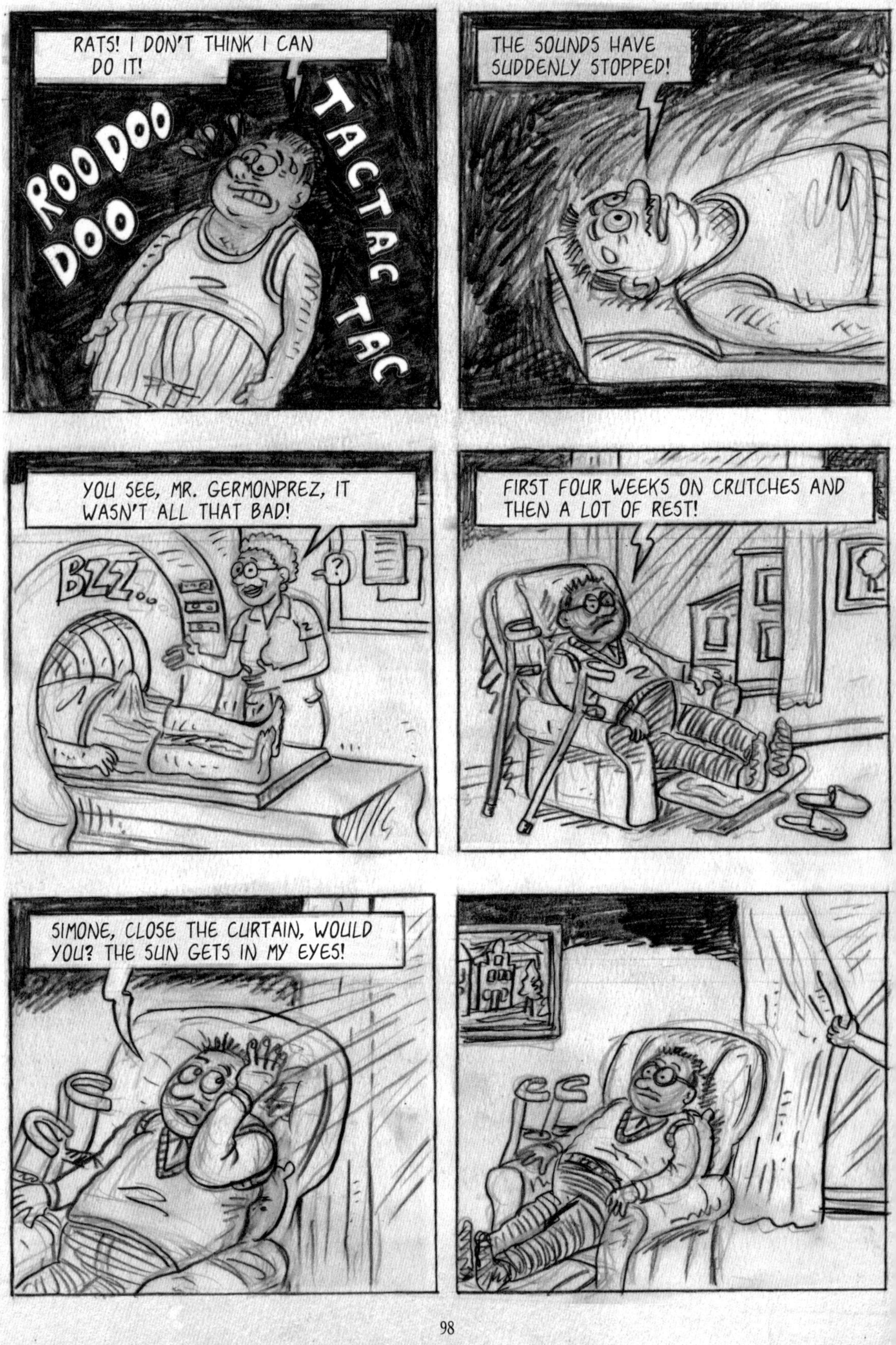
RATS! I DON'T THINK I CAN DO IT!
ROO DOO DOO
TACTAC TAC
THE SOUNDS HAVE SUDDENLY STOPPED!
YOU SEE, MR. GERMONPREZ, IT WASN'T ALL THAT BAD!
BZZ...
?
FIRST FOUR WEEKS ON CRUTCHES AND THEN A LOT OF REST!
SIMONE, CLOSE THE CURTAIN, WOULD YOU? THE SUN GETS IN MY EYES!

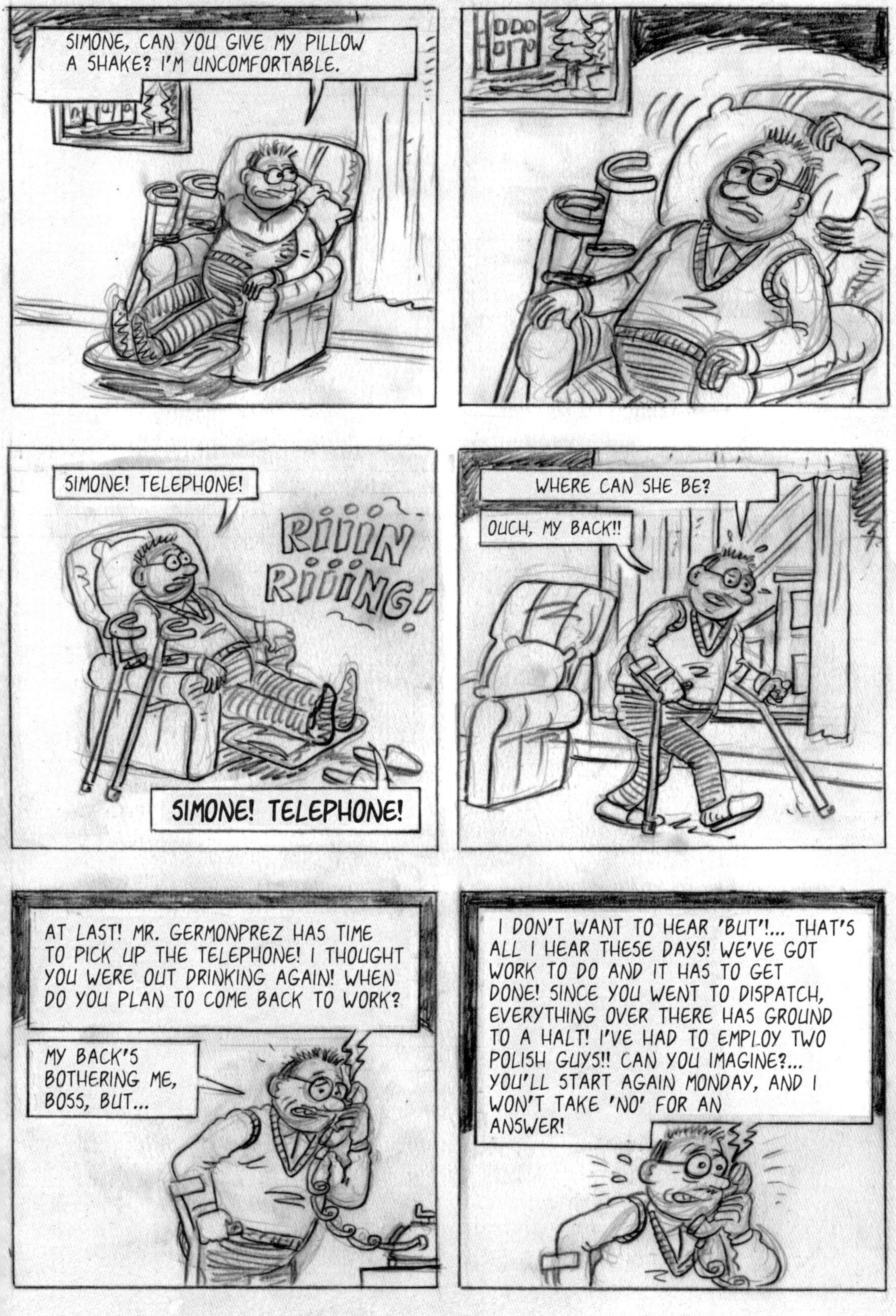

SIMONE, CAN YOU GIVE MY PILLOW A SHAKE? I'M UNCOMFORTABLE.
SIMONE! TELEPHONE!
RIIIN RIIING!
SIMONE! TELEPHONE!
WHERE CAN SHE BE?
OUCH, MY BACK!!
AT LAST! MR. GERMONPREZ HAS TIME TO PICK UP THE TELEPHONE! I THOUGHT YOU WERE OUT DRINKING AGAIN! WHEN DO YOU PLAN TO COME BACK TO WORK?
MY BACK'S BOTHERING ME, BOSS, BUT...
I DON'T WANT TO HEAR 'BUT'!... THAT'S ALL I HEAR THESE DAYS! WE'VE GOT WORK TO DO AND IT HAS TO GET DONE! SINCE YOU WENT TO DISPATCH, EVERYTHING OVER THERE HAS GROUND TO A HALT! I'VE HAD TO EMPLOY TWO POLISH GUYS!! CAN YOU IMAGINE?... YOU'LL START AGAIN MONDAY, AND I WON'T TAKE 'NO' FOR AN ANSWER!

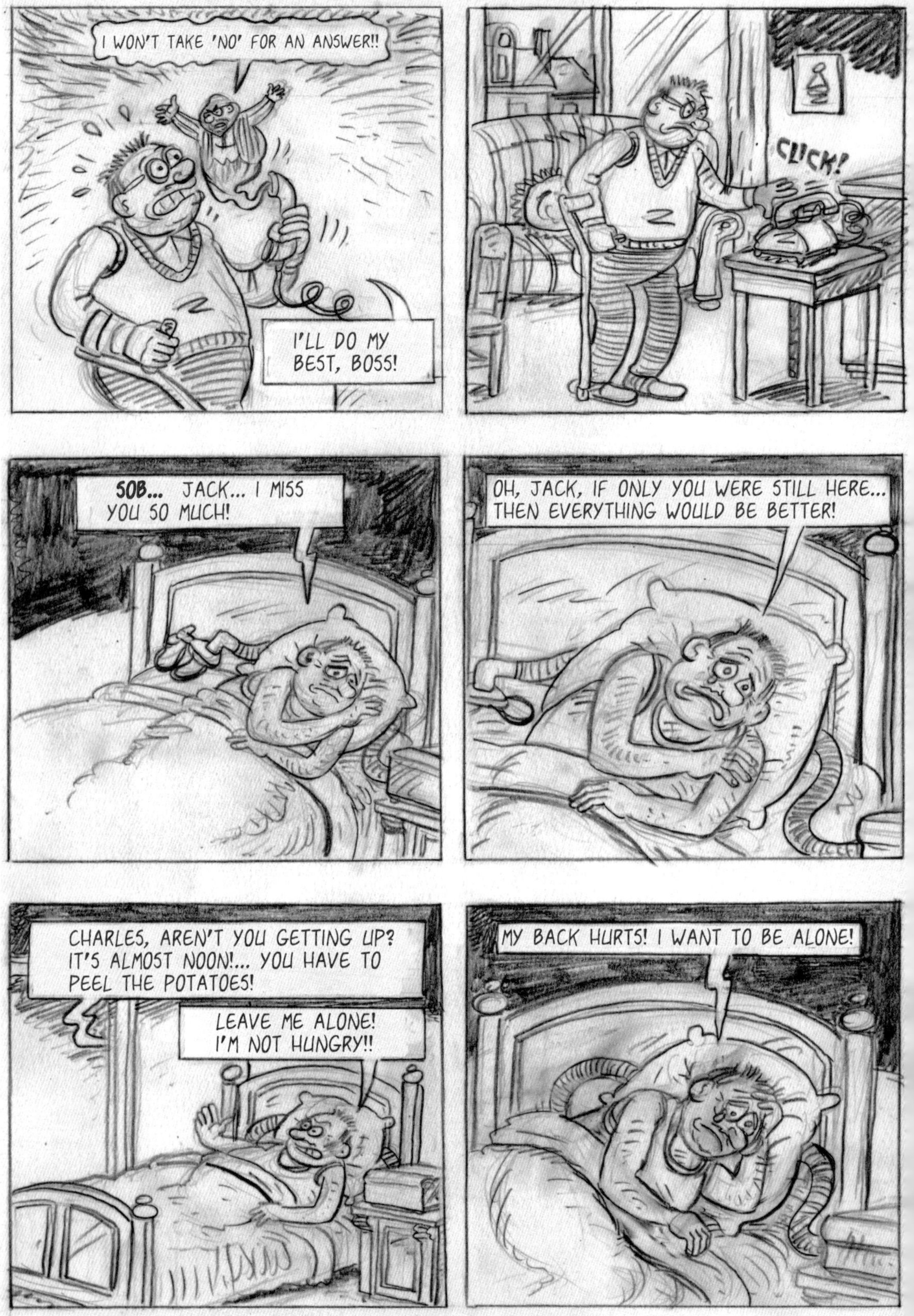
I WON'T TAKE 'NO' FOR AN ANSWER!!
I'LL DO MY BEST, BOSS!
CLICK!
SOB... JACK... I MISS YOU SO MUCH!
OH, JACK, IF ONLY YOU WERE STILL HERE... THEN EVERYTHING WOULD BE BETTER!
CHARLES, AREN'T YOU GETTING UP? IT'S ALMOST NOON!... YOU HAVE TO PEEL THE POTATOES!
LEAVE ME ALONE! I'M NOT HUNGRY!!
MY BACK HURTS! I WANT TO BE ALONE!

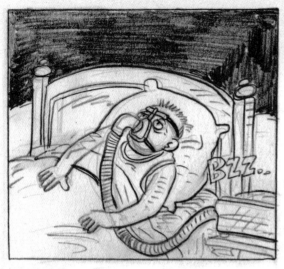

GO AWAY, JACK!

YOU DON'T EXIST, JACK!... DR. DE SMEDT SAYS YOU EXIST ONLY IN MY IMAGINATION.

YOU EVEN AGREE WITH HER!! THEN WHAT ARE YOU DOING HERE?

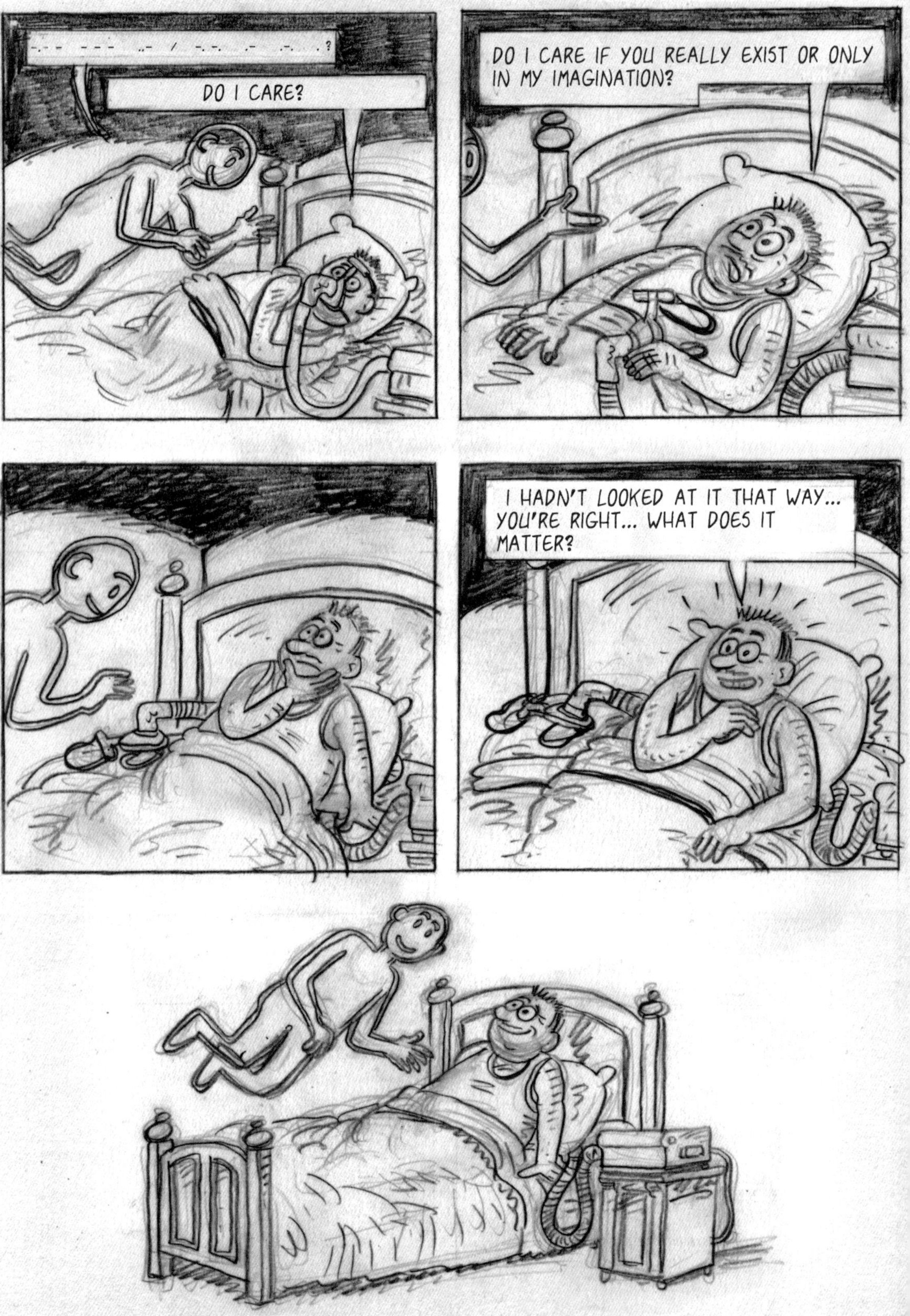
DO I CARE?
DO I CARE IF YOU REALLY EXIST OR ONLY IN MY IMAGINATION?
I HADN'T LOOKED AT IT THAT WAY... YOU'RE RIGHT... WHAT DOES IT MATTER?

CHAPTER 6 – SHREDDED WORDS

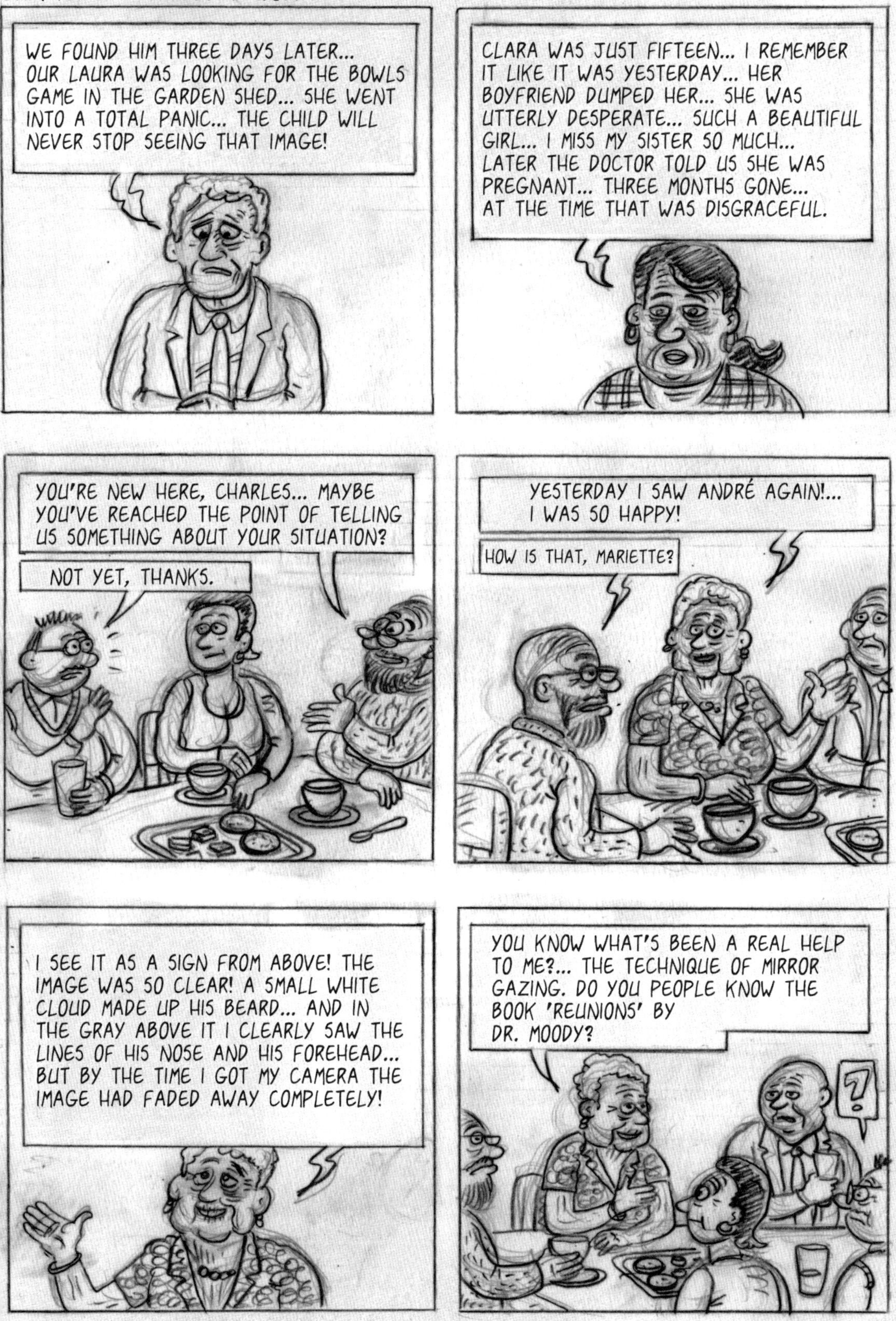
WE FOUND HIM THREE DAYS LATER... OUR LAURA WAS LOOKING FOR THE BOWLS GAME IN THE GARDEN SHED... SHE WENT INTO A TOTAL PANIC... THE CHILD WILL NEVER STOP SEEING THAT IMAGE!
CLARA WAS JUST FIFTEEN... I REMEMBER IT LIKE IT WAS YESTERDAY... HER BOYFRIEND DUMPED HER... SHE WAS UTTERLY DESPERATE... SUCH A BEAUTIFUL GIRL... I MISS MY SISTER SO MUCH... LATER THE DOCTOR TOLD US SHE WAS PREGNANT... THREE MONTHS GONE... AT THE TIME THAT WAS DISGRACEFUL.
YOU'RE NEW HERE, CHARLES... MAYBE YOU'VE REACHED THE POINT OF TELLING US SOMETHING ABOUT YOUR SITUATION?
NOT YET, THANKS.
YESTERDAY I SAW ANDRÉ AGAIN!... I WAS SO HAPPY!
HOW IS THAT, MARIETTE?
I SEE IT AS A SIGN FROM ABOVE! THE IMAGE WAS SO CLEAR! A SMALL WHITE CLOUD MADE UP HIS BEARD... AND IN THE GRAY ABOVE IT I CLEARLY SAW THE LINES OF HIS NOSE AND HIS FOREHEAD... BUT BY THE TIME I GOT MY CAMERA THE IMAGE HAD FADED AWAY COMPLETELY!
YOU KNOW WHAT'S BEEN A REAL HELP TO ME?... THE TECHNIQUE OF MIRROR GAZING. DO YOU PEOPLE KNOW THE BOOK 'REUNIONS' BY DR. MOODY?
?

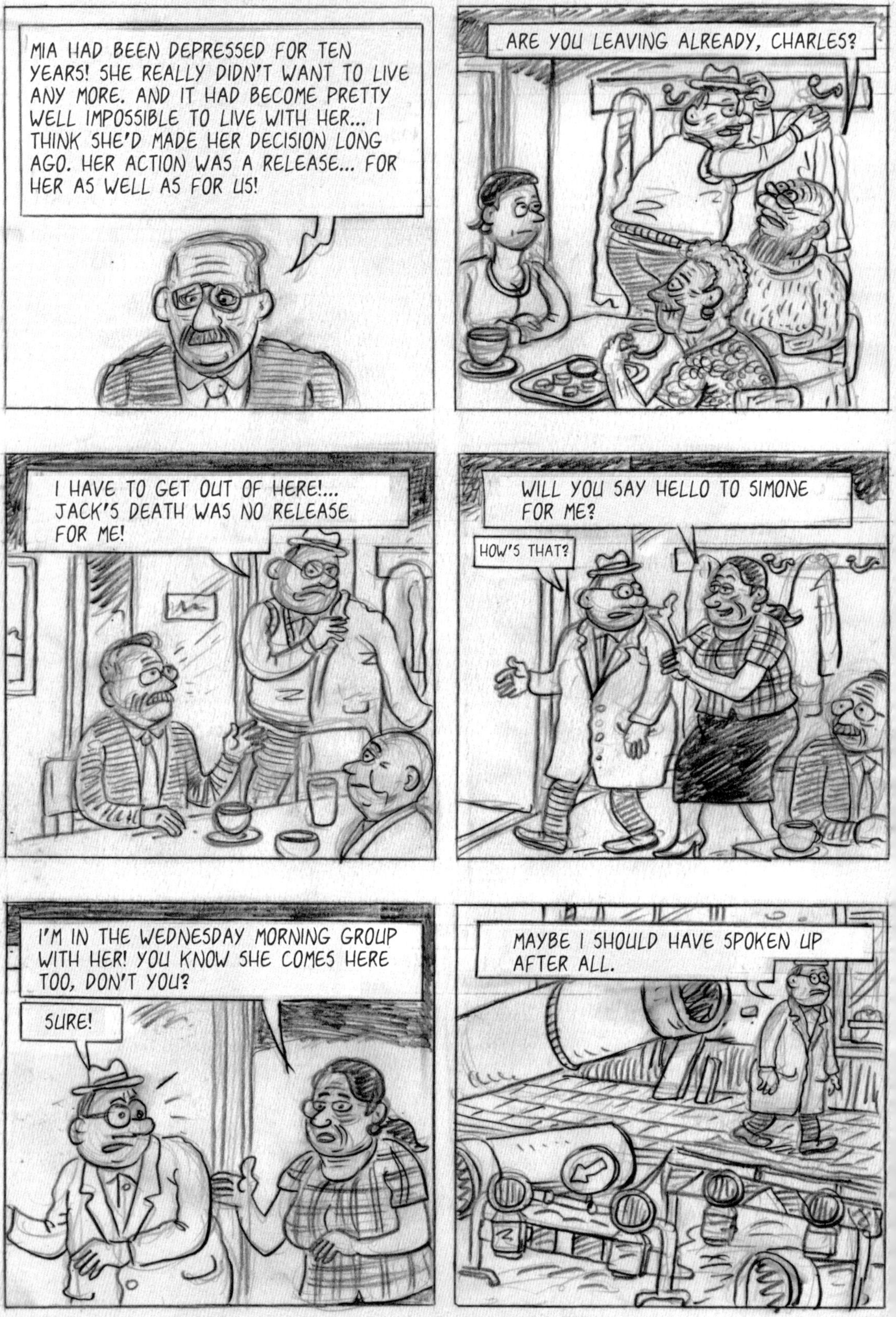
MIA HAD BEEN DEPRESSED FOR TEN YEARS! SHE REALLY DIDN'T WANT TO LIVE ANY MORE. AND IT HAD BECOME PRETTY WELL IMPOSSIBLE TO LIVE WITH HER... I THINK SHE'D MADE HER DECISION LONG AGO. HER ACTION WAS A RELEASE... FOR HER AS WELL AS FOR US!
ARE YOU LEAVING ALREADY, CHARLES?
I HAVE TO GET OUT OF HERE!... JACK'S DEATH WAS NO RELEASE FOR ME!
WILL YOU SAY HELLO TO SIMONE FOR ME?
HOW'S THAT?
I'M IN THE WEDNESDAY MORNING GROUP WITH HER! YOU KNOW SHE COMES HERE TOO, DON'T YOU?
SURE!
MAYBE I SHOULD HAVE SPOKEN UP AFTER ALL.

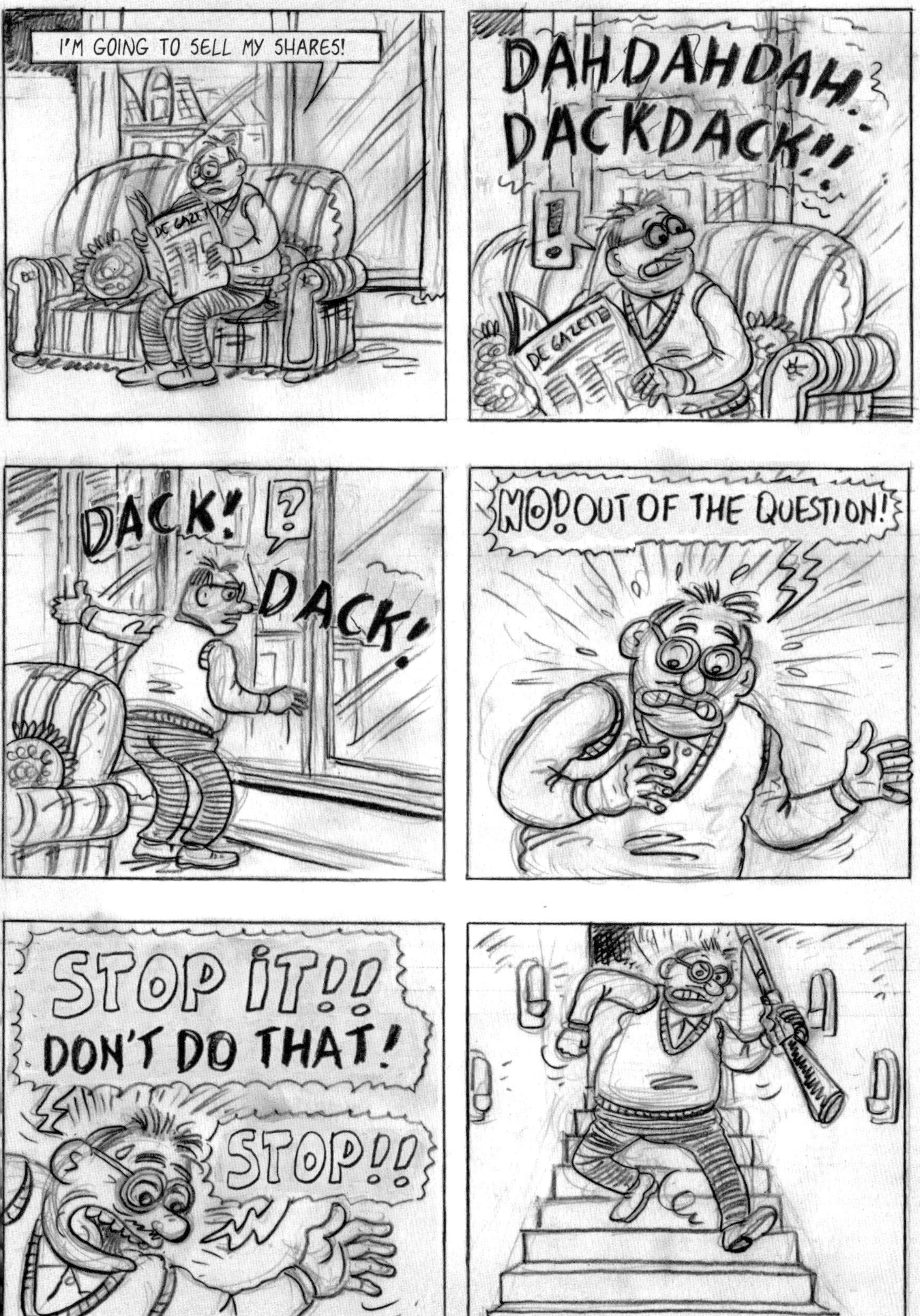
I'M GOING TO SELL MY SHARES!
DE GAZET
DAHDAHDAH DACKDACK!!
DE GAZETT
DACK! DACK!
?
NO! OUT OF THE QUESTION!
STOP IT!!! DON'T DO THAT!
STOP!!

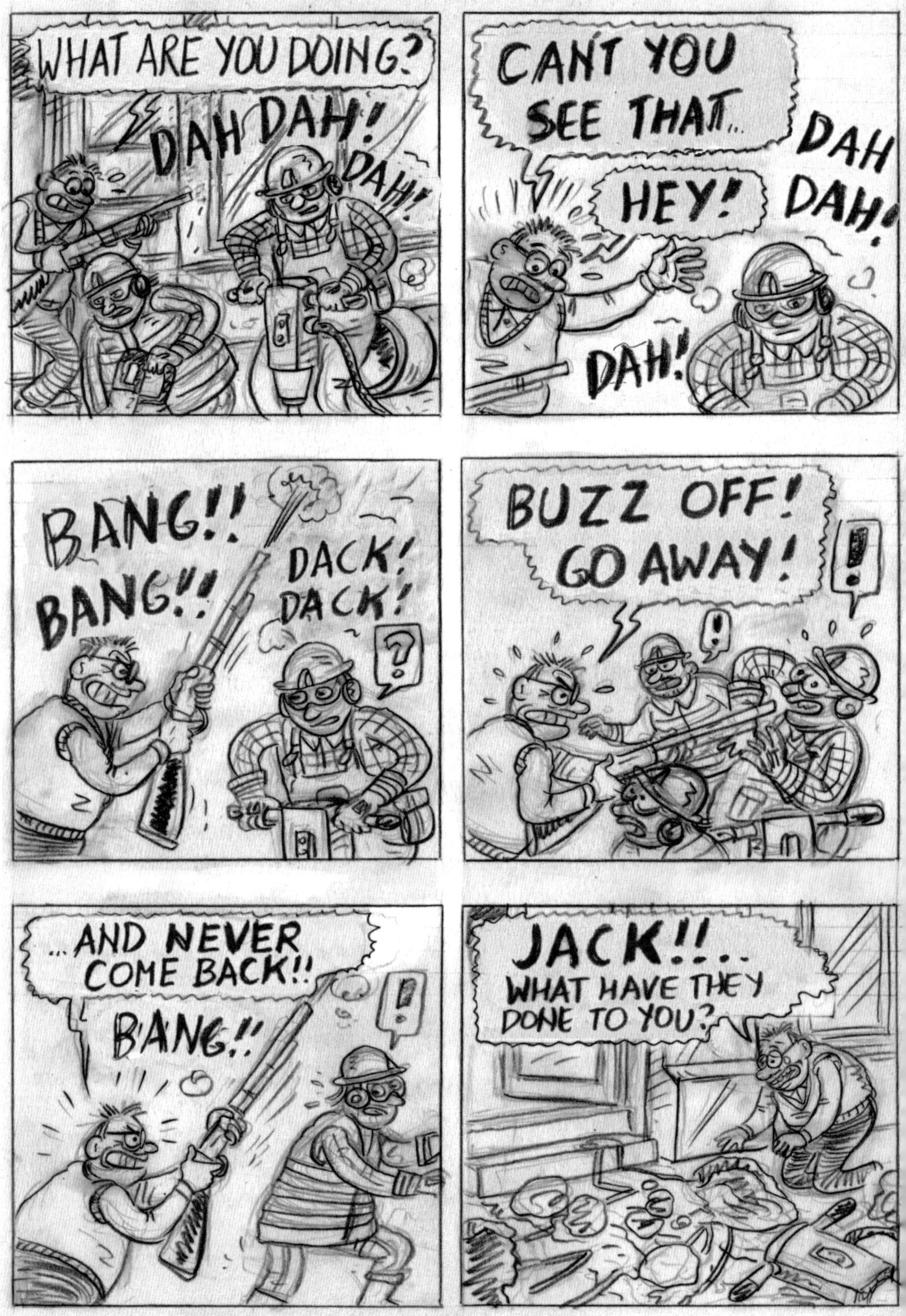
WHAT ARE YOU DOING?
DAH DAH!
DAH!
CAN'T YOU SEE THAT...
HEY!
DAH DAH!
DAH!
BANG!!
BANG!!
DACK! DACK!
?
BUZZ OFF! GO AWAY!
!
!
...AND NEVER COME BACK!!
BANG!!
!
JACK!!...
WHAT HAVE THEY DONE TO YOU?

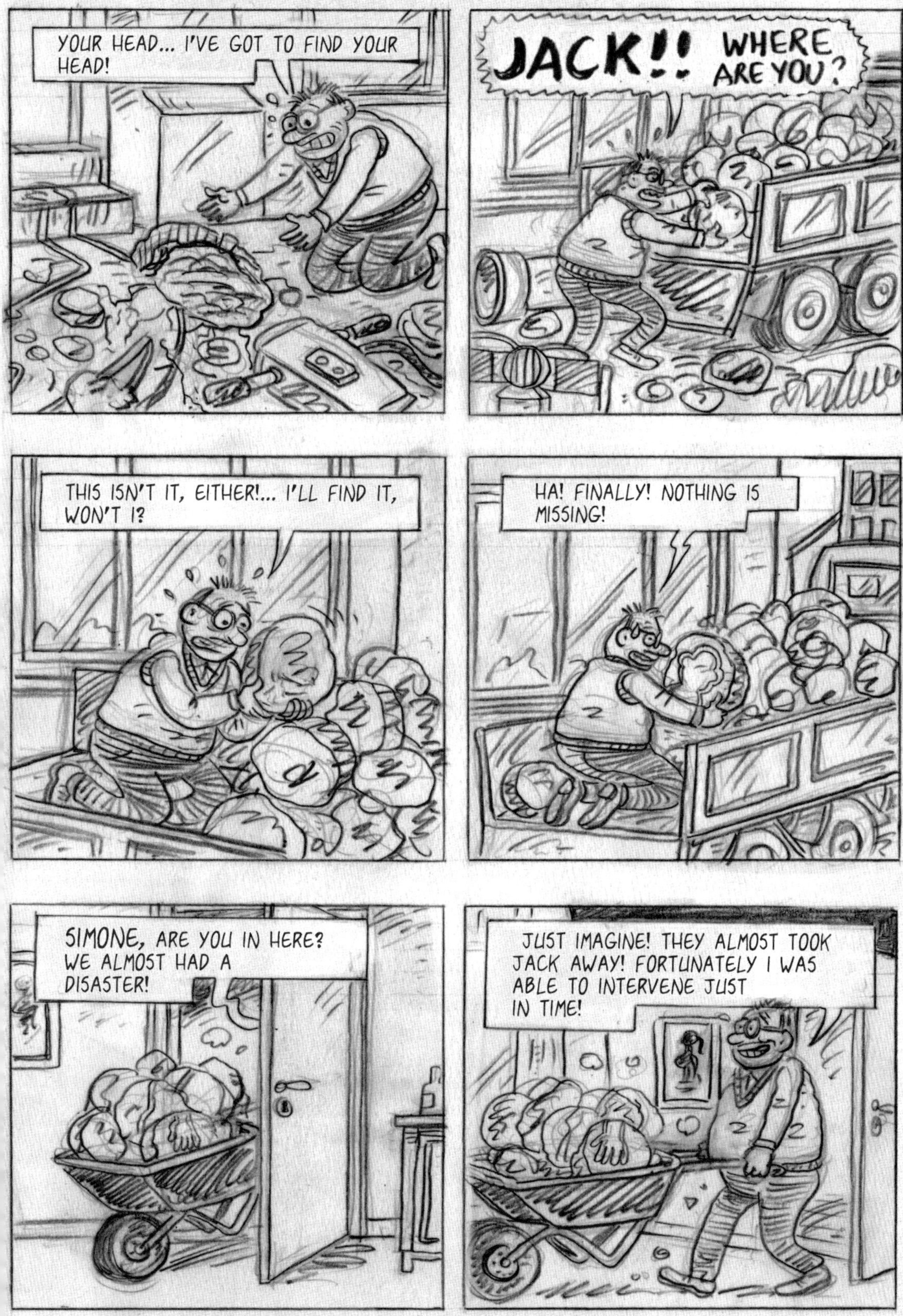
YOUR HEAD... I'VE GOT TO FIND YOUR HEAD!
JACK!! WHERE ARE YOU?
THIS ISN'T IT, EITHER!... I'LL FIND IT, WON'T I?
HA! FINALLY! NOTHING IS MISSING!
SIMONE, ARE YOU IN HERE? WE ALMOST HAD A DISASTER!
JUST IMAGINE! THEY ALMOST TOOK JACK AWAY! FORTUNATELY I WAS ABLE TO INTERVENE JUST IN TIME!

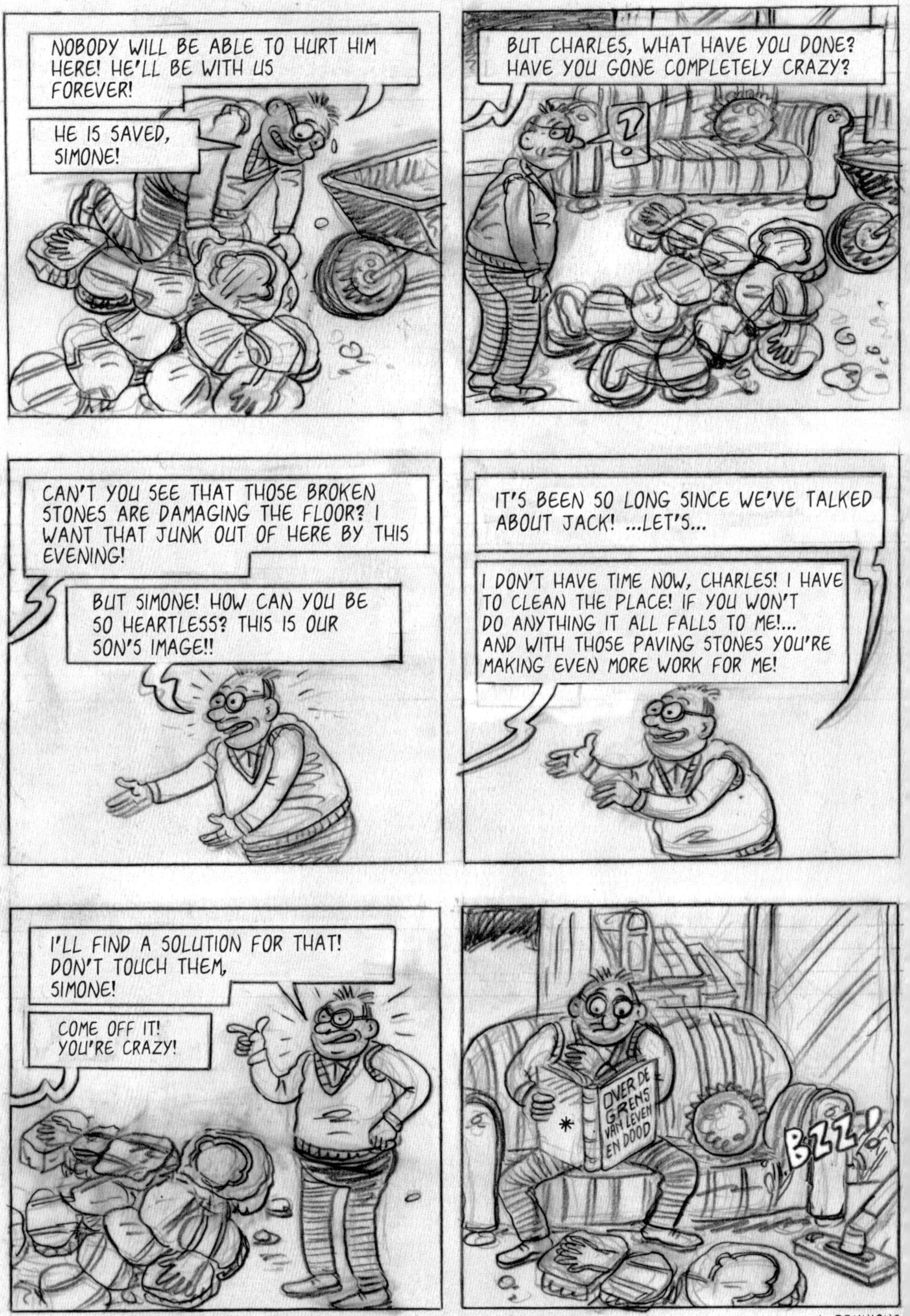
NOBODY WILL BE ABLE TO HURT HIM HERE! HE'LL BE WITH US FOREVER!
HE IS SAVED, SIMONE!
BUT CHARLES, WHAT HAVE YOU DONE? HAVE YOU GONE COMPLETELY CRAZY?
?
CAN'T YOU SEE THAT THOSE BROKEN STONES ARE DAMAGING THE FLOOR? I WANT THAT JUNK OUT OF HERE BY THIS EVENING!
BUT SIMONE! HOW CAN YOU BE SO HEARTLESS? THIS IS OUR SON'S IMAGE!!
IT'S BEEN SO LONG SINCE WE'VE TALKED ABOUT JACK! ...LET'S...
I DON'T HAVE TIME NOW, CHARLES! I HAVE TO CLEAN THE PLACE! IF YOU WON'T DO ANYTHING IT ALL FALLS TO ME!... AND WITH THOSE PAVING STONES YOU'RE MAKING EVEN MORE WORK FOR ME!
I'LL FIND A SOLUTION FOR THAT! DON'T TOUCH THEM, SIMONE!
COME OFF IT! YOU'RE CRAZY!
OVER DE GRENS VAN LEVEN EN DOOD
*
BZZZ!
* REUNIONS

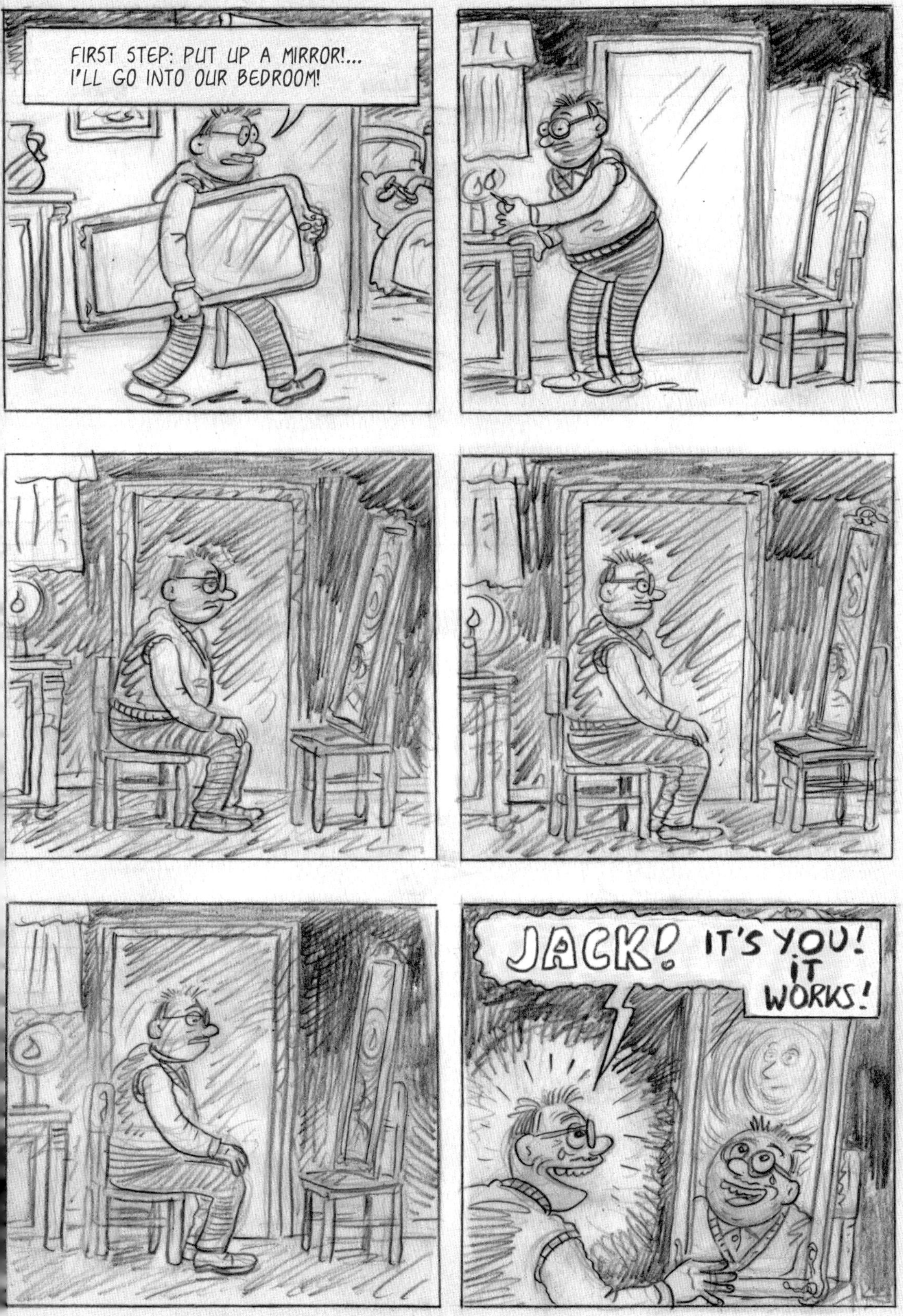
FIRST STEP: PUT UP A MIRROR!...
I'LL GO INTO OUR BEDROOM!
JACK! IT'S YOU! IT WORKS!

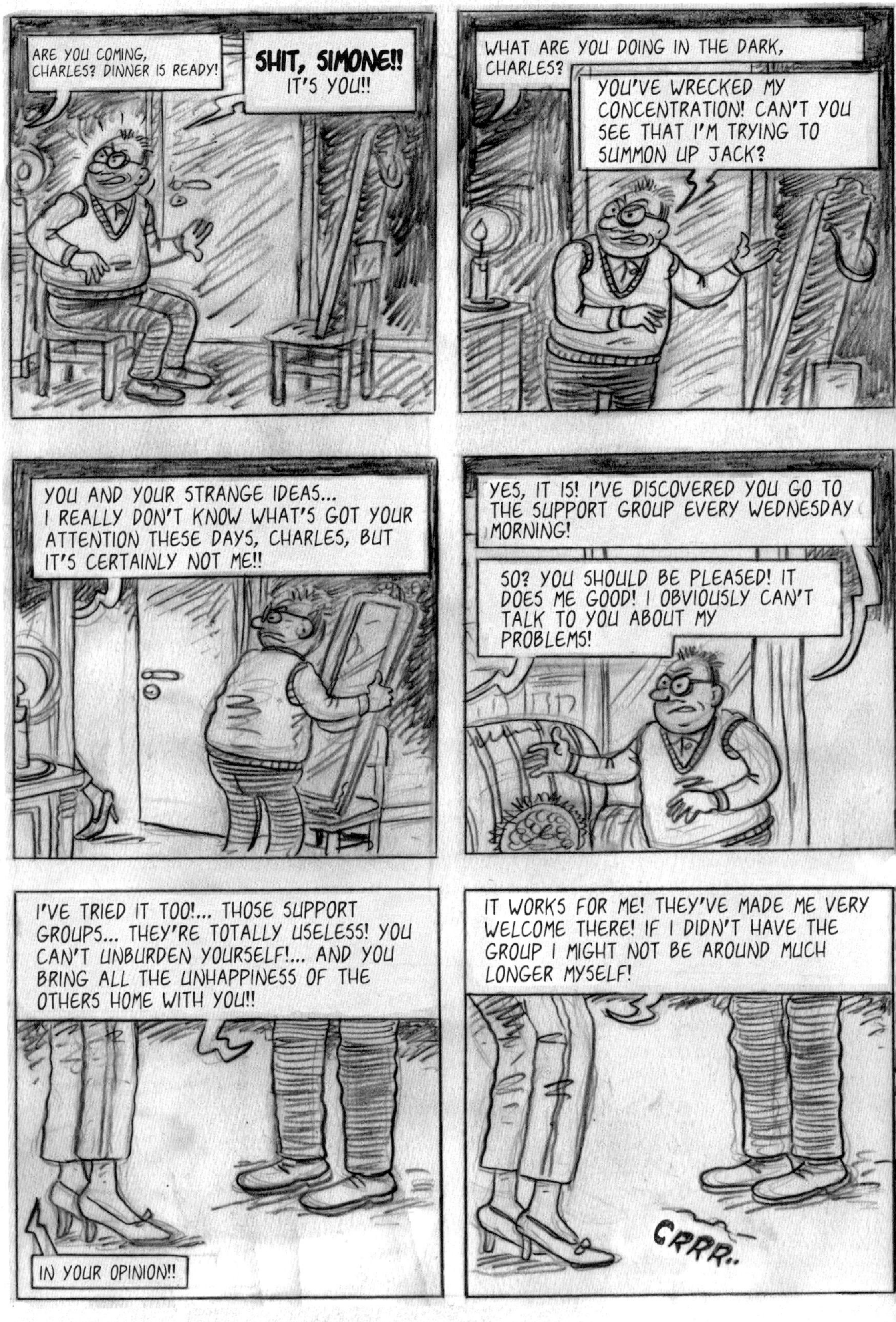
ARE YOU COMING, CHARLES? DINNER IS READY!
SHIT, SIMONE!! IT'S YOU!!
WHAT ARE YOU DOING IN THE DARK, CHARLES?
YOU'VE WRECKED MY CONCENTRATION! CAN'T YOU SEE THAT I'M TRYING TO SUMMON UP JACK?
YOU AND YOUR STRANGE IDEAS... I REALLY DON'T KNOW WHAT'S GOT YOUR ATTENTION THESE DAYS, CHARLES, BUT IT'S CERTAINLY NOT ME!!
YES, IT IS! I'VE DISCOVERED YOU GO TO THE SUPPORT GROUP EVERY WEDNESDAY MORNING!
SO? YOU SHOULD BE PLEASED! IT DOES ME GOOD! I OBVIOUSLY CAN'T TALK TO YOU ABOUT MY PROBLEMS!
I'VE TRIED IT TOO!... THOSE SUPPORT GROUPS... THEY'RE TOTALLY USELESS! YOU CAN'T UNBURDEN YOURSELF!... AND YOU BRING ALL THE UNHAPPINESS OF THE OTHERS HOME WITH YOU!!
IN YOUR OPINION!!
IT WORKS FOR ME! THEY'VE MADE ME VERY WELCOME THERE! IF I DIDN'T HAVE THE GROUP I MIGHT NOT BE AROUND MUCH LONGER MYSELF!
CRRR..

YOU KNOW WHAT ANNOYS ME THE MOST ABOUT YOU, SIMONE?... THAT YOU'RE NEVER REALLY AT HOME. EITHER YOU'RE GABBING IN THE SUPPORT GROUP OR YOU'RE VISITING FAMILY! AND WHEN YOU ARE AT HOME YOU'RE UNAPPROACHABLE!

CRR...

JUST BECAUSE YOU'RE ALWAYS LAZING ON THE SOFA OR SPENDING HOURS IN THE BAR. I DON'T HAVE TO DO THE SAME! I'M ALWAYS PREPARED TO TALK!

CRRRACK!!

YOU KEEP BABBLING BUT YOU TALK ABOUT NOTHING! YOU'D BE BETTER OFF IF YOU DID WHAT I'M DOING... GET HELP FROM PROFESSIONAL THERAPISTS!

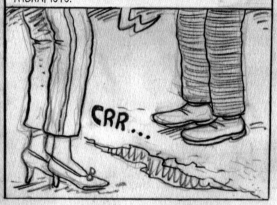

CRR...

I READ BOOKS ABOUT COPING WITH GRIEF!	I READ THE NEWSPAPER!!
I NEED TO KEEP ACTIVE!!	I NEED TIME TO THINK!
I'M HAPPY AT HOME!!	THIS PLACE DRIVES ME CRAZY!!

CRAACK!

THE WORST THING OF ALL WAS THAT I WASN'T ALLOWED TO SEE JACK!... THEY KEPT ME BACK! HIS BODY WAS TOO BATTERED, THEY SAID... I WANTED SO BADLY TO CARESS HIM ONE LAST TIME!

CRRT...

I WANTED TO REMEMBER JACK THE WAY HE WAS WHEN HE WAS ALIVE!

CRACK!

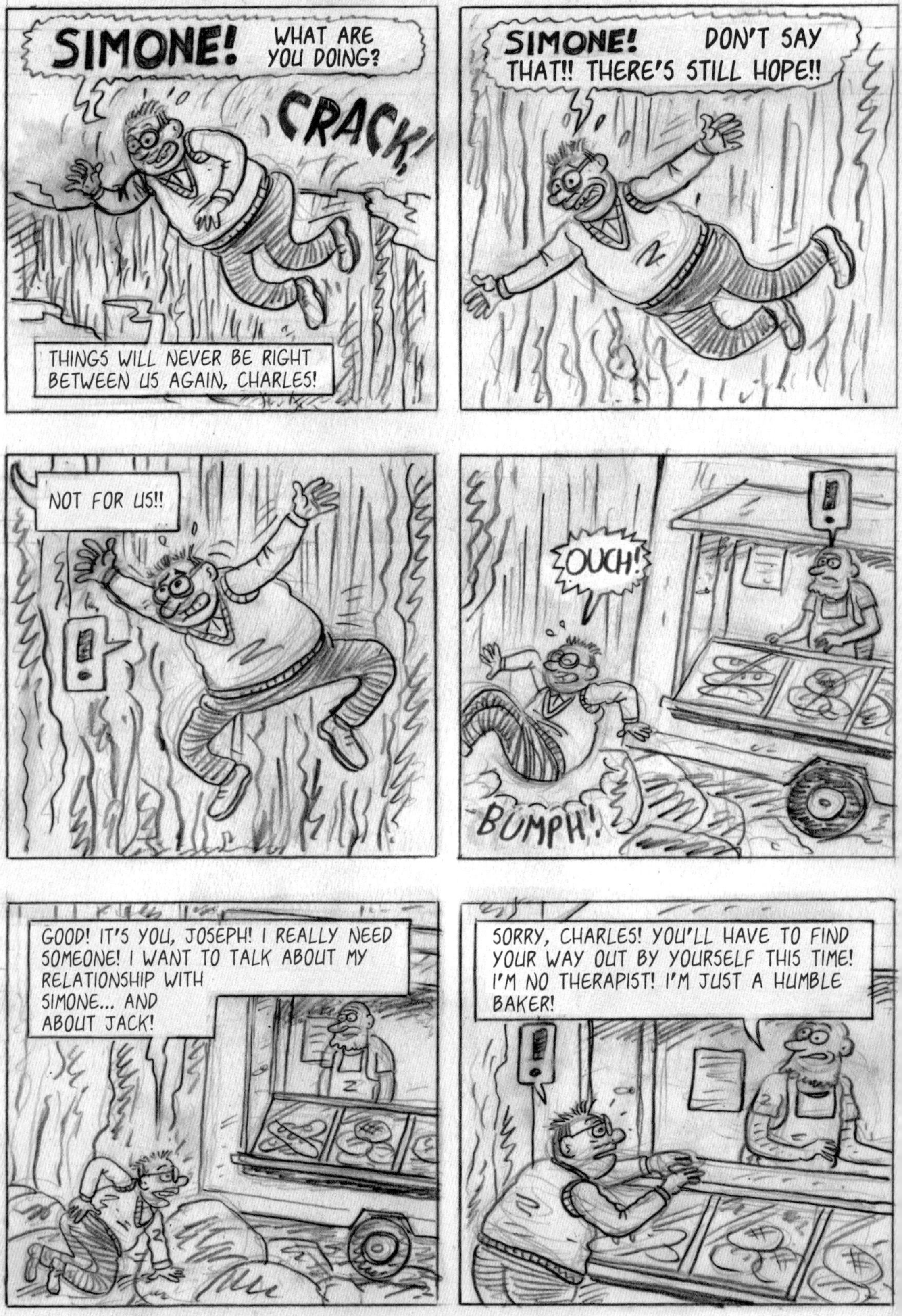
SIMONE! WHAT ARE YOU DOING?
CRACK!
THINGS WILL NEVER BE RIGHT BETWEEN US AGAIN, CHARLES!
SIMONE! DON'T SAY THAT!! THERE'S STILL HOPE!!
NOT FOR US!!
OUCH!
BUMPH!
GOOD! IT'S YOU, JOSEPH! I REALLY NEED SOMEONE! I WANT TO TALK ABOUT MY RELATIONSHIP WITH SIMONE... AND ABOUT JACK!
SORRY, CHARLES! YOU'LL HAVE TO FIND YOUR WAY OUT BY YOURSELF THIS TIME! I'M NO THERAPIST! I'M JUST A HUMBLE BAKER!

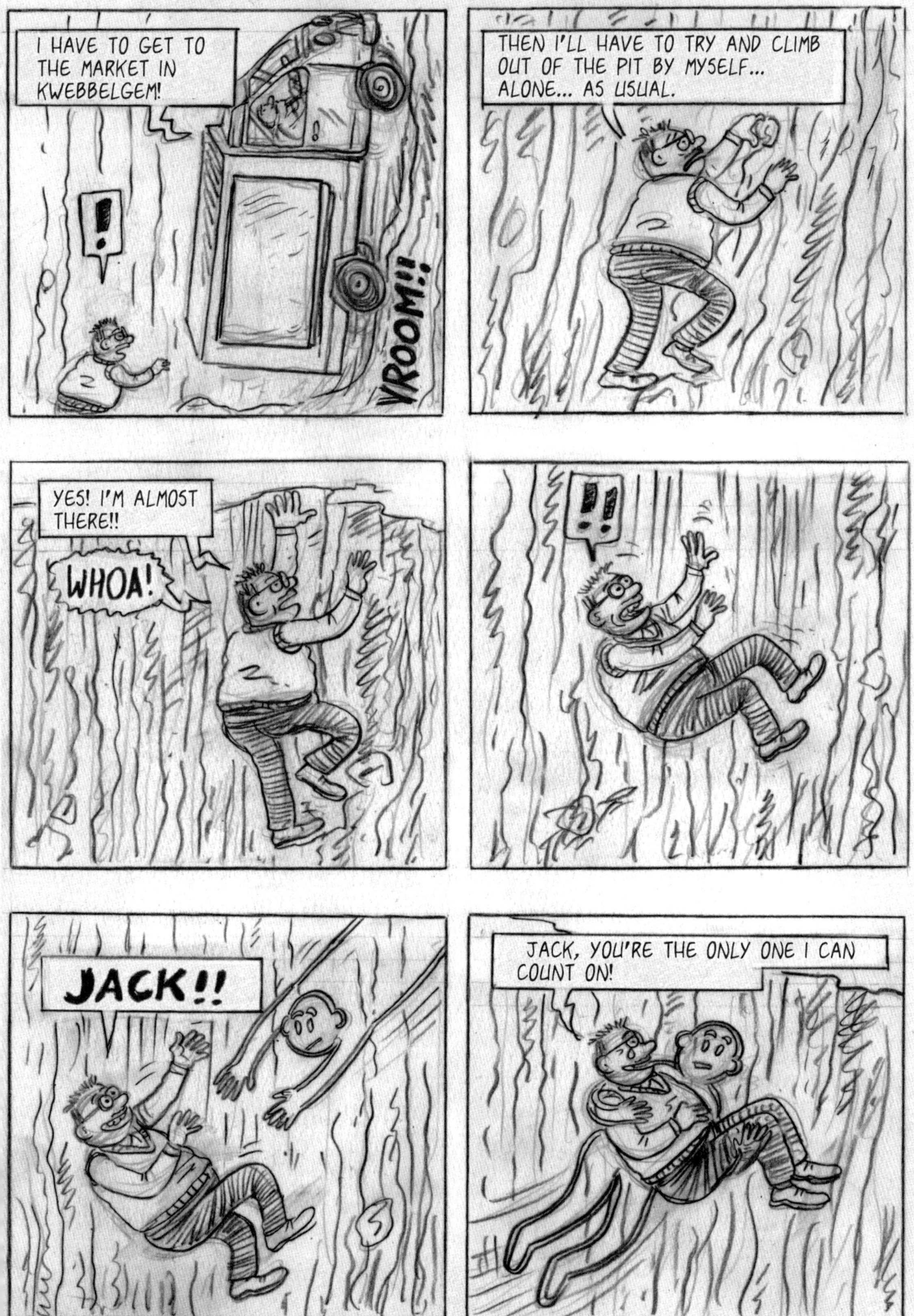

I HAVE TO GET TO THE MARKET IN KWEBBELGEM!
!
VROOM!!
THEN I'LL HAVE TO TRY AND CLIMB OUT OF THE PIT BY MYSELF... ALONE... AS USUAL.
YES! I'M ALMOST THERE!!
WHOA!
!!
JACK!!
JACK, YOU'RE THE ONLY ONE I CAN COUNT ON!

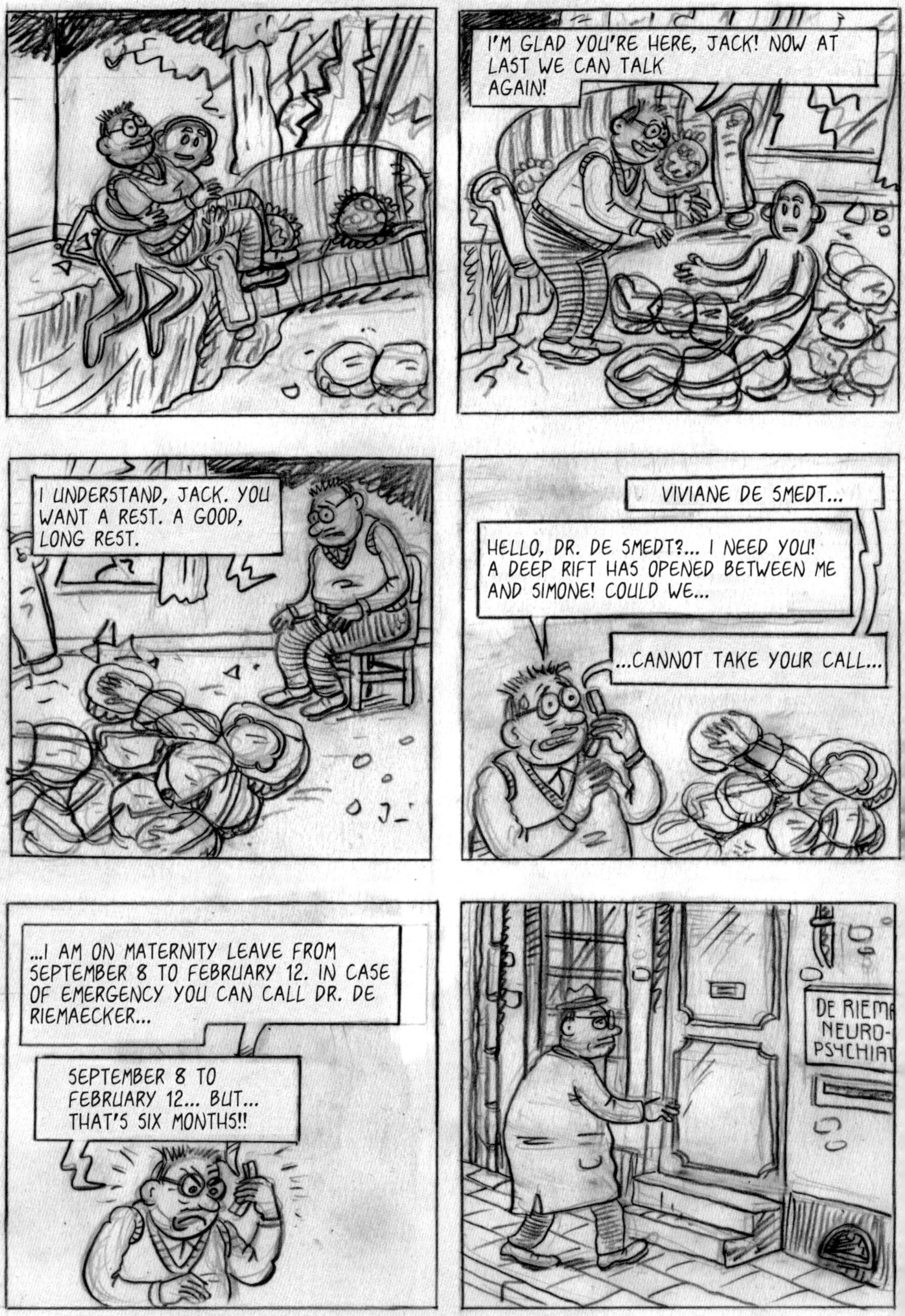

I'M GLAD YOU'RE HERE, JACK! NOW AT LAST WE CAN TALK AGAIN!
I UNDERSTAND, JACK. YOU WANT A REST. A GOOD, LONG REST.
VIVIANE DE SMEDT...
HELLO, DR. DE SMEDT?... I NEED YOU! A DEEP RIFT HAS OPENED BETWEEN ME AND SIMONE! COULD WE...
...CANNOT TAKE YOUR CALL...
...I AM ON MATERNITY LEAVE FROM SEPTEMBER 8 TO FEBRUARY 12. IN CASE OF EMERGENCY YOU CAN CALL DR. DE RIEMAECKER...
SEPTEMBER 8 TO FEBRUARY 12... BUT... THAT'S SIX MONTHS!!
DE RIEMA
NEURO-
PSYCHIAT

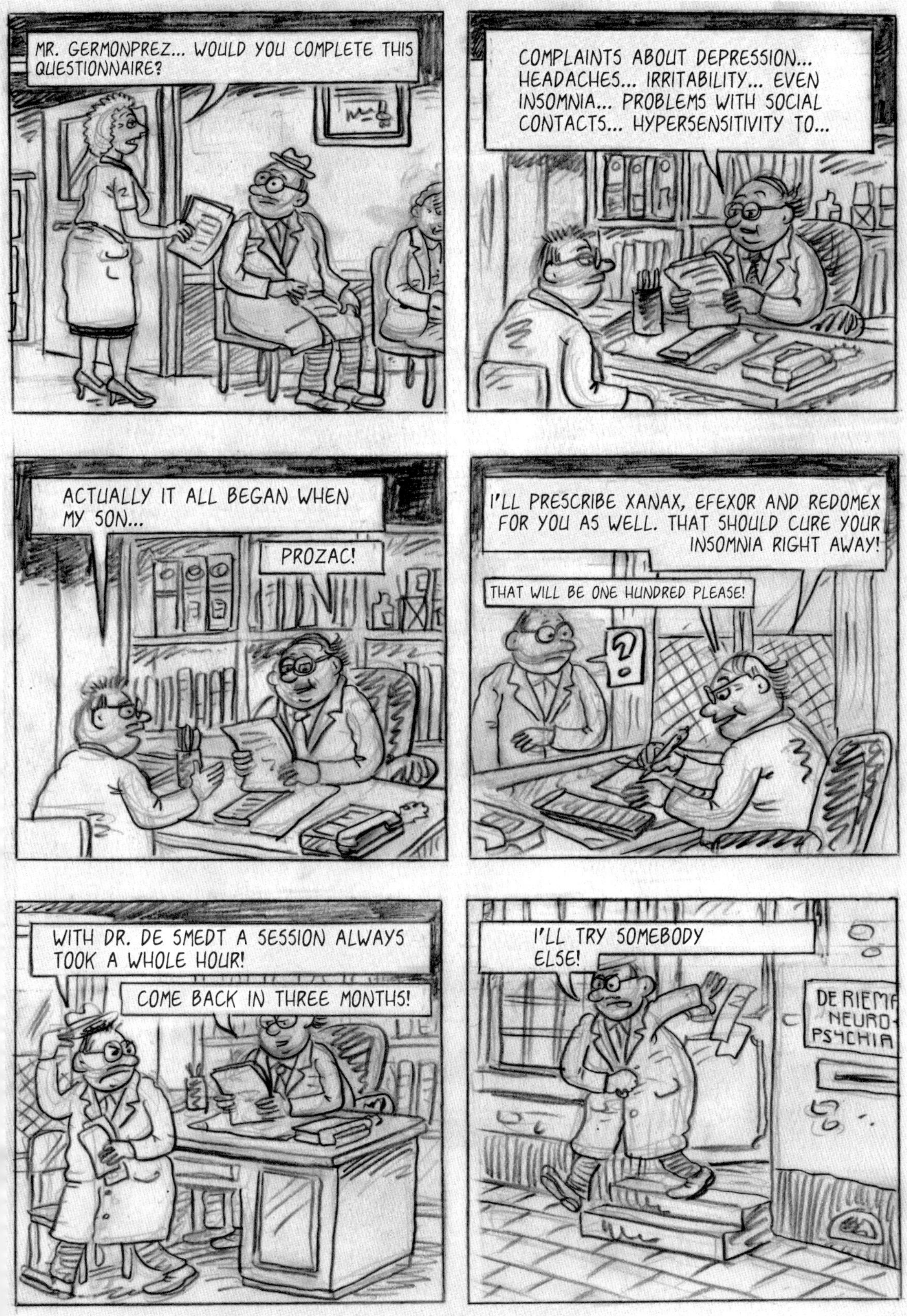

MR. GERMONPREZ... WOULD YOU COMPLETE THIS QUESTIONNAIRE?
COMPLAINTS ABOUT DEPRESSION... HEADACHES... IRRITABILITY... EVEN INSOMNIA... PROBLEMS WITH SOCIAL CONTACTS... HYPERSENSITIVITY TO...
ACTUALLY IT ALL BEGAN WHEN MY SON...
PROZAC!
I'LL PRESCRIBE XANAX, EFEXOR AND REDOMEX FOR YOU AS WELL. THAT SHOULD CURE YOUR INSOMNIA RIGHT AWAY!
THAT WILL BE ONE HUNDRED PLEASE!
?
WITH DR. DE SMEDT A SESSION ALWAYS TOOK A WHOLE HOUR!
COME BACK IN THREE MONTHS!
I'LL TRY SOMEBODY ELSE!
DE RIEMA
NEURO-
PSYCHIA

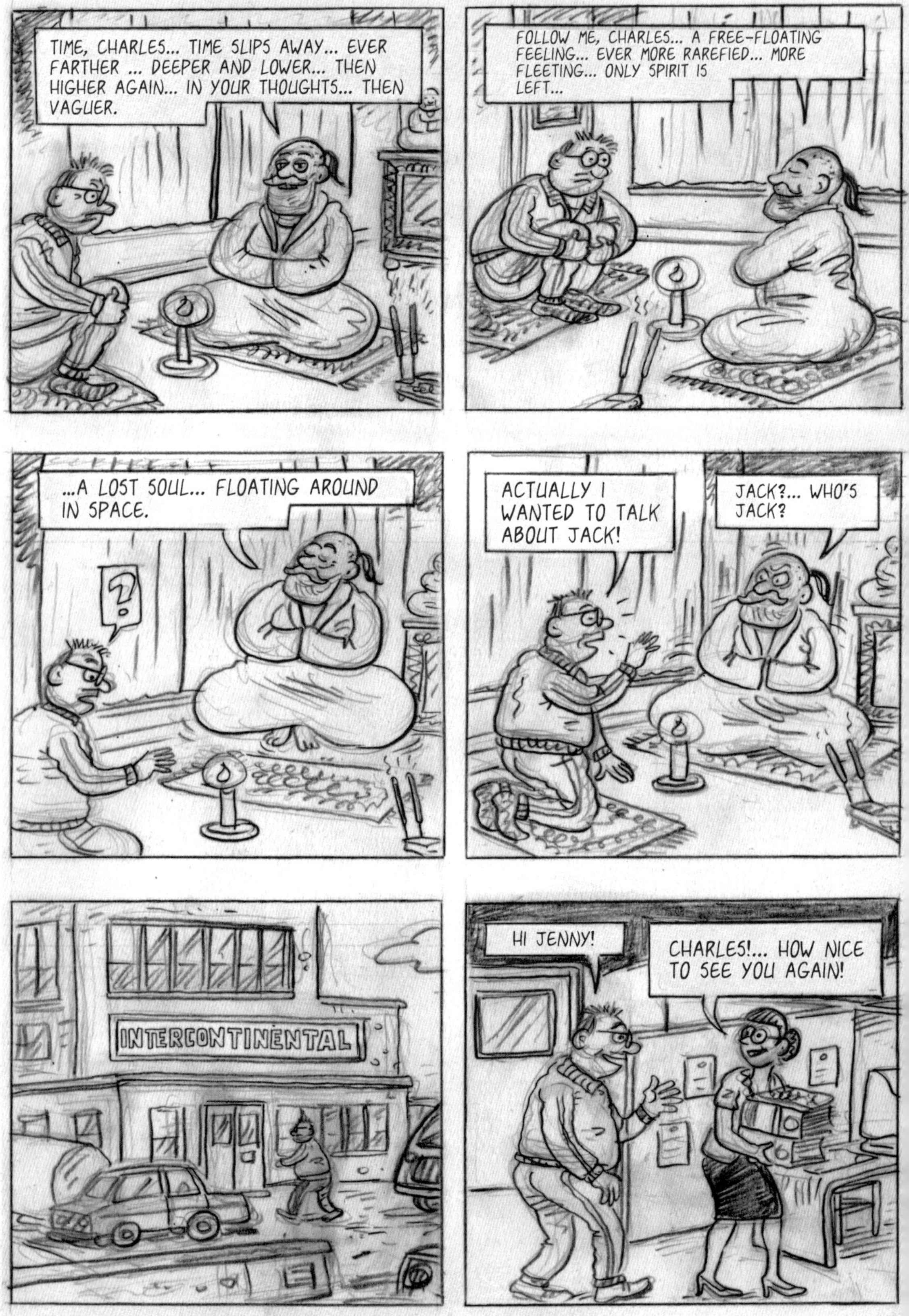
TIME, CHARLES... TIME SLIPS AWAY... EVER FARTHER ... DEEPER AND LOWER... THEN HIGHER AGAIN... IN YOUR THOUGHTS... THEN VAGUER.
FOLLOW ME, CHARLES... A FREE-FLOATING FEELING... EVER MORE RAREFIED... MORE FLEETING... ONLY SPIRIT IS LEFT...
...A LOST SOUL... FLOATING AROUND IN SPACE.
?
ACTUALLY I WANTED TO TALK ABOUT JACK!
JACK?... WHO'S JACK?
INTERCONTINENTAL
HI JENNY!
CHARLES!... HOW NICE TO SEE YOU AGAIN!

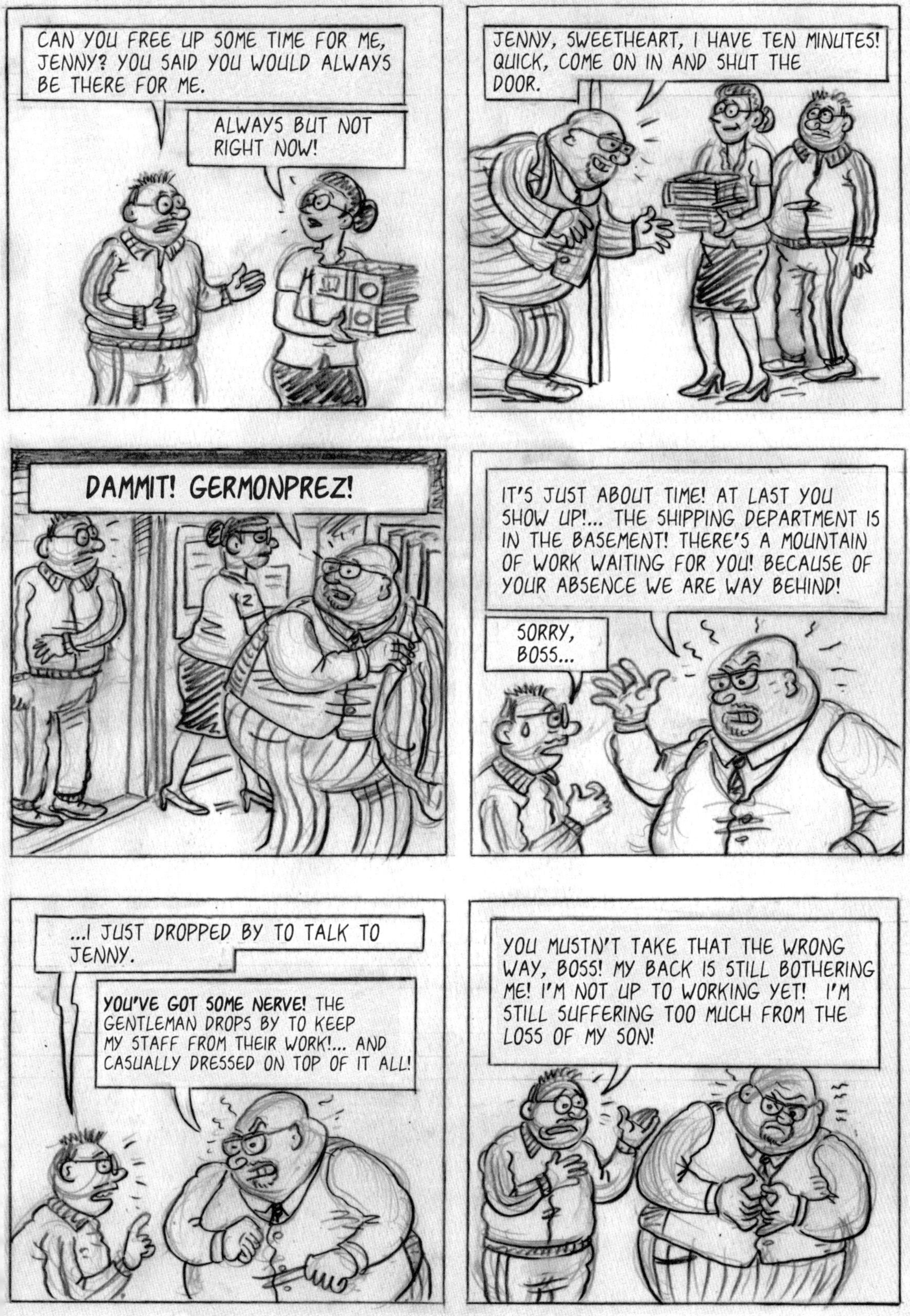
CAN YOU FREE UP SOME TIME FOR ME, JENNY? YOU SAID YOU WOULD ALWAYS BE THERE FOR ME.
ALWAYS BUT NOT RIGHT NOW!
JENNY, SWEETHEART, I HAVE TEN MINUTES! QUICK, COME ON IN AND SHUT THE DOOR.
DAMMIT! GERMONPREZ!
IT'S JUST ABOUT TIME! AT LAST YOU SHOW UP!... THE SHIPPING DEPARTMENT IS IN THE BASEMENT! THERE'S A MOUNTAIN OF WORK WAITING FOR YOU! BECAUSE OF YOUR ABSENCE WE ARE WAY BEHIND!
SORRY, BOSS...
...I JUST DROPPED BY TO TALK TO JENNY.
YOU'VE GOT SOME NERVE! THE GENTLEMAN DROPS BY TO KEEP MY STAFF FROM THEIR WORK!... AND CASUALLY DRESSED ON TOP OF IT ALL!
YOU MUSTN'T TAKE THAT THE WRONG WAY, BOSS! MY BACK IS STILL BOTHERING ME! I'M NOT UP TO WORKING YET! I'M STILL SUFFERING TOO MUCH FROM THE LOSS OF MY SON!

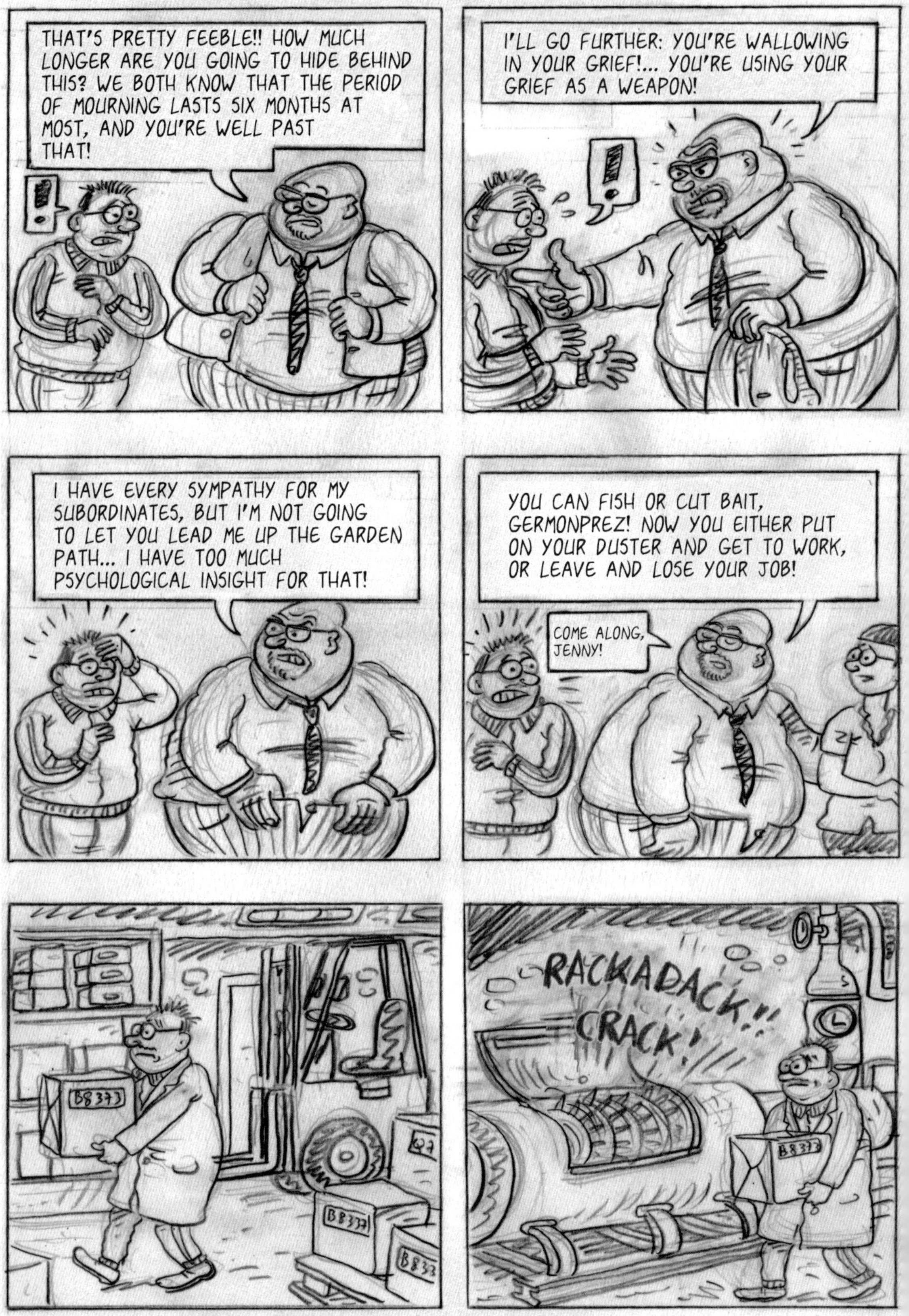
THAT'S PRETTY FEEBLE!! HOW MUCH LONGER ARE YOU GOING TO HIDE BEHIND THIS? WE BOTH KNOW THAT THE PERIOD OF MOURNING LASTS SIX MONTHS AT MOST, AND YOU'RE WELL PAST THAT!
!
I'LL GO FURTHER: YOU'RE WALLOWING IN YOUR GRIEF!... YOU'RE USING YOUR GRIEF AS A WEAPON!
!
I HAVE EVERY SYMPATHY FOR MY SUBORDINATES, BUT I'M NOT GOING TO LET YOU LEAD ME UP THE GARDEN PATH... I HAVE TOO MUCH PSYCHOLOGICAL INSIGHT FOR THAT!
YOU CAN FISH OR CUT BAIT, GERMONPREZ! NOW YOU EITHER PUT ON YOUR DUSTER AND GET TO WORK, OR LEAVE AND LOSE YOUR JOB!
COME ALONG, JENNY!
B8373
B8373
RACKADACK!!
CRACK!
B8373

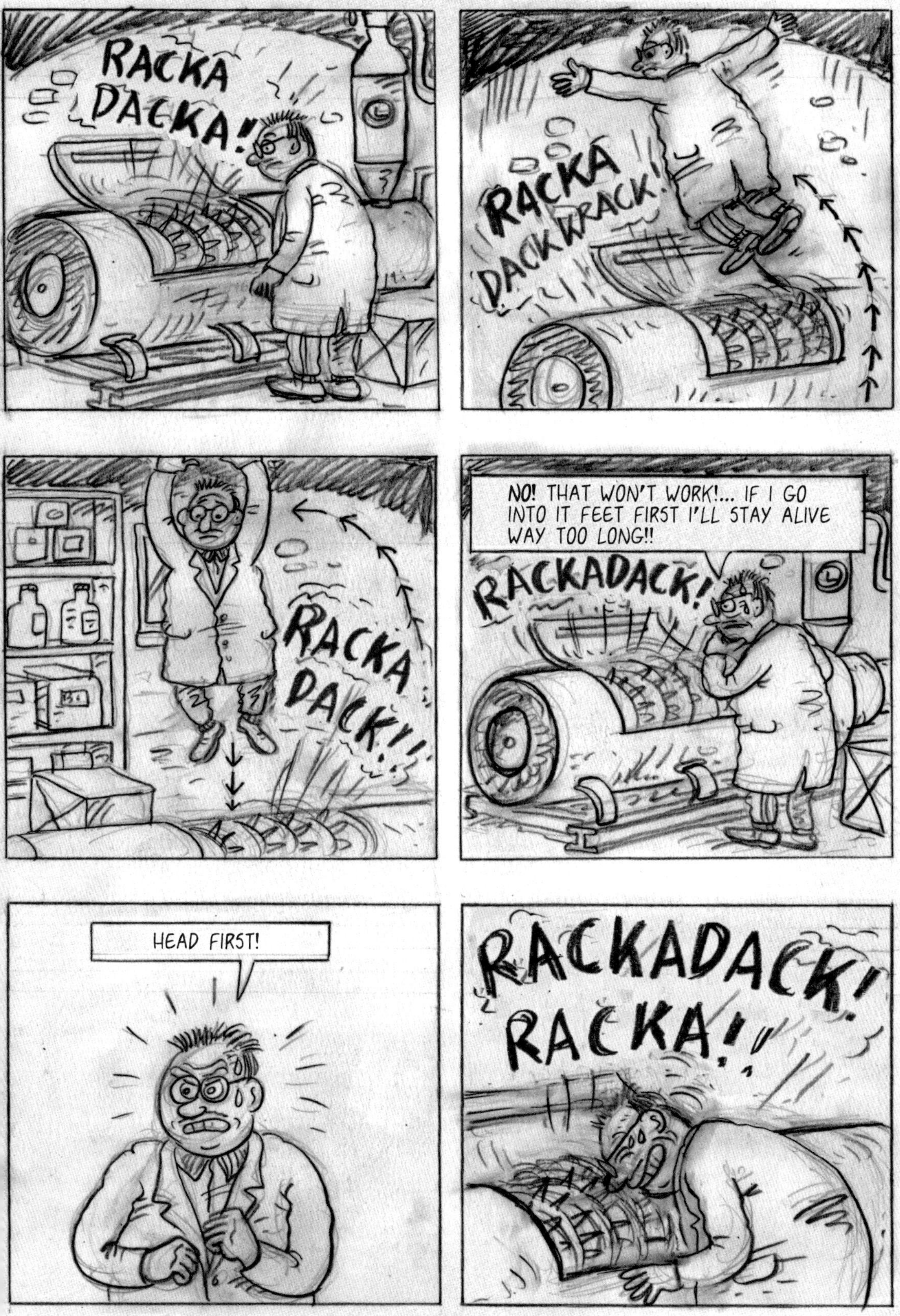
RACKA DACKA!
RACKA DACK WRACK!
RACKA DACK!!
NO! THAT WON'T WORK!... IF I GO INTO IT FEET FIRST I'LL STAY ALIVE WAY TOO LONG!!
RACKADACK!
HEAD FIRST!
RACKADACK!
RACKA!!

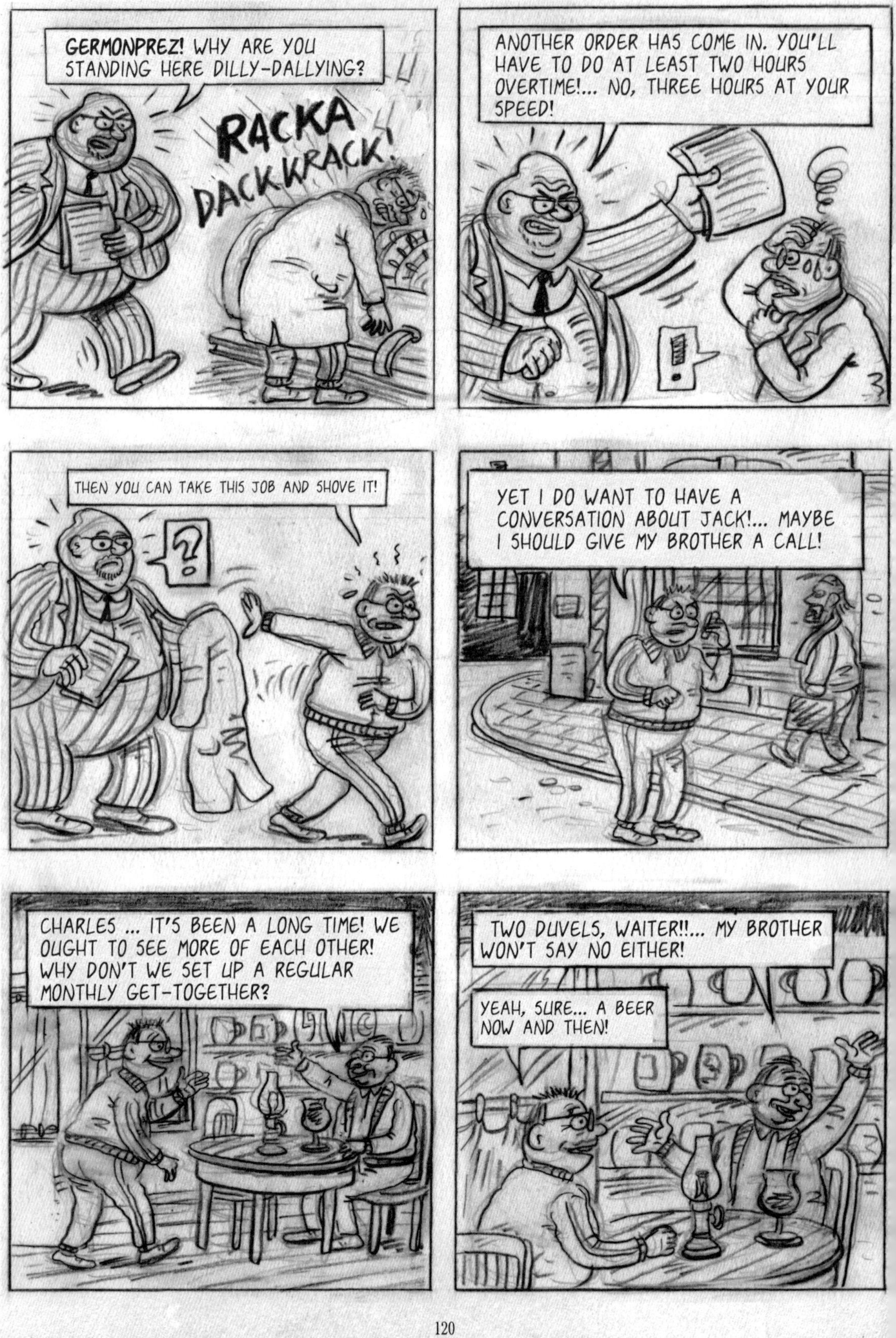
GERMONPREZ! WHY ARE YOU STANDING HERE DILLY-DALLYING?
RACKA DACKKRACK!
ANOTHER ORDER HAS COME IN. YOU'LL HAVE TO DO AT LEAST TWO HOURS OVERTIME!... NO, THREE HOURS AT YOUR SPEED!
!!!!
THEN YOU CAN TAKE THIS JOB AND SHOVE IT!
?
YET I DO WANT TO HAVE A CONVERSATION ABOUT JACK!... MAYBE I SHOULD GIVE MY BROTHER A CALL!
CHARLES ... IT'S BEEN A LONG TIME! WE OUGHT TO SEE MORE OF EACH OTHER! WHY DON'T WE SET UP A REGULAR MONTHLY GET-TOGETHER?
TWO DUVELS, WAITER!!... MY BROTHER WON'T SAY NO EITHER!
YEAH, SURE... A BEER NOW AND THEN!

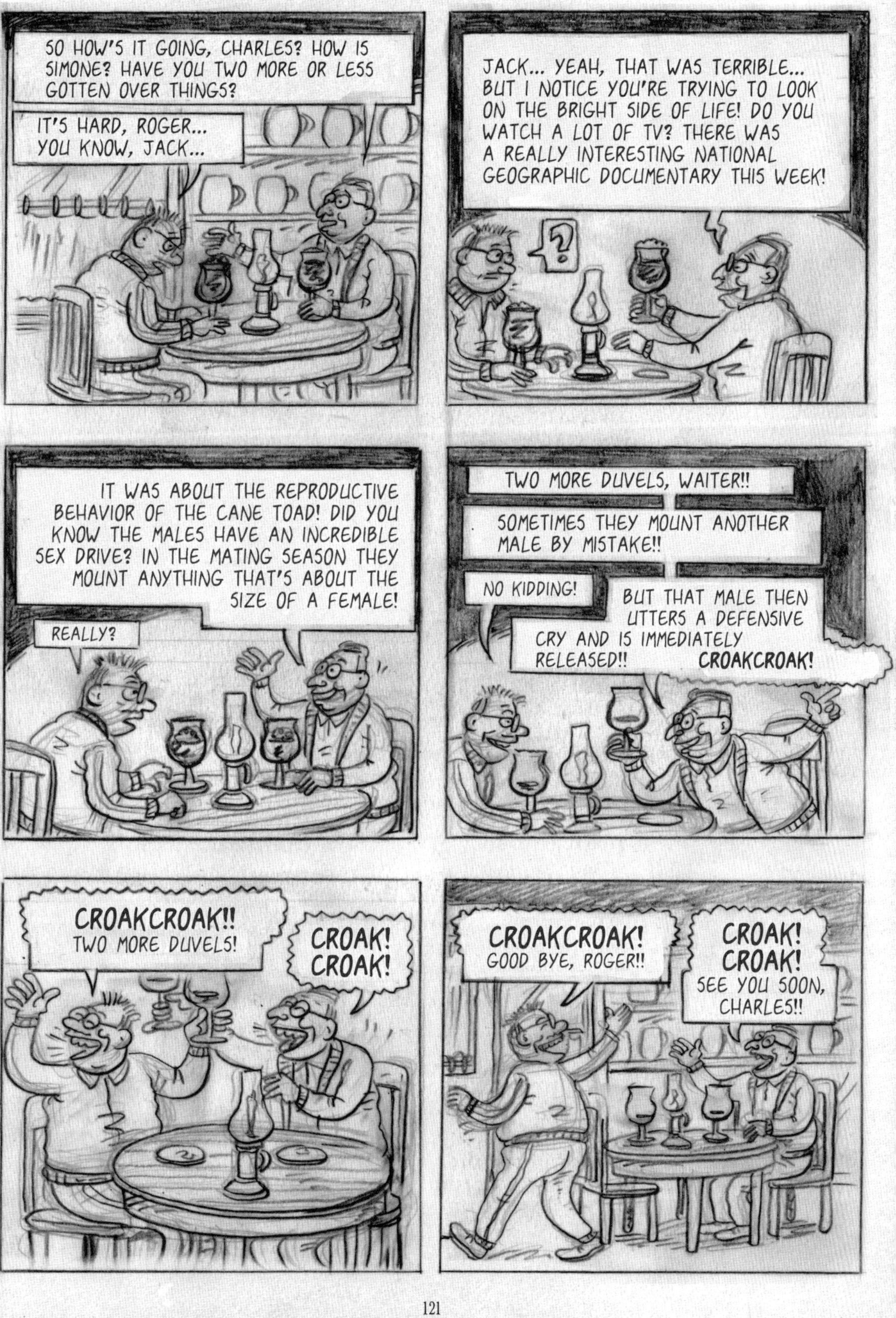

SO HOW'S IT GOING, CHARLES? HOW IS SIMONE? HAVE YOU TWO MORE OR LESS GOTTEN OVER THINGS?
IT'S HARD, ROGER... YOU KNOW, JACK...
JACK... YEAH, THAT WAS TERRIBLE... BUT I NOTICE YOU'RE TRYING TO LOOK ON THE BRIGHT SIDE OF LIFE! DO YOU WATCH A LOT OF TV? THERE WAS A REALLY INTERESTING NATIONAL GEOGRAPHIC DOCUMENTARY THIS WEEK!
?
IT WAS ABOUT THE REPRODUCTIVE BEHAVIOR OF THE CANE TOAD! DID YOU KNOW THE MALES HAVE AN INCREDIBLE SEX DRIVE? IN THE MATING SEASON THEY MOUNT ANYTHING THAT'S ABOUT THE SIZE OF A FEMALE!
REALLY?
TWO MORE DUVELS, WAITER!!
SOMETIMES THEY MOUNT ANOTHER MALE BY MISTAKE!!
NO KIDDING!
BUT THAT MALE THEN UTTERS A DEFENSIVE CRY AND IS IMMEDIATELY RELEASED!! CROAKCROAK!
CROAKCROAK!! TWO MORE DUVELS!
CROAK! CROAK!
CROAKCROAK! GOOD BYE, ROGER!!
CROAK! CROAK! SEE YOU SOON, CHARLES!!

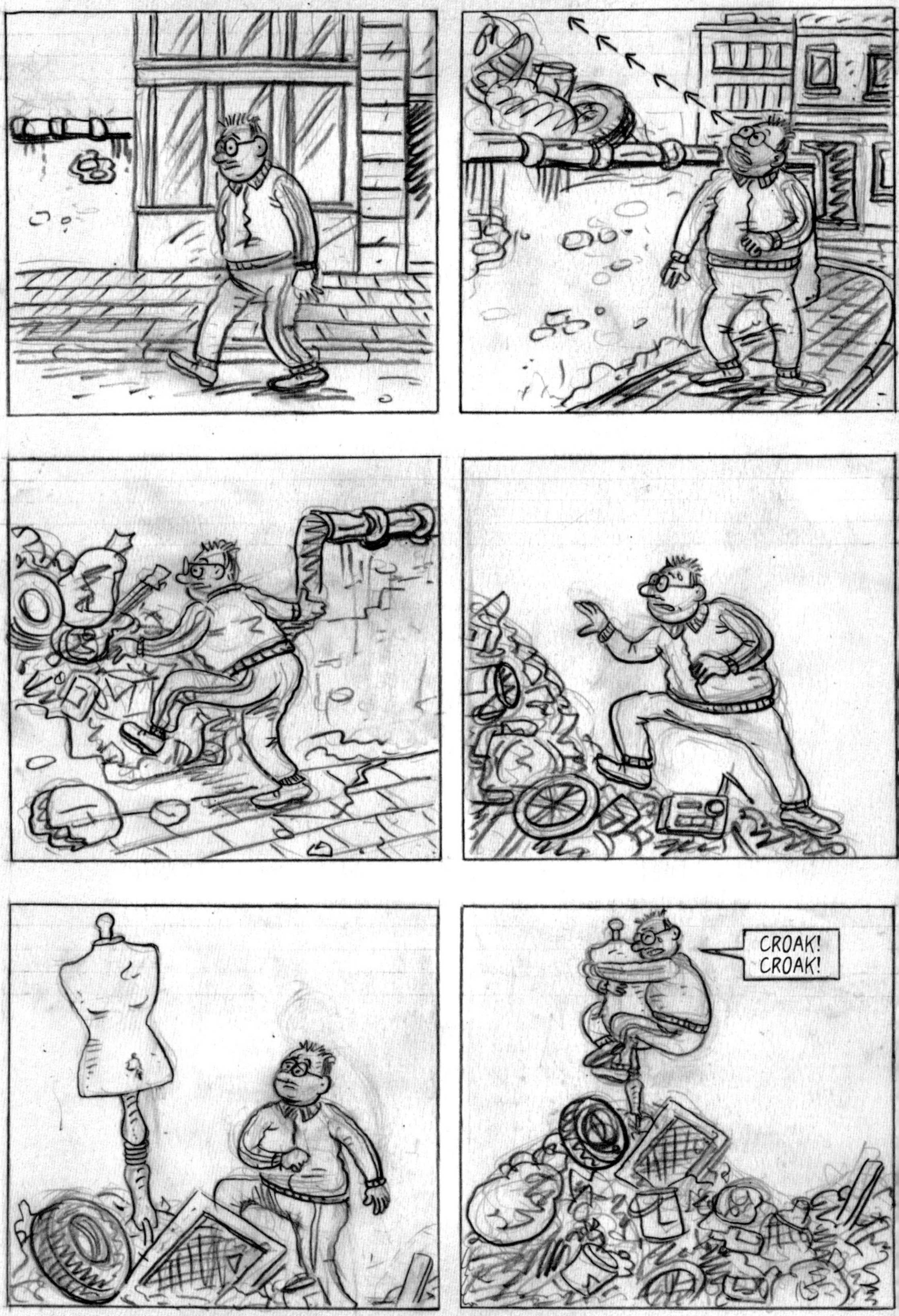
CROAK!
CROAK!

CHAPTER 7 - EUPHORIA

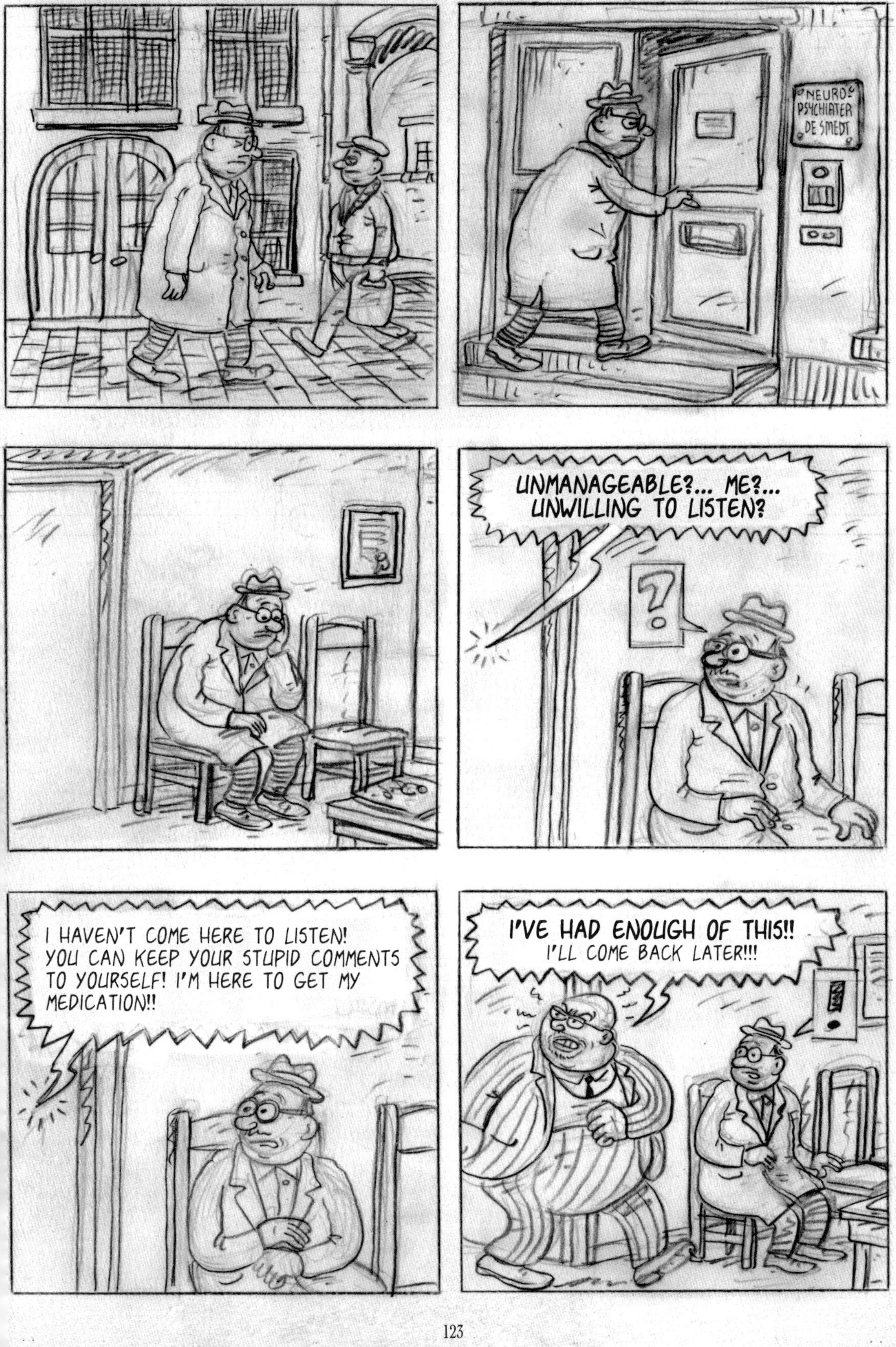
NEURO-PSYCHIATER DE SMEDT
UNMANAGEABLE?... ME?... UNWILLING TO LISTEN?
I HAVEN'T COME HERE TO LISTEN! YOU CAN KEEP YOUR STUPID COMMENTS TO YOURSELF! I'M HERE TO GET MY MEDICATION!!
I'VE HAD ENOUGH OF THIS!! I'LL COME BACK LATER!!!

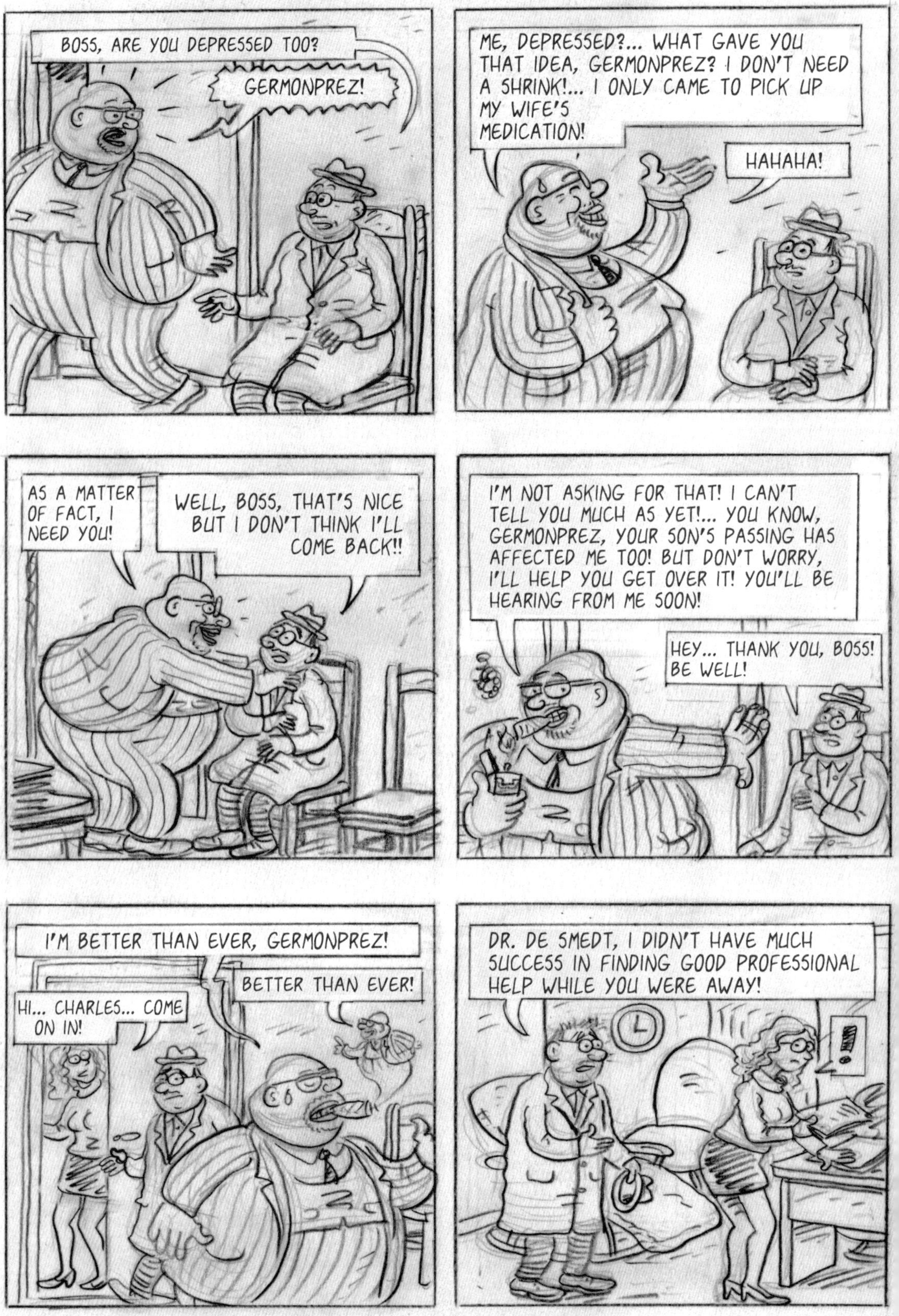
BOSS, ARE YOU DEPRESSED TOO?
GERMONPREZ!
ME, DEPRESSED?... WHAT GAVE YOU THAT IDEA, GERMONPREZ? I DON'T NEED A SHRINK!... I ONLY CAME TO PICK UP MY WIFE'S MEDICATION!
HAHAHA!
AS A MATTER OF FACT, I NEED YOU!
WELL, BOSS, THAT'S NICE BUT I DON'T THINK I'LL COME BACK!!
I'M NOT ASKING FOR THAT! I CAN'T TELL YOU MUCH AS YET!... YOU KNOW, GERMONPREZ, YOUR SON'S PASSING HAS AFFECTED ME TOO! BUT DON'T WORRY, I'LL HELP YOU GET OVER IT! YOU'LL BE HEARING FROM ME SOON!
HEY... THANK YOU, BOSS! BE WELL!
I'M BETTER THAN EVER, GERMONPREZ!
BETTER THAN EVER!
HI... CHARLES... COME ON IN!
DR. DE SMEDT, I DIDN'T HAVE MUCH SUCCESS IN FINDING GOOD PROFESSIONAL HELP WHILE YOU WERE AWAY!
!

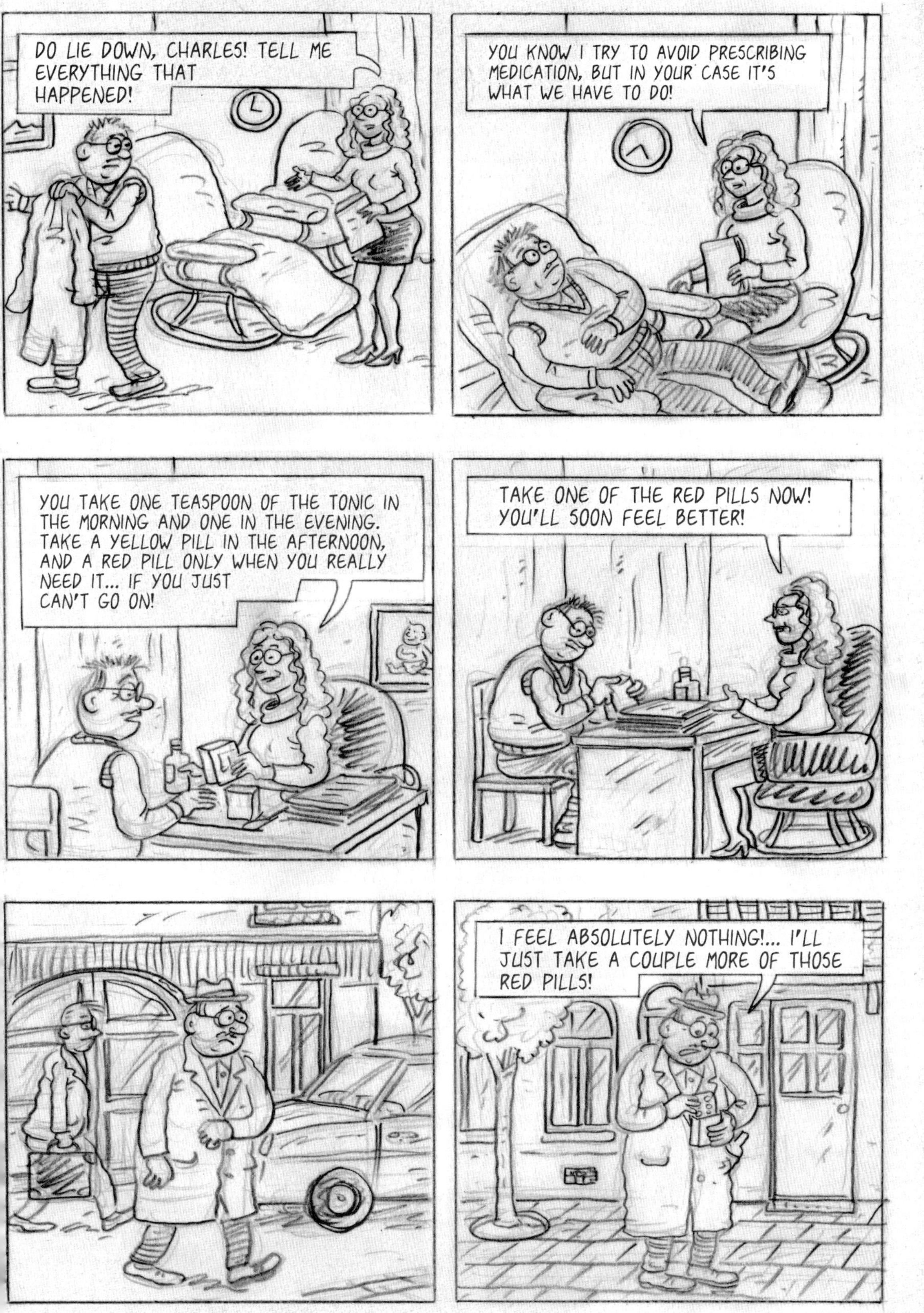
DO LIE DOWN, CHARLES! TELL ME EVERYTHING THAT HAPPENED!
YOU KNOW I TRY TO AVOID PRESCRIBING MEDICATION, BUT IN YOUR CASE IT'S WHAT WE HAVE TO DO!
YOU TAKE ONE TEASPOON OF THE TONIC IN THE MORNING AND ONE IN THE EVENING. TAKE A YELLOW PILL IN THE AFTERNOON, AND A RED PILL ONLY WHEN YOU REALLY NEED IT... IF YOU JUST CAN'T GO ON!
TAKE ONE OF THE RED PILLS NOW! YOU'LL SOON FEEL BETTER!
I FEEL ABSOLUTELY NOTHING!... I'LL JUST TAKE A COUPLE MORE OF THOSE RED PILLS!

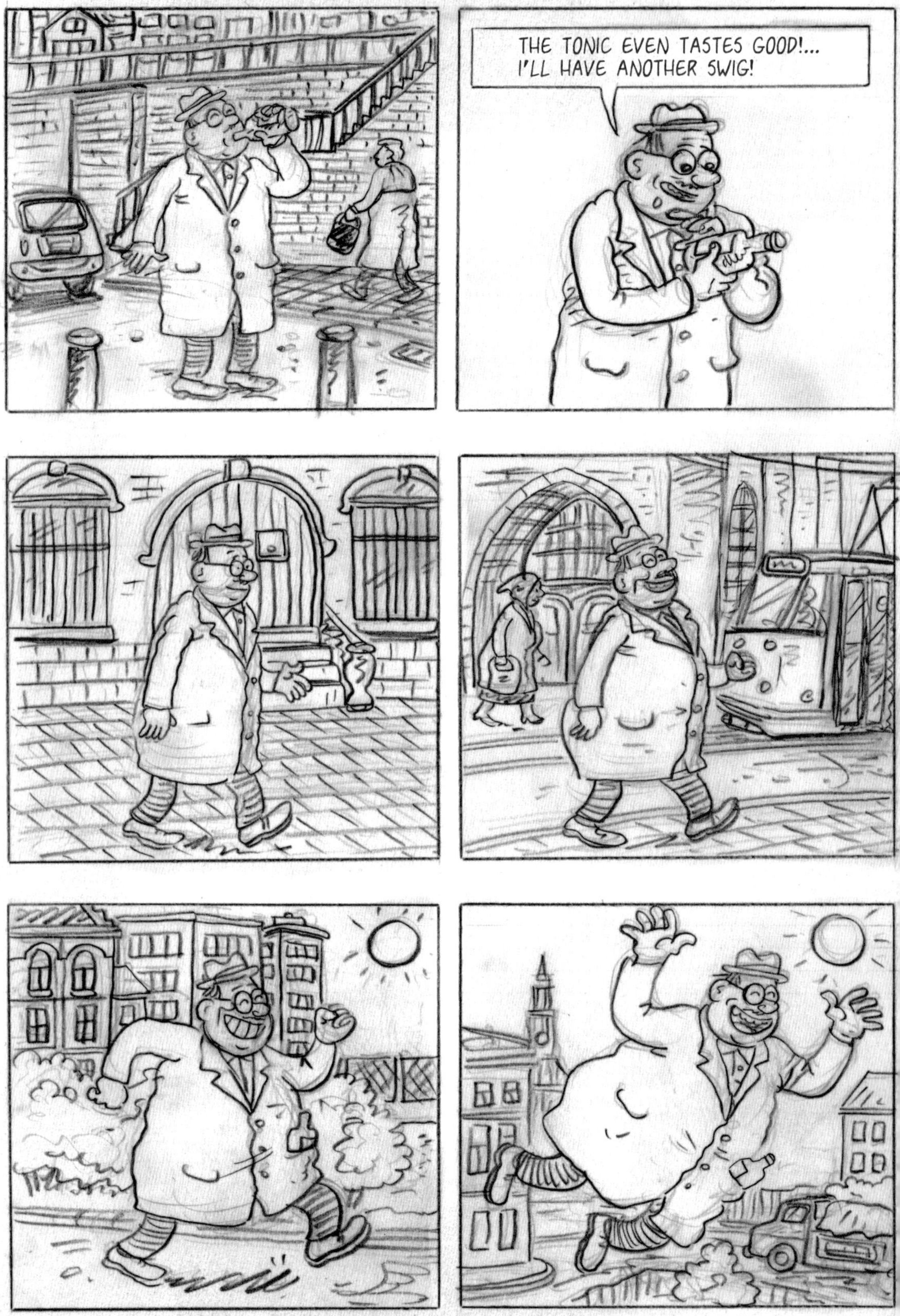
THE TONIC EVEN TASTES GOOD!... I'LL HAVE ANOTHER SWIG!

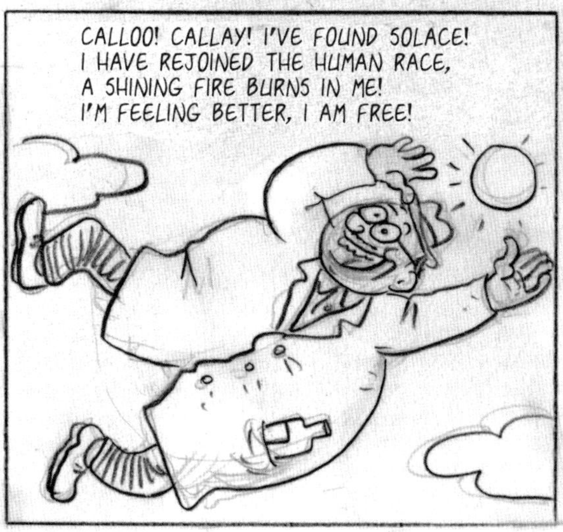
CALLOO! CALLAY! I'VE FOUND SOLACE!
I HAVE REJOINED THE HUMAN RACE,
A SHINING FIRE BURNS IN ME!
I'M FEELING BETTER, I AM FREE!

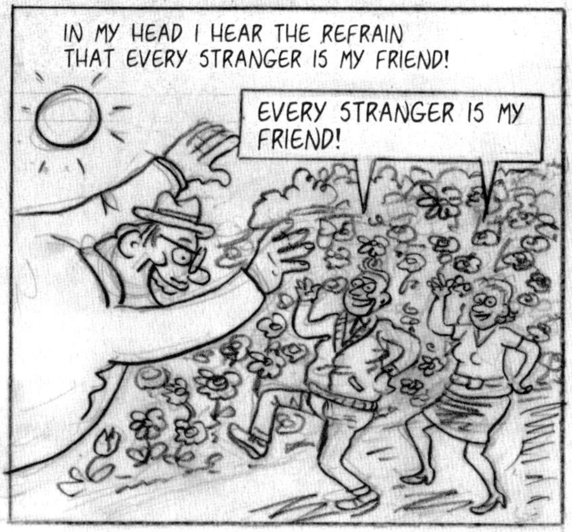
IN MY HEAD I HEAR THE REFRAIN
THAT EVERY STRANGER IS MY FRIEND!
EVERY STRANGER IS MY FRIEND!

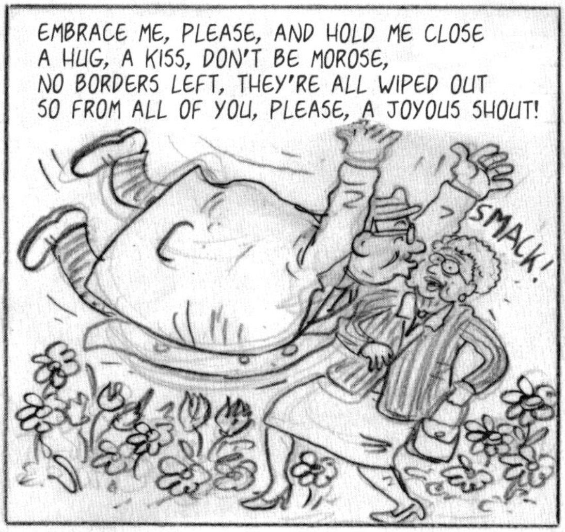
EMBRACE ME, PLEASE, AND HOLD ME CLOSE
A HUG, A KISS, DON'T BE MOROSE,
NO BORDERS LEFT, THEY'RE ALL WIPED OUT
SO FROM ALL OF YOU, PLEASE, A JOYOUS SHOUT!
SMACK!

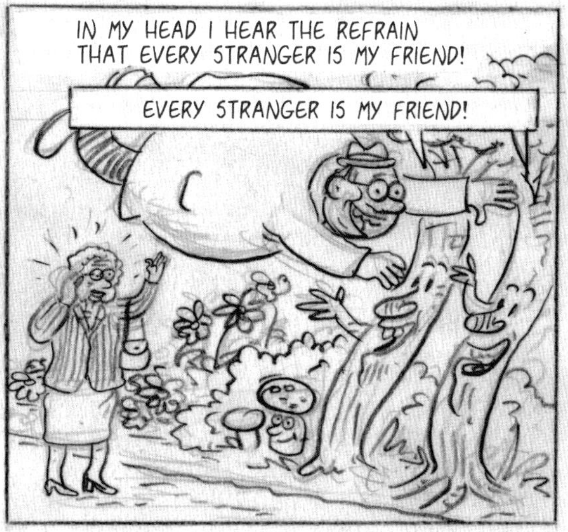
IN MY HEAD I HEAR THE REFRAIN
THAT EVERY STRANGER IS MY FRIEND!
EVERY STRANGER IS MY FRIEND!

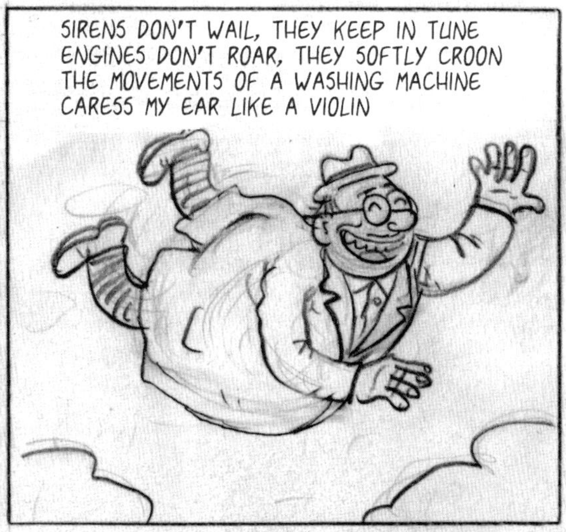
SIRENS DON'T WAIL, THEY KEEP IN TUNE
ENGINES DON'T ROAR, THEY SOFTLY CROON
THE MOVEMENTS OF A WASHING MACHINE
CARESS MY EAR LIKE A VIOLIN

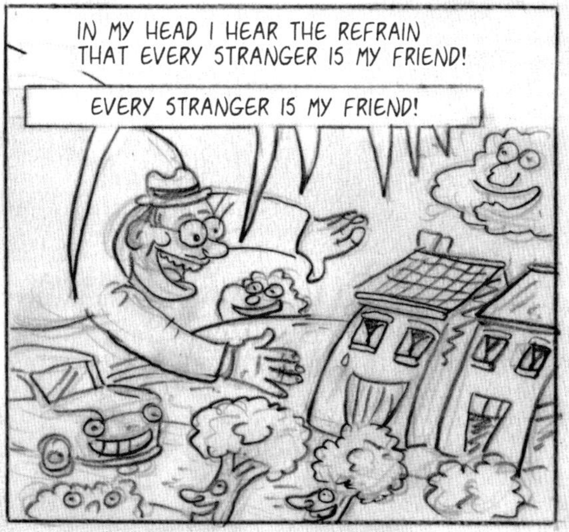
IN MY HEAD I HEAR THE REFRAIN
THAT EVERY STRANGER IS MY FRIEND!
EVERY STRANGER IS MY FRIEND!

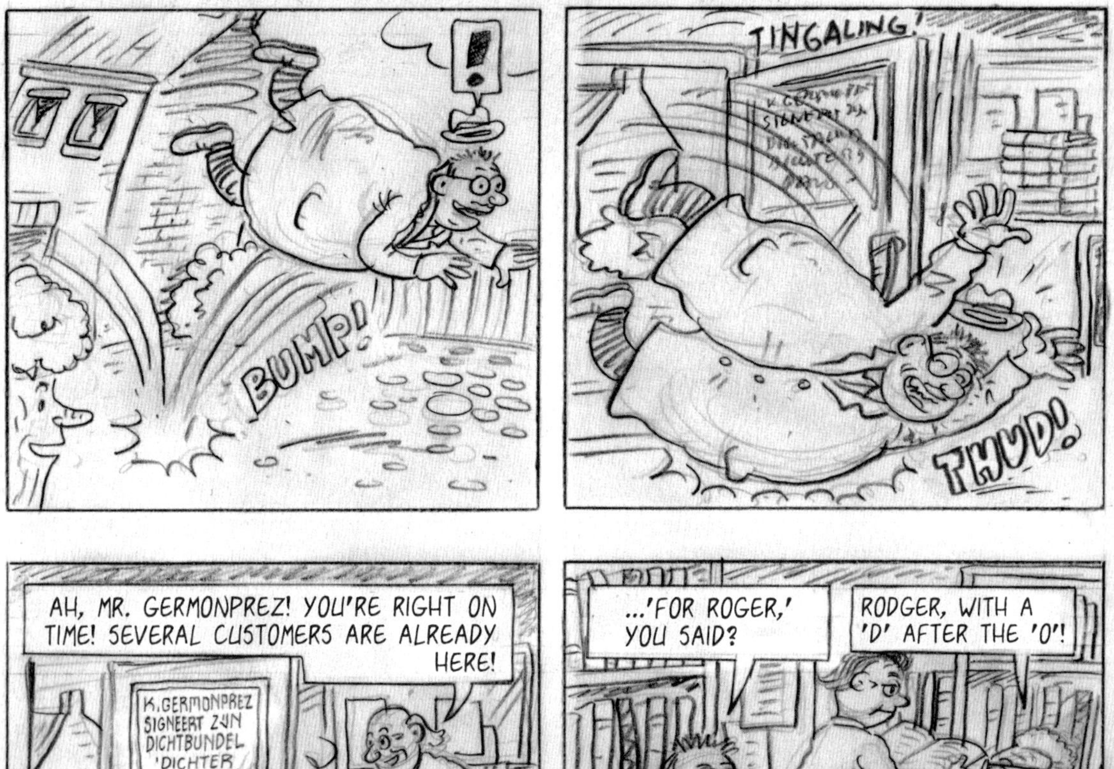
!
BUMP!
TINGALING!
THUD!
AH, MR. GERMONPREZ! YOU'RE RIGHT ON TIME! SEVERAL CUSTOMERS ARE ALREADY HERE!
K. GERMONPREZ SIGNEERT ZIJN DICHTBUNDEL 'DICHTER BIJ DANS'
...'FOR ROGER,' YOU SAID?
RODGER, WITH A 'D' AFTER THE 'O'!

*GERMONPREZ WILL SIGN HIS COLLECTION OF POEMS 'NEARER THE DANCE'

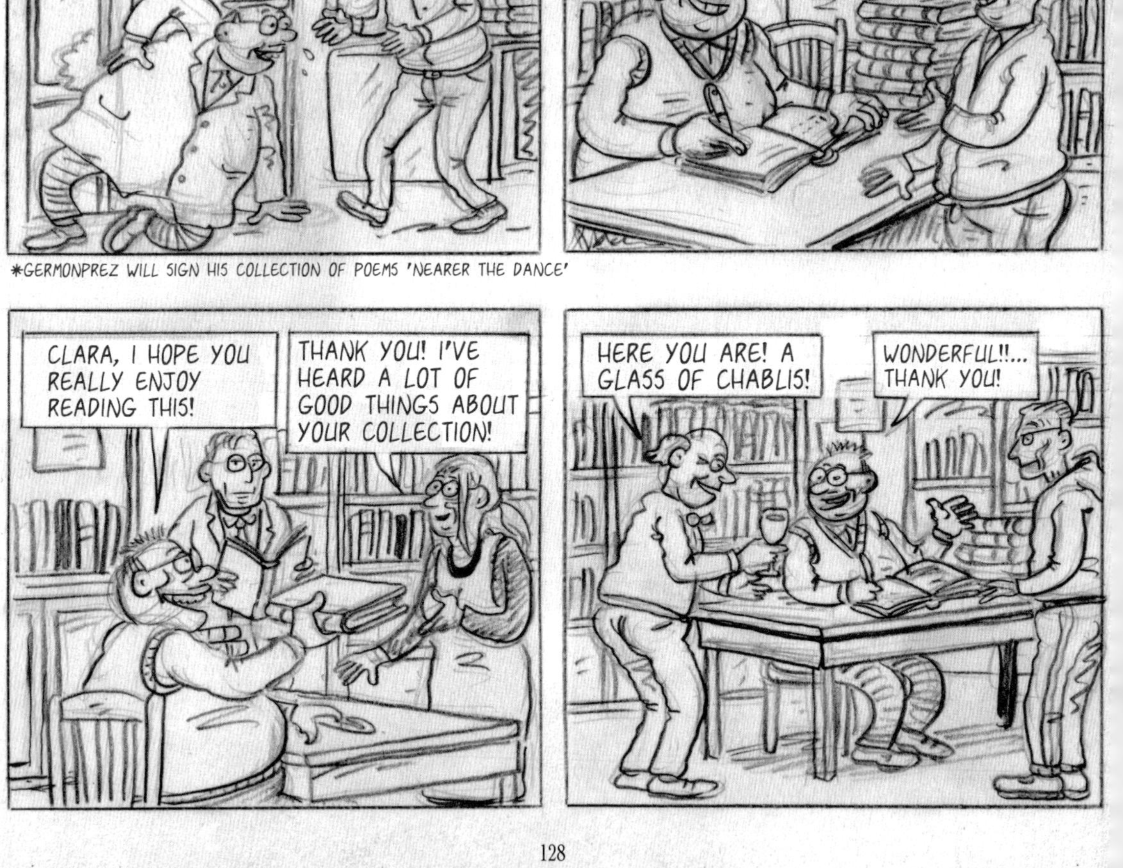
CLARA, I HOPE YOU REALLY ENJOY READING THIS!
THANK YOU! I'VE HEARD A LOT OF GOOD THINGS ABOUT YOUR COLLECTION!
HERE YOU ARE! A GLASS OF CHABLIS!
WONDERFUL!!... THANK YOU!

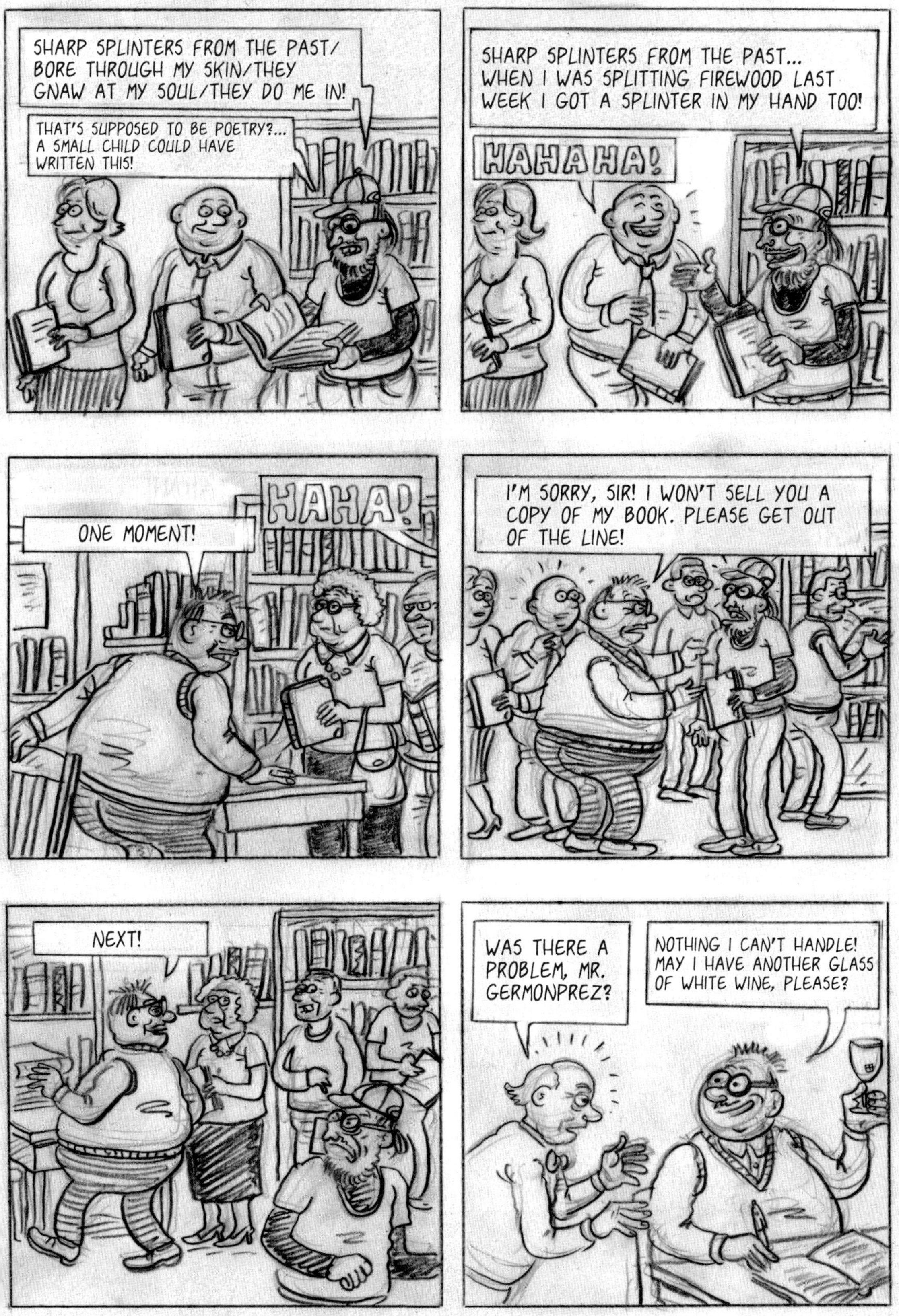
SHARP SPLINTERS FROM THE PAST/ BORE THROUGH MY SKIN/THEY GNAW AT MY SOUL/THEY DO ME IN!
THAT'S SUPPOSED TO BE POETRY?... A SMALL CHILD COULD HAVE WRITTEN THIS!
SHARP SPLINTERS FROM THE PAST... WHEN I WAS SPLITTING FIREWOOD LAST WEEK I GOT A SPLINTER IN MY HAND TOO!
HAHAHA!
HAHA!
ONE MOMENT!
I'M SORRY, SIR! I WON'T SELL YOU A COPY OF MY BOOK. PLEASE GET OUT OF THE LINE!
NEXT!
WAS THERE A PROBLEM, MR. GERMONPREZ?
NOTHING I CAN'T HANDLE! MAY I HAVE ANOTHER GLASS OF WHITE WINE, PLEASE?

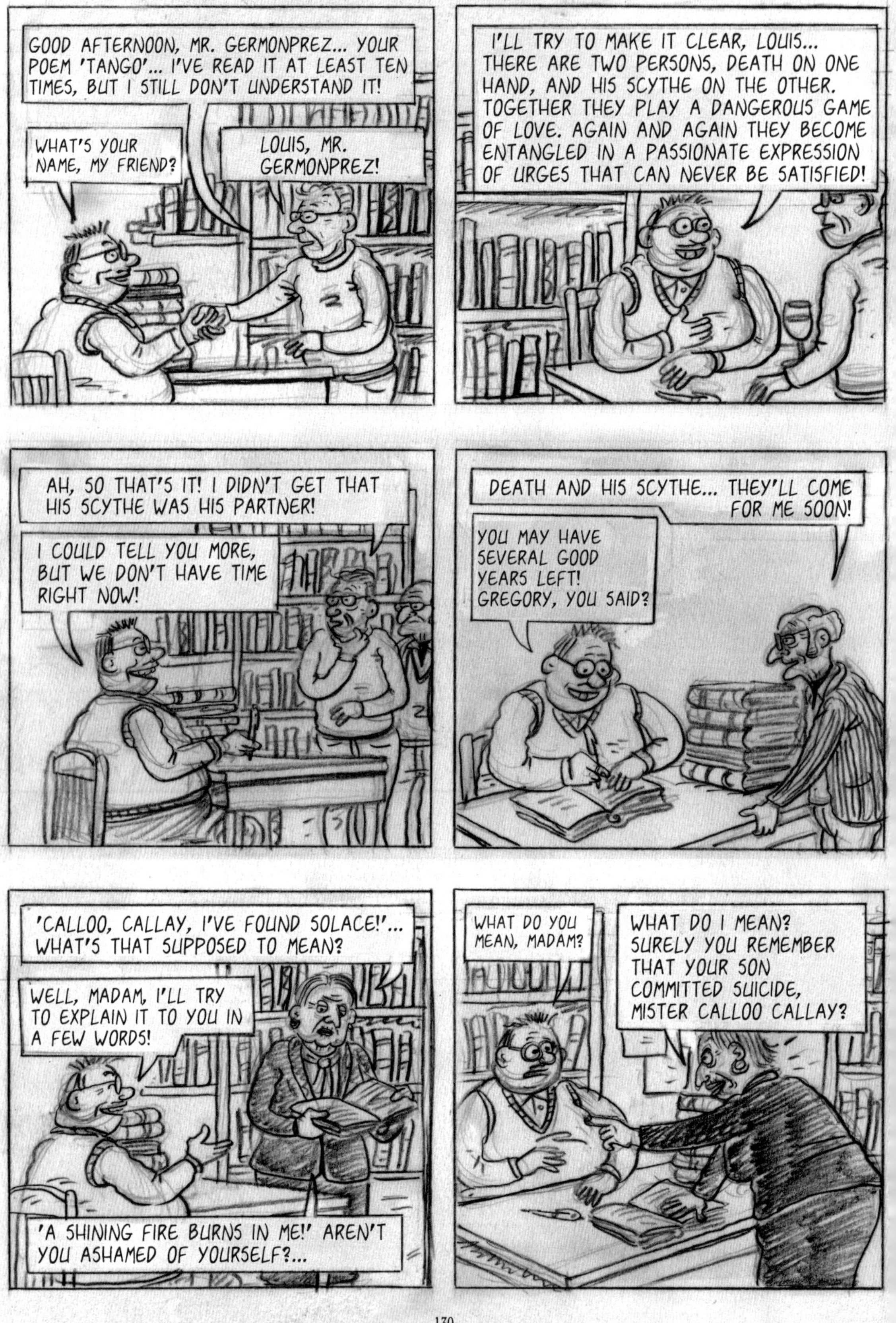
GOOD AFTERNOON, MR. GERMONPREZ... YOUR POEM 'TANGO'... I'VE READ IT AT LEAST TEN TIMES, BUT I STILL DON'T UNDERSTAND IT!
WHAT'S YOUR NAME, MY FRIEND?
LOUIS, MR. GERMONPREZ!
I'LL TRY TO MAKE IT CLEAR, LOUIS... THERE ARE TWO PERSONS, DEATH ON ONE HAND, AND HIS SCYTHE ON THE OTHER. TOGETHER THEY PLAY A DANGEROUS GAME OF LOVE. AGAIN AND AGAIN THEY BECOME ENTANGLED IN A PASSIONATE EXPRESSION OF URGES THAT CAN NEVER BE SATISFIED!
AH, SO THAT'S IT! I DIDN'T GET THAT HIS SCYTHE WAS HIS PARTNER!
I COULD TELL YOU MORE, BUT WE DON'T HAVE TIME RIGHT NOW!
DEATH AND HIS SCYTHE... THEY'LL COME FOR ME SOON!
YOU MAY HAVE SEVERAL GOOD YEARS LEFT! GREGORY, YOU SAID?
'CALLOO, CALLAY, I'VE FOUND SOLACE!'... WHAT'S THAT SUPPOSED TO MEAN?
WELL, MADAM, I'LL TRY TO EXPLAIN IT TO YOU IN A FEW WORDS!
'A SHINING FIRE BURNS IN ME!' AREN'T YOU ASHAMED OF YOURSELF?...
WHAT DO YOU MEAN, MADAM?
WHAT DO I MEAN? SURELY YOU REMEMBER THAT YOUR SON COMMITTED SUICIDE, MISTER CALLOO CALLAY?

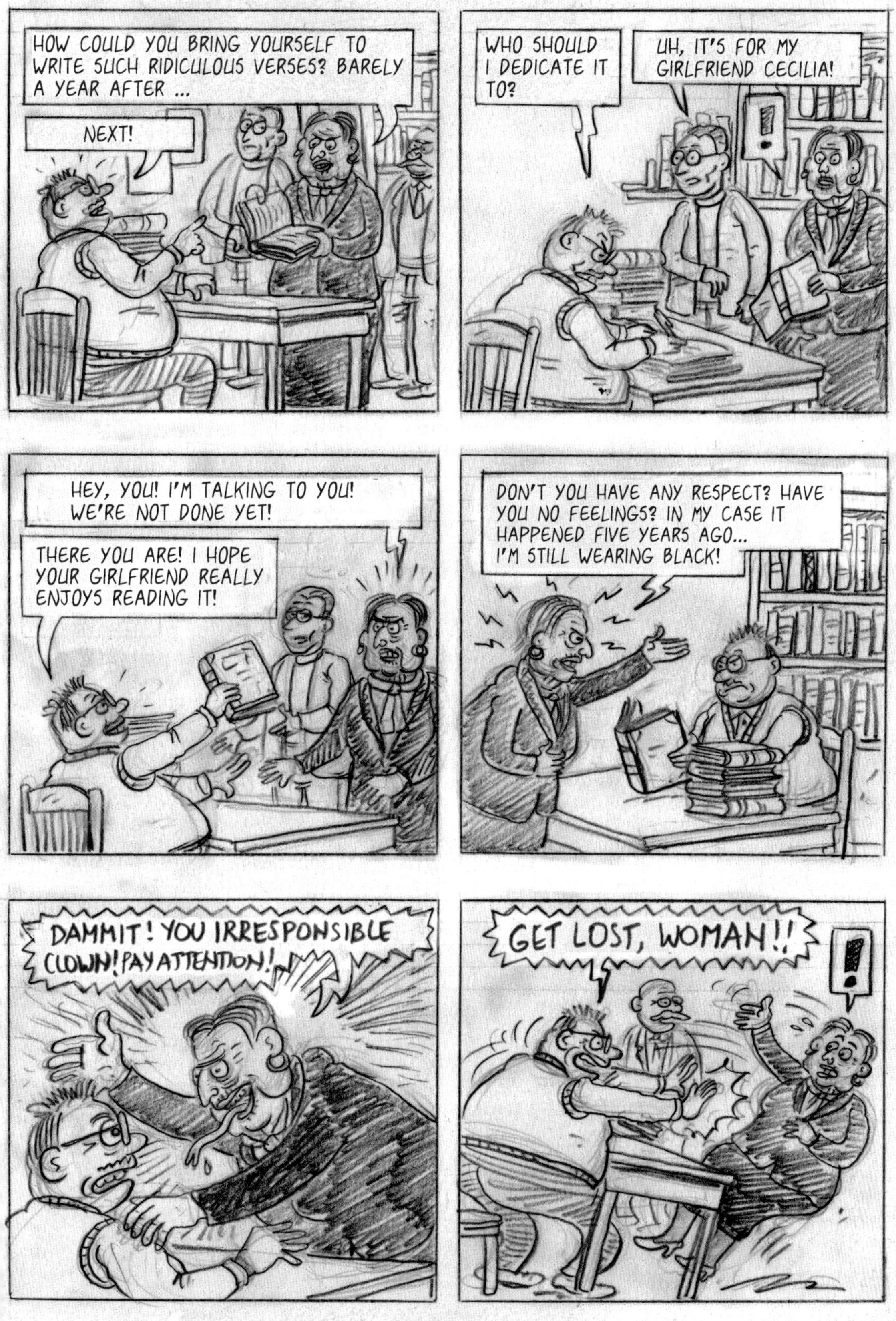
HOW COULD YOU BRING YOURSELF TO WRITE SUCH RIDICULOUS VERSES? BARELY A YEAR AFTER ...
NEXT!
WHO SHOULD I DEDICATE IT TO?
UH, IT'S FOR MY GIRLFRIEND CECILIA!
!
HEY, YOU! I'M TALKING TO YOU! WE'RE NOT DONE YET!
THERE YOU ARE! I HOPE YOUR GIRLFRIEND REALLY ENJOYS READING IT!
DON'T YOU HAVE ANY RESPECT? HAVE YOU NO FEELINGS? IN MY CASE IT HAPPENED FIVE YEARS AGO... I'M STILL WEARING BLACK!
DAMMIT! YOU IRRESPONSIBLE CLOWN! PAY ATTENTION!
GET LOST, WOMAN!!
!

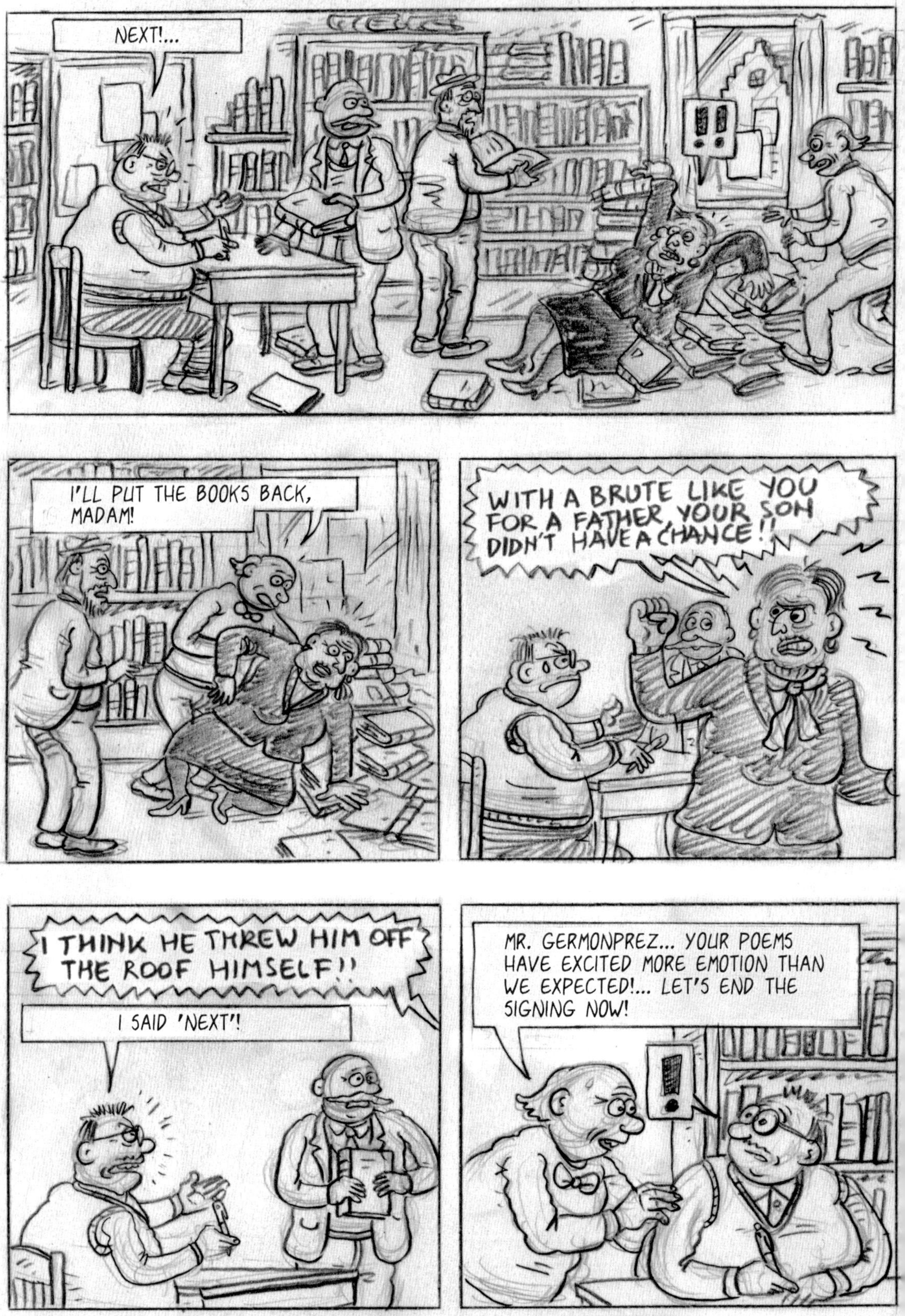
NEXT!...
I'LL PUT THE BOOKS BACK, MADAM!
WITH A BRUTE LIKE YOU FOR A FATHER, YOUR SON DIDN'T HAVE A CHANCE!!
I THINK HE THREW HIM OFF THE ROOF HIMSELF!!
I SAID 'NEXT'!
MR. GERMONPREZ... YOUR POEMS HAVE EXCITED MORE EMOTION THAN WE EXPECTED!... LET'S END THE SIGNING NOW!

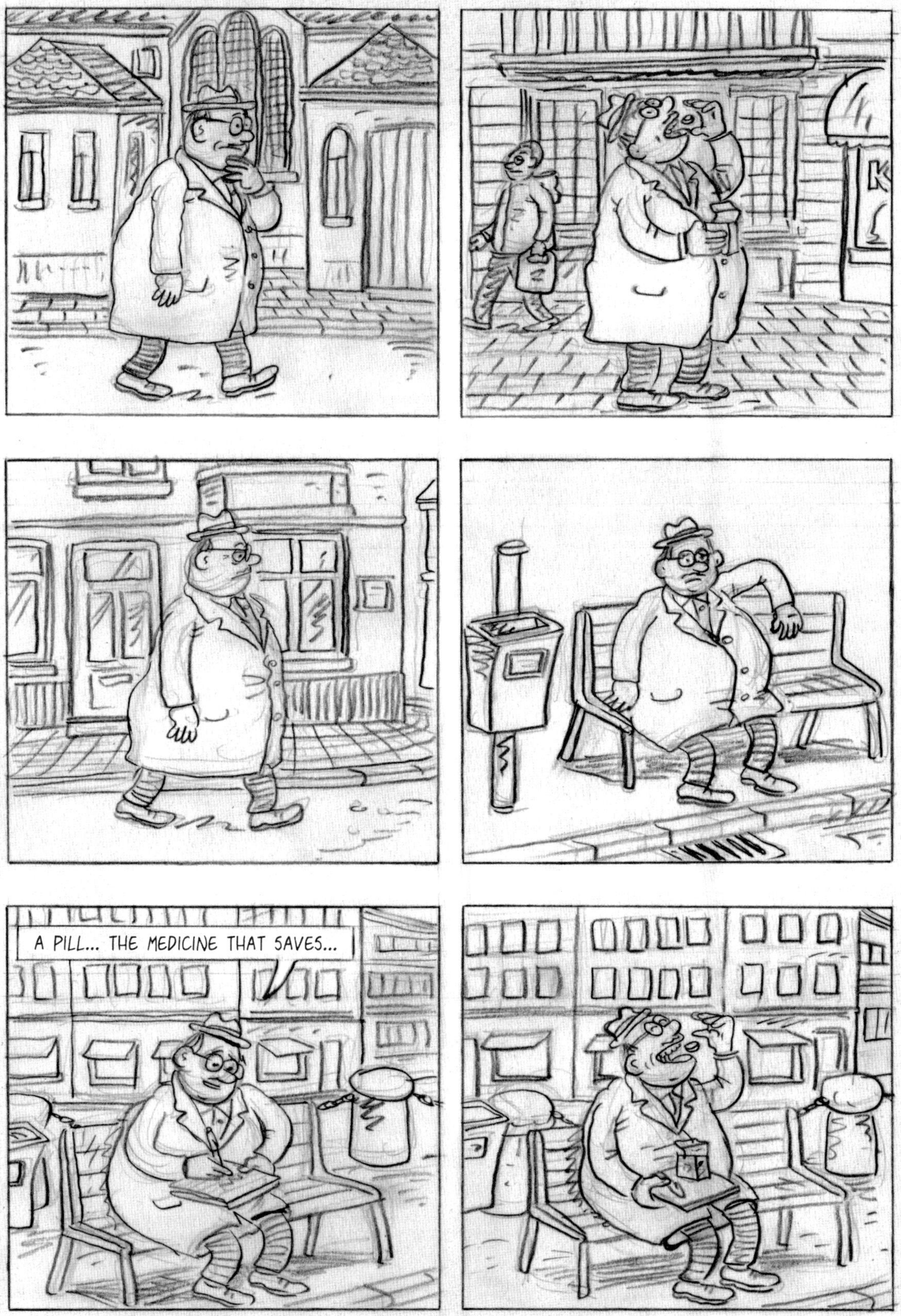
A PILL... THE MEDICINE THAT SAVES...

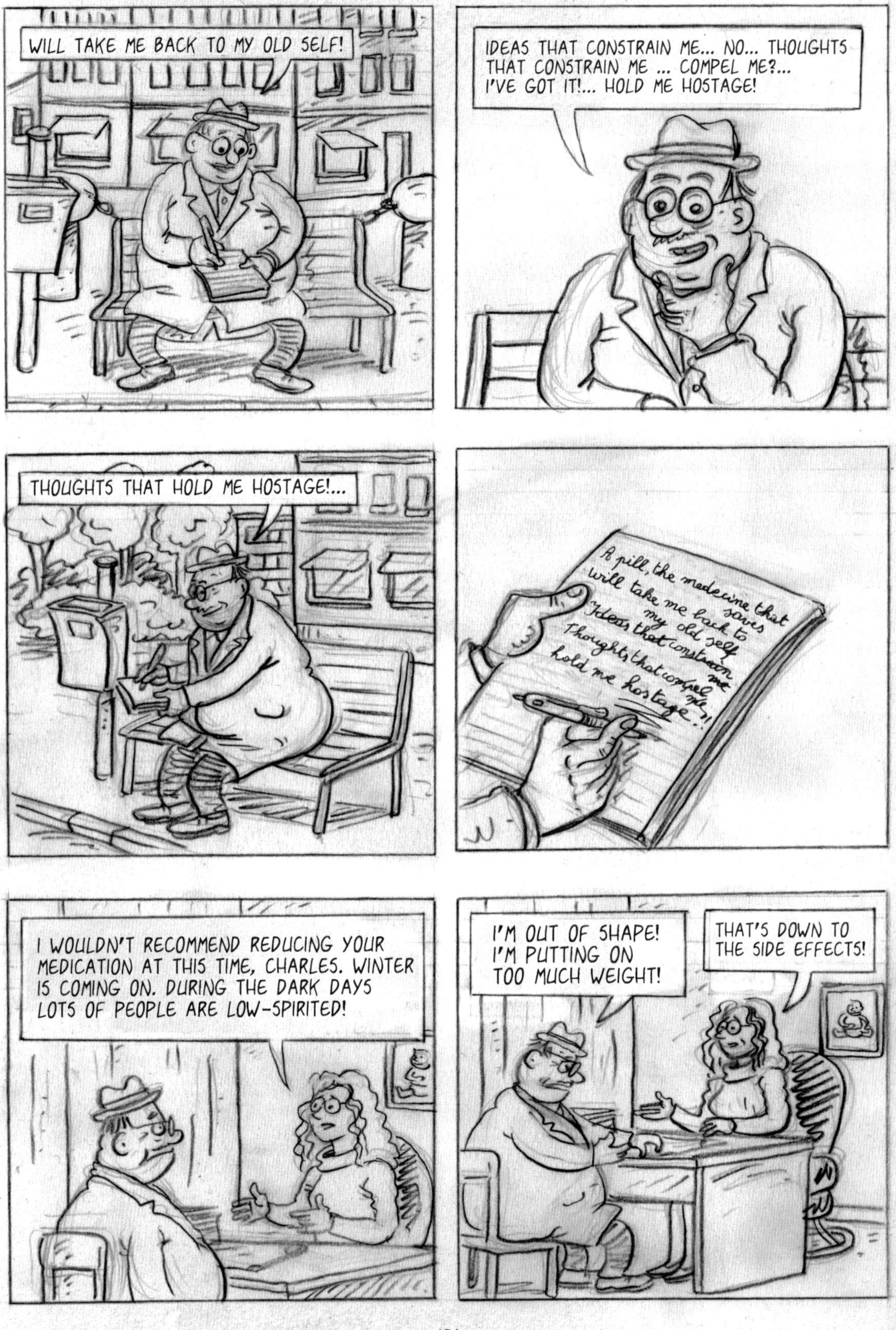
WILL TAKE ME BACK TO MY OLD SELF!
IDEAS THAT CONSTRAIN ME... NO... THOUGHTS THAT CONSTRAIN ME ... COMPEL ME?... I'VE GOT IT!... HOLD ME HOSTAGE!
THOUGHTS THAT HOLD ME HOSTAGE!...
A pill, the medecine that saves
will take me back to my old self
Ideas that constrain me
Thoughts that compel me
hold me hostage!!
I WOULDN'T RECOMMEND REDUCING YOUR MEDICATION AT THIS TIME, CHARLES. WINTER IS COMING ON. DURING THE DARK DAYS LOTS OF PEOPLE ARE LOW-SPIRITED!
I'M OUT OF SHAPE! I'M PUTTING ON TOO MUCH WEIGHT!
THAT'S DOWN TO THE SIDE EFFECTS!

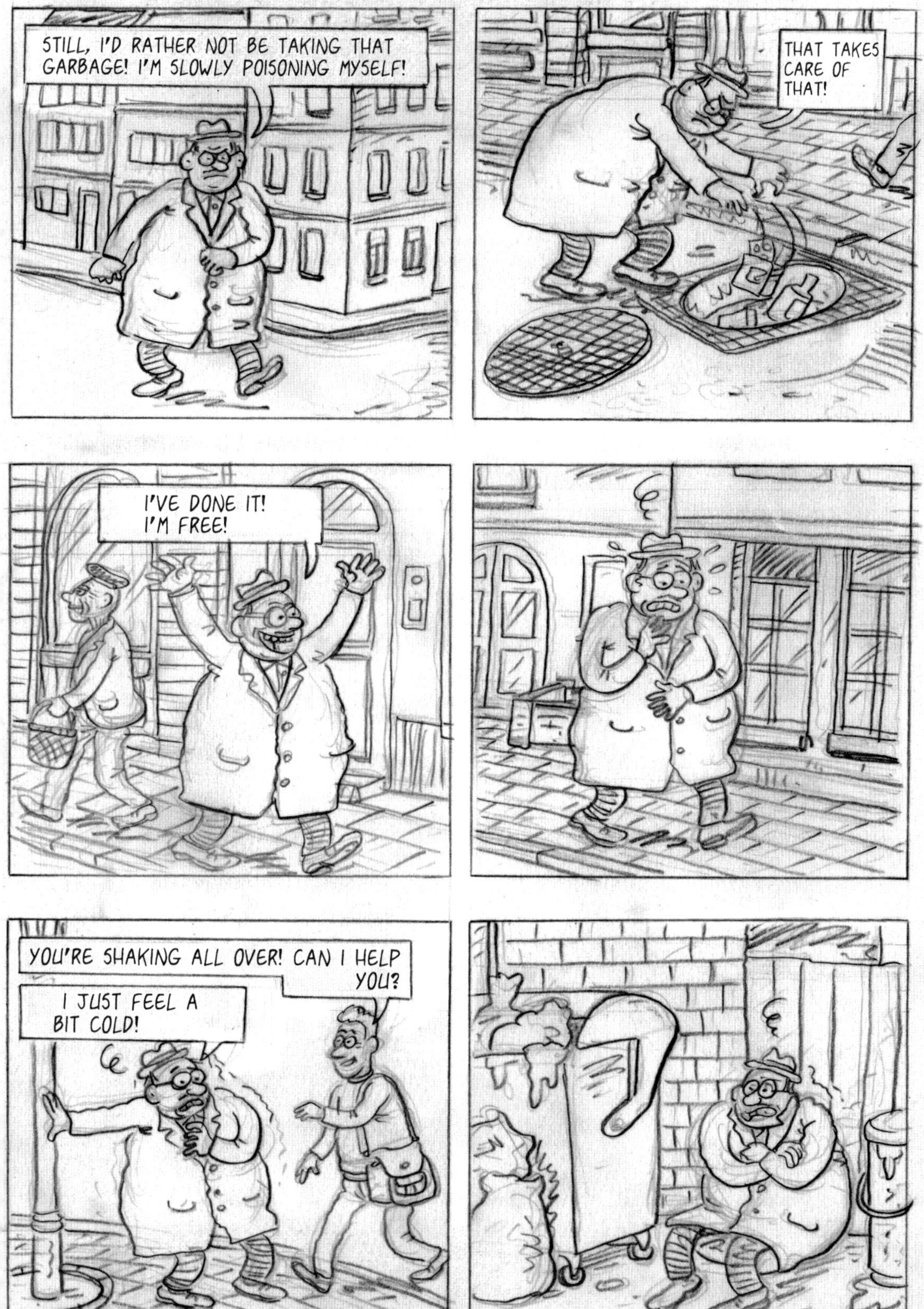
STILL, I'D RATHER NOT BE TAKING THAT GARBAGE! I'M SLOWLY POISONING MYSELF!
THAT TAKES CARE OF THAT!
I'VE DONE IT! I'M FREE!
YOU'RE SHAKING ALL OVER! CAN I HELP YOU?
I JUST FEEL A BIT COLD!

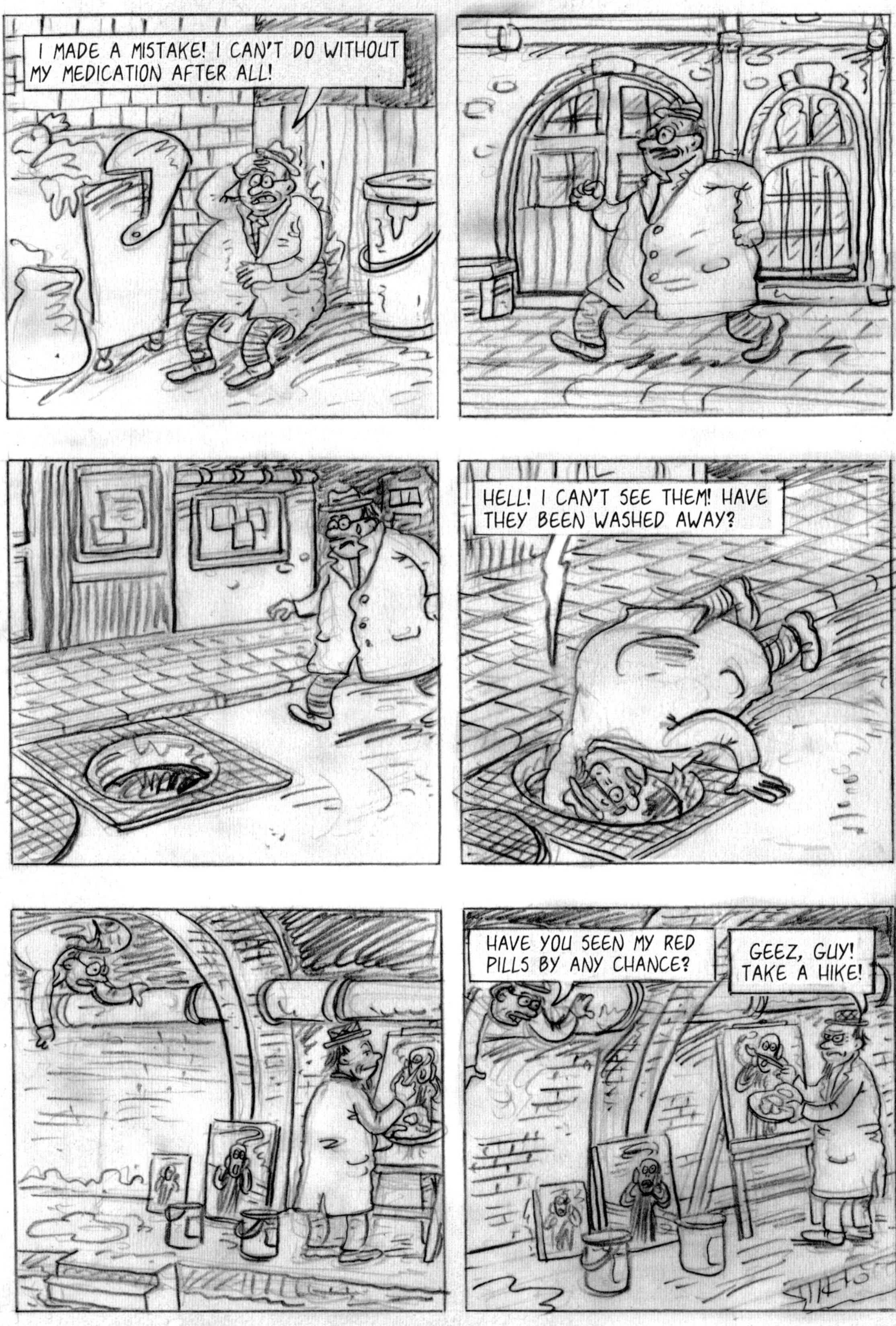
I MADE A MISTAKE! I CAN'T DO WITHOUT MY MEDICATION AFTER ALL!
HELL! I CAN'T SEE THEM! HAVE THEY BEEN WASHED AWAY?
HAVE YOU SEEN MY RED PILLS BY ANY CHANCE?
GEEZ, GUY! TAKE A HIKE!

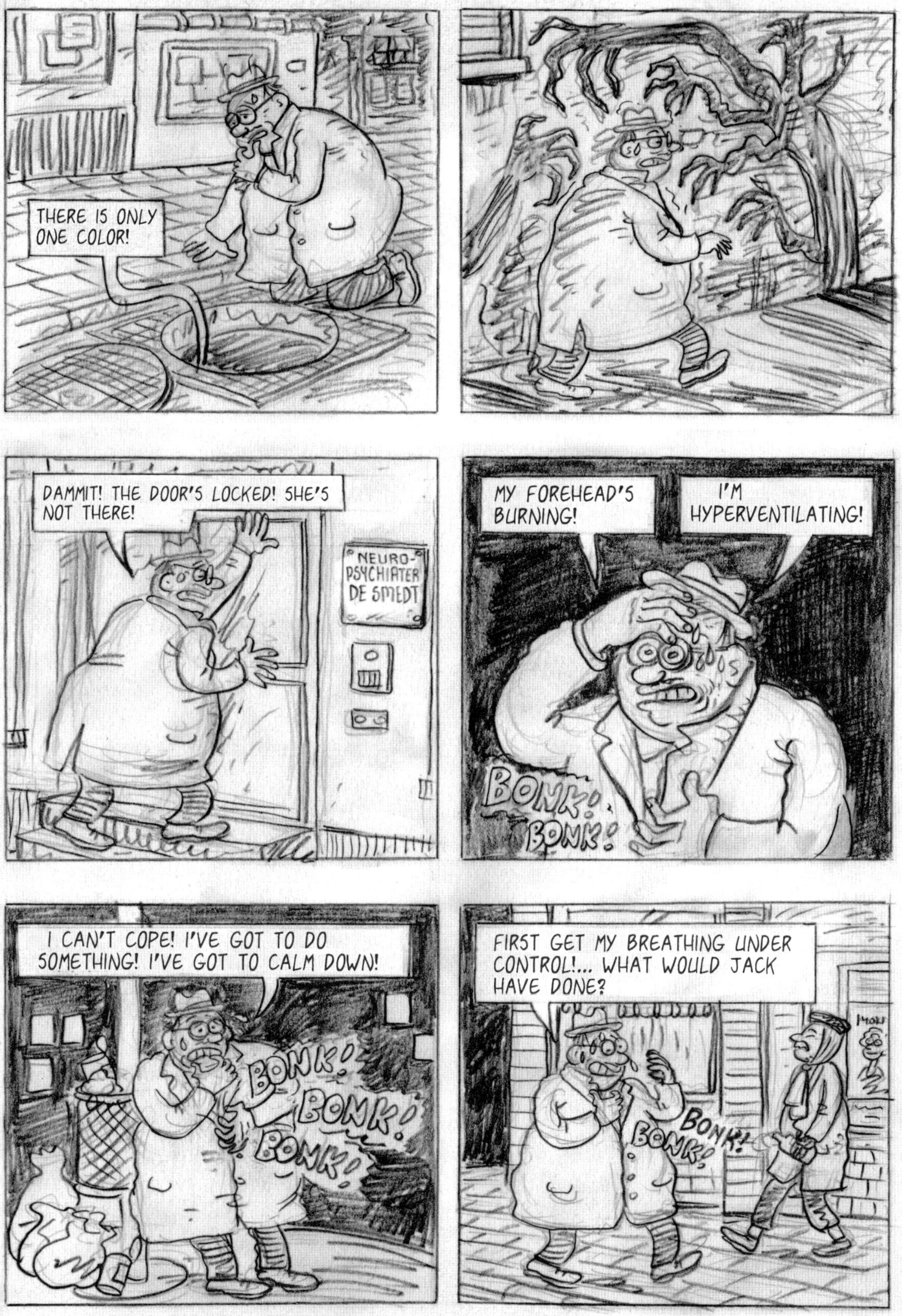
THERE IS ONLY ONE COLOR!
DAMMIT! THE DOOR'S LOCKED! SHE'S NOT THERE!
NEURO-PSYCHIATER DE SMEDT
MY FOREHEAD'S BURNING!
I'M HYPERVENTILATING!
BONK! BONK!
I CAN'T COPE! I'VE GOT TO DO SOMETHING! I'VE GOT TO CALM DOWN!
BONK! BONK! BONK!
FIRST GET MY BREATHING UNDER CONTROL!... WHAT WOULD JACK HAVE DONE?
BONK! BONK!

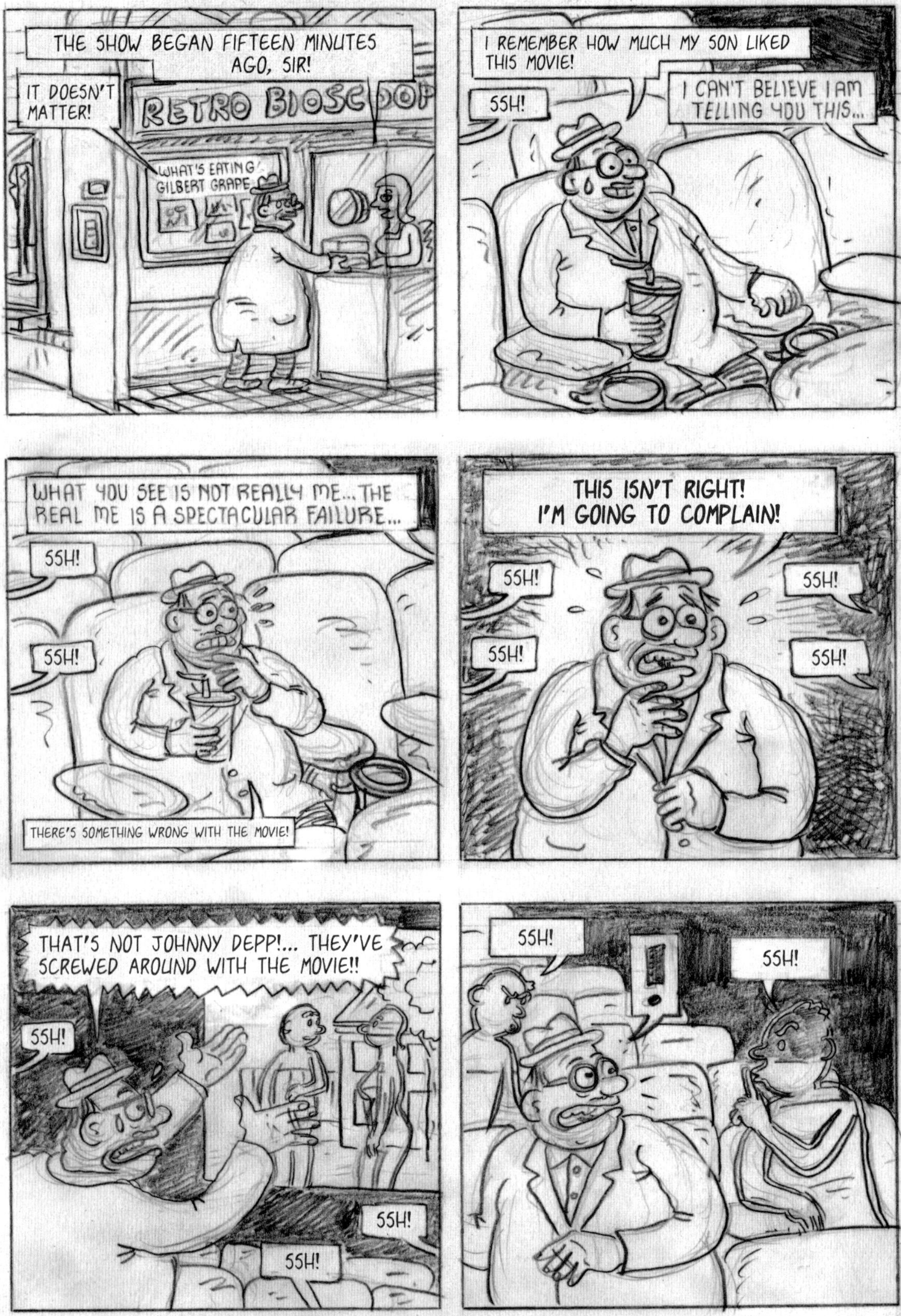
THE SHOW BEGAN FIFTEEN MINUTES AGO, SIR!
IT DOESN'T MATTER!
RETRO BIOSCOOP
WHAT'S EATING GILBERT GRAPE
I REMEMBER HOW MUCH MY SON LIKED THIS MOVIE!
SSH!
I CAN'T BELIEVE I AM TELLING YOU THIS...
WHAT YOU SEE IS NOT REALLY ME... THE REAL ME IS A SPECTACULAR FAILURE...
SSH!
SSH!
THERE'S SOMETHING WRONG WITH THE MOVIE!
THIS ISN'T RIGHT! I'M GOING TO COMPLAIN!
SSH!
SSH!
SSH!
SSH!
THAT'S NOT JOHNNY DEPP!... THEY'VE SCREWED AROUND WITH THE MOVIE!!
SSH!
SSH!
SSH!
SSH!
SSH!

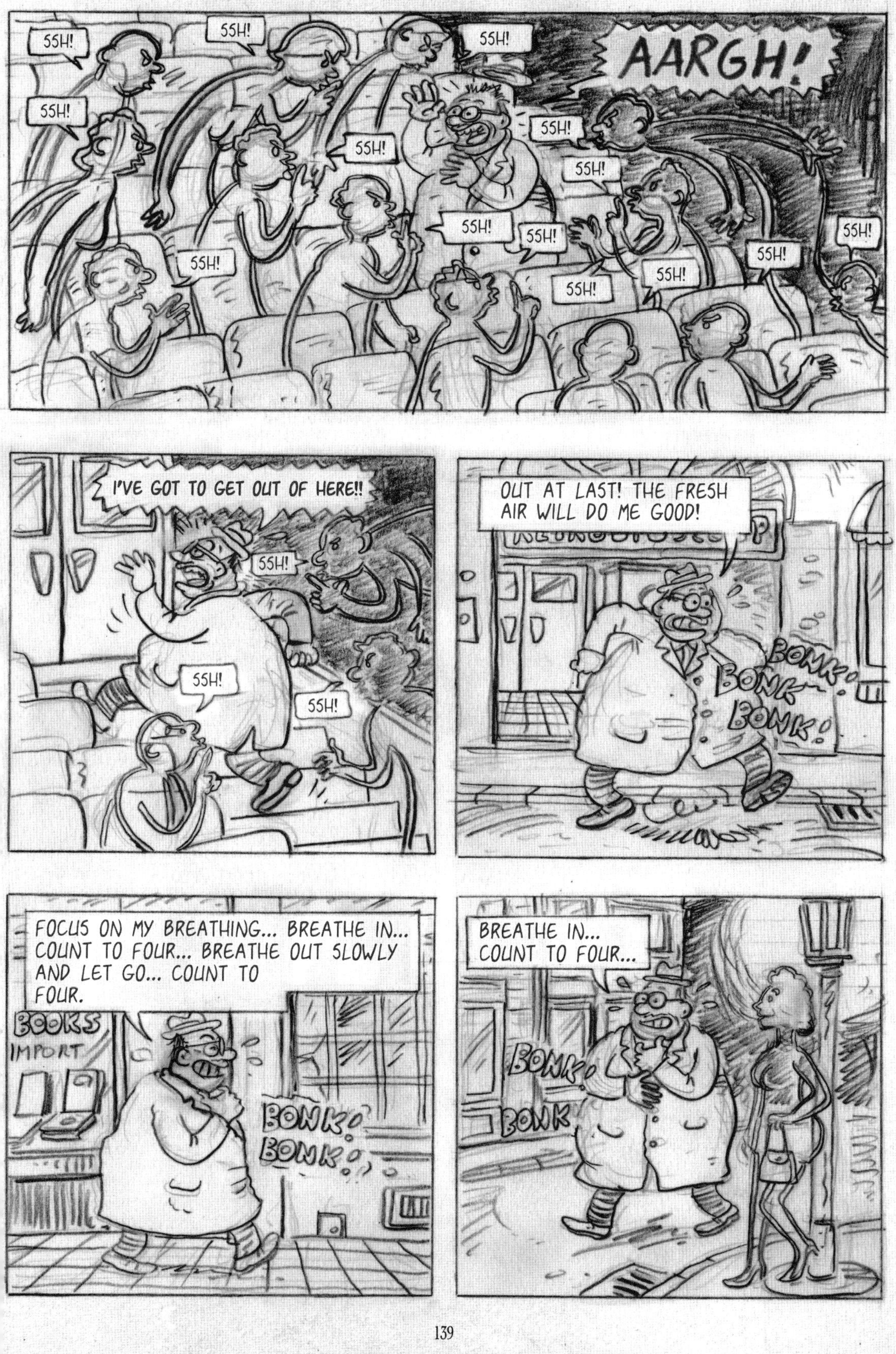
SSH!
SSH!
SSH!
SSH!
SSH!
AARGH!
SSH!
SSH!
SSH!
SSH!
SSH!
SSH!
SSH!
SSH!
SSH!
SSH!
I'VE GOT TO GET OUT OF HERE!!
SSH!
SSH!
SSH!
OUT AT LAST! THE FRESH AIR WILL DO ME GOOD!
BONK!
BONK
BONK!
FOCUS ON MY BREATHING... BREATHE IN... COUNT TO FOUR... BREATHE OUT SLOWLY AND LET GO... COUNT TO FOUR.
BOOKS
IMPORT
BONK!
BONK!
BREATHE IN... COUNT TO FOUR...
BONK!
BONK

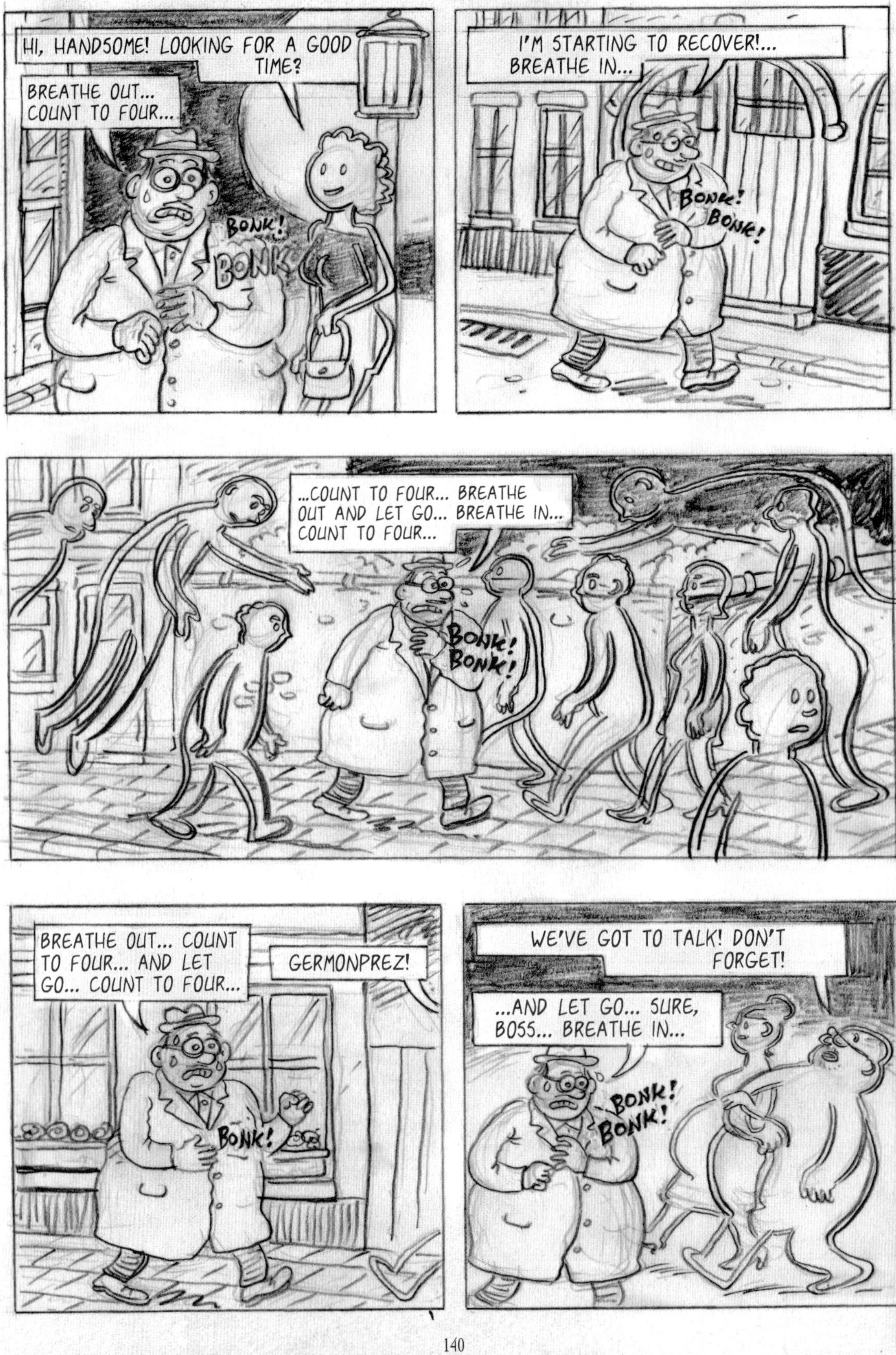
HI, HANDSOME! LOOKING FOR A GOOD TIME?
BREATHE OUT... COUNT TO FOUR...
BONK!
BONK!
I'M STARTING TO RECOVER!... BREATHE IN...
BONK!
BONK!
...COUNT TO FOUR... BREATHE OUT AND LET GO... BREATHE IN... COUNT TO FOUR...
BONK!
BONK!
BREATHE OUT... COUNT TO FOUR... AND LET GO... COUNT TO FOUR...
GERMONPREZ!
BONK!
WE'VE GOT TO TALK! DON'T FORGET!
...AND LET GO... SURE, BOSS... BREATHE IN...
BONK!
BONK!

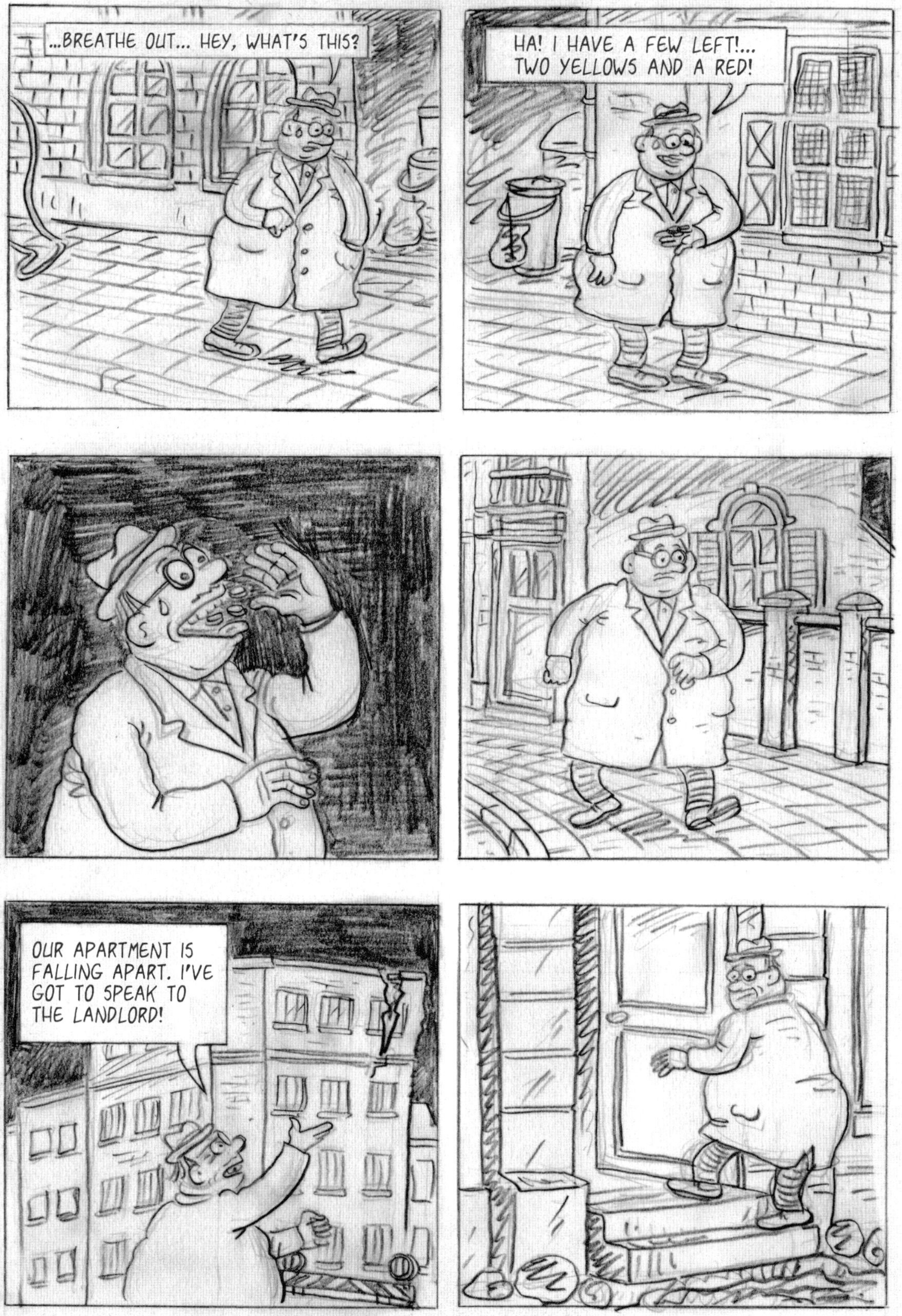
...BREATHE OUT... HEY, WHAT'S THIS?
HA! I HAVE A FEW LEFT!... TWO YELLOWS AND A RED!
OUR APARTMENT IS FALLING APART. I'VE GOT TO SPEAK TO THE LANDLORD!

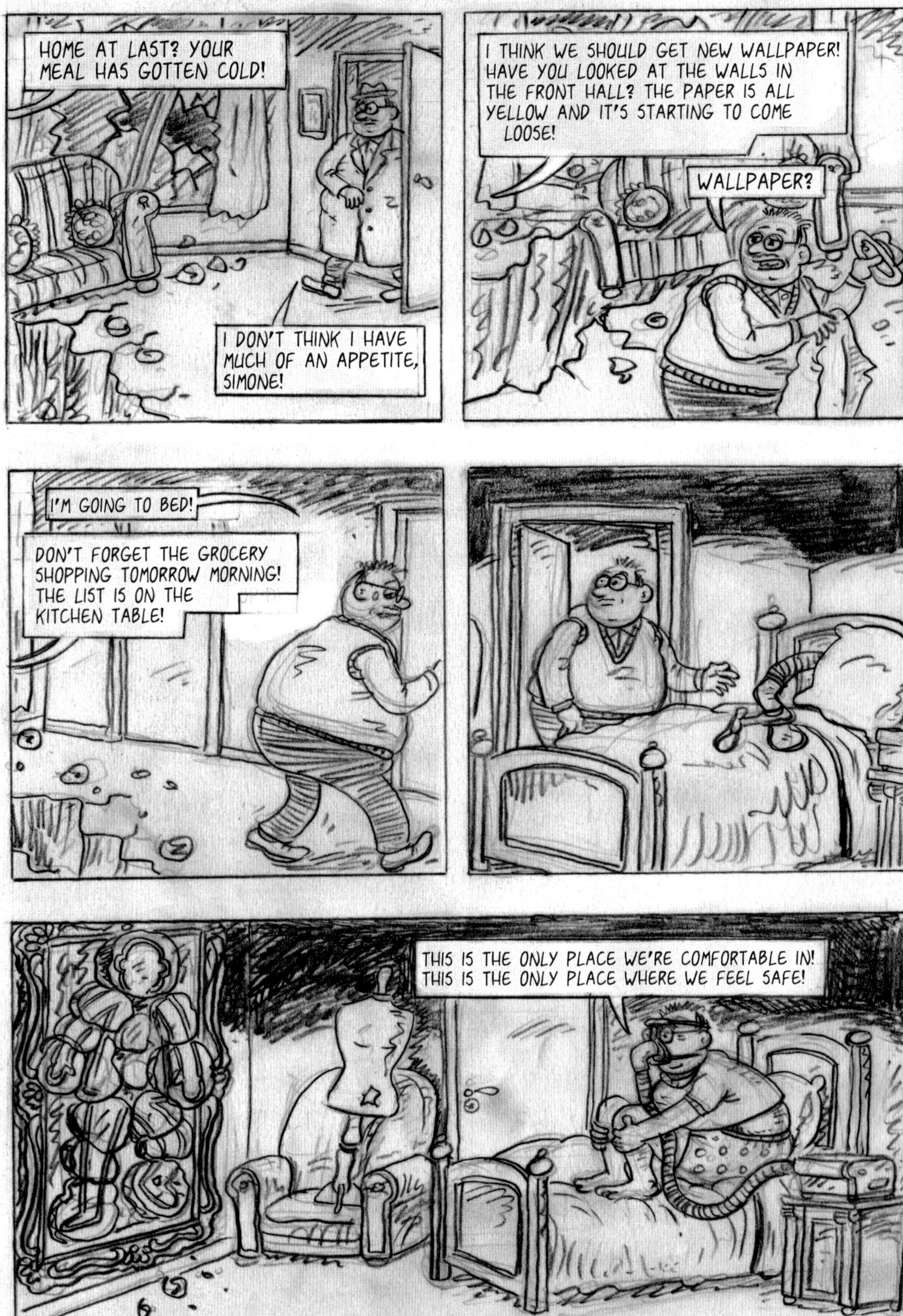
HOME AT LAST? YOUR MEAL HAS GOTTEN COLD!
I DON'T THINK I HAVE MUCH OF AN APPETITE, SIMONE!
I THINK WE SHOULD GET NEW WALLPAPER! HAVE YOU LOOKED AT THE WALLS IN THE FRONT HALL? THE PAPER IS ALL YELLOW AND IT'S STARTING TO COME LOOSE!
WALLPAPER?
I'M GOING TO BED!
DON'T FORGET THE GROCERY SHOPPING TOMORROW MORNING! THE LIST IS ON THE KITCHEN TABLE!
THIS IS THE ONLY PLACE WE'RE COMFORTABLE IN! THIS IS THE ONLY PLACE WHERE WE FEEL SAFE!

CHAPTER 8 – ACROSS THE RIFT

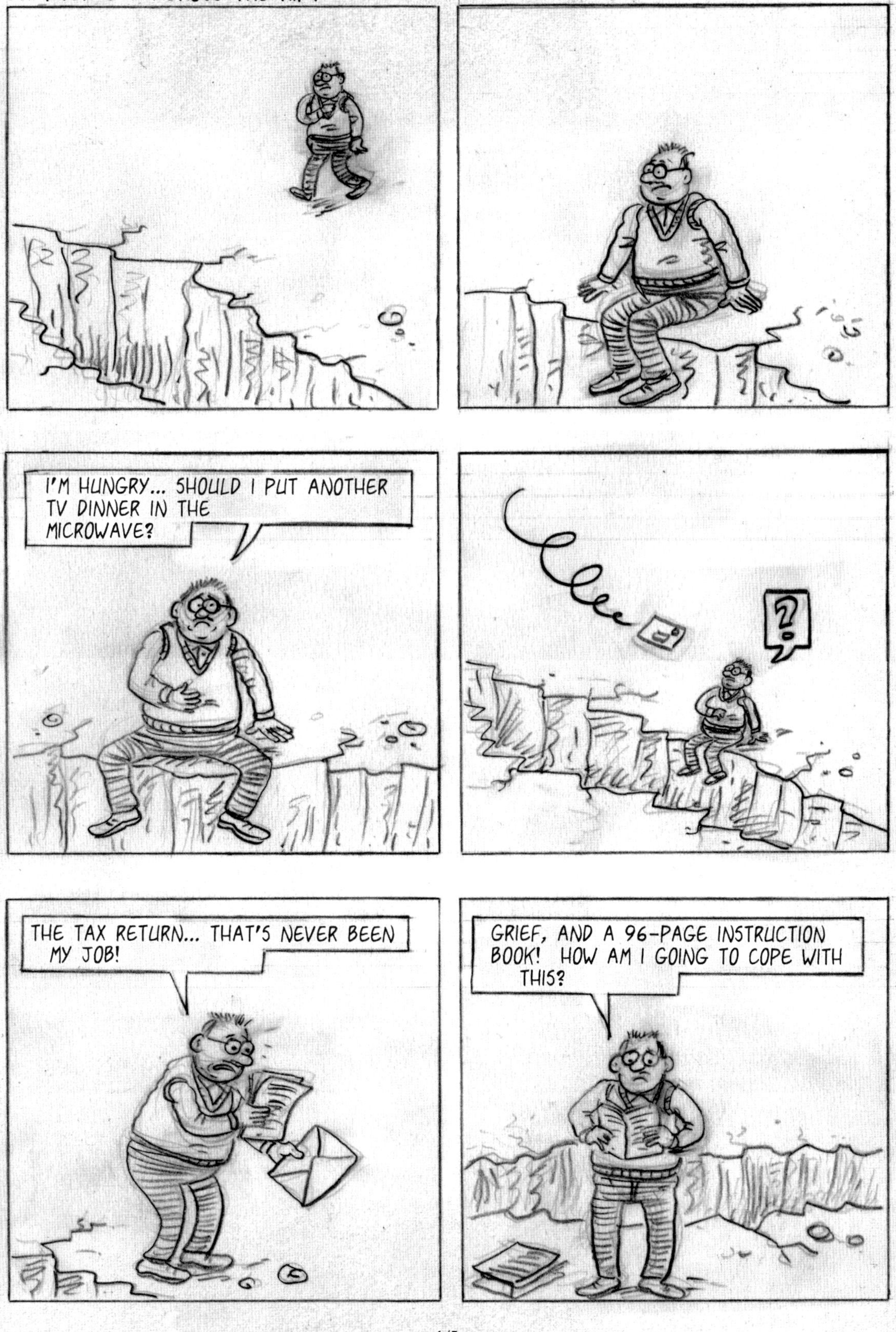

I'M HUNGRY... SHOULD I PUT ANOTHER TV DINNER IN THE MICROWAVE?
?
THE TAX RETURN... THAT'S NEVER BEEN MY JOB!
GRIEF, AND A 96-PAGE INSTRUCTION BOOK! HOW AM I GOING TO COPE WITH THIS?

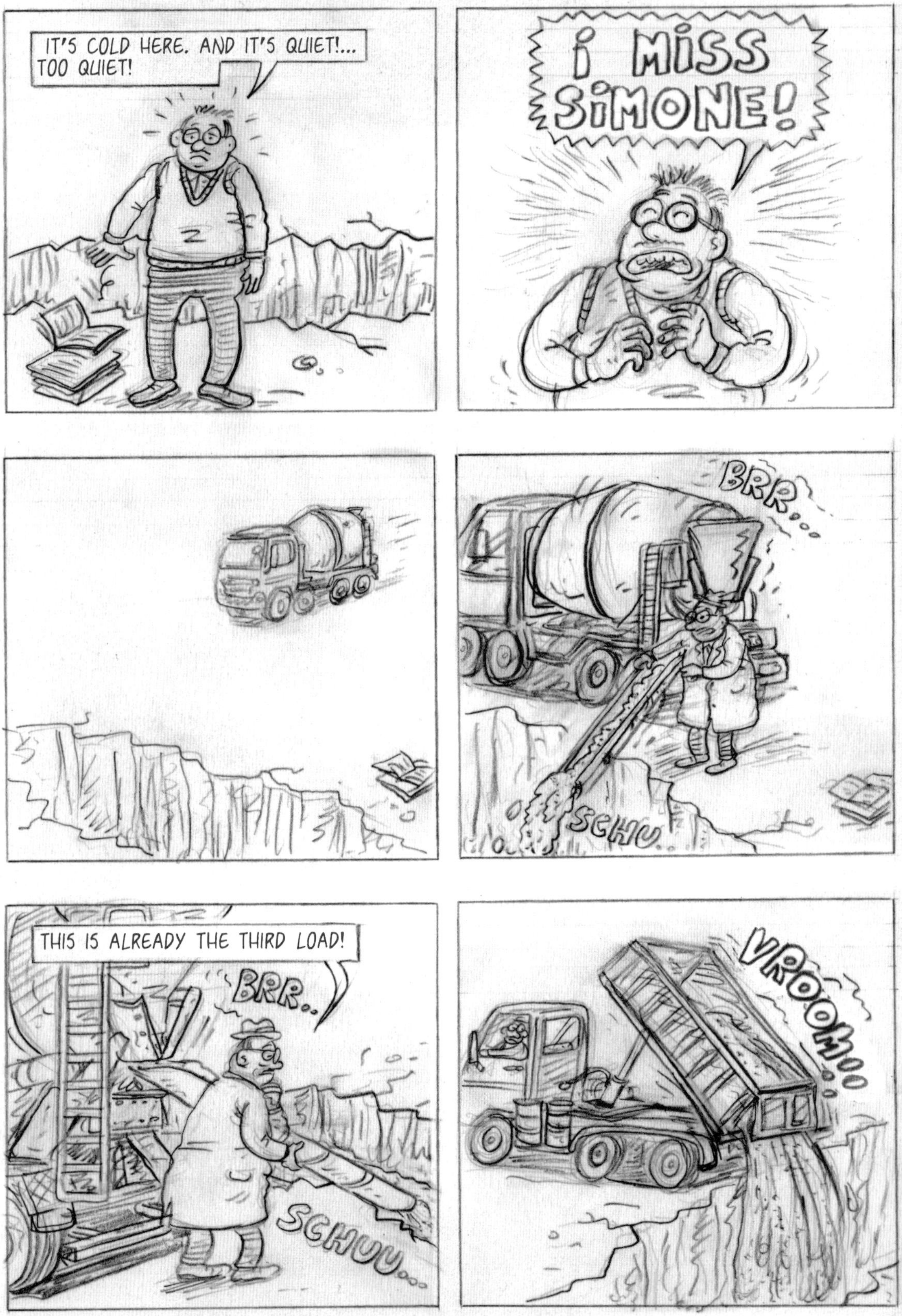
IT'S COLD HERE. AND IT'S QUIET!... TOO QUIET!
I MISS SIMONE!
BRR...
SCHU..
THIS IS ALREADY THE THIRD LOAD!
BRR..
SCHUU...
VROOOM...

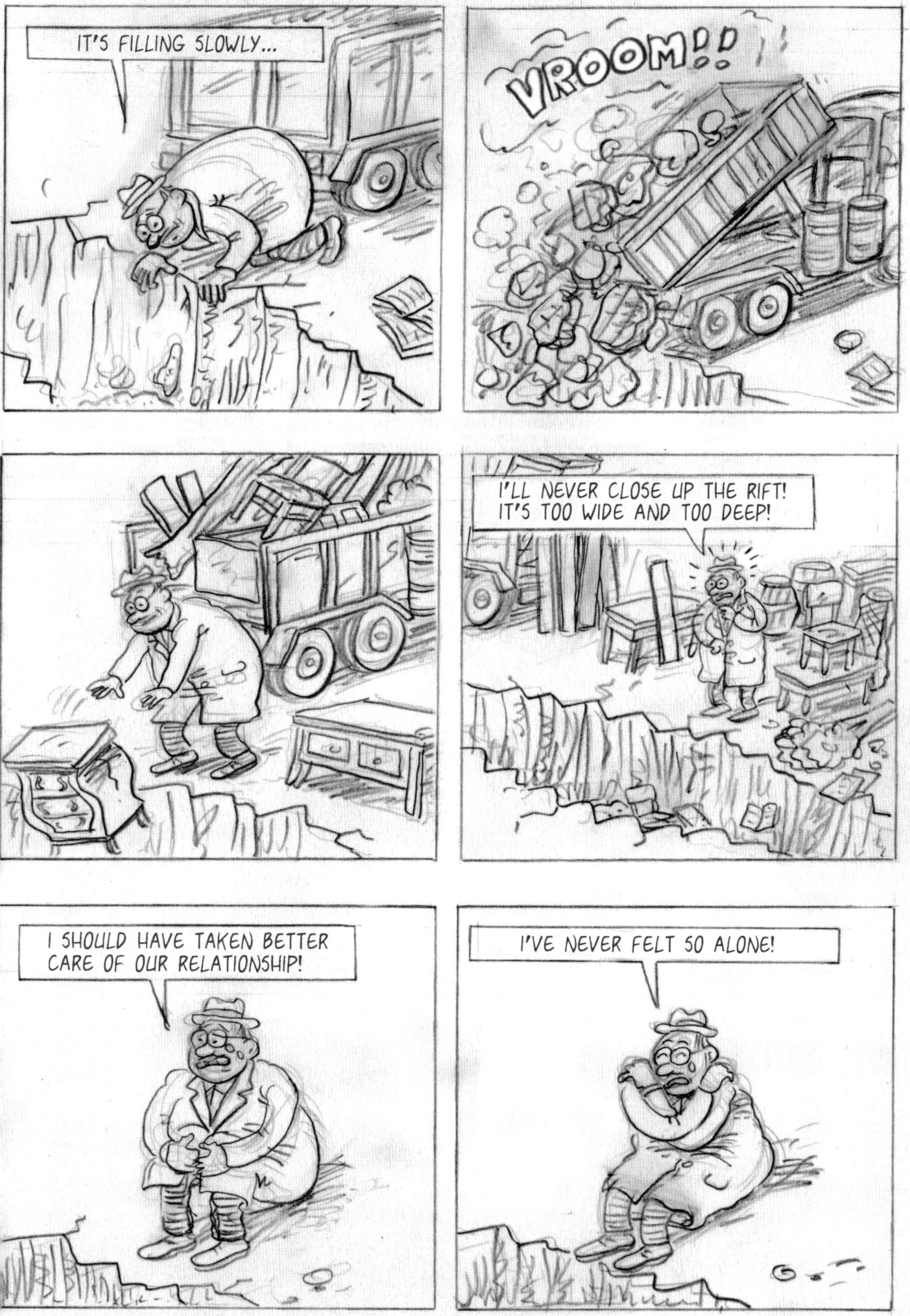
IT'S FILLING SLOWLY...
VROOM!!
I'LL NEVER CLOSE UP THE RIFT! IT'S TOO WIDE AND TOO DEEP!
I SHOULD HAVE TAKEN BETTER CARE OF OUR RELATIONSHIP!
I'VE NEVER FELT SO ALONE!

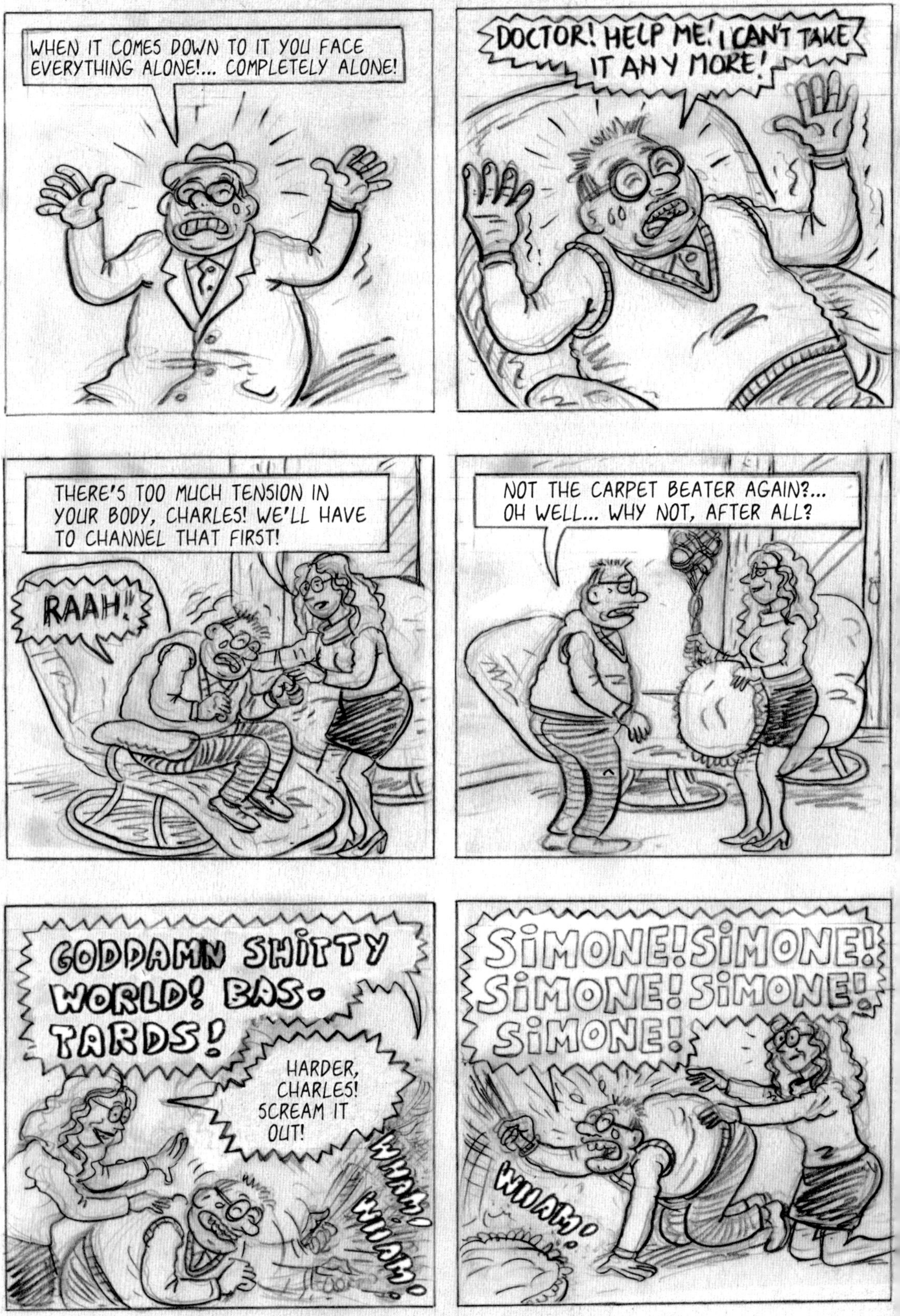

WHEN IT COMES DOWN TO IT YOU FACE EVERYTHING ALONE!... COMPLETELY ALONE!
DOCTOR! HELP ME! I CAN'T TAKE IT ANY MORE!
THERE'S TOO MUCH TENSION IN YOUR BODY, CHARLES! WE'LL HAVE TO CHANNEL THAT FIRST!
RAAH!!
NOT THE CARPET BEATER AGAIN?... OH WELL... WHY NOT, AFTER ALL?
GODDAMN SHITTY WORLD! BAS-TARDS!
HARDER, CHARLES! SCREAM IT OUT!
WHAM!
WHAM!
SIMONE! SIMONE! SIMONE! SIMONE! SIMONE!
WHAM!

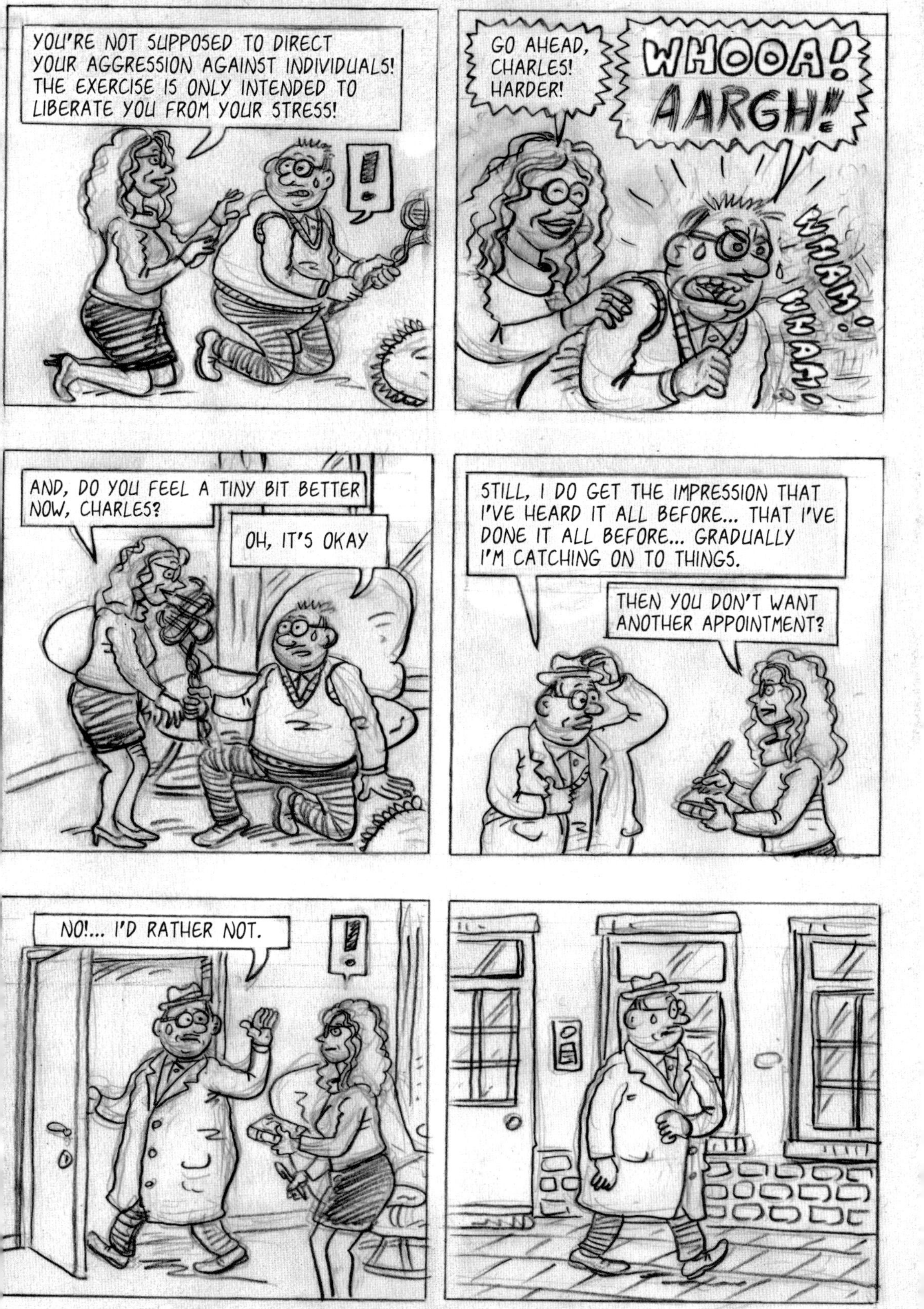
YOU'RE NOT SUPPOSED TO DIRECT YOUR AGGRESSION AGAINST INDIVIDUALS! THE EXERCISE IS ONLY INTENDED TO LIBERATE YOU FROM YOUR STRESS!
GO AHEAD, CHARLES! HARDER!
WHOOA! AARGH!
WHAM! WHAM!
AND, DO YOU FEEL A TINY BIT BETTER NOW, CHARLES?
OH, IT'S OKAY
STILL, I DO GET THE IMPRESSION THAT I'VE HEARD IT ALL BEFORE... THAT I'VE DONE IT ALL BEFORE... GRADUALLY I'M CATCHING ON TO THINGS.
THEN YOU DON'T WANT ANOTHER APPOINTMENT?
NO!... I'D RATHER NOT.

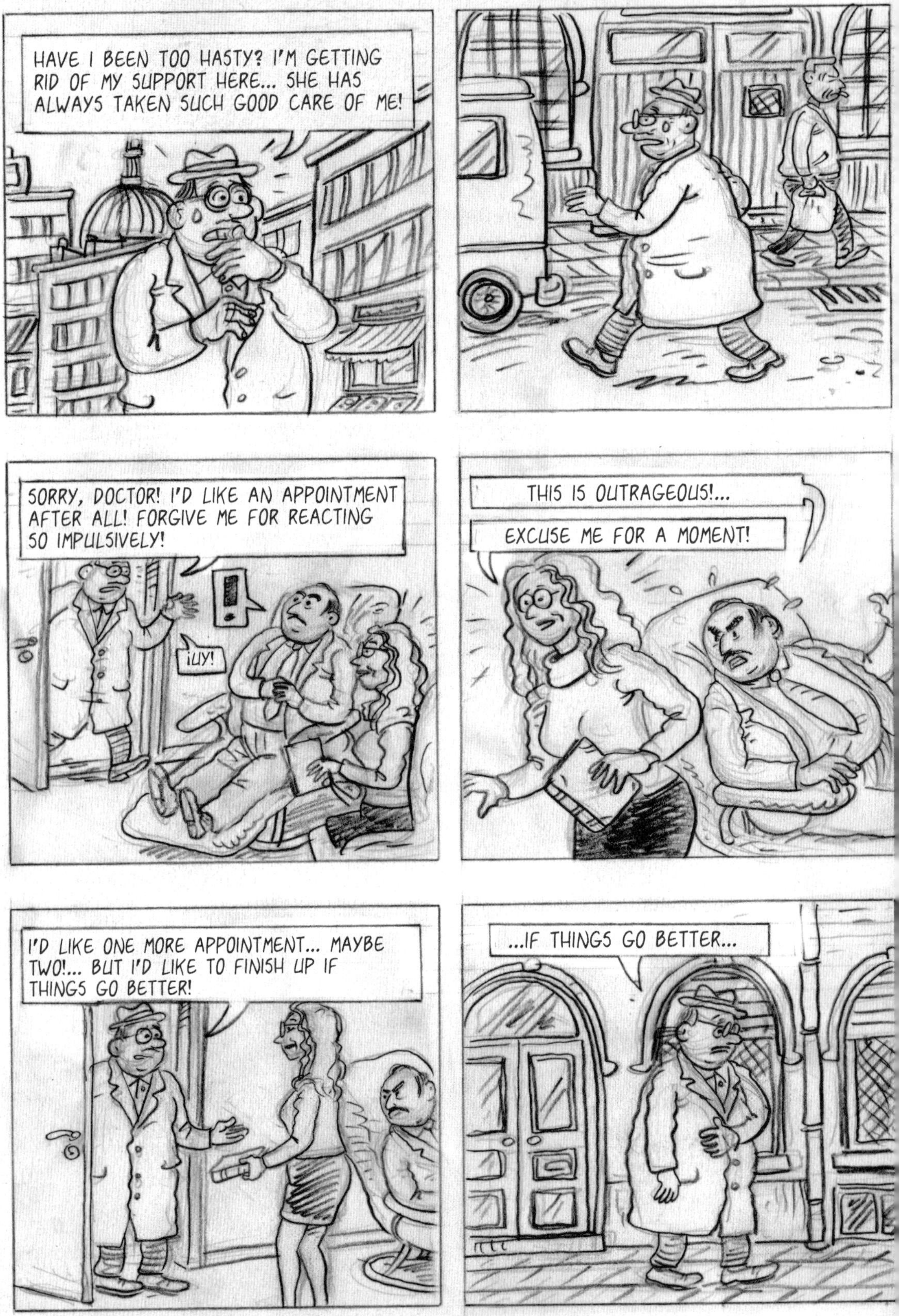
HAVE I BEEN TOO HASTY? I'M GETTING RID OF MY SUPPORT HERE... SHE HAS ALWAYS TAKEN SUCH GOOD CARE OF ME!
SORRY, DOCTOR! I'D LIKE AN APPOINTMENT AFTER ALL! FORGIVE ME FOR REACTING SO IMPULSIVELY!
!
¡UY!
THIS IS OUTRAGEOUS!...
EXCUSE ME FOR A MOMENT!
I'D LIKE ONE MORE APPOINTMENT... MAYBE TWO!... BUT I'D LIKE TO FINISH UP IF THINGS GO BETTER!
...IF THINGS GO BETTER...

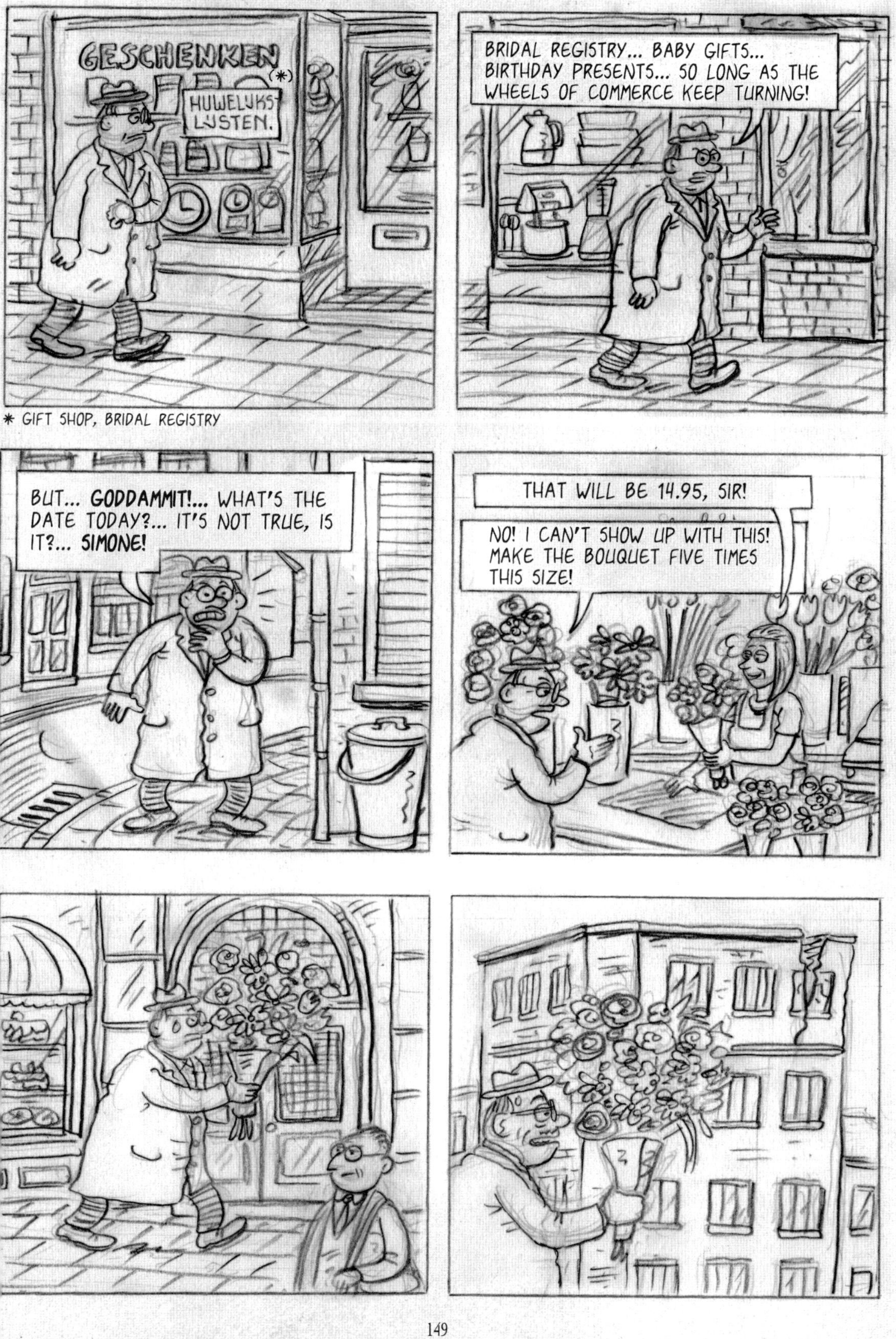
GESCHENKEN (*)
HUWELIJKS-LIJSTEN.
BRIDAL REGISTRY... BABY GIFTS... BIRTHDAY PRESENTS... SO LONG AS THE WHEELS OF COMMERCE KEEP TURNING!
* GIFT SHOP, BRIDAL REGISTRY
BUT... GODDAMMIT!... WHAT'S THE DATE TODAY?... IT'S NOT TRUE, IS IT?... SIMONE!
THAT WILL BE 14.95, SIR!
NO! I CAN'T SHOW UP WITH THIS! MAKE THE BOUQUET FIVE TIMES THIS SIZE!

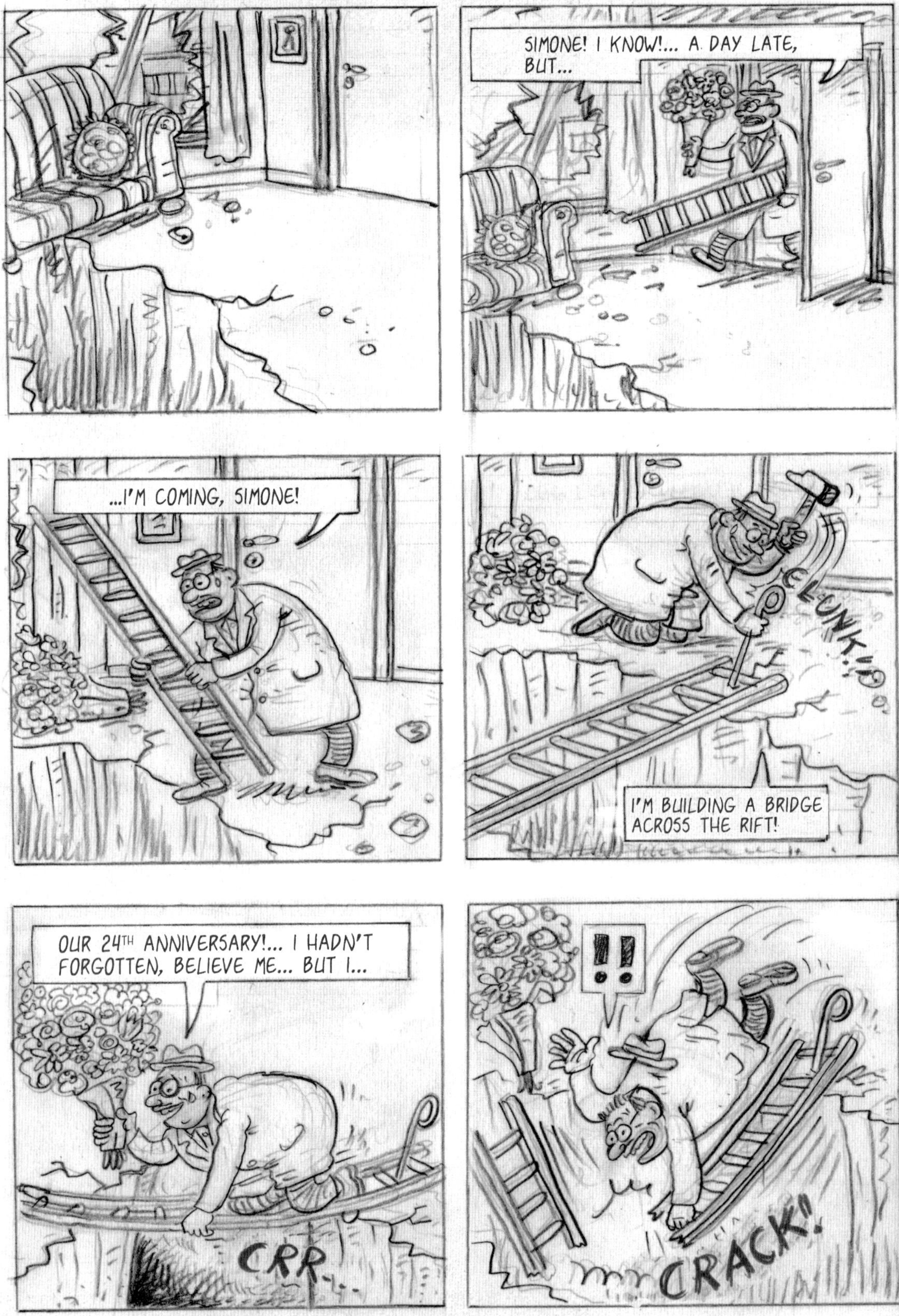
SIMONE! I KNOW!... A DAY LATE, BUT...
...I'M COMING, SIMONE!
CLUNK!!
I'M BUILDING A BRIDGE ACROSS THE RIFT!
OUR 24TH ANNIVERSARY!... I HADN'T FORGOTTEN, BELIEVE ME... BUT I...
CRR
!!
CRACK!

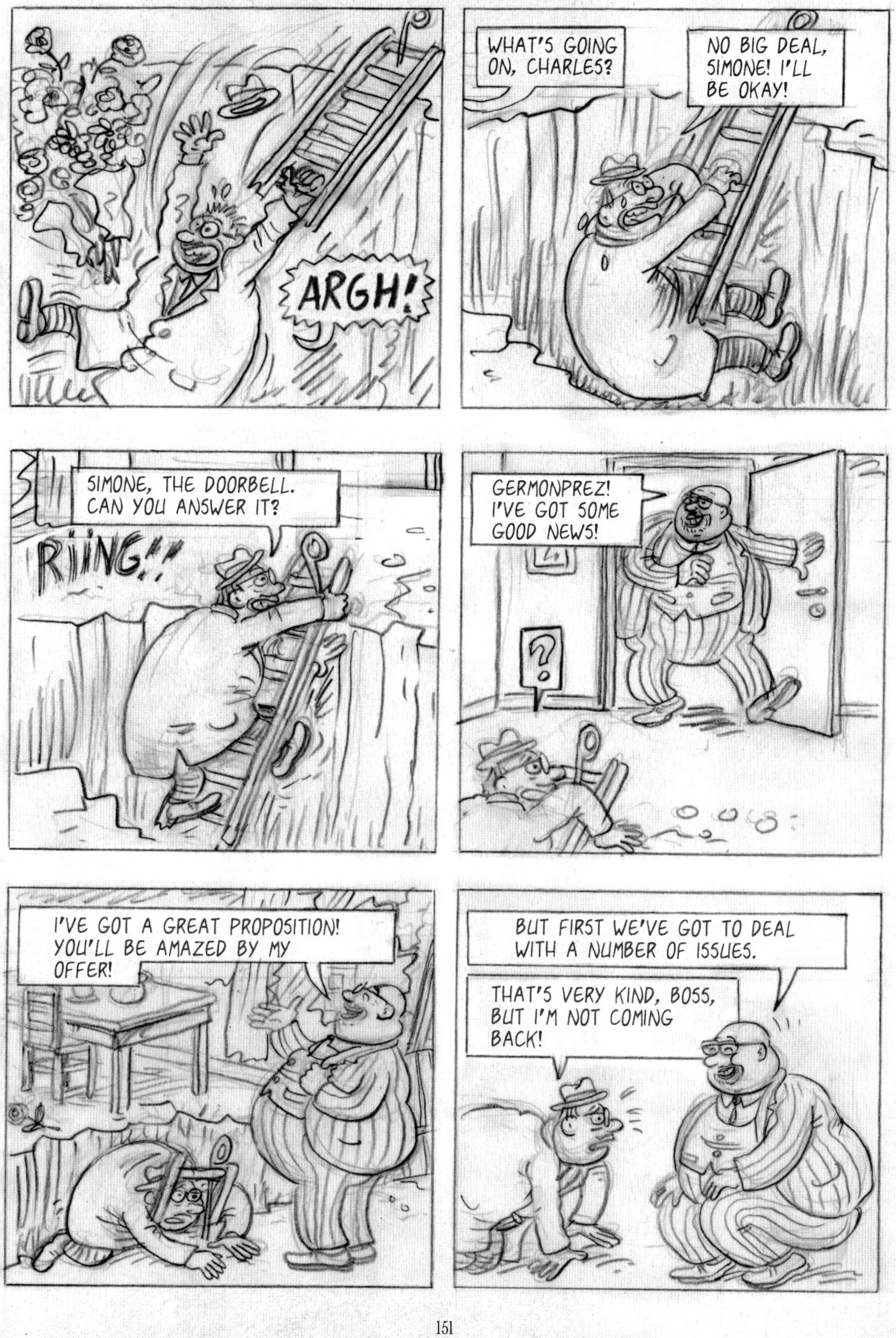
ARGH!
WHAT'S GOING ON, CHARLES?
NO BIG DEAL, SIMONE! I'LL BE OKAY!
SIMONE, THE DOORBELL. CAN YOU ANSWER IT?
RIIING!!
GERMONPREZ! I'VE GOT SOME GOOD NEWS!
?
I'VE GOT A GREAT PROPOSITION! YOU'LL BE AMAZED BY MY OFFER!
BUT FIRST WE'VE GOT TO DEAL WITH A NUMBER OF ISSUES.
THAT'S VERY KIND, BOSS, BUT I'M NOT COMING BACK!

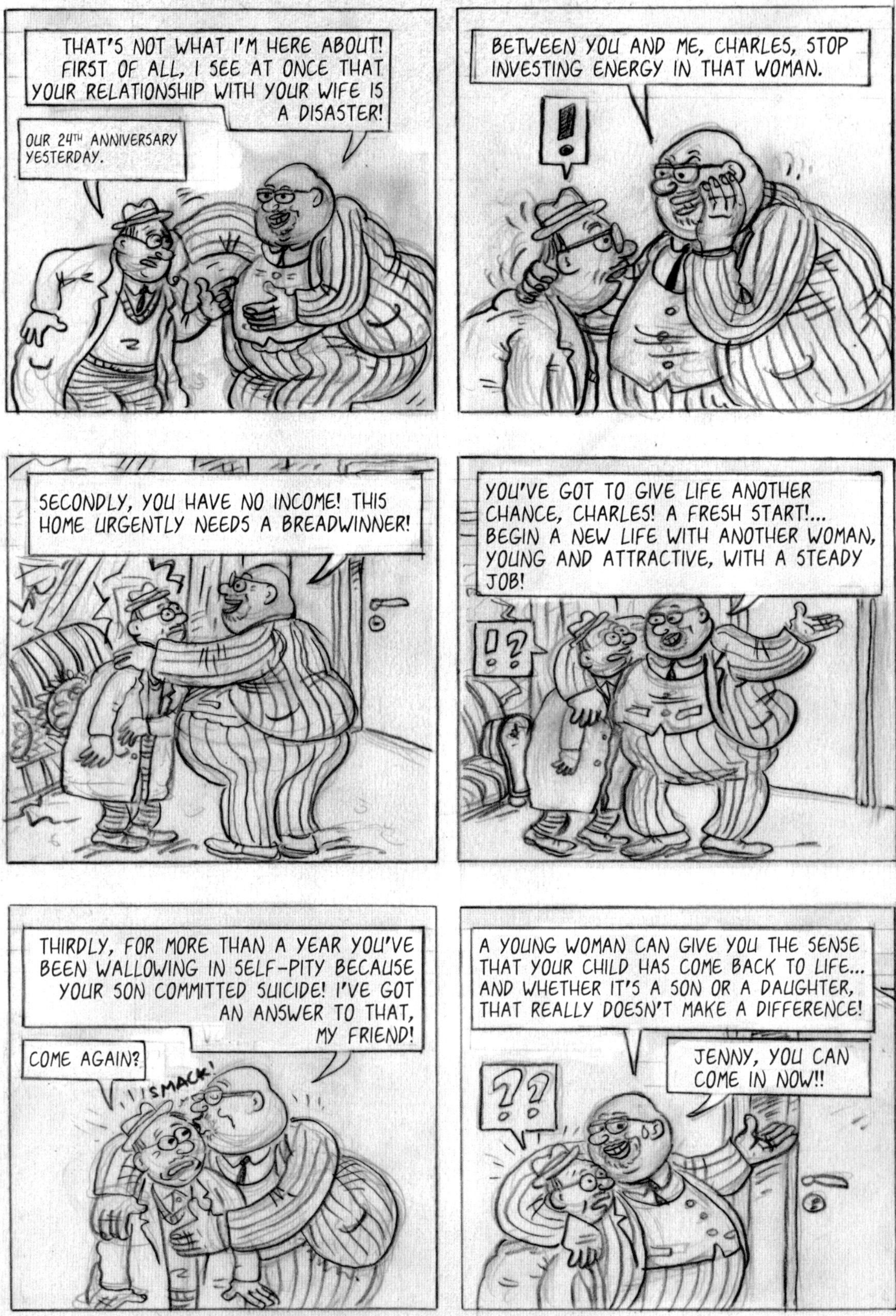
THAT'S NOT WHAT I'M HERE ABOUT! FIRST OF ALL, I SEE AT ONCE THAT YOUR RELATIONSHIP WITH YOUR WIFE IS A DISASTER!
OUR 24TH ANNIVERSARY YESTERDAY.
BETWEEN YOU AND ME, CHARLES, STOP INVESTING ENERGY IN THAT WOMAN.
!
SECONDLY, YOU HAVE NO INCOME! THIS HOME URGENTLY NEEDS A BREADWINNER!
YOU'VE GOT TO GIVE LIFE ANOTHER CHANCE, CHARLES! A FRESH START!... BEGIN A NEW LIFE WITH ANOTHER WOMAN, YOUNG AND ATTRACTIVE, WITH A STEADY JOB!
!?
THIRDLY, FOR MORE THAN A YEAR YOU'VE BEEN WALLOWING IN SELF-PITY BECAUSE YOUR SON COMMITTED SUICIDE! I'VE GOT AN ANSWER TO THAT, MY FRIEND!
COME AGAIN?
SMACK!
A YOUNG WOMAN CAN GIVE YOU THE SENSE THAT YOUR CHILD HAS COME BACK TO LIFE... AND WHETHER IT'S A SON OR A DAUGHTER, THAT REALLY DOESN'T MAKE A DIFFERENCE!
??
JENNY, YOU CAN COME IN NOW!!

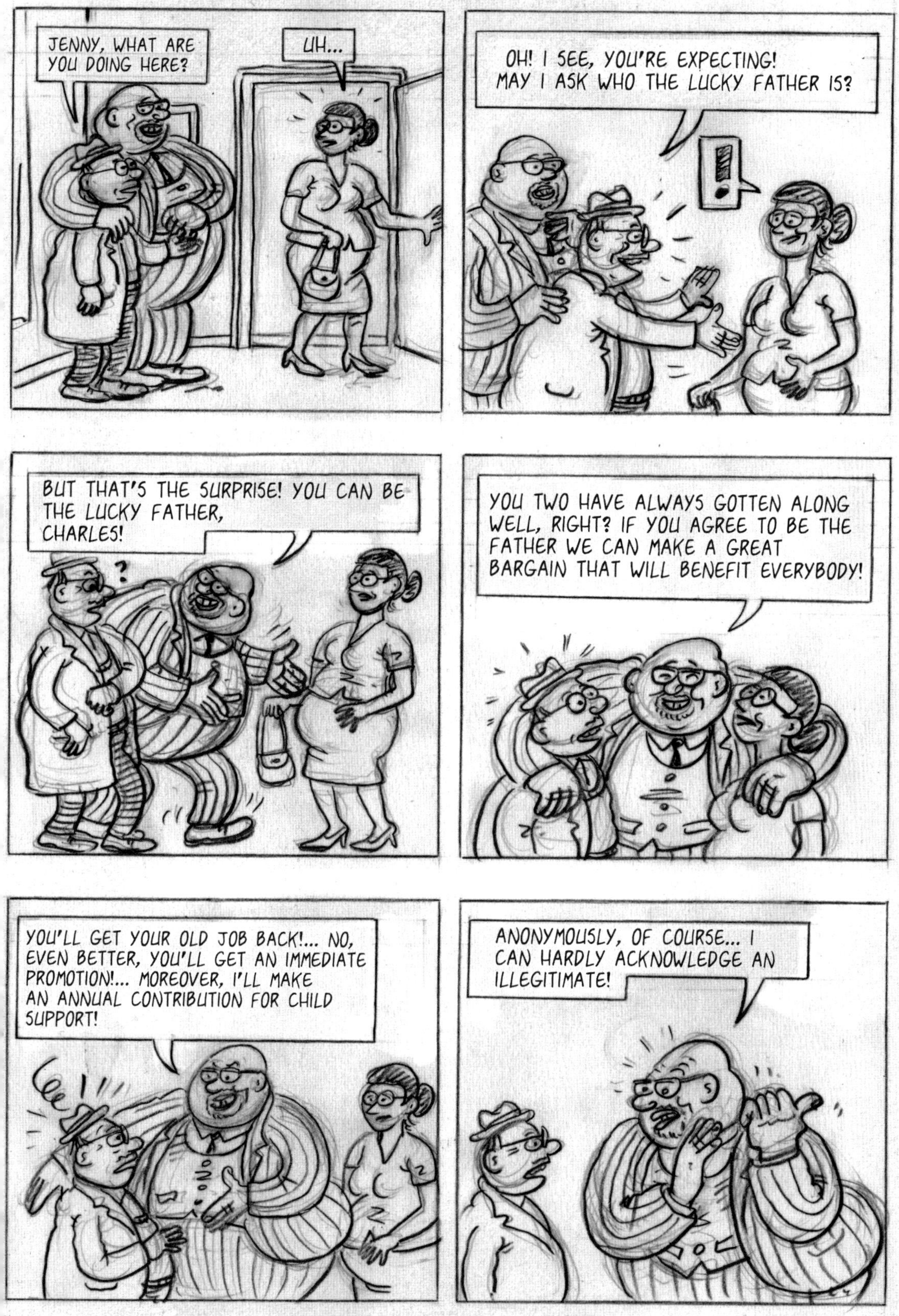
JENNY, WHAT ARE YOU DOING HERE?
UH...
OH! I SEE, YOU'RE EXPECTING! MAY I ASK WHO THE LUCKY FATHER IS?
BUT THAT'S THE SURPRISE! YOU CAN BE THE LUCKY FATHER, CHARLES!
YOU TWO HAVE ALWAYS GOTTEN ALONG WELL, RIGHT? IF YOU AGREE TO BE THE FATHER WE CAN MAKE A GREAT BARGAIN THAT WILL BENEFIT EVERYBODY!
YOU'LL GET YOUR OLD JOB BACK!... NO, EVEN BETTER, YOU'LL GET AN IMMEDIATE PROMOTION!... MOREOVER, I'LL MAKE AN ANNUAL CONTRIBUTION FOR CHILD SUPPORT!
ANONYMOUSLY, OF COURSE... I CAN HARDLY ACKNOWLEDGE AN ILLEGITIMATE!

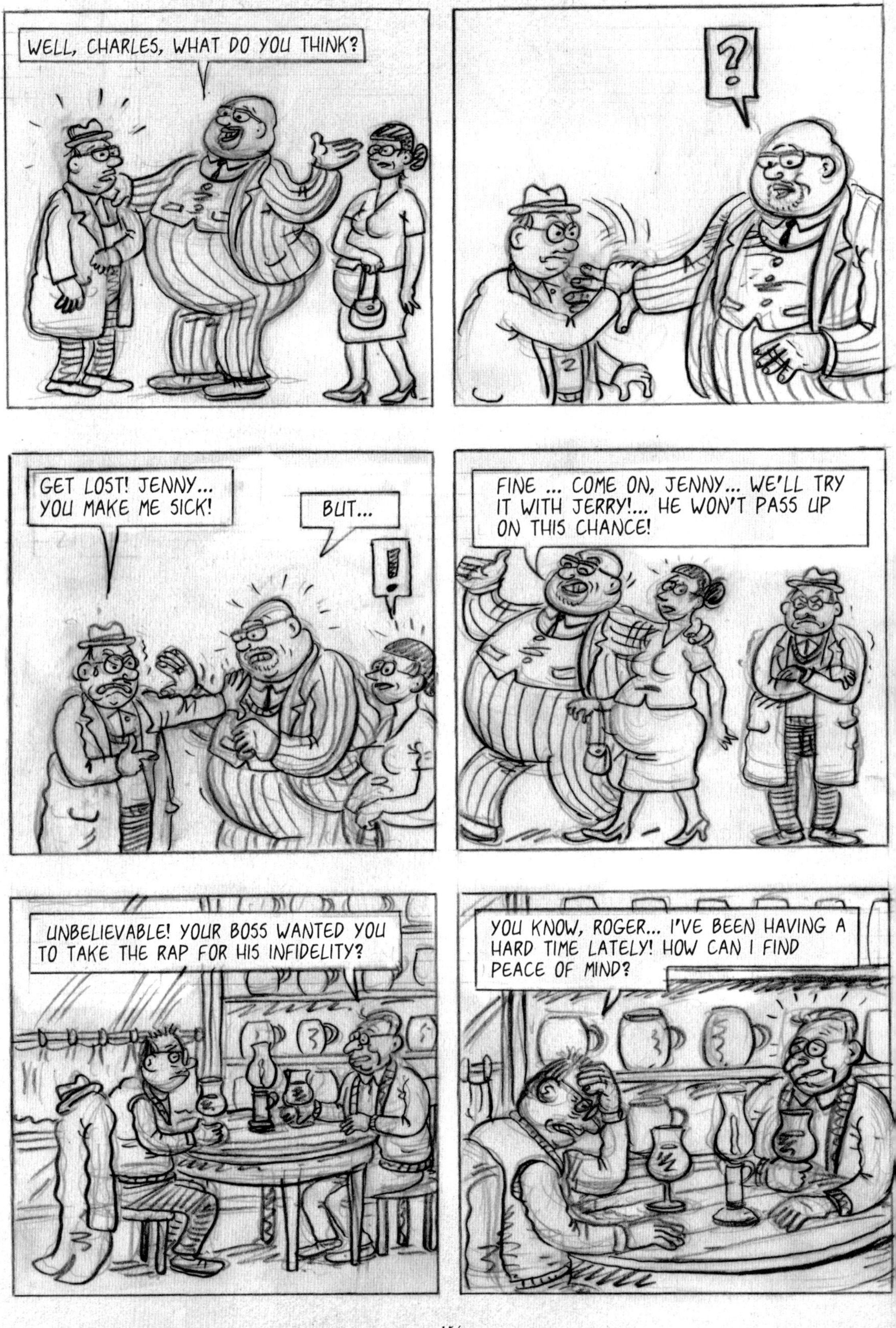
WELL, CHARLES, WHAT DO YOU THINK?
?
GET LOST! JENNY... YOU MAKE ME SICK!
BUT...
!
FINE ... COME ON, JENNY... WE'LL TRY IT WITH JERRY!... HE WON'T PASS UP ON THIS CHANCE!
UNBELIEVABLE! YOUR BOSS WANTED YOU TO TAKE THE RAP FOR HIS INFIDELITY?
YOU KNOW, ROGER... I'VE BEEN HAVING A HARD TIME LATELY! HOW CAN I FIND PEACE OF MIND?

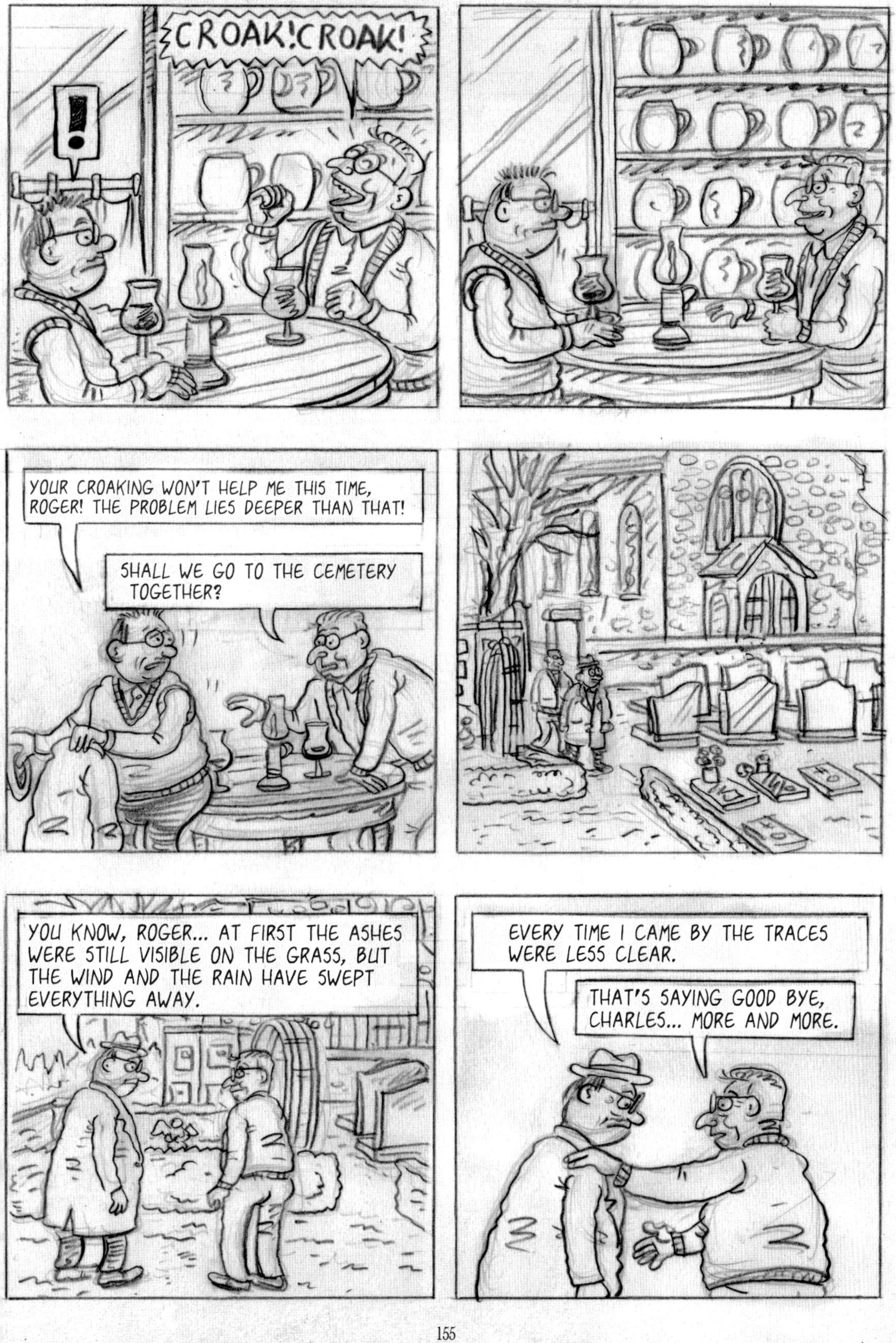
CROAK! CROAK!
!
YOUR CROAKING WON'T HELP ME THIS TIME, ROGER! THE PROBLEM LIES DEEPER THAN THAT!
SHALL WE GO TO THE CEMETERY TOGETHER?
YOU KNOW, ROGER... AT FIRST THE ASHES WERE STILL VISIBLE ON THE GRASS, BUT THE WIND AND THE RAIN HAVE SWEPT EVERYTHING AWAY.
EVERY TIME I CAME BY THE TRACES WERE LESS CLEAR.
THAT'S SAYING GOOD BYE, CHARLES... MORE AND MORE.

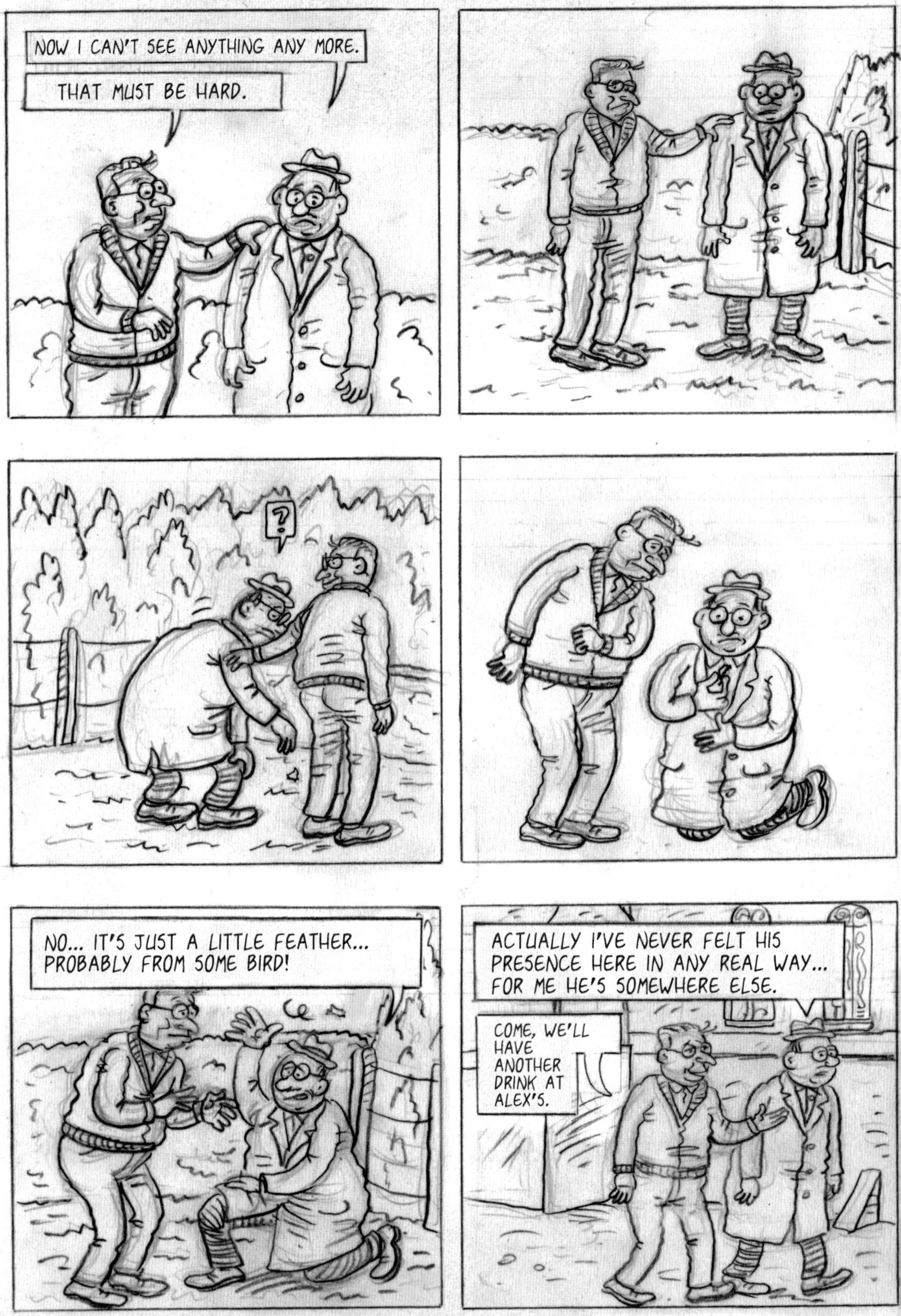
NOW I CAN'T SEE ANYTHING ANY MORE.
THAT MUST BE HARD.
?
NO... IT'S JUST A LITTLE FEATHER... PROBABLY FROM SOME BIRD!
ACTUALLY I'VE NEVER FELT HIS PRESENCE HERE IN ANY REAL WAY... FOR ME HE'S SOMEWHERE ELSE.
COME, WE'LL HAVE ANOTHER DRINK AT ALEX'S.

FOR ME THIS IS THE ONLY PLACE YOU ARE, JACK.
I'M HAPPY TO SEE YOU, JACK! THEY CAN'T TAKE THIS CONNECTION AWAY FROM US!
WE'VE GOT TO TALK, SON! LIFE IS SLIPPING AWAY FROM ME! I DON'T KNOW WHAT I'M SUPPOSED TO BE DOING HERE! WHAT'S THE POINT OF IT ALL? I NEED TO GET A GRIP ON THINGS!
I KNOW, MY BOY! YOU'LL ALWAYS BE HERE FOR ME!

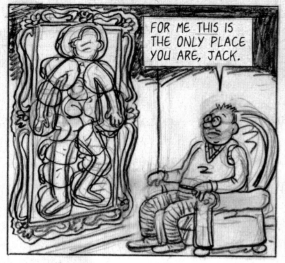

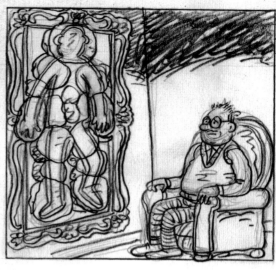

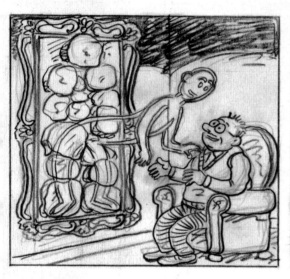

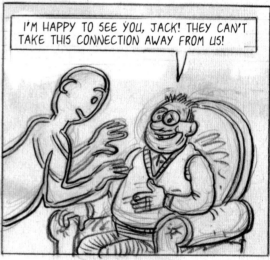

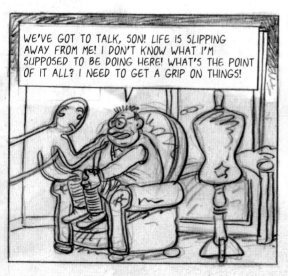

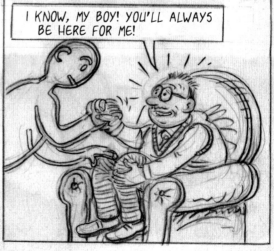

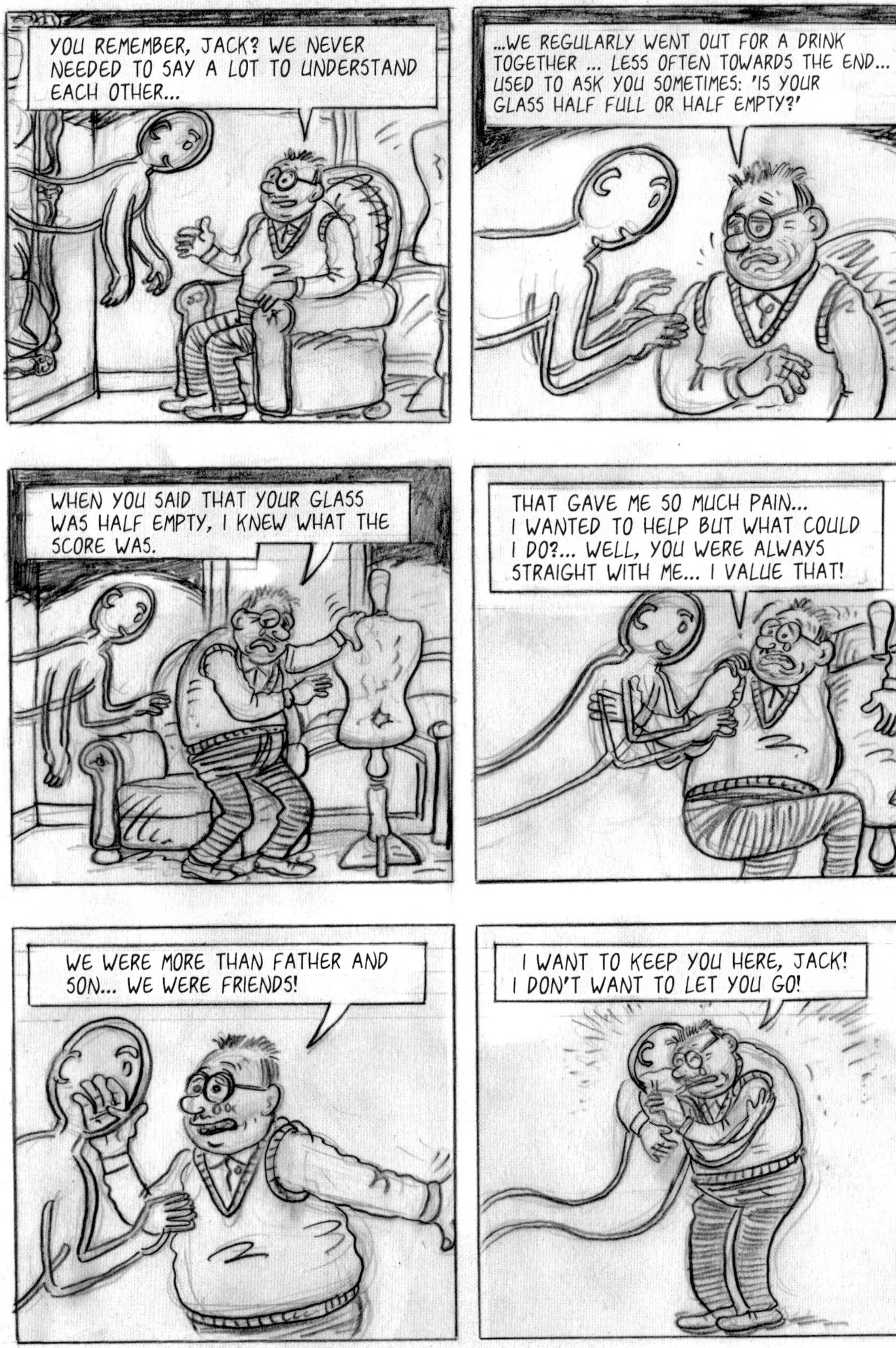
YOU REMEMBER, JACK? WE NEVER NEEDED TO SAY A LOT TO UNDERSTAND EACH OTHER...
...WE REGULARLY WENT OUT FOR A DRINK TOGETHER ... LESS OFTEN TOWARDS THE END... USED TO ASK YOU SOMETIMES: 'IS YOUR GLASS HALF FULL OR HALF EMPTY?'
WHEN YOU SAID THAT YOUR GLASS WAS HALF EMPTY, I KNEW WHAT THE SCORE WAS.
THAT GAVE ME SO MUCH PAIN... I WANTED TO HELP BUT WHAT COULD I DO?... WELL, YOU WERE ALWAYS STRAIGHT WITH ME... I VALUE THAT!
WE WERE MORE THAN FATHER AND SON... WE WERE FRIENDS!
I WANT TO KEEP YOU HERE, JACK! I DON'T WANT TO LET YOU GO!

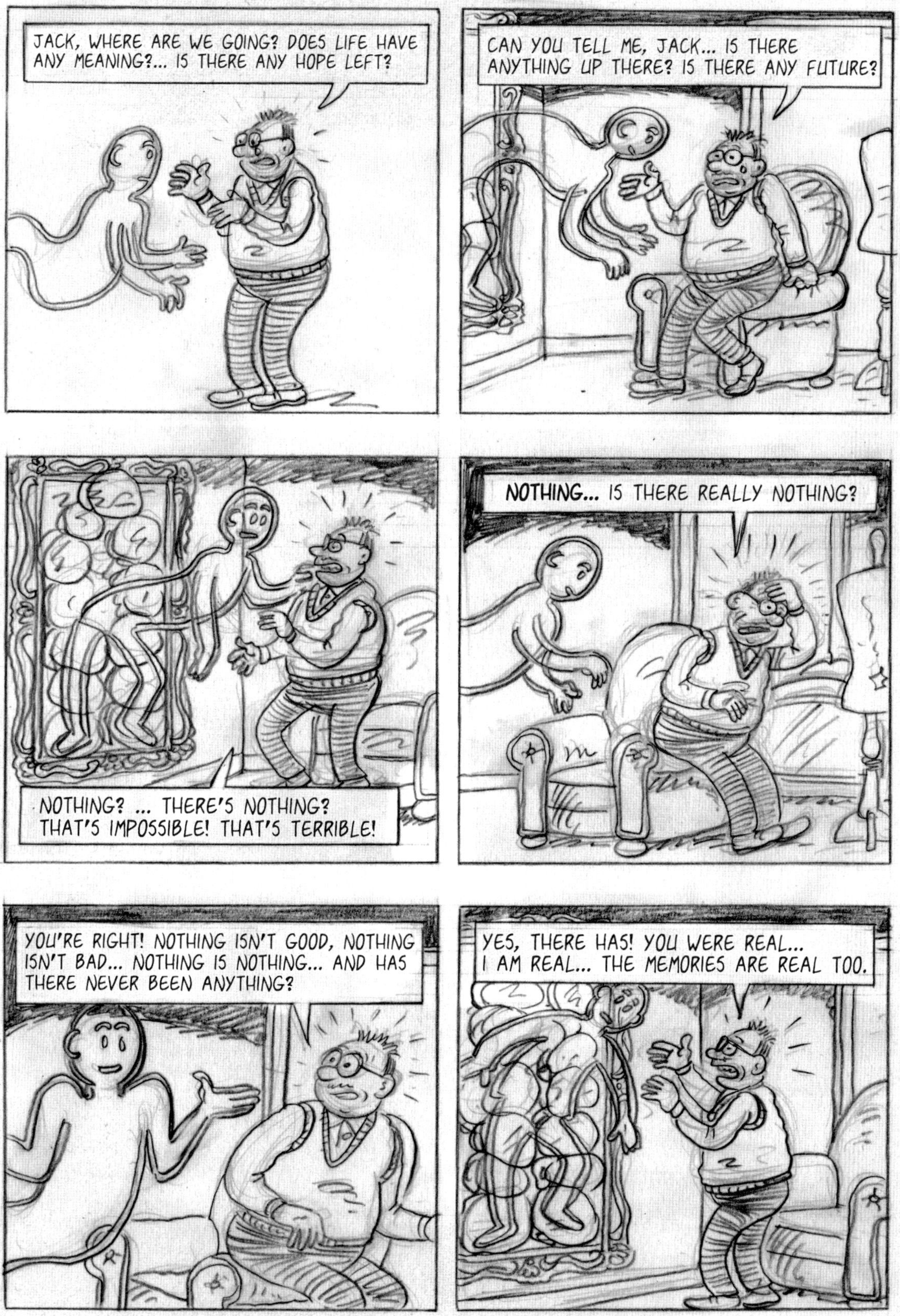
JACK, WHERE ARE WE GOING? DOES LIFE HAVE ANY MEANING?... IS THERE ANY HOPE LEFT?
CAN YOU TELL ME, JACK... IS THERE ANYTHING UP THERE? IS THERE ANY FUTURE?
NOTHING? ... THERE'S NOTHING? THAT'S IMPOSSIBLE! THAT'S TERRIBLE!
NOTHING... IS THERE REALLY NOTHING?
YOU'RE RIGHT! NOTHING ISN'T GOOD, NOTHING ISN'T BAD... NOTHING IS NOTHING... AND HAS THERE NEVER BEEN ANYTHING?
YES, THERE HAS! YOU WERE REAL... I AM REAL... THE MEMORIES ARE REAL TOO.

I'LL CARRY ON WITH WHAT STILL EXISTS!... BUT WHAT DOES STILL EXIST?

SIMONE!

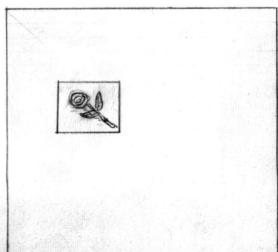

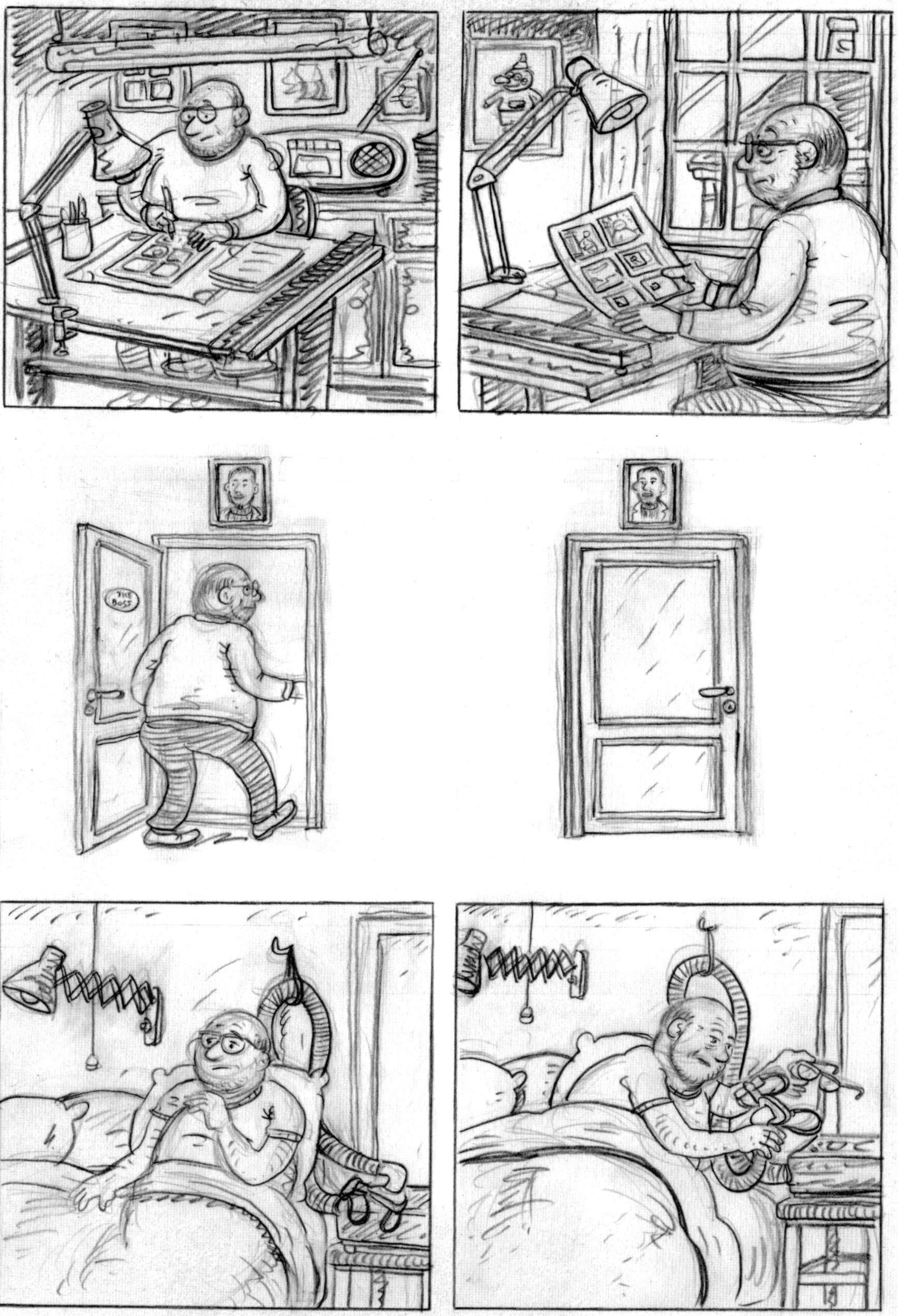
THE BOSS

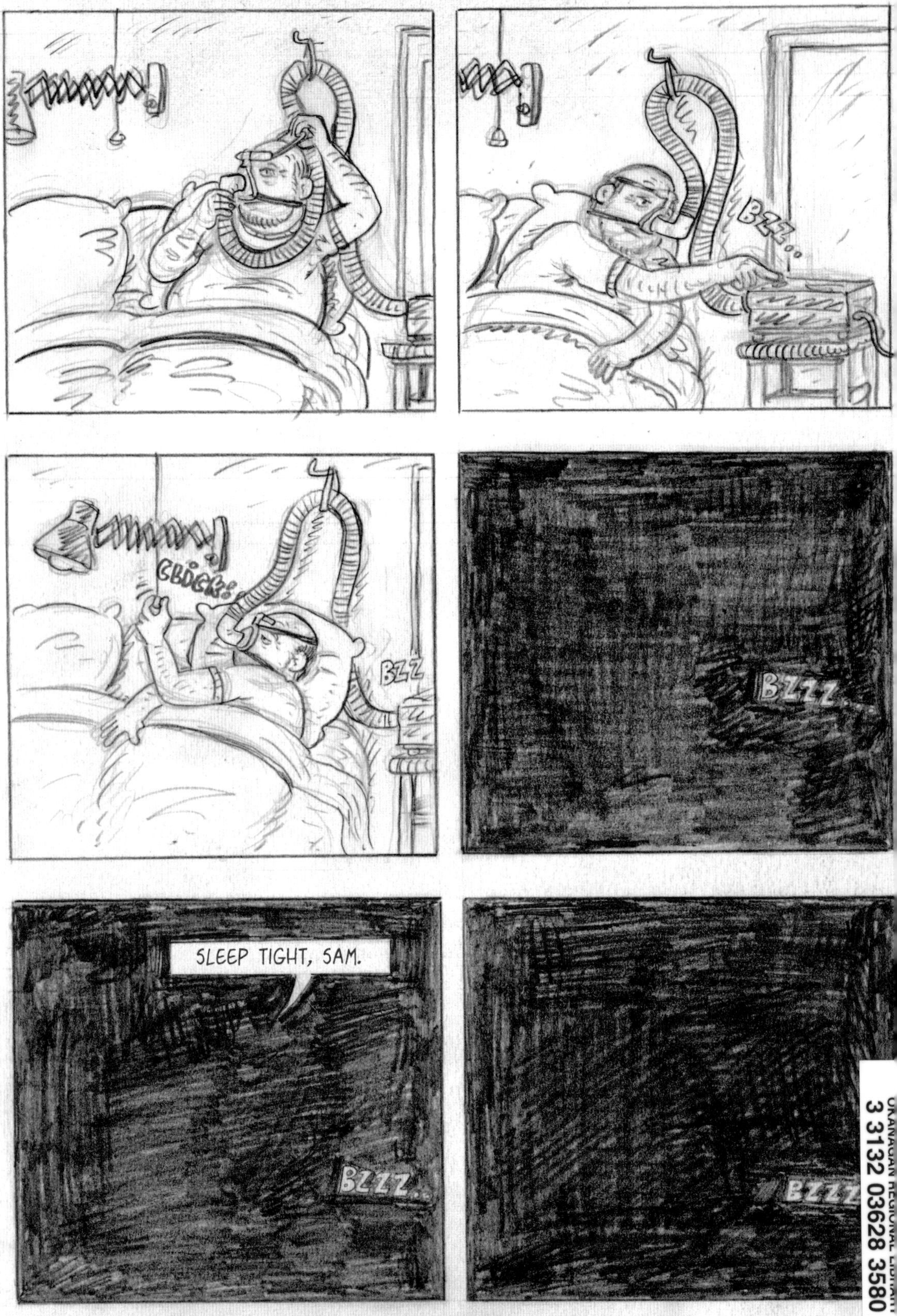
BZZ..
CLICK!
BZZ
BZZZ
SLEEP TIGHT, SAM.
BZZZ..
BZZZ

Message from the Author:

If you have been affected by the events in this book you may wish to visit one of these help organizations:

Australia: http://suicidepreventionaust.org/Home.aspx

Canada: http://www.casp-acps.ca/home.asp

New Zealand: http://www.spinz.org.nz/page/5-Home

U.K.: http://www.uk-sobs.org.uk/

U.S.A.: http://aas.liveelements.net/web/guest/home

**Flemish
Literature
Fund**

*The translation of this book is funded by the Flemish Literature Fund
(Vlaams Fonds voor de Letteren - www.flemishliterature.be)*

*Years of the Elephant was originally published by Bries
in Flemish as an eight parts series.*

Edited by Fanfare

www.ponentmon.com

Graphic adaptation and layout:
Sly Wind Tidings

Corrections: Deb Aoki

ISBN: 978-84-92444-30-4

Produced in China